CHANGING WORLD – UNCHANGING VALUES

Christian Faith in Medical Practice

Published by
International Christian Medical and Dental Association
82-88 Hills Rd, Cambridge CB2 1LQ, UK

Published by
International Christian Medical and Dental Association
82-88 Hills Road
Cambridge CB2 1LQ, UK

1998

ISBN 0 9532690 0 0

Cover photograph: Pictor International

Designed, photoset and printed by
Stanley L. Hunt (Printers) Ltd, Midland Road, Rushden, Northamptonshire

PREFACE

THIS publication coincides with the XI World Congress of the International Christian Medical and Dental Association. It brings together some of the key Bible addresses and papers delivered during the last 35 years, at the 10 previous world congresses and around 50 regional conferences organised on behalf of the Association and its forerunner, the International Congress of Christian Physicians.

The purpose is not to take a nostalgic look backwards, but to affirm the underlying and unchanging Christian principles developed in the papers; to provide inspiration to doctors, dentists and students as they consider healthcare beyond 2000.

It has been extremely difficult to select the contents of the book from the many excellent addresses given at the conferences. Regretfully, many papers have had to be omitted. The editors have endeavoured to provide examples of the application and integration of Christian faith and medical practice from many countries with very differing circumstances, resulting from political, economic and ethnic diversity. However, the examples illustrate principles equally applicable throughout the world.

Despite the many different backgrounds of the contributors the common thread is that all the papers have been written from a firm conviction that the Christian faith remains relevant to changing attitudes within the profession worldwide. The differences in practice of modern medicine lead to ethical dilemmas previously unknown. In reading the papers it is helpful to note the date and location of the presentation, in order to put into the right context the particular viewpoint expressed.

The editors request the understanding of contributors where, in order to achieve the main purpose, it has only been possible to include a short extract or summary. Any reader wishing to have a copy of the full text of any particular paper is invited to write to the ICMDA Secretariat.

With such a delightful transcultural collection modes of expression vary, as does spelling. In this context we wish to record our indebtedness to Mrs Diana Roberts for her expert typing and advice on the format of the manuscript. We also thank Mr David Hunt of Stanley L Hunt (Printers) Ltd for his professional advice.

Janet Goodall and Keith Sanders
Joint Editors

Janet Goodall

Past consultant paediatrician Stoke-on-Trent and senior clinical lecturer, University of Birmingham, UK. One time consultant paediatrician to the Uganda Government. President CMF (UK) 1995–97. ICMDA Vice-President 1994–98. Author *Children and Grieving*.

R Keith M Sanders

Past medical superintendent Duncan Hospital and regional superintendent Emmanuel Hospital Association, India. CMF(UK) General Secretary 1974–90. ICMDA General Secretary 1982–92, Vice-President 1994–98.

CONTENTS

THE INTERNATIONAL CHRISTIAN MEDICAL AND DENTAL ASSOCIATION

ORGANISATIONS of Christian doctors, dentists and students have existed in some countries for over 100 years. In 1963, representatives of seven such organisations met in Amsterdam at the first International Congress of Christian Physicians (ICCP).

From these beginnings, the International Christian Medical and Dental Association (ICMDA) developed as a partnership of representative national Christian medical and dental organisations with the aim of uniting doctors and dentists in promoting Christian faith and practice in the medical and dental professions worldwide. In some countries the membership of the national organisation is restricted to members of the medical and dental professions and their students; in others it is open to members of a variety of healthcare disciplines. In this latter situation the ICMDA relates to the doctor and dentist members.

Where there is no national organisation then individual doctors and dentists who hold a biblically based faith in Jesus Christ may have their names included on a register of interested individuals.

The original objective was to organise a world congress every three years, the joint aims of which were to deepen the spiritual lives of Christians practising in the medical and dental professions and to examine how the Christian faith and ethic could be integrated into professional life and practice. However, the rapid development of science and technology within medicine required a more frequent and ongoing exchange of ideas and information than was possible at a triennial conference. Thus, in 1986 the concept and role of ICCP was redefined to meet these requirements and the name changed to ICMDA.

Alongside the ICCP/ICMDA a comparable student movement, the International Congress of Christian Medical Students (ICCMS) and the International Christian Medical and Dental Students' Association (ICMDSA) developed. Because of the practical difficulties of maintaining a fully independent student organisation it was agreed, in 1990, to merge the student and graduate associations and to develop the student work from a section of ICMDA.

The activities of ICMDA have been an inspiration and support to increasing numbers of physicians and dentists worldwide. On occasion the support of an organisation which was both international and medical has been instrumental in securing permission to arrange conferences or to form a new national organisation. The political changes of the last quarter of the 20th century brought a number of such opportunities. Students have frequently provided that initial vision and enthusiasm which has led to the formation of a national organisation.

By 1997 there were 41 countries in full membership, whilst a further 29 nations maintained links with the Association.

Wherever we come from, the profession not only faces increasing ethical dilemmas but also changes in society's attitudes and its approach to healthcare, the way in which this is provided and the regulations governing the profession. As Christian physicians we have both the responsibility to respond to such pressures for change and also the ability to make a major contribution to the debate. Liaison and co-operation between the national organisations within ICMDA means that we are better able to meet the challenges and use the opportunities. We can learn from and support one another, remembering that such learning and encouragement is a two way process.

The logo of the Association was first used during the 5th World Congress of ICCP, held in Singapore in 1975. Inspired by the account, in John 13, of how Jesus, on the night before he was crucified, washed the feet of his disciples and then wiped them with the towel with which he was girded, it depicts the cross, the bowl and the basin; symbols of Christ's love (supremely described in John 3:16 and 1 John 3:16), humility and service. John 13:16 reminds us that the servant is not greater than his master. With his example before us and his inspiration within us may all those associated with ICMDA, whether as individuals or as National Members seek to serve and support one another in such love.

For God so loved the world that he gave his one and only Son, that whoever believes in him should not perish but have eternal life (John 3:16)

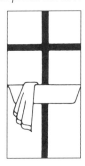

This is how we know what love is; Jesus Christ laid down his life for us. And we ought to lay down our lives for our brothers (1 John 3:16)

The Aims of the Association shall be.

1 to provide for National Christian Medical and Dental Associations a regular means of exchange of views, information and experiences in the field of the medical sciences particularly where these concern Christian faith and ethics;

2 to promote friendship and co-operation amongst Christian medical and dental men and women throughout the world;

3 to examine and test changes in medical thought and action by the principles of the Basis (Clause 6);

4 to disseminate information concerning, and to promote discussion of, the problems which from time to time arise for Christians practising medicine;

5 to deepen the spiritual life of Christians practising medicine and to encourage them to witness within their respective national medical professions;

6 to study, encourage and support the work of Christian medical missions at home and abroad.

The Full Basis of the Association shall be:

'The Revelation of the One true God (Father, Son and Holy Spirit) and the Gospel of man's redemption and regeneration through the death and resurrection of our Lord Jesus Christ, as these are given to us in the Bible, which is the divinely appointed rule for faith and life' (Matthew 28:19,20; John 14:6; 1 Corinthians 15:3–5 and 2 Timothy 3:16,17). The Short Basis, for public use, shall be: 'The revelation of God in the Person of Jesus Christ as we meet him in the Bible' (John 14:6).

From the Constitution of the ICMDA, clauses 5 and 6.

DECLARATION OF ICMDA

From the 9th World Congress of the ICMDA, Seoul, Korea 1990 under the theme *'Biblical ethics and Oriental culture in health care today'*. Written by Dr Paul Brand, President of ICMDA, at the request of and in consultation with Officers of the ICMDA and Congress Committee.

RATIFICATION

Following lectures and opinions expressed by Christian men and women in the medical and dental professions of over 45 countries represented at the Congress, we now wish to:

Reaffirm the aim and the basis of the ICMDA:–

(a) to relate constantly all matters of human health, life and death to the purposes God the Creator intended, as revealed in the life and teaching of Jesus Christ, through whom all things were made and in whose hands all things are held together.

(b) to relate constantly Biblical principles to all aspects of life, recognising the varying gifts of God to different races and people as being true reflections of his presence and power to preserve and to bless the individual, the family and society.

(c) to maintain the independence of the ICMDA from any particular church, religious society or political group.

We affirm our belief:–

(a) that in our Lord Jesus Christ lies the only real hope of bringing true harmony and healing of mind, body and spirit to a hurting world.

(b) that in fulfilling Christ's command to love others as he loved us lies real success; obeying this rule from the heart greatly enhances the fruitfulness of all medical activities and health care, being relevant in all circumstances and in all cultures and economies.

ELABORATION

Following the emphasis during this week of meetings, we need to amplify certain aspects of the above general statement.

The foundation of Christian medical ethics is the recognition of God as the Creator, and of men and women as being uniquely and individually endowed with a mind and spirit, designed for fellowship with God and for living in communities with love and mutual interdependence.

When man rebelled against God and followed selfish and destructive paths, Jesus Christ came to live in human flesh, and sacrificed himself to become our redeemer. His life on earth has become for us an example, and his continuing spirit the motive force that helps us to practise our healing professions according to his will.

At this congress we have appreciated the various ways in which these foundational truths have been interpreted against the background of Eastern and Western cultural heritage.

The nature of man

Modern scientific medicine has progressed so rapidly in terms of chemistry and physics and biology that doctors find it easy to forget the aspects of mind and spirit which do not lend themselves to precise measurements or physical control.

We affirm the primacy of the spirit, for which the mind and body serve as vehicles and instruments. We recognise that if we are to restore real health to men and women we have to be willing to take the time to understand their fears and hopes, their human relationships and the place of God in their lives. We have to realise that physical symptoms may not always lead us to the primary sickness but may mask a spiritual anxiety or dislocation.

Christian doctors and dentists have a special opportunity to help those whose physical sickness may be closely linked with moral failure, as may be the case with alcohol or drug addiction or with today's urgent problem of AIDS. In all these situations we have to avoid a judgmental attitude, but, in the spirit of our Lord Jesus, provide compassionate care even while we make clear that where there has been neglect of God's law, there is also grace for those who repent.

We also know that many of those in most need of healing are some of the least able to pay for their care and treatment. As Christian doctors and dentists we share with all members of the body of Christ the challenge to serve the most needy in the way that Jesus did.

The family

Throughout this conference there has been a recurring emphasis on the importance of the family, as the central unit in God's plan for a healthy society. We deplore the breakdown of the traditional family unit in the West, and trace this to the widespread departure from God's law of faithfulness in marriage. We are seeing the serious effects on today's children and foresee accelerating problems with succeeding generations who grow up with self-gratification as their sole motive, and family loyalty and concern for others forgotten.

While we are glad to note that family solidarity is greater in Eastern cultures, we, from both East and West, look with apprehension on changes in newly industrialised Eastern countries which seem to be following the trends of the West. We join in a plea to the Christian church to stand against this tide and uphold Christian teaching in regard to family morality which leads to family and individual health and wholeness.

Scientific advances

We are thankful for the extent to which new scientific techniques are being developed to heal diseases and to relieve pain and suffering. Scientists are now able to look into the very codes by which life originates, and are able to manipulate them in a way which could affect the very nature of man.

We believe in the sanctity of life and recognise it as a grace of God. We need to accept the ability to combat diseases that threaten life, and to welcome opportunities to improve its quality. But we also need to be alert and oppose attempts to change the primary intent of God the creator, and his perfect plan for humanity. We deplore any insistence on the prolongation of biological life of the body once the mind is dead and the spirit has departed.

Christian medical leaders have been slow to keep pace with the implications of genetic engineering, both for good and for evil, and with those aspects of contraception, and in vitro fertilisation of various sorts, which are so new that they lie in ethically uncharted territory. While we remain unshakably committed to defending the sanctity of life, and therefore in opposition to abortion on demand and to active euthanasia, there are many areas which demand attention and analysis and we must not allow circumstances to overtake us, leaving us impotent because we are undecided and protesting followers when we should be giving leadership.

Politics

We note that the rapid changes in moral outlook in Western countries are being followed by changes in politics and laws which have tended to undermine support of the family and accord acceptance of ways of life that are contrary to God's law and also to health.

We affirm the responsibility of Christian doctors — often looked up to as leaders in society — and Christian Medical and Dental Societies and Fellowships to enter the arena of public debate and accept the responsibility of speaking out for what we believe to be right.

We are encouraged by the way newly liberated communities of Eastern Europe have turned, in the turmoil of their uncertainty, to trusted Christian physicians, members of ICMDA, and propelled them into positions of leadership. Even though our witness today may seem to fall on deaf ears, the time will soon come when the full effect of today's immorality will become evident, through disease and social breakdown. At that time the public will turn in desperation, as they have recently in post-communist countries, to those who have been known for their warnings and for their integrity.

All of us therefore need to look to our public image, and make sure, by the grace of God, that our personal and our family lives stand up to scrutiny, and that they commend our faith and honour the name of Jesus Christ our Lord.

The ICMDA fellowship

ICMDA is concerned with Christian faith and medical practice; but it is also a fellowship based on our love for each other in Jesus Christ. Now as we all return to our various countries we recognise that some of our members are going back to continue their lonely witness in difficult places with little or no Christian fellowship.

We think of some in Eastern Europe, and others in parts of Africa or Latin America, suffering under political persecution or religious discrimination. We affirm our love for you. We salute you for your faithful witness. We are committed to support you in any way we can. We promise to pray for you, that God will bless you, not only in attaining freedom, but also in the painful processes of adapting to new policies.

Section 1

The Firm Foundation

THE UNCHANGING CHRIST

ARNOLD ALDIS

THE PRE-EXISTENT CHRIST

THE theme of this congress is expressed in the overall title 'Saving health in a changing world', and inevitably, therefore, the emphasis in many of the papers and in the discussions will be upon the changes. That we live in a changing world is obvious to all of us. There are political, territorial, economic, social, educational and cultural changes. Christians must know how to react to the changes which are taking place around them, for change is not to be equated with progress, and while some changes are to be welcomed, some are equally to be resisted if Christian values and standards are to be maintained.

If we are to react wisely to change, rather than being swept along in the ever increasing flood, we need some stable base from which the changes can be viewed, some secure and immovable bedrock of conviction and absolute truth upon which we can set our feet while we survey the swirling currents which surround us.

Scripture states, 'Jesus Christ, the same yesterday, and today, and forever' (Heb. 13:8). So the unchanging Christ will be the theme to which we will turn each morning. To do so, however, demands that we should make some division of the subject and there are many ways in which this might be done. We might for example take the text I have already quoted, and (under the headings of 'Yesterday', 'Today', and 'Forever') speak of the Historic Christ, the Christ of Experience, and the Reigning and Triumphant Christ. I have chosen to base these morning Bible studies on a very familiar, but very wonderful, passage of Scripture to be found in Paul's letter to the Philippians chapter 2, verses 5–11. In order that we may savour as much as as we can of the full meaning of these words — which may well be an early Christian hymn — I propose to start each morning by reading the passage in a different

ICCP Davos, Switzerland, 1978. **Arnold Aldis.** *Past consultant surgeon, University Hospital of Wales, and medical post-graduate dean for Wales, UK.*

translation. We begin then this morning with the splendid Elizabethan English of the King James version:

> 'Let this mind be in you which was also in Christ Jesus: who, being in the form of God, thought it not robbery to be equal with God: but made himself of no reputation, and took upon him the form of a servant, and was made in the likeness of men: and being found in fashion as a man, he humbled himself and became obedient unto death, even the death of the cross. Wherefore God also hath highly exalted him, and given him a name which is above every name: that at the name of Jesus every knee should bow, of things in heaven, and things in earth, and things under the earth; and that every tongue should confess that Jesus Christ is Lord, to the glory of God the Father.'

This passage divides naturally into three stanzas: the Pre-existent Christ, verses 5 and 6; the Incarnate Christ, verses 7 and 8; and the Exalted and Victorious Christ, verses 9–11. These will be our three themes.

Attempts to identify the human Jesus

Ever since the publication of Albert Schweitzer's monumental volume *Von Reimarus zu Wrede* in 1906 (with its later English translation, *The Quest of the Historical Jesus*, in 1910) there has been a concentration of interest in the human Christ, the Jesus of history. This concentration of interest on the human Jesus is in part a reflection of the view of many of the writers that Jesus was no more than a man, as argued in a recent theological book which has caused something of a stir in England: *The myth of God incarnate.*

But the unchanging Christ cannot be confined within the narrow limits of a Galilean peasant, the prophet of Nazareth, the great human teacher sent from God, and the revealer of God. His own claim to be more than all of this, the acceptance of that claim by his disciples and the church which he founded, and the apostolic witness to that claim, all forbid us to think of Jesus in purely human terms. The human Jesus is indeed fully and truly human. But he was also God, and if he were not, then he cannot in any sense be the Saviour that Scripture declares him to be and which we have found him to be. Indeed it is this truth which provides us with the assurance of his changelessness. If Jesus was only a man — albeit the best man who ever lived and the highest example of manhood — then he must also share the change and inconsistency which is so characteristic of man. Man changes, but of God it is written, 'I am the Lord, I change not' (Mal. 3:6), or as James puts it in his letter, 'Every good and every perfect gift is from above, coming down from the Father of lights with whom there is no variation or shadow of change' (James 1:17). This is supremely true of God's greatest gift, that of his Son, who shares the changelessness of the giver.

The revealed fact of his deity

To those who seek only the Jesus of history, the idea of pre-existence is meaningless, but to those of us who see in him not only perfect man, but God incarnate, pre-existence is an essential part of our Christology, for truly we can echo the words of Isaiah, 'Unto us a child is born, unto us a son is given: and the government shall be upon his shoulder: and his name shall be called Wonderful Counsellor, The mighty God, The everlasting Father, The Prince of Peace' (Isa. 9:6). The Scriptures leave us in no doubt concerning the pre-existence of Christ and we have not only his claim but also the apostolic teaching. The passage of Scripture around which we are centring our thought begins with his pre-existence in the divine glory which he shared with his Father. 'Have this mind in you which was also in Christ Jesus, who being in the form of God, thought it not robbery to be equal with God', or as the Revised Standard Version puts it, 'did not count equality with God a thing to be grasped'. Jesus Christ was and is God from eternity to eternity. He became man, was not just man, and this is supported by inference in many other New Testament passages such as Romans 8:3, 1 Corinthians 10:4, and Galatians 4:6. Not only so, but Christ himself claims pre-existence with God in many passages in the gospel of John, where indeed it is a theme which runs right through the book.

Those who suggest that the Christology presented in the gospel of John was derived not directly from the teaching of Jesus or the claims he made concerning himself, but evolved slowly under the influence first of Jewish and then of Hellenistic ideas, overlook the post-resurrection teaching of our Lord. Christ claimed to be the Lord during his ministry and the claim was accepted — although not fully understood — by the disciples. This is made clear by the fact that all three synoptic gospels include the great confession of

Peter, 'Thou art the Christ, the Son of the living God'. However in John 16:12 Jesus is recorded as having said to the disciples, 'I have many things to say to you but you cannot bear them now'. Surely he began to say these 'many things' after his resurrection, when, on the walk to Emmaus, 'beginning with Moses and all the prophets he interpreted to them in all the Scriptures the things concerning himself' (Luke 24:27). And later in the upper room he said (vv. 44 –45), 'These are my words which I spoke to you while I was yet with you, that everything written about me in the law of Moses, and the prophets, and the psalms must be fulfilled. Then he opened their minds to understand the Scriptures.' Or as Luke puts it in the opening verses of the Acts, 'To them he presented himself alive after his passion by many proofs, appearing to them during forty days, and speaking of the kingdom of God'. Surely it was these post-resurrection conversations which established the theology and Christology to which the apostles later gave witness in the New Testament writings.

Then, too, the suggestion that the Christology of the New Testament slowly evolved under the influence of extrinsic factors wholly overlooks or underestimates the guidance and direction of the Holy Spirit in these matters. The verse I have already quoted (John 16:12), 'I have many things to say to you but you cannot bear them now', was spoken in the context of the promised gift of the Holy Spirit for the very next verse declares, 'When the Spirit of truth comes, he will guide you into all truth'.

The convincing claims of his pre-existence

Let us turn to the clear statements concerning the pre-existence of Christ recorded by John, both in the words of Jesus himself, and also in John's witness to him. Jesus brings to a close the remarkable conversation with the Jews recorded in John 8 with the astonishing words, 'Truly, truly I say to you, before Abraham was, I am', and it was this claim which led them to seek to stone him for his blasphemy. Again in our Lord's high priestly prayer for his disciples recorded in John 17:5 we have his clear statement, 'Father, glorify thou me in thine own presence with the glory which I had with thee before the world was made'. Or again, the pre-existence of Christ and his equality with God could hardly be more clearly expressed than in the magnificent prologue to the gospel, 'In the beginning was the Word, and the Word was with God and the

Word was God. He was in the beginning with God, all things were made by him and without him was not anything made that was made.'

We have already noted the Pauline teaching on the pre-existence of Christ in the passage of Scripture around which we have been centring our thoughts, but while it is referred to only indirectly there, Paul expounds the doctrine fully in his letter to the church at Colosse. Speaking of Christ he declares, 'He is the image of the invisible God, the firstborn of all creation: for in him all things were created, in heaven and on earth, visible and invisible, whether thrones or dominions or principalities or authorities — all things were created through him and for him. He is before all things and in him all things hold together' (Col. 1:15–17).

Christ Creator and Lord of history

Not only was the unchanging Christ active in creation, but these verses also declare that he is continually active in sustaining and upholding that which he has created, including man himself. The Christian concept of God is very different from that of the deist who believes that God created the universe and left it to its own devices. How good it is to know that the unchanging Christ was not only involved in the creation of all things, but that he is also in control of all things. He upholds all things, and by him all things hold together. What a vision of God Isaiah gives us in his prophecy, 'Lift up your eyes on high and see; who created these, he who brings out their host by number, calling them all by name, by the greatness of his might and because he is strong in power, not one is missing' (Isa. 40:26).

How good to know that God is still on the throne and he holds the whole universe in his hand, and that the whole of history is in a very real sense his story. How good and reassuring that in the exercise of this sustaining, controlling activity of God, the unchanging Christ is eternally involved, and that in him we live and move and have our being; for he not only holds the worlds in his hand, but he holds us in his hand. For Jesus said, 'My sheep hear my voice and I know them and they follow me, and I give unto them eternal life and they shall never perish and no one shall snatch them out of my hand. My Father who has given them unto me is greater than all and no one is able to snatch them out of my Father's hand. I and the Father are one' (John 10:27–30).

The implications of Christ's changelessness

So then we come round to where we began, the unchanging Christ, and we base our assertion that he is indeed unchanging and unchangeable, not primarily on his humanity, but on his deity. Amid the changes and chances of this passing world, and the changing character of man himself, God alone is constant and unchanging; and Jesus Christ, because he is God, shares with his Father the unchanging character of God, and this not only in time but from eternity to eternity.

Thus Christ is unchanging *in the constancy of his love* towards men, for as God's love is unwavering, so the love of Christ, as the perfect reflection of that love, and unlike human love, does not change in the face of man's failure to respond. Paul uses the phrases 'the love of God' and 'the love of Christ' interchangeably, and answers his own question in Romans 8:35, 'Who shall separate us from the love of Christ?' with the exultant reply, 'I am persuaded that neither death nor life, nor angels nor principalities, nor powers, nor things present, nor things to come, nor height nor depth, nor any other creature shall be able to separate us from the love of God, which is in Christ Jesus our Lord.'

Christ is unchanging *in the greatness of his power* for he said, 'All power is given unto me in heaven and on earth' (Mat. 28:18). But the power of God revealed in Christ is not to overawe us, it becomes available for our help, for, though Jesus Christ was and is the creator and sustainer of the universe, yet he marks the sparrow's fall by saying, 'Fear not, ye are of more value than many sparrows' (Luke 12:6–7).

Jesus Christ is unchanging *in the inexhaustibility of his wealth*, for indeed the riches of Christ are unsearchable (Eph. 3:8); they are the very riches of God himself. There is no human need which cannot be met from such an inexhaustible store, and that store has been made available to us in Christ, for, as Paul reminds us, 'You know the grace of our Lord Jesus Christ, that, though he was rich, yet for your sakes he became poor, that ye through his poverty might be rich' (2 Cor. 8:9).

Or, again, Jesus Christ is unchanging *in the divine omniscience of his wisdom,* and once again, not to overawe us, but so that we who lack wisdom might find it in him for 'Christ Jesus is made unto us wisdom' (1 Cor. 1:30).

Or, again, Jesus Christ is unchanging *in the faithfulness of his promises* for 'All the promises of God find their yes in him' (2 Cor. 1:20). And so we may go on until we have exhausted every divine attribute which we can think of, and each will have its perfect reflection in the unchanging Christ, and in him is made relevant to our need.

But in order that this may be so, the unchanging Christ had to be made man. He who is from the beginning in the form of God and who thought it not a thing to be grasped at to be equal with God, had to lay aside that glory in the incarnation and become a man that we, fallen humanity, might recover our true manhood and become his brothers in the family of God. He who is rich beyond all imagining had to become poor that we might be rich. He who is strong above all measure had to become weak and dependent that we might find our strength in him. But even more than this, for, although for mortal man it must be beyond our full understanding, yet we dare to confess reverently and wonderingly that, 'He who knew no sin had to become sin for us that we might be made the righteousness of God in him' (2 Cor. 5:21).

THE INCARNATE CHRIST

ARNOLD ALDIS

'Let Christ Jesus be your example as to what your attitude should be. For he, who had always been God by nature, did not cling to his prerogatives as God's equal, but stripped himself of all privilege by consenting to be a slave by nature and being born as mortal man. And, having become man, he humbled himself by living a life of utter obedience, even to the extent of dying, *and the death he died was the death of a common criminal.* That is why God has now lifted him so high, and has given him a name beyond all names, so that at the name of Jesus "every knee shall bow" whether in Heaven or earth or under the earth. And that is why, in the end, "every tongue shall confess" that Jesus Christ is the Lord, to the glory of God the Father' (paraphrase by J. B. Phillips of Philippians 2:5–11).

Yesterday, we were concerned with the pre-existent Christ, the second person of the Trinity, co-existent and co-equal with God. Today, we are concerned with the Christ who laid aside the glory which he had with his Father and became a man. In becoming a man, he did not come as some great leader or kingly figure, but as a slave. As a slave he lived his life in complete obedience to God, even to the point of death, and that, the death of a criminal.

Man was made in the image of God and for fellowship with God and to be the friend of God, but man fell. The relationship was broken. God became man in Christ to restore that broken relationship. It is idle to speculate what would have happened if man had not fallen, for we simply do not know. Man is a fallen creature and his redemption can only be brought about by God. A part of that redemptive process involved God becoming a man. To use Paul's words, 'When the fullness of the time was come God sent forth his Son, born of a woman, born under the law to redeem those who were under the law, that we might receive the adoption of sons' (Gal. 4:4–5).

The fullness of time
At this point, we might well ask, if God saw that the incarnation was a necessary part of the redemptive process, why it was delayed

so long, and what Paul means when he says 'When the fullness of the time was come'. No doubt with our limited human knowledge and understanding we can never fully answer the question, but as we study God's redemptive plan to restore fallen mankind into fellowship with himself, we discover that redemption is no facile task; it is both costly and time consuming. Long centuries of preparation were needed first. God chose a man and through that man a nation and through that nation he began to teach man by means of history, providence, covenant, law, sacrifices, precepts and prophecy what God was like and what he required of man. Through the law God showed himself to be a holy God, whose moral demands condemned man for his failure to live up to them. So too, God showed himself to be a just God who held man to be responsible for his failure and who could by no means overlook man's sin. But at the same time he showed himself to be a God who was ever willing and ready to forgive in response to man's repentance, for, 'To the Lord our God belong mercies and forgivenesses, though we have rebelled against him; neither have we obeyed the voice of the Lord our God, to walk in his laws, which he set before us by his servants the prophets' (Dan. 9:9–10). But God also showed that forgiveness was costly and that sin needed to be atoned for before it could be forgiven. Such atonement could only be made by God and at the cost of sacrifice and death, for, 'Without shedding of blood there is no remission' (Heb. 9:22).

Slowly — O how slowly — men learnt the lessons which God was trying to teach. Line upon line and precept upon precept and with many a setback because of his unwillingness to learn and his misunderstanding of the teaching, he often deliberately rejected the message of prophet and teacher. But yet at long last God saw that the years of preparation were over and the 'fullness of time had come' or as we should say, 'the time was ripe'. Once again God chose a man — *the Man* — the Man Jesus Christ to be the first of a new race of men, of a redeemed humanity. And so eternity invaded time and the pre-existent Christ became the incarnate Christ, to work out in time that which had been planned in eternity.

The Jesus of the gospels

So we turn to look at the human Jesus, the Jesus of history. In doing so I must make it clear that the only direct evidence of him we have is that provided in the gospels, and that I accept this evidence as reliable. Albert Schweitzer, in his volume *The Quest of the Historical Jesus,* came to the conclusion that it was impossible to arrive at a true picture of the human Jesus and that the gospel records were mostly projections of the evolving Christology of the church back into the narrative, with invented or edited stories of Jesus to support their evolving belief concerning him. Many writers before and since then have taken the same sort of position. Rudolph Bultmann, probably the most influential New Testament scholar of the twentieth century, took much the same view. Over against such weighty opinion I would place three simple observations concerning the gospel records.

First, the synoptic gospels are written in the simple factual style which one would associate with historical records. Furthermore, one of the authors, Luke, is a very reliable historian, as shown by the growing evidence from the Acts of the Apostles. Consider how carefully he puts the story of Jesus into its historical setting. 'Now in the fifteenth year of the reign of Tiberius Caesar, Pontius Pilate being governor of Judaea, and Herod being tetrarch of Galilee, and his brother Philip tetrarch of Iturea and of the region of Trachonitis, and Lysanias the tetrarch of Abilene, Annas and Caiaphas being the high priests, the word of God came to John the son of Zacharias in the wilderness' (Luke 3:1–2).

In the second place, the records are contemporary. They are written by men who were alive during our Lord's ministry on earth, and although Luke did not have the advantage of Matthew and John of actually knowing and living with Christ, he had ample opportunity — which he seems to have used to the full — of talking with those who knew the Lord intimately. It must be admitted that it is hardly possible to write things which are untrue about any person while there are many alive who knew the person concerned and who could refute the errors. Especially is this so in the case of Jesus, when there were the strongest possible reasons for their wishing to do so. So Peter on the day of Pentecost does not have to specify the mighty works of Christ, but says, 'Ye men of Israel, hear these words; Jesus of Nazareth, a man approved of God among you by miracles and wonders and signs, which God did by him in the midst of you, as ye yourselves also know' (Acts 2:22).

Furthermore, in the third place, the gospel records not only purport to be historical and are contemporary, but they are also inspired. In his conversation with the disciples in the upper room and on the way to Gethsemane, our Lord promised the gift of the Holy Spirit, and assured them that one of the functions of the Holy Spirit would be 'to teach you all things and bring all things to your remembrance, whatever I have said to you' (John 14:26).

Thus, in speaking of the incarnate Christ, the human Jesus, or the Jesus of history, I do so, accepting the gospel records at their face value, not indeed as a complete biography of our Lord, but as a sufficient, reliable and inspired record. I have spent a little time on this point, for it is often said that the historicity of the gospels is of no importance, since it is the ideas which the gospels enshrine which really matter, not the historical facts they purport to describe. But this I believe is to mistake the nature of the Christian faith. When we say, as we often do, that Christianity is an historic faith, we mean that it is not simply a set of ideas about God and about man, but a faith founded on historic facts. Of course the Faith itself goes beyond the historic facts, but none the less it is tied to the facts, and rests on them.

If the facts can be shown to be untrue, then the faith which rests on them is likewise overthrown. That Jesus was born in Bethlehem is a claimed fact of history which is open to historical research as any fact of history, but that he was the Son of God is an article of faith which no amount of historical research can either prove or disprove. That he was crucified under Pontius Pilate again is an historical statement which is open to historical investigation, but that he was delivered for our offences (Rom. 4:25) is an article of faith upon which historical research is not qualified to pronounce. That Jesus rose from the dead on the first Easter morning is an historic fact upon which the disciples were prepared to hazard their lives, but that he was raised for our justification (Rom. 4:25) is a matter of faith which history can neither confirm nor deny. To think otherwise is to deny the clear statement made by Paul: 'If Christ be not raised, your faith is in vain; ye are yet in your sins' (1 Cor. 15:17).

Before we look at the gospel records, however, we must notice that Christ voluntarily became man. It is true that the Father sent the Son, but Paul makes it clear that Christ humbled himself, and made himself of no reputation, and took upon himself the form of a servant. This is a point of considerable importance for this characterised the whole life of Jesus. His words and his actions were truly his, and yet at the same time they were the words and actions of the one who sent him (John 5:19; 10:25; 12:50; 14:23–24).

The humanity of Jesus

Turning to the gospel records themselves, how far do they confirm the truth that Paul speaks of in our passage of Scripture when he says that the pre-existent Christ who was equal with God, became man? How far was Jesus truly human? At once we may say in a word that the gospel records portray Christ as sharing the whole range of human experience apart from sin.

First, he was born as men are born, a helpless dependent baby. True his birth was unique in that he was born of a virgin, for Jesus was God's new man, God's perfect man, and there had to be a break in the inherited bias towards sin which all other men share because of their continuity with fallen Adam.

He grew both in body and in mind as any human child grows (Luke 2:52). He lived as a man and shared with men all the varied experiences which are common to man. He was weary (Luke 8:23; John 4:6). He was hungry (Luke 4:2). He was thirsty (John 4:7; 19:28). He could, and did, rejoice with those that rejoiced and wept with those that wept (John 2:2; 11:35). He was tempted in all points as we are (Heb. 4:15; Luke 4:2). He was a man of sorrows and acquainted with grief (Mat. 26:38), and yet knew what it was to rejoice (Luke 10:21). He died, as all men die, and was buried (Mat. 27:50; 59–60). In all these ways Jesus was truly human and in becoming a man he humbled himself and took upon himself the form of a servant (Luke 22:27; John 13:4–5).

The uniqueness of his life

Having said this, however, we must go on to say that the life of Jesus, though truly human, was also unique. We have mentioned already his unique birth, but we must go on to notice the unique features of his life. He was unique in his words, for the gospel records make it clear that, 'Never man spake like this man' (John 7:46), and that he taught with authority and not as the scribes (Mark 1:22), and that men 'wondered at the gracious words which proceeded out of his mouth' (Luke 4:22). At this point it is important to consider to what extent the wisdom and knowledge of Jesus was limited by his true humanity. It is clear from our passage of Scripture that in becoming a man he voluntarily laid aside the attributes of deity including omniscience. We must believe — for the Scriptures tell us so — that he grew in stature and wisdom as an ordinary child grows (Luke 2:46; 2:52), and yet his growth was in some senses unique. Thus at the age of twelve, in the temple in Jerusalem, we read: 'All who heard him were amazed by his understanding and his answers' (Luke 2:47), and the Jews listening to his teaching in the temple later said: 'How is it that this man has learning when he has never studied?' (John 7:15). In saying that Jesus grew in wisdom and knowledge and in self-awareness is one thing, but it is quite another to say that he was therefore also subject to human error, and this I believe is quite unjustified.

It is often said today that Jesus was a man of his time and was subject to the errors and misunderstandings of his age, but this does not follow. That he laid aside his omniscience, and willed not to know in a supernatural way, we may surely accept. But that he also willed to be misled by human error is quite another matter and surely the evidence of the gospel record is clearly against any such view. He certainly accused others of error when he said, 'Ye do err, not knowing the Scriptures' (Mat. 22:29), but claimed himself to speak with authority, 'We speak that we do know and testify that we have seen' (John 3:11). Many indeed sought to trap him in his speech by putting to him hard questions, but went away wondering at the answers they received. In this connection I have often thought it remarkable that words which we so commonly have to use such as 'I think' or 'maybe' or 'perhaps' are never found on the lips of our Lord in the gospel records. He did not have to use them; his speech was 'Truly, truly I say unto you'.

But if he was unique in his words he was also unique in his works. He proved himself to have authority over the forces of nature and it was said of him, 'He has done all things well, he even makes the deaf to hear and the dumb speak' (Mark 7:37), and, 'Who then is this that even wind and sea obey him?' (Mark 4:41).

Then again he was unique in his sinlessness. That he was tempted the Scriptures assure us and that the temptations were fiercer than we can ever understand is also plain — as witness his agony in the Garden of Gethsemane. That he was the friend of sinners was a charge which was frequently levelled at him, but it is equally clear that he never shared their sin. He was on the one hand 'the friend of sinners' but, on the other hand, he was 'holy, harmless and undefiled, and separate from sinners' (Luke 7:34; Heb. 7:26).

The uniqueness of his death

Then he was unique in his death, not in the manner of his dying, but in his control of the situation. On the Mount of Transfiguration Moses and Elijah appeared and spoke with him, and Luke tells us the subject of their conversation, 'They spoke of his decease' (*exodus* is the word used) which he should accomplish at Jerusalem. Death is something that happens to us; for him it was something that he accomplished. Or again Jesus says, 'No one takes my life from me, but I lay it down of my own accord. I have power to lay it down and power to take it again' (John 10:18). Note here again that although the laying down of his life was his own action, it was also the Father's will, for he adds, 'This commandment have I received of my Father'.

But the unique character of his death does not reside only in the fact that his death was entirely under his own control, but far more in the fact that his death was intimately linked with our salvation. Death came into the world through sin as the Scriptures make clear, and thus death became the universal experience of man, for all have sinned. But as I have said — and the gospel records declare — Christ was free from taint of sin, a friend of sinners indeed, and yet without sin in himself. Furthermore he was free, by reason of his unique birth, from the hereditary bias to sin which we all share, and as such death had no claim upon him. And yet he died, voluntarily and purposefully, for this was a part of the eternal plan.

No doubt it is impossible for human language and understanding to encompass the full and complete meaning of the death of Christ and no doubt this is why the Scriptures use so many different ways of speaking of his death. No theory of the atonement will ever exhaust the content of that death, but surely three truths concerning his death shine clearly out of Scripture.

First, *it was necessary.* Jesus Christ did not come simply to live a perfect human life, to show man what God expected him to be. He was not merely an example for us to follow, as some would have us believe. He came to die and his awareness of this fact was a dominating influence in his life. He spoke of it to his disciples repeatedly and set his face to go to Jerusalem, knowing what was to happen to him there (Mark 10:33–34). Not that Jesus had any sort of 'death wish' for as a real man he shrank from it, as his agony in the Garden of Gethsemane makes clear, and yet he accepted it as a necessary part of the divine plan.

Secondly, *it was vicarious*. He died for us and on our behalf. So Paul writes to the church in Rome, 'God commends his love towards us in that while we were yet sinners Christ died for us' (Rom. 5:8), and Peter declares, 'Christ also hath once suffered for sins, the just for the unjust' (1 Pet. 3:18), and Christ himself says, 'The Son of Man came not to be ministered unto but to minister and to give his life a ransom for many' (Mat. 20:28). His death was for us. This was in a personal as well as a corporate sense, not just for mankind but for man as an individual so that Paul is able to speak of Christ as 'the Son of God who loved me and gave himself for me' (Gal. 2:20).

Thirdly, *it was substitutionary*. Instead of us, he died that we might live, and his death was intimately connected with our sin. I have said that the human life of Jesus was unique in its sinlessness, but he who knew no sin in his own life, yet entered into even this experience of human life on the cross — not his own sin but ours. At this point we probe the mystery of the atonement to a point where human understanding fails, but in reverent and wondering faith we read and accept. 'He his own self bare our sins in his own body on the tree' (1 Pet. 2:24) and, 'God made him to be sin for us who knew no sin that we might be made the righteousness of God in him' (2 Cor. 5:21). The deep agony of this truth can perhaps be seen and felt in the cry of dereliction from the cross. 'My God, my God, why hast thou forsaken me?' (Mark 15:34). Not that the death of Christ was a sacrifice to appease an angry and wrathful God, for 'God was in Christ reconciling the world unto himself' (2 Cor. 5:19), and the love which went all the way to Calvary for us was as much the Father's love as it was the love of Christ.

Both God and man

So the incarnate, unchanging Christ was fully human and truly became man, but he was also unique. If he had not been fully human he could not have been man's representative in his life and in his death. But having said this we must also say that the incarnate Christ was not only human but also divine. When he laid aside the attributes of God and humbled himself, he did not lay aside his deity. When God became man, he did not cease to be God — such is the central paradox of the Christian faith. Doubtless with our finite minds we are unable to begin to comprehend this and yet the Scriptures are insistent in claiming the deity of Christ and there are many examples in the gospel records where the truth is implicit if not explicit. Thus his mighty works proclaim his divine power. Not that we believe that Jesus is God because of his miracles, since our Lord himself made it clear that supernatural powers might have another source than God when he said, 'If I by Beelzebub cast out devils, by whom do your sons cast them out? But if I with the finger of God cast out devils, no doubt the kingdom of God is come among you' (Mat. 12:27–28), but the miracles are consistent with his claims. Then he claimed and exercised the right to forgive sins, which is God's prerogative, as the doctors of the law rightly declared and before whom our Lord defended his word of forgiveness to the palsied man, 'That ye may know that the Son of Man hath power on earth to forgive sins, he saith to the sick of the palsy, "Rise, take up thy bed and walk" ' (Luke 5:24). Then he received worship from men as his due, and no word of rebuke was spoken to Thomas, the twin, when he fell at his feet with the words, 'My Lord and my God' (John 20:28). Once, too, during his lifetime something of the glory that was his by right shone through the veil of his flesh. Peter never forgot that moment and writing of it later he says: 'We were eyewitnesses of his majesty — for we were with him on the holy mountain' (2 Pet. 1:16, 18).

This leads me finally to say a word about how we are to hold at one and the same time to the truth of the incarnate Christ's real humanity and his true deity. The human mind is as averse to paradoxes as nature is to a vacuum, and the Christian faith is full of paradoxes. The paradox of predestination and free will, the paradox of losing one's life to gain it, and the great central paradox of the incarnation. Usually the human mind tends to deal with paradoxes in one of two ways. *Either* it cleaves to one half of the paradox and seeks to ignore or play down the other; thus, throughout history, the church has repeatedly polarised into one or other of the two sides of the paradox, now stressing the human Jesus to the virtual denial of his deity, and now stressing his deity to such an extent that his humanity is regarded simply as an appearance. *Or*, on the other hand, it may tend to try and find some compromise between the two extremes of the paradox which virtually denies both.

But the truth does not lie in one half of the paradox or in some middle ground between but, as Charles Simeon of Cambridge used to say, 'in both extremes'. We must hold both truths in tension, not seeking overmuch to reconcile them because now we see through a glass darkly and are waiting until we see him face to face. Perhaps the nearest we can come to understanding the mystery of the incarnation is along the lines of the analogy of grace. Note the paradox of grace in the life of a Christian, so well expressed by Paul when he says, 'I am crucified with Christ, nevertheless I live, yet not I, but Christ liveth in me' (Gal. 2:20). Man is never more human than when his actions are truly his own and yet he acts in complete obedience to the will of God. Such a state of complete unity with the will of God and the leading of the Holy Spirit is never, alas, true of us, but was it not true of Christ who said, 'I do always the will of him that sent me' (John 5:30)? Jesus Christ did not live his perfect human life by calling on special divine resources which are not available to us, but by using to the full the resources of prayer, the Scriptures, dependence and obedience, so that it could surely be said of him, 'Not I, but God lives in me'.

THE EXALTED AND VICTORIOUS CHRIST

ARNOLD ALDIS

> 'Your attitude should be the kind that was shown us by Jesus Christ, who, though he was God, did not demand or cling to his rights as God, but laid aside his mighty power and glory, taking the disguise of a slave and becoming like men. And he humbled himself even further, going so far as actually to die a criminal's death on a cross. Yet it was because of this that God raised him up to the heights of heaven and gave him a name that is above every name, that at the name of Jesus every knee should bow, in heaven and on earth and under the earth, and every tongue shall confess that Jesus Christ is Lord to the glory of God the Father.' (Phil. 2:5–11 from *The Living Bible*)

Under the overall title of 'The Unchanging Christ' we have considered the pre-existent Christ, eternally one with the Father, who did not use his equality with God as an opportunity to establish his rights in opposition to God, but who voluntarily humbled himself and became obedient unto death. We have considered also the human Jesus in his life of perfect obedience even unto death, the death of the cross. And now we turn to the last theme which speaks of the exaltation and glorification of Christ to his rightful position on the throne of the universe in equality with God.

We have spoken of the true humanity of the incarnate Christ, which is so clearly emphasised by Paul in Philippians 2. He makes the point by saying the same thing in several different ways, so that there could be no misunderstanding. 'He made himself of no reputation. He took upon him the form of a servant. He was made in the likeness of men. He was found in fashion as a man.' But, while the life of our Lord was a truly human life, it was at the same time a unique life, unique in his birth, unique in his life and unique in his death. But the earthly life of the unchanging Christ was unique supremely in his resurrection from the dead, and to this we now turn as we look at the last section of our reading.

Christ exalted

> 'Wherefore God also hath highly exalted him, and given him a name that is above every name: that at the name of Jesus every

> knee should bow, of things in heaven, and things in earth and things under the earth; and that every tongue should confess that Jesus Christ is Lord, to the glory of God the Father' (AV).

While these verses refer in large part to the ascension and exaltation of Christ and his future triumph and reign, they clearly also include his resurrection, for in this God vindicated his son and set his seal upon his life and atoning death. But before considering the glorious statements of our passage of Scripture by confirming and amplifying them, let us look for a moment at the word which opens this section: 'Wherefore' — 'Wherefore God has highly exalted him.' Read like this it would be easy to see the exaltation of Christ as some sort of reward given by God for his obedience unto death. This however would, I think, be a false reading and would convey the wrong idea. Rather, it is that the exaltation and glorification of Christ is the natural and logical outcome of his perfect life in obedience. His place at the Father's side and on the throne was his, and his by right. He did not earn it, but resumed it. As one of the best known hymns in the English language puts it: 'The highest place that heaven affords, is his by sovereign right, The King of kings and Lord of lords, and heaven's eternal light'.

The effects of the resurrection of Christ

Let us now look at the glorious theme of the resurrection of Jesus and his exaltation and triumph. The resurrection has been the subject of more attacks than perhaps any other Christian belief. As many of the opponents of the Christian faith have seen more clearly than some of its professed friends, the resurrection is crucial to the faith, for as Paul puts it, 'If Christ be not risen from the dead, your faith is in vain, ye are yet in your sins' (1 Cor. 15:14). The bodily resurrection of Christ is of course one of those historic facts upon which Christianity rests, and it is open to historical investigation. It is not my purpose at this point — nor would there be time — to pursue the subject of the evidences for the resurrection. They have, in any case, been very adequately set out elsewhere by a number of authors, and are, I believe, sufficient to satisfy all except those who are determined not to believe whatever the evidence.

First of all then let us note that the resurrection of Christ, as with the whole of his life and death, is set forth in Scripture as being

Christ's own action and at the same time the work of God. Thus in John 10 Jesus says, 'No man taketh my life from me, I lay it down of myself. I have power to lay it down and I have power to take it again.' Again in John 2:19, in answer to the challenge of the Jews concerning his authority in cleansing the temple, Jesus says, 'Destroy this temple, and in three days I will raise it again'. Yet in the Acts and the Epistles the resurrection of Christ is consistently ascribed to God. Thus in Peter's sermon on the day of Pentecost he says, 'this Jesus hath God raised up, whereof we are all witnesses' (Acts 2:32), and in the same sermon he quotes from the Messianic Psalm 16, 'Thou wilt not leave my soul in Hades neither wilt thou suffer thy Holy One to see corruption'. Or again in the simple confession of faith for the believer given by Paul in Romans 10:9 we read, 'If thou shalt confess with thy mouth Jesus as Lord, and believe in thy heart that God has raised him from the dead, thou shalt be saved'. So once again we find the actions of God and the actions of Jesus identified and used interchangeably.

Then note, too, that the resurrection was the crowning evidence that Jesus was who he claimed to be, the very Son of God. It was the evidence which he himself submitted. And so, Paul, opening his letter to the Christians in Rome, writes of Christ that 'He is declared to be the Son of God with power by his resurrection from the dead'.

Then notice that, as with his death, the resurrection of Christ was for us, for, 'He was delivered for our offences and was raised for our justification' (Rom. 4:25). So as the believer sees in the crucified Christ his sin-bearer, he sees in the risen Christ his justifier before God. As in the cross the sinner finds forgiveness, so in the resurrection he finds justification. This means that the believer's standing before God depends on the twin central facts of the gospel, the death and the resurrection of Jesus Christ, not on his death alone but also on his risen life. How clearly Paul puts this in Romans 5:10 when he writes, 'For if while we were enemies we were reconciled to God by the death of his Son, much more, now that we are reconciled, shall we be saved by his life'.

So, too, the resurrection provides the dynamic for Christian living and Paul prays for the Ephesian Christians, that 'they might know what is the immeasurable greatness of his power in us who believe, according to the working of his great might, which he accomplished in Christ when he raised him from the dead'

(Eph. 1:20–21) and prays for himself that 'he might know the power of his resurrection' (Phil. 3:10). And all this is brought about by the believer's identification with Christ both in his death and in his resurrection, so that Paul writes, 'We were buried therefore with Christ by baptism into death, so that as Christ was raised from the dead by the glory of the Father, we too might walk in newness of life. For if we have been united with him in a death like his we shall certainly be united with him in a resurrection like his' (Rom. 6:4–5). So, too, Paul writes concerning his own life, 'I am crucified with Christ, nevertheless I live, yet not I but Christ liveth in me' (Gal. 2:20). That this identification with the resurrection of Christ is not simply a hope for the future — as the use of the future tense in Romans 6:5 might suggest — but a present reality, is made clear in Ephesians where Paul speaks of God having 'raised us up with Christ and made us sit with him in the heavenly places in Christ Jesus' (Eph. 2:6).

The results of the exaltation

Although our identification with the resurrection is a present reality, the believer may also rejoice that it awaits a future fulfilment for Christ was raised 'to be the firstfruits of them that sleep' (1 Cor. 15:20). Death is not final for the Christian, but the prelude to a resurrection of glory 'when we shall be like him, for we shall see him as he is' (1 Jn. 3:2). We have the direct assurance of Jesus himself as to this in those strong words of hope, 'I am the resurrection and the life, he that believeth in me, though he were dead yet shall he live, and he that liveth and believeth in me shall never die' (John 11:25–26). Again three times in John 6 Jesus speaks of raising up the believer at the last day (John 6:40, 44, 54). So the unchanging Christ is now the exalted and glorified Christ, set at God's right hand. Once again it is for us, for he is there ever representing us and pleading our cause before the Father.

If we fall into sin he is there as our advocate with the Father, pleading his atonement as the ground for our forgiveness and his imputed righteousness as the ground for our acceptance (1 Jn. 2:1–2). Not only so but 'He is able to save to the uttermost all who come unto God by him, seeing he ever liveth to make intercession for us' (Heb. 7:25). Jesus once said to Peter, 'Simon, Simon, behold Satan demanded to have you that he might sift you like wheat, but I have prayed for you, that your faith fail not'

(Luke 22:31), and in his high priestly prayer for the disciples recorded in John 17 our Lord says, 'Neither pray I for these alone, but also for those who believe on me through their word' (John 17:20). We all now share a place for all time in the prayers of the risen and exalted Christ and who can tell how much the perseverance of the saints is dependent on the intercessions of the Saviour. But the resurrection of Christ is also the guarantee of final judgement. For Paul preaching before the Areopagus on Mars Hill declares, 'God now commands men everywhere to repent, because he has fixed a day on which he will judge the world in righteousness by a man whom he has appointed, and of this he has given assurance to all men by raising him from the dead' (Acts 17:30–31). Sin will not forever go unpunished, wickedness will not forever triumph, but wrongs will be righted and justice done by the unchanging Christ.

The resurrection, however, was only the first step in the exaltation and glorification of Christ which took place at the ascension. I have often wondered whether we are right to emphasise the resurrection almost to the exclusion of the ascension, for clearly our Lord himself regarded the ascension as the moment of his exaltation. Thus, to Mary in the garden the risen Jesus says, 'Do not hold me, for I have not yet ascended to the Father, but go to my brethren and say unto them, I am ascending to my Father and your Father, to my God and your God' (John 20:17). So too in the Epistles the writers make much of what has been called the 'heavenly session' of Christ. Paul writes, 'God raised him from the dead and made him sit at his right hand in the heavenly places, far above all rule and authority and power and dominion and above every name that is named, not only in this age, but in the age which is to come' (Eph. 1:20–21), and the passage of Scripture from which we are working speaks of God having 'highly exalted him and given him a name that is above every name'.

So Christ, who in his incarnation humbled himself and became man, is now exalted and set at God's right hand far above all, but he is the same unchanging Christ, and in resuming the place that was his by right with all the attributes which he laid aside in his incarnation, he did not discard his humanity. It is important to say this, for many have thought, and seem to think today, that Jesus, the pre-existent Christ, became man for the brief period of his life on earth and then became God again at his resurrection and ascension. But this is not what the Scripture teaches. It tells us that the pre-existent Christ became man and is now and forever both God and man, so that in a very real sense there is a man in heaven today on the throne of the universe, so that the faithful Stephen, as he was being stoned, could say, 'Behold I see the heavens opened and the Son of Man standing at the right hand of God' (Acts 7:56). Or again the aged apostle John in exile on Patmos has a vision of heaven and sees a Lamb standing by the throne as though it had been slain (Rev. 5:6). The presence of a man, the man Christ Jesus, in heaven today is the guarantee that there will be many with him there one day, for he is the firstborn of many brethren and it is his purpose to bring many sons unto glory (Rom. 8:29; Heb. 2:10).

The final authority of Christ

The exaltation and glorification of Christ has a further purpose, as our passage of Scripture tells us, and it is that 'at the name of Jesus every knee should bow whether in heaven or on earth or under the earth, and every tongue confess that Jesus Christ is Lord to the glory of God the Father'. In his resurrection and ascension Christ triumphed over all the forces of evil, over sin and over death for, 'When he ascended on high he led a host of captives and gave gifts to men' (Eph. 4:8) and his victory will one day be recognised by all. He was born to be King and indeed he is the King of kings and Lord of lords, and one day his kingship will be recognised by all for 'the kingdoms of this world are to become the kingdoms of our God and of his Christ, and he shall reign for ever and ever' (Rev. 11:15). Clearly, however, this moment has not yet arrived and Scripture confirms that there is a future consummation for which we will have to wait. As the writer of the epistle to the Hebrews puts it when speaking of Christ, 'Thou didst make him for a little while lower than the angels, thou hast crowned him with glory and honour putting everything in subjection under his feet. As it is we do not yet see everything in subjection to him, but we see Jesus crowned with glory and honour' (Heb. 2:7–9).

How then is the unchanging Christ to establish his kingdom and become effectively King of kings and Lord of lords so that every knee shall bow and every tongue confess him Lord? Surely this is by a process culminating in a crisis. The process is taking place now, and we who meet here are a part of that process. Jesus Christ came to be the founder of a new race of men, a redeemed humanity, and he himself was the first of that race for he is the first-born of many brethren. To his disciples, who were among the first to enter the kingdom through the response of faith to the calling and election of God, he gave the task of proclaiming to the world that entrance to the kingdom was now indeed open to all on the same basis. As that great early Christian hymn the 'Te Deum' puts it, 'When thou hadst overcome the sharpness of death, thou didst open the kingdom of heaven to all believers'. In this sense the kingdom of God already exists and has been growing down the centuries for in a very real sense, as Jesus said, 'The kingdom of God is within you' (Luke 17:21). Every believer who confesses Jesus as Lord and submits to his kingship is a part of that kingdom.

Sometimes the growth has been painfully slow, sometimes dramatic and exciting, sometimes in one part of the field which is the world, and sometimes in another. But always where the seed has been sown — if it has indeed been the good seed of the Word — some has fallen on good ground and has taken root and grown, watered by the Holy Spirit. And so the kingdom of God has grown by an organic living process and continues to do so. Some would have it that this is the whole story and that in the process of time the kingdom of God will be ushered in when all men have responded to the gospel.

This, however, is not the picture which the incarnate Christ, whose kingdom it is, gives to his disciples and us. True, he speaks of sowing the seed and the growth of the crop, but he speaks also of a harvest, a great climax to the ages, when the kingdom will reach its consummation, and he makes it clear that at the harvest there will still be wheat and weeds growing side by side. In the human analogy it is not possible for weeds to change into wheat, but gloriously in its Christian counterpart this is happening every day, for 'if any man be in Christ he is a new creature' (2 Cor. 5:17). Christ never gave us reason to believe that all men would respond to the gospel, the opportunity to do so is indeed available to all, but human free will is still respected and in this gospel-age God will never force any man to bow the knee and confess that Jesus is Lord. The task of the church is not to Christianise the world but to evangelise it; the first is an impossible task, but the second is gloriously possible and who can say how close it is to fulfilment?

The return of the triumphant Christ

How then is the climax of the ages, this harvest of the ripening grain, to take place? Surely the answer is to be found in the coming Christ. It is to me a very sad fact that the eager expectation of the second coming of Christ has so largely disappeared from so many churches today. It is rare to hear a sermon or address today which even mentions it, and yet Scripture is full of it. Perhaps this is one reason why the church is so often despondent and depressed today, for in the New Testament the second coming of Christ is held out as the great hope before the church. Paul writing to Titus says, 'We should live sober, upright and godly lives in this present world awaiting our blessed hope and the glorious appearing of our great God and Saviour Jesus Christ' (Titus 2:12–13).

There are I know some very obvious reasons why the doctrine of the Second Coming is so neglected today. In the first place, the doctrine bristles with problems and difficulties, partly by reason of the strange and unfamiliar apocalyptic language in which it is often presented in Scripture, and partly because it deals with matters of which we have no present experience and which are no doubt beyond our finite minds, limited as they are by concepts of time and space. But the fact that we are unable fully to comprehend the truth is no reason for discarding the truth itself, for, after all, the other doctrines of Scripture such as the Incarnation, and the Trinity are also beyond human comprehension but we do not discard them on that account.

Then, in the second place, the doctrine has been done a great disservice by those who have sought to find dogmatic answers to the riddle of the apocalyptic language and have ventured to draw up detailed interpretations and timetables which have often been conflicting and contradictory, and so the doctrine itself has suffered. But this is no reason for not accepting what is clear in Scripture concerning the second coming — and there is much that is clear beyond reasonable doubt. It may be profitable for us to look at some of these certainties before we close these studies on the unchanging Christ.

First, then, the return of Christ is certain for he promised it himself in memorable words to his disciples, 'Let not your hearts be troubled, believe in God, believe also in me. In my Father's house are many rooms, if it were not so I would have told you. I go to prepare a place for you. And when I go and prepare a place for you, I will come again and will take you to myself, that where I am, ye may be also' (John 14:1–3).

Secondly, it is the unchanging Christ, human and divine, who is coming, as the angelic messengers on the Mount of Olives are careful to insist: 'This same Jesus, which is taken from you into heaven, shall so come in like manner as ye have seen him go into heaven' (Acts 1:11).

Thirdly, it will be a visible bodily return as the angels' words make clear and as Jesus himself taught in his answer to the high priest's challenge at his trial. ' "Are you the Christ, the Son of the Blessed?" And Jesus said, "I am, and you will see the Son of Man sitting at the right hand of power, and coming with the clouds of heaven" ' (Mark 14:61–62).

Fourthly, he is coming to complete our salvation. Not that anything further has to be done over and above what he has done already; our salvation is assured by that one perfect and sufficient sacrifice made once for all on the cross. But our experience of that salvation is still only partial and incomplete. Paul reminds us that 'We have this treasure in earthen vessels' (2 Cor. 4:7). So, too, the writer of the epistle to the Hebrews declares, 'So Christ having been offered once to bear the sins of many, will appear a second time, not to deal with sin but to save those who are eagerly waiting for him' (Heb. 9:28).

Fifthly, he is coming to reward his servants. This is made clear in many of the parables of the kingdom which fell from his lips and which are recorded in the gospels. There is a tendency among Christians to disclaim any idea of reward, and of course it is true that after we have done all that is commanded we remain unworthy servants (Luke 17:10), and the thought of reward should not be the motive for our service. But we would be very wrong to despise the reward. Paul, as he reached the end of his life, writes to his son in the faith, Timothy, 'I have fought the good fight, I have finished my course, I have kept the faith. Henceforth there is laid up for me a crown of righteousness, which the Lord, the righteous judge shall give me on that day, and not to me only but unto all those who love his appearing' (2 Tim. 4:7–8).

He is coming to judge the living and the dead. The Scriptures make it quite clear that Christ is the appointed judge, 'The Father judges no one but has given all judgment to the Son' (John 5:22). Since the judgment has been committed to the unchanging Christ whose love knows no bounds we may be assured that that judgment will combine both perfect justice and perfect love.

He is coming to meet and to claim his bride, the Church, which on that day will be 'without spot or wrinkle or any such thing, but holy and without blemish' (Eph. 5:27), just as its members will be 'presented faultless before the presence of his glory with rejoicing' (Jude 24). What a glorious prospect this is for us, 'for we shall see him as he is, face to face, whom we now see through a glass darkly' — or 'as in a mirror dimly' as the RSV has it (1 Cor. 13:12). How perfectly Job expresses this hope although he wrote centuries before the coming of Christ, 'I know that my redeemer liveth, and that in my flesh shall I see God, and not as a stranger but as a friend' (Job 19:25–27).

Finally, he is coming to set up his kingdom which shall have no end. Words fail to describe what this will be like and the Bible resorts to pictorial language to portray it. We can have little conception as to what the reality will be like or how it will come about, but of its certainty there can be no doubt. He was born to be king, and King he will be. It will be the unchanging Christ, the same yesterday and today and forever who will reign. To that glad day and joyful reunion let us eagerly look forward, active in his service till he comes.

'I cannot tell how all the lands shall worship
When at his bidding every storm is stilled,
Nor yet how great the sound of jubilation
When all the hearts of men with love are filled.
But this I know, the skies will thrill with splendour
And myriad, myriad human voices sing,
And earth to heaven and heaven to earth make answer
At last, the Saviour, Saviour of the world is KING.'

Section 2

Relationships

Spiritual, personal, social and professional

CHANGE OF PERSONAL IDENTITY

PABLO MARTINEZ

Introduction

THE first morning we considered how being united with Christ, being in Christ, produces certain changes in our person. We saw how it affects our past and delivers us from the burden of our past, then opens a new window with three different landscapes outside. The first had to do with our relationship with God. We have a new relationship with God, the thirst and love for God. Secondly, we saw how this affects our relationships with others — the social implication of the change. There is also a third area where the Gospel, being in Christ and with Christ, brings forth dramatic and big changes. This is in the relationship with oneself, the matter of personal identity.

Knowledge of self

What is my identity? Who am I? What is my value? How should I view myself? Am I important? Why am I important? I believe this is a crucial subject in a society that has come to replace the knowledge of God with the knowledge of man. Certainly there is a place for us to get to know ourselves. We cannot condemn completely a certain amount of self-knowledge. The old Greek phrase says, 'Know thyself'. This is right to a certain degree, but when knowledge of ourselves becomes our goal then it has become an idol, which is wrong. This is what we see in our society today — self glorification, the cult of selfism or self-worship.

There are many psychiatrists and psychologists who say you are able to do whatever you want to do. Just close your eyes and dream a dream and go after it because you have the self drive to get what you want. This self glorification in human power has an emphasis which is totally wrong and unfortunately it is affecting our churches. Secularism today is pervading our Christian life and our churches. I think the so-called 'psychologisation' of Christian

ICMDA European Congress, Balatonoliga, Hungary, 1996. **Pablo Martinez.** *Clinical psychiatrist, church elder, Barcelona. Chairman of UME Spain.*

faith or 'psychologisation' of the church has rightly been criticised. We cannot replace the knowledge of God with introspection and self analysis, we cannot transform small Bible study groups into places for group dynamics and we cannot convert worship into personal catharsis.

We have to be very careful. What do we put first? Ourselves? Self-knowledge, which is ultimately self-worship, or God? This is one extreme but we have to be equally careful with the other extreme, which says psychology is evil! Christian psychologists and psychiatrists are in great risk of being heretics! 'How can you be a Christian and a psychiatrist?' people often ask me. They wonder how I can stand firm in my faith. The answer is, 'Give unto Caesar what is Caesar's and give to God what is God's.' The problem in our society is that we have lost the balance and we are giving to Caesar too much of what belongs to God.

Knowledge of God's Word
Let us look at Isaiah 43:1–5. Let these words really sink in. When the Word of God reaches the depths of our heart it is not something cold and intellectual but personal and it makes a difference. Christ being in us has something to say to our identity and self-esteem and who we are in Christ. It is here that we reach the great therapeutic value of the Gospel.

Firstly an introductory note to Isaiah 43. This is a promise that was primarily addressed to the people of Israel, so we need to remember the principle of hermeneutics which says that we have the freedom to use the promises in the Old Testament addressed to the people of Israel, and apply them to ourselves today. What do we find in this passage? Where is our identity to be found and founded? There are only two possible answers to this.

Either our identity is founded on our achievements, on our value of ourselves (and this is humanism) or our identity is founded on God himself.

Identity founded on self
It is interesting to see how existentialism brought forth two branches, one of which was the atheistic branch of existentialism with Jean-Paul Sartre, Camus and others. Furthermore it is interesting to read Jean-Paul Sartre's work and to note that some-times he had doubts as an atheist. Atheists also doubt in the same

way that Christians sometimes doubt, and at certain stages in his life Sartre wondered whether instead he should believe in God. Why was this?

Another great psychologist said, 'The problem in the 19th century was God's death, and the problem in the 20th century is man's death.' Unfortunately he did not see the relationship between the two facts. When you build up your identity solely on yourself, sooner or later you come to a great identity crisis. It is striking to realise how many bright intellectuals have ended their lives by committing suicide, or have had psychological disturbances and turmoil, from Nietzsche, Arthur Koestler and Hemingway to Sartre himself. When you have built up your identity on your own achievements, sooner or later you will reach an identity crisis. Who am I, what is the sense of life?

Identity founded on God
The other option is to base our identity on God himself. In this passage in Isaiah we find two supports which sustain our identity. Firstly, our identity is based on God's very identity, or what God is for us. Secondly, our identity is based on God's opinion of who we are, in other words our identity in God's eyes. Let us look at these two means of support.

Our identity is based on God's identity
We find four words in these verses in Isaiah that give us the key. These four words can be linked into pairs, so there are actually two attributes of God's identity that are therapeutic to us.

First, God is *creator* and *the one who forms us;* in Latin we could say *formator.* It is interesting that God does not refer only to himself as creator. There is something else besides creation. Why? If he only used the word creator it could give us the impression that this was just a moment or point in time, making it seem that 'God created us and left us alone, lost in the immense space of life'.

So the word creator is followed by another very important attribute of God — the one who forms you, and that makes the world of difference. Could you tell me what is the difference between a biological father and a real parent? How long does it take to make a child? No more than one minute. How long does it take to form, to shape, to mould, to educate a child? Ten years, twenty years? *Creating* is somehow easy but *forming, moulding and shaping*, the continuous action that a parent imparts to a child, is far more difficult. God is not only a biological father, a creator, he is the one who forms us like a potter with the clay vessel at the wheel. God forges our personality and our character and he is like the sculptor working with a chisel.

Ephesians 2:10 springs to mind, that we are 'God's workmanship'. The original word in Greek means we are God's poem. Do we really believe that? When I say this among circles of young people, some of them protest and say that, 'If I am God's poem, he didn't write a very good one.' Whether we like it or not we are God's craftsmanship and poem and he continues to sustain us and mould us with certain specific purposes. So the first feature of God's identity is that he is creator and he continues to form us.

Secondly, the other attribute is that God is *redeemer* and *saviour.* Let us read verses 1 and 3 of Isaiah 43.

> 'But now, this is what the Lord says—
> he who created you …
> he who formed you …
> "Fear not, for I have redeemed you …
> For I am the Lord, your God, the Holy One of Israel,
> your Saviour …" '

These two words go together again because we cannot separate them, in the same way that we cannot separate the creator from the one who forms, nor can we separate the saviour from the redeemer.

Now we all know about the word redemption. To redeem in the old Greek world meant to buy a slave and to give him freedom. Therefore the basic idea behind redemption is freedom. We should not forget this even though we know it very well. God's intention for our identity is freedom and deliverance. It is most interesting to realise how the International Association of Psychoanalysts (there are several of them with different names) has chosen as their motto the verse, 'You shall know the truth and the truth shall make you free.' A non-Christian organisation has this motto! The aim of psychoanalysis is deliverance and making us free. This is exactly the same idea that lies behind the message of the gospel, that of freedom and deliverance.

How sad it is to see Christians in churches who are so burdened by their problems, even by their Christian rules and regulations, that they look like small birds in a cage. They are like prisoners who go to church in a very unhappy way. Where is the deliverance and freedom for those Christians and for those churches? So we are created and formed by God, saved and redeemed to have freedom and free lives.

A deep relationship. God continues, 'I called you by name.' There is a signature to these attributes. It is not only that God is creator or that he redeemed us but that there is a deep personal relationship. 'I call you by name.' Calling someone by name is a symptom of intimacy to a point that when two lovers, a husband and a wife, have a deep intimate relationship when they are engaged or married, they have certain names for each other that no one else in the world knows. I wouldn't know the English words but there are some sweet Spanish words for lovers. Calling someone by name is an expression of intimacy. Nineteen times in these five verses the idea of relationship appears — you, with me, with you. There is a constant personal relationship. God knows my name and calls me by name. When we are in heaven we will all have our own name as an expression of intimacy.

You are mine. We close this first point with another sentence from these verses. '... You are mine', verse 1. I wish for a moment that we could have music for this passage because there is a crescendo and the intensity grows. God is your creator, he forms you, he saves you, he calls you by name, he says, you are mine. This is exactly what a husband and wife tell each other, you are mine and no one else's. There is such intimacy in a married relationship that they feel they belong to each other; you are mine. This is exactly the same idea in our relationship with God, that of intimacy.

This has some ethical implications that we will not consider now but we need to mention. We are God's property for two reasons, the right of creation and the right of redemption. Because of this it gives us great security and certainty. 'My sheep are mine and no one will steal them from my hand' (John 10:27–28) is a great comfort and at the same time a duty and responsibility. I cannot do with my life what I want.

So, the first support for our identity is God's own identity. We must now move to the second one.

Our identity in God's sight

There are three sentences that we now have to read. What does God say to you and me? Verse 4, '… you are precious and honoured in my sight, and … I love you'. Before we consider this passage notice the very small statement 'in my sight'. This is God's opinion and what he thinks of you and me. Your opinion is secondary and does not matter as much as God's opinion of ourselves.

I remember a young man who was a patient once coming to me and telling me, 'I feel like a mosquito'. I was surprised by the comparison; I have heard patients comparing themselves to dogs or cats but never mosquitoes! This aroused my interest and I asked him why. He said, 'What do you do when you kill a mosquito? You just kill it and nothing happens, no one knows or cares. This is exactly how I feel.' He was a Christian and I told him it was interesting to hear his opinion of himself, but I said, 'Do you really believe that God thinks you are a mosquito?' He opened his eyes and did not answer. Some time later he came to me and said, 'I realise that feeling like a mosquito was insulting God. I am not a mosquito any more, I am a person.' I was relieved to hear of this change.

The most important thing ultimately is God's opinion and not ours. In his sight you are, first of all, *'precious'*. This means costly, high priced and God had to pay a high price for us. Secondly, *'honoured'*, of great value. We are worthy of receiving honour. This is followed by the conclusion, *'I love you'*. It is here that we need to grasp these sentences in a very personal way. Can you imagine the voice of the Lord telling you these three sentences?

Let us pause for a moment. God is telling you and me that in his eyes we are precious, honourable, and that he loves us. If we come to experience that reality in our life it will have revolutionary effects from an emotional and existential viewpoint, unrelated to materialism and humanism.

Kodak, the founder of the famous American photograph and film enterprise, died by committing suicide. He said, 'Nothing in this life gave me satisfaction.' Goethe, the German philosopher and writer, who was probably one of the brightest minds in the last century, said on his seventy-fifth birthday: 'In 75 years I have never enjoyed one day of real happiness.'

What and where is our identity based upon? God is telling you and me we are precious and honoured and that he loves us. That, little by little will substitute for your ideas about yourself — 'I am good for nothing', 'I am a disaster', 'no one loves me, no one cares'. So many people in our society are crippled by feelings of inferiority and low self-esteem and they look for affection anywhere, for example in Buddhism, New Age philosophy or in erotic sexuality. Chesterton was very right when he said: 'When man ceases believing in God, it is not so much that he believes nothing but that he believes anything.'

Men and women are searching for identity in dry, arid places. Our identity is ultimately built upon these two supportive columns. God tells you and me, 'I created you, I continue to shape and mould you, I saved you by redeeming you and therefore freedom is the aim of your life. I call you by name and you are mine, and in my opinion you are precious and honoured and I love you.'

Of course, our achievements and what we do in life are important, but let us remember that ultimately the meaning of life and the sense of our identity is not found in ourselves, but in God alone.

MEDICAL SERVICE WHICH SPELLS FREEDOM

JOHN WHITE

THIS morning we will think about how to use and maintain our freedom, how to learn and serve joyfully and effectively, how to find the place of service that God has for each one of us.

Maintaining freedom

Let me begin with how to use and maintain our freedom. Let us glance once again at Galatians 5:1,13,16,25. In verse 1 we learn what Christ has done. 'Christ set us free to be free men. Stand firm then and refuse to be tied to the yoke of slavery again.' Christ has given us freedom and we are to maintain that freedom. We are urged not to lose it. Of course it is essential that we understand again the nature of the freedom. Freedom from what? What was Paul writing to the Galatians about? He had been teaching them about freedom from the need to justify themselves by keeping the law.

Have you not felt as I have felt that I was inadequate as a Christian and that I could not meet the standards required of me, that I would be judged and that I would be failed? This is the kind of thing that Paul is talking about. We do not need to justify ourselves before God any more. God is perfectly satisfied with what Christ has done, and to discover that is to discover what it means to be free and to be holy. Of course I have to go on applying the lesson again and again. But that truth is the constant source of my own deliverance from bondage, the bondage to sin and the bondage of having to keep the law in order to please God.

Free to love

How do we guard that freedom? There are certain things we must not do, other things that we must do. In Galatians 5:13 we read, 'You, my friends, were called to be free men, only do not turn your freedom into licence for your lower nature, but be servants to one

ICCMS Oxford, UK, 1980. **John White.** *Associate professor of psychiatry, University of Manitoba, Canada.*

another in love' (*agape* love). In being loving servants to one another and to the world, we will maintain that freedom that Christ has given.

There are problems here and the first is how do I love? How do I love the obnoxious Christian students who always get in the way of God's work in my medical school? How do I love the stupid committee members who have such wild ideas which are neither biblical nor practical and yet they insist on them? How shall I love my old-fashioned church members who don't seem to understand what my job is?

Here are some pointers which I can give you. I suppose it is always easier to love when I know that I am loved. People who come from families where there is real parental love find it easier to get on with people and to love people, so in the degree that the Holy Spirit reveals to us how much God loves each one of us, we will have greater freedom in loving other people. Again, if we recognise that Christ loved some of the stupid people with whom we are surrounded, it will be easier for us to love them too. The critical point is that we act in love towards them. We often confuse love with liking. God does not call on us to like stupid people and if we are surrounded by them it may be that we do not feel attracted to them, but we must show love to them. God does not call on us to like ugliness, but he does call on us to love ugly people and in order to learn to love we must act as though we do love. We will find that if we obey the Holy Spirit and act towards somebody as though we love them, then feelings will follow on. We are not to wait for loving feelings, we are first to act in love. So the three little pointers are:

- *first, to ask the Holy Spirit to teach you from the Scriptures how much God loves you;*
- *second, to realise how Christ loves the very people you do not like; and*
- *third, to act in love whether you feel love in your heart or not.*

The Holy Spirit our teacher

To safeguard our freedom we must be guided by the Holy Spirit. This is repeated in Galatians 5:16,25. Verse 16 says, 'I mean this, if you are guided by the Spirit, you will be freed from (or not fulfil) the desires of your nature.' In verse 25, 'If the Spirit is the source of our life, let the Spirit also direct our cause.' Sometimes we are inclined to think that there is a mysterious process whereby in yielding blindly to the Holy Spirit we will become holy. On the contrary, the Holy Spirit is presented to us in this and other passages primarily as our guide in the sense of being our teacher, that is, the one who supervises the development of progress in holiness.

We submit to the Holy Spirit as our clinical director, our instructor, the one who tells us what to do on the job and this is a moment by moment thing. Whether we like it or not we will find that the Holy Spirit is telling us what to do and only by closing our mind to him will we escape from him. We may not have realised whose the voice was, but increasingly as our life goes on he will remind us of Scripture. He will say do this and we will say, I can't and he says, never mind whether you can or you can't, do it. As we obey, we develop the skills of Christian living. It is something which has to be learned. Holiness is not a theory, it is practice.

Guided by him we find that we are not giving way to our lower nature, but every time we do, we know that the blood of Jesus is still available, the death of Christ still satisfies God. We are not learning holiness in order to justify ourselves before God, but having been justified he wants to train us so that we may learn our freedom.

Singleminded service

While we use and maintain our freedom, we are also called to serve joyfully and effectively. Look at Ephesians 6:5–8. The context is obedience to earthly masters on the part of slaves; the principles apply not only to our earthly masters but to our fellow-Christians and to non-Christians. We are servants. How can we avoid service becoming a chore? 'Slaves, obey your earthly masters with fear and trembling. Singlemindedly, as serving Christ, do not merely offer the outward show of service to curry favour with men but as slaves of Christ do wholeheartedly the will of God. Give the cheerful service of those who serve the Lord, not men, for you know that whatever good each man may do, slave or free, will be repaid him by the Lord.' Now the basic principle is repeated four times in these four verses. We must do our service for the Lord Jesus Christ. Although I may outwardly be serving my patient, or anyone else, I must do it as though I were serving the Lord himself. If I am working for someone I dislike, it is as though the Lord says to me,

'Do it for me. You may not feel like it but do it for me.' We must do our service for the Lord Jesus Christ, because in so doing we please him.

You will notice that he says in verse 5, 'Singlemindedness, as serving Christ'; in verse 6, 'As the slaves of Christ'; in verse 7, 'As those who serve the Lord', and in verse 8 he reminds us that because we are serving him we will be paid by him. So Paul emphasises this principle, that we are to serve the Lord, and if we find it difficult to serve others, we must remember it is work for the Lord and that will make it easier. We are not serving to impress other people. We can even use the word 'testimony' wrongly; sometimes by testimony we mean am I impressing non-Christians? We are not called upon to impress non-Christians. Witness and testimony are God's goodness shining through while others simply will perceive our weaknesses.

Let us look at the tests by which we may know whether in serving others we are truly serving Christ. The first thing Paul mentions in verse 5 is that our service should be with fear and with trembling. The fear and trembling is before the Lord, and this is our reaction because we are aware of the greatness and the solemnity of our task. Most of us have a happy, jolly kind of approach to Christian service, unaware of the profound issues that are at stake. If we do not fear and tremble as we go to serve others, it is because we have not realised what we are doing.

We are also told to serve singlemindedly. The real difficulty most of us have in serving others is our ambivalence. We are not sure whether we really want to do it or not. We need to commit ourselves wholeheartedly to this service of the Lord, knowing that it will bring glory to him and that it is the best thing for others and for ourselves. Therefore, we must do it wholeheartedly, cheerfully, gladly and freely, a cheerful service because we serve the Lord, not men.

Guidance for the future

How can I know what God has for me in the future? Let me comment on the nature of guidance. One of the principles in guidance is that God's Word, the principles of Scripture, are a lamp to our feet and a light to our path (Ps. 119:105). The Word of God is not a searchlight that picks out the end of our path. God will not necessarily reveal to us what we are going to be doing 30 or 40 years from now; rather, it is his will to show us what we must do today and how to apply moral principles to our daily, step-by-step walk. If we keep on the pathway — and in our case it is to be the pathway of righteousness — we will end up in the right place. If, step by step, we please the Lord, we will have far fewer problems about long-range guidance.

As we consciously think about the future, how are we going to know the right way? The key is to have confidence in God because God wants you to find that place far more than you do. He is deeply concerned about your future and he is not going to let you go. Christian guidance is not walking a tightrope but a path. If we get into the bushes we will find that the Holy Spirit will come after us and will say, 'No, no. You go this way.' Many of our anxieties are because we do not understand God's purposes for us.

It is in order to understand God that we need to look at Hebrews 12:1. With all these witnesses to faith around us like a cloud we must throw off every encumbrance, every sin to which we cling, and run with resolution the race for which we are entered. We must have confidence in God. We are surrounded by all sorts of men and women who have down the ages, through the Holy Spirit, brought Scripture to us. *The thrust of their message is that God is a holy, a loving and a just God.* This is a most basic lesson about guidance. God is to be trusted, he will indeed lead, he will indeed guide, he will indeed bring us to the place where he wants us to be. Therefore, let us pay heed to this great crowd of witnesses. They are telling us that they understand how we feel; they were human too, and still are. As feeble human beings with all the difficulties we face, they found that God is wholly reliable. Therefore, let us rely upon him as they urge us to.

The second thing we are told if we are to be guided aright is to throw away all the encumbrances and the sins to which we cling. Mark that the verse is talking about things which we cling to. God has his own order in dealing with sin in our lives, and it is not always the same order as ours. Some habits humiliate us and we wish that we could get rid of them so that we could feel all right about ourselves, and we wonder why God does not deal with those besetting sins, as we call them. What we must do is to throw away attitudes to which we are clinging, those which we could give up but are unwilling to. One example is an unforgiving spirit. Sometimes I feel resentful towards certain people. It may be painful but I must forgive them and I must give up my unforgiving attitude.

Thirdly, we are to run with resolution. The Greek word here means 'stickability', the capacity to hang on in the face of discouragement. For of course the enemy of our souls wants us to become discouraged. How can I know what my future will be? Will I ever get through my medical studies? How can I possibly both serve God and be a physician or a surgeon? How can I be serving the Lord when I fail so often? The resolution springs from knowing the faithfulness of God. We must run with resolve. Only as the difficulties arise will we learn the capacity to run on determinedly. He wants us to have that faith that endures, not the faith which is great in a religious meeting but disappears the moment I come face to face with a problem.

Finally, we are to run looking unto Jesus. We remember that he is still a human being and that he has faced the difficulties that we face here on earth, therefore he understands. We do not have a high priest who 'cannot be touched with the feelings of our infirmities', but one who was 'in all points tempted like as we are, yet without sin' (Heb. 4:15). Whatever our temptation is, he has felt that temptation. We must look to him and remind ourselves that we walk in his footsteps. We remember, too, that he is interceding for us. The Captain of our salvation pleads for us at the right hand of the Father here and now, so, 'looking unto him, let us run with patience' (Heb. 12:1). The Lord Jesus plans before us a pathway of service in the freedom that he has given us.

As the Holy Spirit brings these and other scriptures to our minds he will teach us all a glorious freedom in a loving service.

CONSTRAINTS FOR CHRISTIANS IN PRACTICE

RONALD WINTON

Introduction

CONSTRAINTS on a doctor in practice would seem to me to be in two main areas. The first area is within the practice. The second area is outside the practice.

Constraints within the practice relate particularly to the doctor's relationship with patients, his relationship with patients' relatives, and relationships with his medical colleagues and the other health professionals with whom he works.

Constraints outside the practice relate to the community. They include such things as medical politics, social and community issues, and many aspects of ethics.

Constraints outside the practice

My brief is to set you thinking about the Christian doctor's place in the wider sphere of activity — constraints outside the practice. My qualification for talking about this is that for some thirty years of my medical career, I was observing medicine and the medical profession from the vantage point of an editorial chair. This was both in my own country and on an international level through my involvement in the World Medical Association. I was close to the leaders of the profession, with their involvement in medical politics, in social and community issues and in medical ethics. I was close to those involved in investigation and research, with all their implications, especially ethical, for the community. I was close to those who were in the thick of the actual professional game of medical practice.

If you look at the written constitution of most general medical organisations, particularly national medical associations, you will see at the beginning the stated objectives of the organisation. The first of these objectives is likely to be expressed in some such words as this: 'The promotion of the medical sciences and the mainte-

ICMDA Cancun, Mexico, 1986. **Ronald R. Winton.** *Past editor* Medical Journal of Australia *and formerly Chairman World Medical Association and WMA Committee for medical ethics. ICMDA Chairman 1980–86, Vice-President 1986–94.*

nance of the honour and interests of the medical profession'. That covers most of the ground that I was talking about here. The point is that somebody has to be actively concerned with it. Who should this be?

Some doctors give a great deal of time and thought to these wider fields, involving, as they do, medical politics, social and community issues, medical ethics, and the like. Their work is voluntary and normally unpaid. It is often costly to their working time, to their income and to their leisure. It may be costly to their family life and even to their personal reputations and popularity. Medical politics, in particular, can be a demanding area. And at times it can be a rough and tumble game.

Why do they do it? Some would say that it is because they are concerned about medicine and the delivery of good health care. Some would say simply that they wish to look after the best interests, financial and social, of themselves and their colleagues. Some would admit that they enjoy it. And for some it is an ego booster.

What about the Christian doctor? Has he or she a place in this rough and tumble game? Is there a specific Christian contribution to be made? I suggest that we have a duty to answer these questions individually to ourselves, so far as we can.

BASIC ATTITUDES

Six basic attitudes come to my mind as possibilities for the Christian doctor. Most of them are options open to any doctor, but there are Christian ways of looking at them. The six attitudes are: 1 opt out; 2 criticise; 3 pray; 4 do something else; 5 give support; and 6 get involved.

Opt out

There are a number of reasons for having nothing to do with medicopolitical matters and social issues. The most common reason is general apathy and purely selfish preoccupation with one's own affairs, while expecting others to do the dirty work. Such attitudes are, I suggest, indefensible for anyone. They are surely incompatible with any Christian sense of duty. It may not be possible to do very much. Sheer busyness, family responsibilities or a limited capacity arising from such personal factors as ill health can be overwhelming. But it may still be possible to take an interest.

The specific question taken by some Christians is that medical politics and even social issues, like all politics and various other public matters, are 'worldly' and so they are 'out' for the Christian. This attitude centres on what the individual Christian understands by 'worldliness' and 'separation', especially in terms of scriptural passages where the Christian is told not to be unequally yoked together with unbelievers and is warned against love of the world.

We may understand these passages in different ways. They certainly tell the Christian to mind his step. But it would not be true to the fuller context of the Scriptures to see them as the basis of a sort of monasticism or opting out. Our Lord's prayer to his Father for his followers was:

> 'I do not pray that you should take them out of the world, but that you should keep them from evil. They are not of the world, even as I am not of the world … As you sent me into the world, so I have sent them into the world.' (John 17:15–19)

He was not joking when he laid on his followers — on us — the responsibility of being the light of the world and the salt of the earth. If we are to be of practical use, a light has to be where things are dark, and salt needs to be right in the soup.

It is true that in general mankind and human society are in rebellion against God. It is true that the one who is called the prince of this world manages to maintain a good deal of his usurped power, for Satan is a usurper. Nor can we expect God's complete rule to be restored until he chooses to take over. Nevertheless, this is God's world. And God's people have every right and responsibility in their everyday life to assert his sovereignty, as well as the validity and relevance of his ways and will. We have to recognise the plurality in our society. But that must not bluff us into silence.

In medicine it should be appreciated that to be a practitioner in isolation is virtually impossible. What goes on in the profession and in the community must impinge on the individual medical practice, indeed on any aspect of medical activity, whether clinical or not. Anyone who elects to enter medicine enters a broad field of trusteeship, which is not to be denied. Medicine is a trust, we are the trustees, and trustees are both guardians and servants of their trust.

Discharge of this trust is first of all to the individual patient. But it must also, I believe, involve an obligation towards medicine as a whole — the quality of health care delivered to the community, the standards and conditions of medical practice, the nature and limits of medical research, and so on. No medical man or woman is a medical island. And the Christian often has a very special contribution to make. Don't opt out.

Criticise

Destructive criticism is easy. Anyone can do it. It requires neither special training nor great effort, though a strong streak of irresponsibility helps a lot. For a Christian, destructive criticism is indefensible.

Constructive criticism is a different matter. It is, of course, harder and rarer, and it is more likely to be accompanied by, or followed by, constructive action. It has merit, provided it is informed and not pontifical. It is usually welcomed, even if only because it indicates interest and perhaps sympathy.

Pray

By all means let us pray — for patients, for staff, for colleagues at home and abroad, for the profession, for medicine and its development, and for everything to do with it. By all means, let us pray about medical politics and about specific issues as they come to the fore. Let us pray believing.

At the same time it is a waste of effort to pray cheap prayers, and by cheap prayers I mean prayers devised simply to pass the buck. Prayers are real only if they are about things which really concern us, things which concern us enough for us to be willing to be involved in the answer, if God so wills. With many things that we pray for, there seems little if any way in which we can be helpfully involved in the answer. We would if we could if we care. Rightly then, we look to God, and he cares. But we cannot expect a prayer to go beyond the ceiling, or indeed past the tops of our heads, if it is seen as a quick and easy way out.

Do something else

What do I mean by that? A good deal of argument goes on these days (including among Christians) between advocates of two schools of action on social and political matters. These are the 'symptom-treatment' and the 'cure' schools of action. Some enthusiastic activists lump together as 'band-aid' treatment the kind of charitable work and upholding of moral standards on which Christians have tended to concentrate in the past. They want action that goes deeper, they want to change the system.

Well, by all means, let us change the system if we are sure, quite sure, that we have a better one to adopt. But it seems rather rash to denigrate the so-called 'expedients', the charity, by means of which people of compassion and integrity have been meeting immediate human need in a practical way for a long time. No experienced doctor underrates the value of symptomatic treatment, even while he is carrying out genuine curative measures. Moreover, it is a sad fact of human experience that any social system, whether established or dazzling new, stands or fails by the qualities of those who administer it. Change does not guarantee improvement. In the world of medical politics, plans of this sort have to be thought through and assessed.

The thick of this battle is not every doctor's place, whether or not he wants to see the system changed. But that does not leave him with nothing to do. There are things to do with ensuring that patients receive truly caring attention within the available facilities, that hospitals run as smoothly as they can, that those who might miss out — the inadequate, the frightened and the shy, the ignorant, the stranger and the immigrant — are helped to get the care that most of us tend to assume they get. In this the Christian doctor has a great resource.

1 Corinthians 13 is God's prescription for living. The Christian will find ways of applying it — ways that will lift him out of the ghetto of mere pietism to assert, albeit simply and quietly, that Jesus Christ is Lord in all parts of God's world.

Give support

Nothing can make the campaigner for any worthwhile cause so sick at heart as the apathy of good people. He understands — and sometimes respects — his opponents. He discounts — and probably despises — the selfish and irresponsible. But he does hope for the support of men and women of goodwill, whom he has believed to have integrity and ideals and a thoughtful sense of responsibility (a description that should fit Christians). If they agree with what he is doing and the way he is doing it, he hopes that they will tell him. If they disagree, in whole or in part, he still hopes that they will tell him, and that they will explain their disagreement with understanding and charity.

This is very relevant in medical politics, where by the very nature of things every doctor is in some way implicated. Leaders of the profession are aware of this, and they reasonably expect some form of interest to flow from it. If they find their colleagues quite indifferent to what they are seeking to do, they need to be very dedicated and very patient — or very thick-skinned — if they are to carry on. The patient and dedicated people warrant honest support, with the offering of a frank and constructive expression of opinion.

This means that those in the support line must be informed and responsible and fair. Is it too much to expect that when people of integrity and good purpose accept leadership in our profession, they should be able to look to their Christian colleagues, just because they are Christian, for responsible, fair and charitable support and counsel? If so, that support and counsel must also be informed. If they do not see any point in looking to their Christian colleagues in this way, is there not something seriously wrong? Isn't this a breakdown in Christian witness? We should want to help here in this support area. There are lots of ways of doing it which, without being sanctimonious, are honouring to the Christ we are known to profess to serve.

Get involved

The idea of being 'involved' in anything scares some people. John Stott, in one of his books, relates the true story of the murder of a decent young woman in a New York street early one March morning in 1964. Within walking distance of her apartment she was stabbed by a man in three separate attacks. The police found that at least 38 respectable, middle-class, law-abiding citizens had heard the woman's screams and had from their windows watched her being stabbed, but had done nothing about it. They gave various reasons for their inaction. But, according to a police officer, 'the word we kept hearing from witnesses was "involved". People told us they just did not want to get involved.'

But not only fear of danger stimulates reluctance to being involved. Some Christians just say, 'If we get involved, where will it stop?' They forget that God will never ask us to do more than he gives us grace to cope with. Is there any reason to be scared of involvement in medical politics and in community issues? It may be demanding of time and effort, and sometimes of financial progress. It may do no good to our personal popularity, though the opposite can be the case. But it is scarcely terrifying.

Perhaps the Christian fears that it will land him or her in situations that will be embarrassing or that will be frankly incompatible with what he or she — rightly or wrongly, but sincerely — conceives to be a Christian way of life. Perhaps, if he sticks to his principles and convictions, the heat will be too much. He may then find himself thinking of a favourite phrase of President Harry Truman: 'If you can't stand the heat, stay out of the kitchen.' For the Christian it is more to the point to recall Shadrach, Meshach and Abednego in the burning fiery furnace — and the fourth figure that Nebuchadnezzar saw in the fire with them (Dan. 3). Even medical politics will never be as hot as that! And we are never left alone by God.

Above and beyond all that, we must never forget the costly involvement of God in his creation and the self-sacrificial involvement of the Son of God in mankind for our redemption. The servant is not greater than his master. If God so loved us, we ought also to love one another. That kind of love means involvement.

CHRISTIAN CHALLENGES TO LIFE

PAULOS GREGORIOS

Biblical realities

D R Gregorios read from the prologue to St John's Gospel (John 1:1–5) and from the beginning of St John's first letter (1 Jn. 1:1–9). In particular he referred to four realities in those passages (he preferred to say 'realities' rather than 'words'), Logos, Life, Light, Love, and to the way in which those realities related to a healing ministry as well as to our lives. We continue with his commentary:

One of the tragedies of our language is that a word like 'logos' is translated as 'word'. Words can become cheap and lose their value. But Logos is a rich concept. It means the self-communicating, sustaining, creative power of God. We tend to think we are here and God is there, somewhere else. Sometimes we treat God as if he were another man like us, as if there were just two people dealing with each other. We forget that our age would not exist except for the creative word of Logos. Our own very existence could not have happened without the Logos. Nor could anybody or anything else around us exist without the Logos. Unless we saw that true kind of Logos, we would have a very cheap concept.

The next of the four realities, Life: Do we know what life is? It is more within the range of knowledge of physicians and surgeons. But I have been thinking about it for years and have not been able to understand it. I have tried to find a definition of Life — at conferences, with experts, with biologists, with physicists, with medical people — but I have not found it. For me, when I come across a word I cannot define, I suspect it has something to do with the character of God. Life is something very deep. The only kind of life known here to us is life subject to death. But the apostles saw the reality of Jesus Christ and another kind of life that was not subject to death. They felt it and heard it and could tell about it.

The next reality is Light. Creation began with light — the Light

ICCP Bangalore, India, 1982. **Paulos Mar Gregorios.** *Metropolitan of the Orthodox Syrian Church of the East, India.*

to light all other lights. As a young theologian, the first chapter of Genesis thrilled me. What God said was primary. Darkness was on the face of the earth, but God spoke and dispelled it. The Scripture tells us that when we moved away from God, darkness was there. God with his creative power dispelled it. The most important enemy of light was hatred and bitterness. Light had to do with life; darkness had to do with hatred, bitterness and enmity. Light was God's creative energy. Peter, James and John saw it on Mount Tabor when the clothes of the Son of God became dazzling. Moses saw it in the burning bush.

Light has a great deal to do with the way we live our lives. It has a lot to do with truth. Falsehood, when something is covered up, is darkness. It is the biggest block to God's life flowing through us. That life has to be released where it has been blocked and obstructed, through illness or sin.

If doctors took care of all their patients, that would take a lot of energy. By not caring they could economise on their emotions. If doctors really care for their patients, that has great healing power.

Love is another cheapened word in our language. It most closely denotes the character of God. In St John's words, 'God is love'. Unhappily love has been perverted. Talking about love and not being genuine is to be hypocritical in our love. To help the patient to love is one of the most powerful forces in the world.

Love is a power. Life is a power. Light is a power. The woman with a chronic haemorrhage (Luke 8) touched the Lord's garment in a crowd, and he asked who had touched him. 'What a question to ask', said the disciples, 'as the crowd is squeezing you.' 'No,' he said, 'somebody touched me in a special way, because power has gone out of me.'

What is that power? Where do we get that power? Even lay people can become dynamos of that energy which flows out from you. To be a healer is to bring the light and life of God to all places where there is darkness.

What it means to know Christ

For this morning's meditation, I have chosen a passage from the fourth chapter of Paul's epistle to the Ephesians, verses 9–24. Here is a fresh paraphrase:

'It says he went back up … What does this mean unless he first came down into the lowest level of the earth? The one who came down is the same one who has now gone back up above all heaven that he may fulfil and perfect the whole universe. He has also given to some to be apostles, to others to be prophets, and to others evangelists, still others to be shepherds and teachers, for the equipment of the whole body of holy ones for the work of serving, for the upbuilding of the body of Christ and making it grow until all of us together gain the oneness of unity in deep knowledge of the love of God; so that we would become a single, mature human being, measuring up to the stature of the fullness of Jesus Christ. There is no need to be tossed about in this way and that way by every passing wind of teaching, devised by the craftiness of human beings or by cleverness and trickery of argument in order to make us deviate from the truth. No, let us be true to each other in love, let us keep growing into Christ, along with all things; for Christ is the centre from which the whole body is co-ordinated, and tied together through every sinew and joint. The energy is supplied in right measure to each part; that makes growth for the whole body and enables its building in love.

So then, I say this on the authority of the Lord; do not conduct yourself like the rest of the world, who in the emptiness of their mind and darkening of perception, are alienated from the love of God through the enormity of their ignorance and the sclerosis of their inner being. They have lost all sensitivity and have given themselves over to sensual gratification in working out their unclean lusts. This is not the way you were taught Christ; assuming that you have heard him and been instructed by the truth in Jesus; you have been instructed to divest yourself of such a way of life, casting off the old humanity which is disintegrating; rather you have been taught to be renewed by the Spirit of God in your inner being and to clothe yourself with the new humanity which is built of the very nature of God, in righteousness and by purity of truth.'

We need have no fear of anything in the world

Now about knowing Christ. It is not something that you can pick up in a classroom but it is a process of growing into this knowledge. First of all, the Scriptures say that Christ is already gone into all the worlds there are. It says that the origin of all creation has now descended into the lowest levels of that creation as incarnate God and that is an unusual and amazing thing. Even though he is the origin of the whole thing and he created all things and he sustains all things, he now, as a human being, has come and descended into the lowest levels of that creation and then he has passed through the levels of that creation back to the Father. This makes a difference. God in his mercy has come through the lowest levels and by his grace has reconciled it all to himself.

This is something that must be remembered; and it must be remembered that no part of this creation can now frighten you. And this means that you, the beloved, have absolutely no power, whether government or demon, to be afraid of. This confidence is very important. Otherwise it can be very frightening in that you may worry that you will lose your prestige or that you can lose your practitioner's licence or be otherwise harmed by what somebody might do to you on account of your convictions, or just because you did the right thing. So you can be unafraid of anything, governments, demons, powers. There is nothing, we must realise, nothing, that is not subject to Jesus Christ.

We share Christ's humanity

One of the things that I can never stop wondering about is that at the right hand of God today is seated a human being; this Jesus Christ is not just God, he is a human being. Now what does it mean, sitting at the right hand of God? To us it probably makes almost no sense to sit at the right hand of God unless you know something about an Oriental durbar. When a king conducts his business, the individual who sits on his right hand side is the Grand Vizier. It is this individual, the Grand Vizier, who gives instructions to the ministers as to what to do, while the king listens, approves by his silence.

Now we must remember that this human being who sits at the right hand of God has the whole universe subject to him. This was not done for the angels. This was done for the human being that came and dwelt among us. It is a human being to whom the universe has been made subject. Now as God, everything is subject to Christ so that nothing has been *made* subject to him. But as an incarnate human being, this subjection has been given to him and this is where the sharing of the Christian occurs in this Lordship, in this Kingship of Christ as ruler of the universe. How fantastic! Think of that.

What a risk God takes! Think of you and me sharing in this regal task! This is a creative God doing much more than just saving us from hell. It is the eternal God's pleasure that we co-operate with Jesus Christ and become members of his body and share in Christ's Kingship of the universe. Everything that is Christ's is also ours. And likewise the universe is not only a subject of my scientific investigation as an object but is now, along with me, part of what has been redeemed by Christ and is subjected to him.

Christ's gifts and how to use them

Another thing I want to speak of is the gifts that he has given. To some to be apostles, to some to be prophets, to some to be evangelists, to some to be shepherds and teachers. Praise God that through the Holy Spirit he can give you new gifts for new times and new places. So don't say that these listed are the only gifts, that no other gifts can exist.

Now as to the first gift, we can no longer get that because you must have been with the Lord to have been an apostle, because that commission must have been received directly from Christ. Poor Paul, he only half qualified for this gift. He received a commission from Christ but he had never been with Christ during his earthly ministry. So his was a big fight all along for Paul to prove that he was an apostle. There were at least five hundred apostles, but the twelve were a special group. Apostles are special people, one who can say, 'we have seen with our eyes and we have heard with our ears and we have touched with our hand, the Lord'. They are the prime witnesses. Only they can say to you 'I have seen the risen Christ'. Only a first generation of five hundred people qualified for it, which had seen with their eyes the risen Lord and who had been with the Lord; their testimony is the basis of our faith. What the apostles have testified, what they have told us, we accept as the foundation for our faith.

Now what is the difference between an apostle and an evangelist? Only this, the apostle is a first-hand witness while the evangelist is second hand. The apostle says 'Jesus Christ is risen, I have seen him'; the evangelist says 'based on the testimony of the apostles I declare unto you that Jesus Christ is risen'. That is the difference between the apostle and the evangelists. The evangelist is dependent on the testimony of the apostle for his own testimony. He is not an eyewitness but he is sent out by the church to witness to its faith, the church that has faith in the testimony of the apostles. The shepherds and the teachers were people who continued the work guiding the people, building them up, instructing them. It doesn't mean that they didn't need the Spirit, but the foundation had already been laid by the prophetic testimony in the first generation in the churches.

Let me say three things about these gifts. First, no gift of the Spirit is for the benefit of the person who receives it. Rather it is for the building up of the body of Christ. It is very important that we realise this. We will get very disoriented in our spirituality if we take these gifts for our own spiritual benefit. Don't seek them for your own benefit, rather seek gifts in order that you may be equipped with these gifts to serve. Not that one does not receive benefits when the gifts are given from the Spirit.

We had an experience in India, about foreign money. We told the Government that we used this money for giving jobs to people of all religions. The Foreign Minister of our Government pointed out that this put more power in our hands than we deserved. The minister said, 'The power is yours; you hand out the jobs to the people.' So sometimes when you are given a gift, even of the Spirit, that is designed to serve the people, you also receive some benefit from it yourself. But don't concentrate on this part of it. Don't concentrate on the benefits that the receiver of the gift can get for himself.

Another thing I want to say about gifts is that there is no general gift given to everybody other than love; so also there is no other specific gift that is given to everybody alike. So each different person receives a different gift. And you shouldn't be jealous of another's gift. Take for example the gift of healing. If you insist that everybody should be a healer this will not work. Now the healing gifts are there but you cannot say that everybody should be a healer. He gives the gifts for the benefit of the whole.

Another thing I would like to stress is something that Paul says very strongly. He says that no gift is of any use without the general gift of love. He says this very strongly in 1 Corinthians 13. If you have no love, however many gifts you do have, they will not be used for the building up of the body of Christ. One can almost say that giving the gift to someone who has no love is like trying to operate on a dead body. You can do the surgical operation but there won't be any healing or activity resulting because the reality of life is not there. So the life force of love must be the base for other gifts.

The church, the body of Christ

I wish to say that these gifts are given for the building up of one single body of Christ. A building up of a unified body of Christ, which spans all the generations. A single unified body which grows into a mature body, composed of human beings. When we all grow in integrity, it constructs the singleness of this body, which I feel means we become one single human body, which for the trained Western mind is difficult to conceive. It is difficult to understand how this can be the case. That all of us, you and I and those who have lived before and those who will come later are alike cells in a single being. We are in touch with one another and we function as one. And the function is one single unit of energy in Jesus Christ. He is the perfect man and he has chosen not only to become one of us but to make us also part of him. Integrity, wholeness, this is the great mystery of Christ. This is the great thing which I have not yet fathomed and I still stand before it in wonder. How Christ can incorporate into himself all of us. He still remains in the process of growing us into himself, uniting us in faith and in the love of Christ which is the ultimate knowledge of him and through that we are to become completely one with him. Thus, we become a human being only in the fullness of Jesus Christ.

Truth is in the growing human body, namely Jesus Christ. Therefore, I am in him a new creature. There I stand and the powers of the Holy Spirit are operating in me. This means that being true to each other in him, we have to keep growing as a community of truth and love. We must continue growing by receiving energy from the Christ, the head from which the whole body is tied together and co-ordinated through every very helpful joint; those connections between free human beings. It is through such inter-human relations that the energy of Christ flows.

Now I would try to draw your attention to something very provocative. You know the first major presentation of the gospel was by Stephen who said, 'God does not dwell in temples made by hands, but he lives in the house not made by hands *(acheropioton)*'. That was the main thrust of his whole speech. The temple of God is the church as a community of human beings. God was not in the Jerusalem temple, but is in the risen body of Christ, that is what Stephen wanted to say. That is what also Jesus, himself, says, 'Destroy this temple and in three days I will raise it up.' He spoke about his body. 'You have made my Father's house a den of thieves.' What is 'my Father's house'? Of course, here the temple in Jerusalem. In my Father's house are many abiding places. Where is that abiding place? Where is my Father's house? You say heaven. But Christ meant the body of Christ. That is the new temple, that is 'my Father's house'. That's where there are plenty of abiding places. That is where Christ abides in you and you abide in Christ and the Father in us. Now that is the mystery which we don't quite see. What we see is the visible phase of this body which is people like you and me. That phase of the church is very disfigured. This great reality of the disfigured church was planted smack in the middle of creation and is the place from which the truth of the Spirit must begin again to become related to the world. That will happen again when the ligaments of caring and the joints of love are functioning properly.

When the energy flow within the community itself becomes unimpeded and unobstructed, that will make it possible for us to bear fruit. Bearing fruit is a very important thing. No tree that I know eats its own fruit. The fruit of the tree is not for itself. Thus the church, the great mystery of the body of Christ, the centre of reality, must bear fruit.

Love, joy, peace, these are the main fruits and they are to be accessible to the rest of the world. It is for the world also that we bear fruit, not for ourselves or just for the church. The gifts of the Spirit are for the common good of the growth of the body. The fruit of the Spirit is for the world to enjoy.

Let us pray:

Christ our God, who became one of us that we may become like thee, take us out from our alienation from thee and from this darkness that is detaining us and destroying us, preventing us from receiving thy gifts and building up the body of Christ. Unite us to thyself that we may know thee and by the power of the Spirit that lives in us, bear fruit for the life of the world. In Christ our Lord. Amen.

THE DOCTOR IN RELATION TO HIM/HERSELF

PABLO MARTINEZ

Introduction
- The need to care for our own garden: '. . . *my own vineyard I neglected'* (SS 1:6b)
- Jesus referred to physicians only twice. One of these times it was precisely to remember the old Greek proverb: *'Doctor, heal yourself'*. From ancient times this was a duty.
- Some people never think of others: they are the paradigm of selfishness; but some people never think of themselves: they are the paradigm of stress . . .!

'VIRUSES' IN A DOCTOR'S LIFE

Frequent 'infections'
They are progressive and interrelated; one leads to the other:

Self ambition: 'too busy'
- Doctors married to work; they don't work for a living but live for working.
- The need to review our theology of work: work is not an end in itself. It is an instrument not for self-fulfilment but to accomplish God's plan and will for our life.
- The pressure to become the best number one in our realm, e.g. Bjorn Borg, the tennis player. It has a high cost. The philosophy of being a 'winner' also permeates Christian doctors.

Isolation: 'too lonely'
- Stopping relationships which are not professionally related; where are all those 'old friends'? Where are those books and readings?
- The 'underdeveloped personality': existence is only for professional purposes. Ultimately this leads to . . .

ICMDA Stavanger, Norway, 1990. **Pablo Martinez.** *Clinical psychiatrist, church elder, Barcelona. Chairman of UME Spain.*

Bitterness: 'too disappointed'
- A spirit of emptiness (similar to that of Ecclesiastes).
- Specially true in mid-life.
- But it is difficult to accept our own part in the guilt — we project it upon others: 'all the others have disappointed me.' We become cynical and hypercritical.

The empty pool syndrome
- In all professions you have to give: a certain amount of energy is always required to perform our work adequately.
- But in the caring professions this is generally increased because you give not only something but yourself. Take the example of Jesus: *'power has gone out of me'* (Luke 8:46).
- To be able to give, you need to receive first. An ancient Latin proverb: *'Nemo dat quod non habet'* ('no one can give me what he does not have'). It is only in the measure that we are full, that we will be able to share. *'For no one is able to lead others further than he is himself'* (Paul Tournier).
- In this sense, we can compare our life to a swimming-pool and our energy to its water: two streams of water need to occur at the same time; *output* (water coming out) but also *input* (water coming in). Whenever the output is bigger than the input, little by little the pool gets empty: this is sometimes the doctor's life.
- This reality comes from *nature: 'the principle of the two movements'* — in nature everything has its rhythms which alternate and are complementary: winter follows summer, night follows day. As doctors, we can see it very well in our hearts: contraction (systole) follows expansion (diastole). The two movements are successive and complementary. Firstly the heart receives blood, then it may distribute it.
- Teilhard de Chardin: *'The secret of balance and happiness consists in centering on oneself, decentering on one's neighbour and super-centering on one greater than oneself: God' ('Le milieu divin').*
- Pascal: *'Most of the misfortunes of man come from the inability to stop and rest'.*

Identifying our pool before it gets empty
How do we recognise stress? Amongst other symptoms, we mention three:

- Irritability: nervousness, fatigue, harsh words, especially when you 'lower the guard' (in the family);
- Inability to enjoy life outside work: little things are not beautiful (unlike Schumacher); loss of gladness — 'gloomy Sunday afternoons'.
- Introversion, self-centredness — we become absentminded; our thoughts are many miles away . . .

In a doctor's life this is especially increased because of his contact with human suffering and death. The doctor has an extra amount of stress (Pasternak, American specialist on the topic).

Three 'highways' to stress

Perfectionism:

- There is a difference between the *search for excellence* and *compulsive perfectionism.* The search for excellence related to spiritual maturity seeks to please God. Compulsive perfectionism related to insecurity seeks to please men.
- A piece of advice: 'Enough is enough'.

Hurry:

- Working or living in a race against the clock is a constant feature in doctors.
- Working a lot is tiring, but working in a hurry is draining.
- We never give the impression that we care when we are in a hurry.
- Jung said: *'Hurry is not of the Devil; it is the Devil!'*

Dispersion:

- Being involved in too many front lines leads to frenetic activism. This problem may be due to:
  (i)   the lack of clear objectives and goals in life. We need a 'road-map' to run the race of life;
  (ii) the difficulty of saying 'no'. When I say 'no', I feel guilty. Learning to say 'no' is essential to health.
- The message of Ecclesiastes 4:6 *'Better one handful of tranquillity than two handfuls with toil and chasing after the wind'.*
- Robert Murray McCheyne, a young Scottish minister, lay dying at the age of 29; he turned to a friend and said: *'God*

gave me a message to deliver and a horse to ride. Alas, I have killed the horse and now I cannot deliver the message.'

- We have to accept our limitations and control our fantasies of omnipotence because we are not superhuman.

THE DUTIES IN THE 'GARDEN'
If we don't want to neglect our garden, we have to do three things:

Cutting
Any gardener has to prune (cut) trees so that they grow healthier. 'Cutting' in a doctor's life may imply:
- Renouncing: small things; radical, big areas
- Changing: our circumstances if possible; our attitudes towards circumstances.

Sometimes the origins of stress may lie outside ourselves, but its treatment always starts inside us. Stress is not the disease itself; it is the symptom of a deeper problem.

Caring
- 1 Tim. 4:16. At the age of 35, Timothy receives this exhortation from his teacher Paul. It is striking to see the order: first the man is to be right, and then his work (teaching, in this case) is to be right. But if the man himself is not right, the work will suffer from it.
- 1 Thes. 4:11: three points:
  It is an important priority: 'search after, desire'.
  Tranquillity is not automatic but related to . . .
  Minding *your own* business.
- The doctor has to treat himself with the same compassion he offers his patients.
- His own business is health in his whole person: he should be caring for: body; mind; spirit.

Growing
- In the same way that in medicine we need a permanent training, a constant updating of our knowledge and skill, we do need the same as persons.
- Otherwise we become 'museum Christians', fossilised Christian doctors.
- Permanent renewal is *sine qua non* to a Christian doctor.

NEEDS OF THE GARDENER

To be whole (complete), integrity; To be holy; To be healthy.

- In the Bible, three concepts go together, you cannot separate them, like the angles in a triangle:
  truth; peace (see Jer. 33:3); health.
- Peace *(shalom)* and health *(shalem)*, ultimately twin sisters, always come from God's truth, not from human resources. Because introspection does not throw any light on oneself. A French writer said: *'Merely by looking at ourselves, we falsify ourselves'* (Paul Claudel).

Conclusion

Before you continue the race of life:

stop (be quiet and silent);
watch (examine, be alert);
walk;

'and you will find rest for your souls' (Jer. 6:16).

The challenge of self-preservation. What makes a doctor decide where to practise? For example, there are more Thai doctors in the United States than there are in Thailand itself and 90% of those in Thailand work in Bangkok, leaving millions of people uncared for. This is a worldwide problem — where money is to be gained and life is relatively comfortable, that is where the doctors wish to work and remote villages and inner cities are neglected. This is not always due to self-interest but can often be for self-preservation. Of course *what* is practised is also open to the same kind of influence. People may not wish to enter the 'Cinderella specialties' because they are not so rewarding, comfortable or enjoyable as the others.

GORDON STIRRAT

ICCMS Oxford, UK, 1980. **Gordon Stirrat.** *Clinical reader in obstetrics and gynaecology, University of Oxford, UK.*

OUR FAMILIES

MERVILLE VINCENT

Introduction

I THINK I am safe in assuming that it would be axiomatic for physicians as spouses and parents to see their goal as the formation and maintenance of healthy families. I believe I do not have to spend time convincing this audience that Scripture teaches the ideal of marriage as a God-ordained relationship, a relationship of mutual love, caring and submission (Eph. 5:21). Also, we are to love our spouses as Christ loved the church, that is with unconditional, sacrificial love.

Nor do I have to convince you that we as parents are co-creators with God of the children we produce. They are ours, but they are also God's. He loves them. He depends on us to love them. To love them, we must be aware of their needs, whether these needs be physical, emotional, intellectual or spiritual. Then, we must take the time and effort to see that these needs are met. Our love for God is shown as much by the love and caring that we demonstrate to our families as it is shown by our commitment to our patients or to our profession.

If the goal is a healthy family, the next question is: what are the characteristics of healthy families? Perhaps I should indicate what I mean by 'a healthy family' in our North American culture. It is simply a family in which the parents preserve their sanity and maintain warm relationships that encourage the personal growth of both parents and produces children who are competent and reasonably autonomous and independent.

The changing family

In the past there were often thought to be five major functions, all of which tended to hold the family together, although they have now been largely superseded:

ICMDA Cancun, Mexico, 1986. **Merville Vincent.** *Superintendent of psychiatry, Homewood, Guelph, Canada.*

- *Economic:* Today everyone can get by on their own;
- *Protection:* Today we look to social agencies, police and government for this;
- *Religious:* Today we have turned this over to the churches or denied its necessity;
- *Education:* We've turned over to the school system;
- *Status and job training:* This is obtained much less from the family than from money, occupation or looks.

Therefore, certain functions that were in the background of families in the past are now in the forefront. These are largely relational functions, that is to love and be loved rather than to be fed or not fed. Intimacy is of more concern than protection. The result is that presently if one feels lonely, isolated, or alienated in a marriage, then solace may be sought elsewhere such as in work, alcohol, other relationships, or the end may be depression, chemical dependency or even suicide. I believe healthy families are important because they nurture the well-being of all their members.

There is considerable evidence that the quality of family life is extremely important to our emotional well-being, our happiness and our mental health as individuals. We know that poor relationships within the family are very strongly related to many of the problems in society, such as juvenile delinquency. Families are the vital cells that constitute the flesh and blood of our society. When one family disintegrates so does a part of our society.

Healthy families — research findings

A good relationship between marital partners characterizes healthy marriages

The research work of Jerry Lewis and his group once again established the importance of the marital relationship in healthy families. The better the marital relationship, the healthier the family. Healthy marriages were characterized by flexibly shared power and deep levels of intimacy. The partners liked each other and were good friends. While in a very close relationship they were still unique individuals but could tolerate and relish their differences. They had good sexual relations. They were open with their feelings and intimate. Problems of course occurred, but they were quickly identified and generally resolved quickly.

Noting that the average duration of marriage in the USA is 9.4 years, Jeannette and Robert Lauer studied 351 couples married over some years. Three hundred of those couples considered themselves happily married. The top seven reasons given by both husbands and wives for their marriage lasting were as follows:

(a)   My spouse is my best friend;
(b)   I like my spouse as a person;
(c)   Marriage is a long-term commitment;
(d)   Marriage is sacred;
(e)   We agree on aims and goals;
(f)   My spouse has grown more interesting;
(g)   I want the relationship to succeed.

The authors noted three findings that run contrary to much common mythology:

- Couples with enduring marriages had not made a practice of either fighting or suppressing anger. Their motto was not 'the family that fights together stays together'.

- Secondly, they did not see marriage as a 50-50 proposition with a 50-50 divide on everything. There was a tendency for each person to emphasize periods of giving and periods of receiving. They seemed prepared to give more than they received in the relationship. The result appeared to be very close to equality of giving and receiving over the long run.

- Thirdly, they tried to spend as much time together and share as many activities as possible. Preference for shared rather than separate activities was seen as a richness and fulfillment in the relationship rather than a loss of identity.

The healthy family spends time together including leisure time

Those families who spent time together genuinely enjoyed being together and structured their lives so it could happen. They realized it does not happen spontaneously. Togetherness was in all areas of their lives: eating meals, recreation and work. Couples who spent a lot of time away from each other — took separate vacations, had separate friends, dined apart frequently — had a lower survival rate.

When time is spent together it allows some of the other things to happen that are important for families, such as the balanced interaction between members of the family without the family breaking up into cliques or coalitions at times of difficulty, or parents turning to a particular child to have their needs met. This shared time is where a sense of humor and a sense of play can happen and these, too, are associated with family health.

The overworked parents expend so much energy and time on their occupations, their personal status and family requirements that there is often little time left for concern about human needs, such as love and sharing. The result is often tired, exhausted, burnt-out fathers and mothers. Conflict and anger result from this overload. There is little time for togetherness as a family. When there is very little time together it is the positive emotions that are not expressed. That takes time. There is only time to discipline, to complain and to correct. Family interactions become tense and infrequent. Individuals seek refuge in their own interests — sport, TV, crafts and other isolation chambers. Not that these activities are inherently bad, but they often become substitutes for interacting with family members. Other stresses include less time for togetherness between spouses on different work schedules, frequent separation of parents and children through the use of child care institutions and the insistence on instant gratification in family life.

Healthy families have good communication patterns

Members of healthy families spend time talking with each other and this is closely related to the fact that they spend a lot of time together. They have good communication patterns, with shared thoughts and feelings and are also good listeners. In this way individuals indicate that they value the messenger, they value the message and they value themselves, even if they are differing with someone.

This communication occurs best in families that are not authoritarian, where power is shared but not abdicated by the parents. Both positive verbal and nonverbal communication is important. In addition to sheer busyness, television can be a major obstacle to communication in the home. This is at all ages and stages. It led one wife to comment that she was more worried if there was life after TV than if there is life after death.

The healthy family shows appreciation for one another

Family members demonstrate empathy and unconditional love. They support, validate and nurture each other's emotional needs.

The individual is affirmed for who he or she is and not for looks, money, accomplishments or any form of productivity. This led family sociologist Urie Bronfenbrenner to define the family as 'a group which possesses and implements an irrational commitment to the well-being of its members'. The implications of this irrational commitment could be for me to go to a ballet with my wife or my wife to go to a hockey game with me.

The craving to be appreciated is a basic human need and the deepest principle of human nature. When the physician fails to set priorities and has little time or energy left for family members, it is not surprising that they experience this as not being appreciated. Just as appreciation is often reciprocated in human relationships, so is the lack of it reciprocated. Too soon the doctor no longer experiences appreciation at home and finds that he is getting much more appreciation in his work. It is then tempting to involve himself in even more work; the vicious cycle is compounded, often resulting in many unmet needs in the medical family — for everyone. In the short run, there is actually more admiration with less responsibility in the medical activities than there is in the activities of the family. I would suggest that there is potentially more reward in participating in a healthy family than there is in an excessive commitment to one's professional life, with the probable cost of failed family relationships.

Healthy families develop a sense of trust

In healthy families, husbands and wives trust each other deeply. Children are gradually given more opportunity to learn trust. The family does not break trust for the amusement of others, which means that they do not tell secrets about each other or stories that humiliate one another. This is an expression of their caring and empathy. The family realizes that broken trust happens on occasion and can be mended. In such a family, both parents and children become trustworthy.

Physicians must repeatedly ask themselves if they have set reasonable priorities for their own family relationships. Only then will they keep promises for time-consuming commitments with their spouse and children. This doesn't necessarily end after the children have left the nest. My adult children in the last year let me know that I was spending too much time with my nose in a paper or journal when they were visiting. Healthy families promote high levels of both closeness and individuality. They learn that it is safe to express one's feelings openly. Children who learn to experience a high level of trusting within the family tend to have higher levels of trusting relationships outside the family.

Healthy families often have a shared religious core

Healthy families tend to be religious. They share a religious core of values and philosophy of life.

These families often have a strong sense of family in which rituals and traditions abound. This encourages a sense of belonging — of roots. Rituals around special religious occasions and holidays increase the sense of identity and belonging; so do special celebrations of birthdays or anniversaries. Part of this is getting together as a family. This also means that these occasions which are partly religious and partly family are important enough to parents so that they arrange not to be on call, or say no to a particular responsibility, so they can be available for such occasions. The message for healthy families is that there appears to be truth in the dictum to 'love God with all your heart, soul and mind and your neighbor as yourself' (Luke 10:27). The important addendum might be not to forget that your closest neighbors are your spouse and children.

Healthy families admit to and seek help with problems

Particularly in medical families it is important to be reminded that healthy families admit, expect and face problems. They seek to solve problems in a variety of ways rather than to avoid them. They don't deny them or hope that they will go away without our 'bothering' anyone, or being embarrassed by any self-disclosure.

A concluding thought

Most of you don't look as if you come from perfect families. Have I discouraged you? I didn't mean to. Actually none of you have perfect families. I didn't come from a perfect family. I'm not the husband and father in a perfect family. I haven't used the word perfect — just healthy. If some of the characteristics have sounded like perfections, they have been so described only to point you clearly in the right direction. When you don't know where you are going, it's impossible to get to your destination. I've tried to point out some directions toward which we should be aiming if our goal is to be moving toward that ever moving target of healthier families.

THE PHYSICIAN AND HIS FAMILY

NARAIN NAMBUDRIPAD

Introduction

FOR thirty-eight years I was a Hindu Brahmin and we had lots of theories. We had far too many theories about life, man and God, and I became quite fed up. Finally, I had nothing to do with religion. I don't know if I became an atheist or not. I left for England to study surgery so that I might become better equipped to serve my people. It was there that I came to know that Jesus Christ was not just a wonderful person, but God's Son.

This happened in very extraordinary circumstances. I had decided that I would not take alcohol because I had seen people doing all sorts of awful, stupid things under the influence of alcohol. At a party I was drinking orange juice and I thought I was the only one who was doing that. There was a nursing sister who was drinking orange juice and I asked her, 'Why do you drink orange juice?' And she said, 'I am a Christian.' I said, 'But these people are all Christians.' (I thought every white man was a Christian, brown men were all Hindus.) She said, 'That's not true; many of them wouldn't confess Jesus Christ as their Saviour.' This was a new thing to me. Then we had a long chat about Jesus Christ. I said, 'I love this man, I have learned to respect him, and there are many Hindus who do. But I find it difficult to believe that he rose again. It's very extraordinary; nobody lives again when he is dead.'

I read John's gospel over the next couple of weeks. As I read I appreciated two things. Firstly, that this man John had had an experience of God which I did not have. I had all the philosophies but no experience; my heart was empty. Secondly, I felt that this man had been an eyewitness. It was true; it was not a 'cock and bull' story, a fable, which is what most of Hinduism is all about.

I soon noticed that Jesus said radical things. He said, 'I and God are one.' No Hindu teacher has said that. No Buddhist has said

ICCP Toronto, Canada, 1972. **K. Narain Nambudripad**. *Director neurosurgery, Christian Medical College, Ludhiana, India.*

that — Buddha never said it. Mohammed never said it; he said, 'I am a prophet.' But Jesus said, 'I and God are one — we are one.' That's a pretty tall claim. He must be either a liar or an impostor or slightly mad — or he must be what he claimed to be. But I saw too that his character was quite contrary to that of a deluded man. Then I discovered that no liar gives his life for a lie, so that he couldn't have been a liar. And I came to the conclusion that Jesus Christ must be what he claims to be, and I didn't understand this.

Conversion and subsequent experience

This obsession with Jesus Christ became very real in my life. What shall I do with Jesus? I must either accept or reject him. It was as if a person was beside me, forcing me to make a decision — which I did. I knelt down and said, 'Lord Jesus I *will* have you. Whatever happens doesn't matter, for I am sure you are reliable.' That was in February 1959. I have never regretted that decision.

The following October I was baptised in Bristol. And when my people heard this they were very angry. Hindu Brahmins are not converted to Christianity — the last convert was about a thousand years ago. They sent two of my relatives to Bristol in November and they took me back to India. I could have stayed in Bristol, I suppose, but I felt I should go to my people and tell them about Jesus Christ. So I went.

I was warned that things would be bad. I thought, 'My family loves me very much, they won't do such things to me.' But I discovered that this was not true. For ten days they were very nice to me; after that they became quite tough. In short, they put me into a psychiatric clinic. They thought I was not right because they said there were only three reasons why a Hindu becomes a Christian: one — love of money; two — love of a woman; and three — insanity. So when they decided that I had nothing to gain either from money or from a woman, they concluded something must be wrong with my mind. 'Much reading hath made you mad.' So they put me in a psychiatric clinic and I had three ECTs. However, after this the psychiatrists said, 'We are very sorry to have done this to you, Dr Nambudripad; we ask your forgiveness. What shall we do now to help you?' And I said, 'You can help me very practically to get away from my family to the Christian Medical College, Vellore.' So I went there in 1960 and was there for two and a half years.

At first my wife would not join me. She thought that I was an outcaste and wouldn't have anything to do with me. Usually Hindus marry women they never see; the women are covered before they are brought for marriage. I had never seen my wife before marriage. After my marriage, of course, I saw her, which is a great thing. But I discovered then that I had nothing in common with my wife — in ideals, education, ambitions, aims. However, since at that time our ideological differences were not very great, we had pulled on without much quarrelling. But now, when my wife decided to join me in March or April of 1960, she had a feeling that I had rejected her and her people and her religion. I had a feeling that we had nothing in common, with now the added problem of a different religion. So we started life together again in 1960 with a great disadvantage.

Now it's twelve years ago that this happened and I want to say God has helped us to live a family life which has been very useful to me as a Christian physician. When I was converted, my eldest son was thirteen years old; now he is twenty-six. My daughter was the first one to be interested in Christianity, followed by my wife and my two younger children. All except the eldest are now converted; gradually they became interested in the claims of Jesus Christ. They saw that he can solve problems and he can give love. This is the basis of my experience. I have found that this is reliable.

I find in Genesis 2 there are relevant scriptures for a physician and his family. Genesis 2:18 reads, 'And the Lord God said, "It is not good that man should be alone; I will make him an help meet for him".' God, when he had made man in his own image and he saw all the beautiful creations, came to one conclusion: the species, *homo sapiens*, needs a helpmate. Biologically, socially, in every way, it is necessary that man should have a helpmate.

Should a Christian physician marry? Should he have a family at all? I believe God's wisdom has provided that he should have a family unless God specially ordains that an individual should remain unmarried. The Lord Jesus Christ himself made this very clear. He said there are three kinds of eunuchs: those who are born eunuchs, those who are made eunuchs by other men and those who choose for themselves a sexless life. And of course he included himself in that third category. It is God's general order in the universe that a man should have a helpmate. In Mark 10:6 Jesus says, 'But from the beginning of the creation, God made them male and female, and the twain shall become one flesh.'

As I told you, I did not fall in love with my wife before I married her. We had so little in common, and yet now I find her presence and her help a real spiritual blessing. Many people tell me that I am what I am because of my wife. She is not very accomplished; she is not very sophisticated. If she came here she would find it very difficult to mix with you. She cannot eat meat. But she is a real help to me, and if I can minister in any capacity it's because of her help. This is because this is God's order. This is the biological order. This is the spiritual order.

I think this, in my experience, poses several problems. Whom should one marry? While in the West it is customary to fall in love and marry, I don't think this is a foolproof order. Looking at the divorce rate here, it is not a foolproof system. You can make mistakes. How can you judge another person when that other person and you are attracted to each other? You each put on your best front; the worst things are hidden. It's only in the trials of life that they start coming up. Now, in our society, it is the custom for the parents to choose the wife. That is also not right because they make 'matches' as we call it — arrangements based on money and family prestige. That's not good either.

Who should choose our partners? GOD should choose our partners; I believe God knows what is best for me and I am sure he chose my wife. He knew I was an impossible person, so he gave me a very patient wife. God gives whatever is good for us. That is what the Bible teaches, and I believe that the longer I live the more I understand how very wise God is. I never thought so ten years ago. I used to pray, 'Why did you give me this wife?' And I said to God, 'Either take me away or take her away; it is impossible.' But the Lord said, 'No. Love your neighbour. If you cannot love your wife, how can you love someone else?' And the Lord taught me this is true. So, at breakfast, at dinner, I prayed, 'Lord, give me love for my wife, so that I may love my neighbour.' This is very true. If I cannot love my wife and children, how can I love you?

Whom should we marry? God's choice. You have to ask God whom you should marry, because God knows — he made us. God knows what is good. We don't accept this — we are too civilised; we are too cultured; we know everything. So we think, 'Some things we know, some things God knows.' If we don't know something, then we go to God. This is not God's intention; I don't see it that way. Whom should we marry? I think believers should marry believers. I don't believe that sexual attraction is the most important thing. I feel that it is a spiritual attraction, it is a person's character attracting another person's character, if you can put it in human terms. Character is the thing that's inside.

What should our attitude to children be? I have learned a great deal about this. In Colossians 3:21 Paul says, 'Fathers, provoke not your children.' Much of family disturbance is due to provoking the children, goading them unnecessarily to anger — a very bad practice. Love your children, don't provoke your children, and of course, love your wife. This is God's order of family life.

Ninety per cent of the effectiveness of my ministry is due to my family. My wife, my children, they are praying for me now. Their support is with me. People may reject me, but they accept me. They are humble people, simple people, several thousand miles away, but I know God will listen to their prayers.

All Christian physicians, married or single, need this kind of loving prayer support from family and fellow Christians. Otherwise their ministry will have no spiritual impact, but will simply follow the patterns set by physicians without faith.

CHRISTIAN DOCTORS AND MARRIAGE

KURUVILLA VARKEY

Introduction

I AM no expert on marriage: I have experience of only one marriage, and that is probably the only qualification I have to speak on this topic. People married for longer periods have more experience to share. Before my marriage I had no opportunity to discuss the subject. It was not thought proper in India to talk about sex, love or marriage in forums like this, or in the church. I am glad that times have changed and that I am able to share with you some thoughts on marriage in the light of the Bible.

Purposes of marriage

At the outset, the main biblical text which helps us to understand marriage is from Genesis and is quoted three times in the New Testament: 'Therefore shall a man leave his father and mother, and shall cleave unto his wife: and they shall be one flesh' (Gen. 2:24). When God created the world, it is written that at the end of every day he made an assessment of his work and said it was very good. But there was something that was not very good: Adam was alone. His loneliness is recorded as not good, and so God created Eve.

A question has recently arisen amongst young people in the western world as to whether or not there should still be marriage. This question is not so worrying in India, where marriage is still considered relevant. Marriage has three main purposes: companionship, establishment of the home, and sexual fulfilment.

Companionship

God made Eve not from the head of Adam so that she would overrule him, nor from his foot so that he could trample on her, but from his side so that she could be a companion to him. In marriage, each partner must supplement the other so there is interdependence of the man and the woman, both being dependent on God. It is interesting that Satan came to tempt Eve when she was alone.

ICCMS Bangalore, India, 1983. **Kuruvilla Varkey.** *Medical superintendent and consultant physician, Christian Fellowship Hospital, Oddanchatram, India.*

Perhaps if Adam had been there he might not have allowed Eve to be tempted. Conversely, if Satan had come to tempt Adam, Eve might have been an encouragement to him.

Establishment of the home

We realise the value of vision only when we become blind. When we consider the many broken homes and the children from them who have become a problem to society, it is then that we realise the value of marriage and the establishment of the home. The parents of this generation are making a big mistake. Their children will look back and blame them for giving them the stone of worldly success when they asked for the bread of life. One patriarch has said, 'Give your children great things, not small things'. Where is the possibility of giving great things if there is no Christian home? Where is the chance of giving this heritage to the children? How important is the home! — and how badly the evil one would attack the home that is not firmly established.

Sexual fulfilment

The Bible makes it plain that sexual fulfilment is part of God's provision and within his will. It is natural, like other appetites, for food and so on. Sex as created by God is pure and legitimate. There is nothing evil connected with it within the framework of marriage.

The physical aspects of marriage are not ignored in the Bible. The sexual union of husband and wife must be symbolic of the far deeper union that already exists between their inner lives. Marriage is therefore a state in which the husband and wife express their desire to give themselves to each other totally, not only physically but in every other aspect of their lives.

The Bible glorifies sexual love in marriage. The whole of the Song of Solomon is about two lovers (see also Isa. 62:5; Prov. 5:18–19; 1 Cor. 7:5). Paul in particular compared the life between husband and wife to the association between the Lord Jesus Christ and the church. Family life is taken as the foretaste of the life of Christ and the church. Ephesians 5:22–33 also speaks of this though it might be hard to understand. Will the ladies here agree to submitting to their husbands as to the Lord? Is it possible for the husband to be head of the wife? The answer to everything is in verse 25, where it says that the husband should love the wife as

Christ loved the church. He gave his life for the church. This love is to be like that with which he washed the disciples' feet and died on the cross.

Marriage as completeness

Marriage makes a man complete. One translation of God's finding a suitable helper for Adam is that he wanted to make the man complete. Walter Trobisch has described the Christian concept of marriage as a triangle, the three points of which are leaving, cleaving and becoming one flesh.

Leaving is essential, physically and psychologically, for a couple to make their own home. Where family ties are very close, it is quite difficult to leave and break them. Leaving does not mean abandoning or discarding these ties, but finding freedom for maturity and growth. Leaving indicates the legal aspect of marriage, important as a public act in our social living. Society knows that the couple are married and can support the family in times of trouble. A Christian society can pray for them. In times of stress the couple can say, 'It is not an illusion that we are married'.

Cleaving implies closeness, being glued together with nothing in between. There is a closeness to each other, closer than anything else, than anyone else. This implies love.

Becoming one flesh indicates the physical aspects of marriage. Moreover, it also shows how husband and wife become one in body, in mind and in spirit. The other aspect of cleaving is love. Love strengthens marriage, marriage strengthens love, love helps in physical union, physical union in return strengthens marriage and marriage gives security for physical union. So there is an interaction, a dynamic action, where each angle of the triangle supports, gets and gives. Faithfulness in responsibility and tender intimacy add other dimensions to the triangle.

A word to the unmarried

One must be called to be celibate. There is nothing virtuous about it, but it is a very specific gift from God. Those who are unmarried must believe that God has a plan for their lives and avoid being restless about it.

God gave Eve to Adam when he was sleeping. It is not implied that we should rest all the time and hope to get good wives or husbands, but the relaxed atmosphere in which you can wait on

God will prove that God is able to give you a partner. Never be in haste. They say that if you marry in haste you repent at leisure.

The order of priority in looking at areas for compatibility in marriage is first the spirit, second the mind and third the physical aspect. We must first ask whether the person is a committed Christian, one who has the experience of Christ living in him or her. People sometimes wish to marry unbelievers, hoping to convert them after marriage, but it is often the other way round. It is easier for you to pull me down from the platform than it is for me to pull you up. It is not very easy to convert anyone after marriage. The problem is, how can we assess the spirituality of a person? They come to conferences and are good in Bible studies, but the only proof would be to see if there are fruits of love, or fruits of the Spirit in them, rather than activity alone.

As to the mind, there must be something in common. You must be able to talk the same language and your mental age should be the same. Emotions are also important and should be compatible. There should be no domineering. To quote Walter Trobisch, 'She must challenge me to the highest through absolutely honest criticism of me. When she is disappointed in me, she should never withdraw her confidence. Untiringly she must help to uncover my weakness, not pretend, and tell me honestly when I hurt her.'

We are human and there must be physical attraction, but it must take the tertiary place, after the spiritual and mental aspects. It is preferable that the man should be a little older than the woman, as it is said that men mature at a slower pace, though of course this varies.

Is it possible to find such a person, who is suitable spiritually, intellectually and physically? It is reassuring that there is no one who can be called the perfect wife or the perfect husband. Yet we must strive to look for this and seek the approval of parents, even if we may have to wait a few years. God speaks even through them. Although they may sometimes object to your decision, made in a good spirit, it has been the experience of many of us that, given patience, thought and prayer, they will come to bless that marriage.

The picture of the marriage at Cana shows that there are imperfections in marriage but, given to God, it can eventually be made perfect — if we sincerely seek his will in the matter.

SEXUAL GUILT IN EMOTIONAL DISORDERS

ORVILLE WALTERS

OUR decade is described as an era in which morals are widely held to be both private and relative, in which pleasure is increasingly considered an almost constitutional right rather than a privilege, in which self-denial is increasingly seen as foolishness rather than virtue.

From many serious studies reviewing current trends in premarital pregnancies, illegitimate births and extramarital activity, it is clear that America is indeed adrift in a sea of permissiveness.

This paper will argue that, as a consequence of this permissiveness, sexual guilt is on the increase, and that guilt tends to increase in step with sexual laxity. In support of this position will be cited:

- the incidence of sexual guilt in university students;
- the contemporary prevalence of anxiety;
- the influence of psychoanalysis in lessening controls;
- the failure of naturalistic therapies to abate guilt.

Since guilt is central in neurosis it may be concluded that an increase in guilt is associated with a corresponding increase in neurotic disorders.

Sexual guilt

In a study of University of Illinois students seeking psychiatric consultation, a representative sampling disclosed that more than one-third, without any questioning that might lead in that direction, presented statements or symptoms indicating sexual guilt. When anxiety and depression as well as sexual guilt were tabulated as presenting symptoms, the great majority of students seeking psychiatric consultation were included. While this study provides no control figures, the prominence of sexual guilt is striking.

Anxiety

The prevalence of anxiety in our time is a form of indirect evidence for an increase in guilt. Tillich described the anxiety of guilt as being characteristic of the medieval era and the anxiety of

*ICCP Oxford, UK, 1966. **Orville Walters**. Director of Health Services, Urbana, USA.*

meaninglessness as predominant in our time. Spiritual emptiness seems to be more prominent than guilt in contemporary life.

Freud himself considered guilt 'nothing but a topographic variety of anxiety'. Many of our university students exhibited a sense of futility and emptiness, but these, too, are often a byproduct of guilt, which carries its complement of depression and self-depreciation. It is therefore reasonable to conclude that the pervasive anxiety of our time is at least in part the expression of increased guilt.

Every view of guilt presupposes some theory of personality. Man's freedom with its seemingly unlimited options, accompanied by the necessity of choice, produces anxiety, as does the threat of a potentially harmful world. This anxiety is not itself sinful, but to alleviate his anxiety, man is tempted to sin. He responds in the pride of self-sufficiency to the threat of nature's contingencies, and often sins further by flight into sensuality in an effort to neutralize his insecurity and anxiety.

Guilt is an objective condition, arising because of departure from some standard of value, in consequence of which an individual becomes responsible or blameworthy. It may be looked upon as a built-in moral alarm reaction which protests about any violation of a standard held to be right. Guilt feeling is a psychological state, a form of anxiety, which has no necessary relation to objective guilt and may be disproportionate or unrealistic in the neurotic and the psychotic.

Conscience

Christian thought teaches that there is a sense of 'ought' in every man — 'the law written in their hearts, their conscience also bearing them witness' (Rom. 2:15). This innate sense is only one element of conscience, the other being the result of social conditioning.

There is a current tendency to deny the innate element in conscience, which may be described as the obligation to discover and fulfil the greatest good for those affected by one's conduct. Although many dissimilarities exist in social conditioning in different cultures, none is without basic conceptions of right and duty.

Conscience has been defined by Berdyaev as 'the organ of perception of the religious revelation, of goodness, righteousness and truth in its entirety. It is not a special department or function of human nature, but the wholeness of man's spiritual being, its centre or its heart.'

The association of guilt with sexuality is traceable to the biblical account of the Fall, and shame has been almost universally associated with sexuality. Because of this, the church has been accused of fostering sexual guilt. However, theology has always taught that the primary sin is rebellion against God, and that sensuality is secondary to it. In Augustine's words, 'The corruptible flesh made not the soul to sin, but the sinning soul made the flesh corruptible ... the flesh is good.' Guilt and shame have become associated with sexuality, not because of repression by the church but because excessive sexuality has been a frequent resort to avoid the responsibility of freedom, just as drunkenness is. This misuse of freedom to alleviate anxiety leads man into guilt, which only intensifies his anxiety. Thus the spiral of anxiety–guilt–greater anxiety–greater guilt is on its way.

Influence of psychoanalysis

Psychoanalysis, which has influenced our culture and our psychology so profoundly, also has its doctrine of man. In the development of psychoanalytic psychology, sexuality was from the beginning given a central place. By 1905 Freud had arrived at a firm doctrine: 'No neurosis is possible with a normal sex life.' The sexual phases of development were considered to be universal. In neurosis or psychosis, regression to an earlier stage of development was assumed to occur. In the same way, personality disorder was produced by fixation at an immature stage. A sexual 'explanation' could be found for every disorder.

Freud acknowledged that the sense of guilt is the most important problem in the evolution of culture, and he derived guilt directly from sexual conflict. He traced its origin to the fanciful killing of a primal father by his sons because of sexual rivalry. The superego was declared to be the residual precipitate of the oedipal conflict.

Freud also recognized the primacy of guilt in neurotic conflict, saying that every neurosis masks a degree of unconscious guilt. He asserted that the demands of both the individual and the cultural superego are frequently overly severe, in which case therapy should seek to moderate it.

The view that guilt should be alleviated by moderating the demands of the superego encourages broader self-indulgence, and psychoanalysis must bear its share of responsibility for the growth of sexual laxity. At the same time, if guilt and anxiety are indeed on the increase, it may well be questioned whether 'doing battle with the superego' has been at all effective in relieving guilt.

Failure of naturalistic therapies to abate guilt

The Christian view of man was examined and repudiated by Freud. 'One may reject the suggestion of an original — as one might say, natural — capacity for discriminating between good and evil,' he wrote, although he later added that 'the formation of the superego and the development of conscience are determined in part by innate constitutional factors and in part by the influence of the natural environment.' He knew of the concern of religions 'to save mankind from this sense of guilt, which they call sin', as well as the teaching of Christianity that the common guilt of all was taken by the sacrificial death of one. However, he repudiated the command to love our neighbors as ourselves because it 'is impossible to fulfil' and is 'a superlative example of the unpsychological attitude of the cultural superego'.

Not all of Freud's followers joined him in rejecting the traditional Christian view of conscience and guilt. Rank expressed approval of the inner voice of the individual's conscience as indicated in the Christian religion. He pointed out that most of Freud's patients were already suffering because of conflict with the kind of morality that he prescribed for them.

Putnam, Freud's most influential supporter in America, held that 'every man ... has a sense of being able to effect something through his "will" ... and with these feelings comes a deep sense of obligation ... It almost always happens that there are some features in the patient's case which can be best defined in moral terms. The patient "ought" or "ought not" to do this or that ... The conflicts to which all men find themselves subjected must be considered, in the last analysis, as conflicts of an ethical description.'

Oskar Pfister believed that the repressed conscience plays a still more troublesome role than the known conscience, and considered it an essential function of psychoanalysis to cultivate a clear voice of conscience. Stekel also described neurosis as the disease of a bad conscience and charged the therapist with responsibility to help his patients to restore the ideals which, deliberately or under compulsion, they have destroyed.

Runestam as early as 1932 asked whether 'it is not religious and moral forces in man that are repressed instead of being the repressing forces ... May it not be that these higher instincts, needs and forces, the religious and moral, have suffered damage, and that repression and neuroses have their bases just in this?' Accordingly, he held, the conquering of the neurosis is an ethical assignment.

Psychoanalysis was never prepared to handle ethical questions. Freud renounced any concern over his patients' ethical problems, and analysts have ever since professed to remain aloof from value judgements. In recent years, the impossibility of maintaining such a posture in the psychotherapeutic situation has become widely recognized, and only the most naïve psychotherapist will make such a claim.

Dealing with guilt

Freud acknowledged guilt as basic to neurosis but discovered no way by which guilt could be resolved. By seeking to moderate the demands of the superego in therapy and pronouncing the practice of Christian love impossible to fulfil, psychoanalysis took its stand in favor of diminished controls and increased self-indulgence. Furthermore, by characterizing religion as collective neurosis, Freud did a disservice to the one movement that has through the centuries been more successful than any other in resolving guilt.

While the church has continued its mediatorial function in commending the *agape* of God as the antidote to man's rebellion and alienation, naturalistic systems of psychology and psychotherapy have persisted in constructing mechanistic models of human nature and have refused to concede the validity of man's transcendental dimension. Indeed, short of personal commitment, it is impossible to understand divine grace, which expresses God's undeserved love and favor, and which brings sinful man into a right relationship with him through Jesus Christ. What man cannot expiate by penance, nor earn by good works, God freely grants — the forgiveness of sin, the cancelling of guilt and the dispensing of mercy in the place of justice.

SEXUALITY AND HOMOSEXUALITY

MONTY BARKER

Introduction

SEXUALITY is not to be equated with *genitality*. All of us are created with the capacity of maleness and femaleness in a variety of ways. Our maleness and femaleness is not exclusively bound to our genital expression of this. Some people may never know genital acts with another person, but that does not mean that they are asexual and cannot express themselves in a very fulfilling way as men and women.

Homosexuality is the emotional and sexual attraction to persons of the same sex. A person can be so oriented and yet never engage in homosexual acts. A person can also be heterosexually oriented with some homosexual feelings which may be latent or suppressed but become more conscious and clamant in situations of special stress or opportunity.

Causation

There is little evidence for any genetic factors. There is some evidence not yet proven that homosexual orientation can be produced by special hormonal influences during pregnancy, or later as an unusual occurrence. Animal studies only have been done here.

Special family influences have been suggested as being important, such as a dominant mother or ineffective father in the production of homosexual feelings in males, and the converse in females.

A more recent view is that some individuals have an emotional deficit in the relationship with the parent of the same sex, and that this searching for such a relationship becomes bound up with sexual desire at the time of puberty.

It may well be that exposure to homosexual experiences in childhood predisposes to the repetition of such experiences later. This is far from being inevitable.

ICMDA Stavanger, Norway, 1994. **Monty Barker.** *Consultant psychiatrist and lecturer, University of Bristol, UK.*

There are probably many different factors at work from our early childhood. Possibly only four percent of men have homosexual feelings exclusively and rather fewer women.

The church's attitude
From Jerome onwards the church's attitude to all things sexual was far from biblical. In addition, homosexual acts were looked upon as being the most sinful of acts. There is a great deal of fear, prejudice and misunderstanding directed towards people with homosexual feelings. Some countries have more stringent laws against homosexual acts than others.

More recently there have been pressure groups within Western churches to deny the Bible teachings against homosexual acts. Some would say that they were 'created' that way, therefore it is not contrary to nature and homosexual acts in certain contexts are not contrary to Scripture.

Biblical teaching
Only homosexual *acts* are commented on in Scripture. There is no comment made about people who may have homosexual feelings but do not practise genital contact. Ezekiel chapter 16 indicates that homosexuality was only one of the sins of Sodom. 1 Corinthians 6:9–10 likewise includes homosexual acts along with other sins.

Romans 1:24–28 indicates that homosexual acts are seen as a perversion of created order and an example of how man's sin has gone against God's order, e.g. man worships the creature rather than the Creator, and uses sexual activity in a way which is the opposite of anatomical function; male and female homosexual acts are noted.

Treatment
Homosexual acts are not an indication of illness, and therefore there is no treatment as such. However, some people with homosexual orientation do become depressed in relation to their conflicts and require treatment for the depression itself.

Counselling and psychotherapy can also be indicated, but with specific goals and not intended as a 'cure'. This therapy is often directed towards dealing with relationships generally.

Helping

Singleness does not necessarily mean loneliness. Many are involuntarily celibate and cannot marry whether homosexual or heterosexual. The church has a poor record of incorporating the single person within the 'family of God'.

Appropriate teaching is needed about sexuality and family life. These issues are often avoided within the church context, leading to the continuing of prejudice and to fear of rejection by singles and in particular homosexually orientated people.

All of us, whatever our sexual orientation, indulge in sexual behaviour which though involuntary is nonetheless culpable. This is part of our sinful tendency, whether we are homosexually or heterosexually orientated. Many of those claiming that homosexual orientation is a normal variant of sexuality deny the impact of our fallen natures here. They refuse to accept that this might be regarded as leading to a handicap in life.

Support is essential. For some the ability to share with someone who is trusted will be enough. For others a special support structure may be essential, e.g. True Freedom Trust*, in the UK. This allows the fellowship of people who understand, share the same difficulty and offer companionship for holidays, etc, without either having recourse to the gay scene or maintaining total secrecy regarding their orientation.

* Address of True Freedom Trust, PO Box 592, London SE4 1EF, UK

HEALTH AND FAMILY LIFE

MONTY BARKER

IT has often been said that family life is under attack today in a new way. What is under attack is the structure of family life, which has been changing rapidly in this century. That to some extent is because of relative affluence and the much higher mobility of our modern society. Similar changes to those happening in the West are occurring elsewhere in the world, but even more rapidly due to the rate of change in those societies. The demand by some to go back to a supposedly biblical past of the extended family is rightly attacked by an Indian Christian, who points out that such prescriptions are not inherently biblical as a pattern for all time, and in any case even in the East are disintegrating. He rightly points out that the idea of the extended family operates in the West, in that it incorporates an idea of family which includes those who may live at a distance and independently. What he does not say, but which other Eastern writers comment upon, is the often stifling and inhibiting tyranny of the extended family under one roof which is far from the biblical teaching on personhood and family. The role of the domineering mother-in-law and the high rate of suicide in young Asian brides is well researched. The high incidence of mental stress among family carers of aged and dementing relatives is causing concern in India, as the number of elderly people has dramatically risen in an increasingly mobile society. The Family Education Department of the World Council of Churches is seeking to foster a worldwide network of family pastoral counsellors. Most of its publications are on families in transition in Africa, Asia and South America.

What we must also remember is that when Paul wrote his letters to the early churches he was writing to people who themselves were often the products of chaotic family lives, especially if they came from a Gentile background and in cities such as Corinth. Our society happens to be changing very rapidly throughout the world

ICMDA Stavanger, Norway, 1994. **Monty Barker.** *Consultant psychiatrist and lecturer, University of Bristol, UK.*

at this time: we are much more aware now of the specific health factors arising out of stable and unstable family lives. Our tasks as Christian doctors are to examine our own family lives to see what model we produce for others, and to examine how far in our own practices we are unconsciously adopting an underlying philosophy of humanity, personhood and relationships which comes from a pagan society. It is then for us to see where our own gifts and opportunities lie in terms of bringing these issues before colleagues, within our own communities and in our direct contact with patients. It was John Stott who entitled his commentary on Ephesians *God's New Society.* It is only as the church truly becomes that new society that we can influence the larger society around.

❖

Is your house a home? If one is really serious about having family unity, then you must begin at the beginning. You must make first things first. The Scriptures say seek ye first the kingdom of God. Parents individually must recommit themselves to the Lord and to the efforts in parenting. And that's where the work begins. It doesn't begin in your spouse. It doesn't begin with talking to your children. It begins with your own attitude and a realization that this is God's will, for you to live a sane and balanced life and not to become a workaholic.

I would like to comment on the statement, 'It's not the quantity of time, but the quality of time that counts'. I don't believe that. I think it's been a rationalization for physicians to remain in an overcrowded lifestyle. Certainly quality time is important but there is no way to equate an elaborate expensive vacation once a year with a day to day, even-flow of an interaction between a child and a parent that is so necessary for correct role modeling and self esteem. It is in these times together that an informal bond of love between a child and a parent transpires, that in effect says to the child 'I delight in you'. 'You are delightful. You are loved.'

The time to begin to establish your priorities is while your children are young and impressionable. Life is not like a video tape. You will never be able to go back and reclaim these years of your little ones.

ALAN NELSON

ICMDA Cancun, Mexico, 1986. **Alan Nelson.** *Family physician, USA.*

❖

HEALTH AND LIFESTYLE

OLAF HILMER IVERSEN

WE seek health for one's own person, for the family, for society, and for future generations. We need a definition of health. WHO has defined health not only as an absence of disease or infirmity, but as a condition of complete physical, mental and social wellbeing. This is of course an unattainable ideal.

We are an *international* Christian physicians' association, and we must work out a definition of health that can be used all over the world under different social conditions, in richness and poverty. It becomes obvious that each society and its living conditions heavily influences a workable definition of health. But what is the relationship between lifestyle and health in Rwanda, in part of Yugoslavia, in the dry areas of Africa with famine, in societies where tuberculosis and leprosy dominate, and in societies where HIV and AIDS are prominent diseases?

A useful definition might be that one is healthy when one wakes up in the morning, looking forward to the day's work, and has some energy for family and relaxation. But a good definition of health might also include the life of many people who are more or less handicapped. Mother Theresa, for instance, is said to have heart trouble, Paul had a thorn in the flesh, and our well-known member, the late Denis Burkitt, did a tremendous job as a surgeon with only one eye since childhood. One of the most well-known blind persons of Norway, who has done a lot of work for other blind people and for all other handicapped persons, always said about himself: 'I am healthy, but blind.' Hence, health is something special for each single person in each particular setting in different social situations.

Disease must be defined as something that impairs health, preventing one from doing good and productive work in the widest context, making it impossible to do what one wishes to do. Health is not in itself a goal for life, but an important means to fulfil the spiritual meaning of life.

ICMDA Stavanger, Norway, 1994. **Olaf Hilmer Iversen.** *Past professor of pathology, University Hospital of Norway, Oslo. ICMDA Chairman 1969–72, Vice-President 1975–94.*

Superstition, with lack of information and education, reduce heavily the possibility of each individual person selecting a lifestyle that protects his own health. Therefore in such areas physicians and other health workers have enormous possibilities for good deeds. It is a duty for all of them to take part in the healing activity. It comprises preventive medicine with vaccination programmes, surgery, medicine, oncology, pain relief, and psychiatry.

But it is also the duty of the physician to help to inform each person in society through the media, TV, radio, newspapers, posters, lectures, pamphlets and practical work. This way of influencing people's lifestyle for the better is certainly a part of a doctor's responsibility, and Christian doctors especially should feel a strong duty to be active in all such fields.

But the doctor's own lifestyle should also be a good example for others. We, who have received so much, should not think too much about protecting ourselves, but, on the contrary, should work to the limits of our ability. The Bible says in Paul's letter to the Ephesians in chapter 2 that 'we are his workmanship, created in Jesus Christ for good works, which God prepared beforehand, that we should walk in them'. A good example contributing to a good and health-promoting lifestyle among others is also that the doctor is an active churchgoer.

CHANGE AFFECTS ALL OUR RELATIONSHIPS

PABLO MARTINEZ

' IF anyone is in Christ he is a new creation, old things are passed away, all are made new (2 Cor. 5:17).'

Introduction

The first thing to be made new is our relationship with God. The first test to measure the degree of change in our relationship with God is our attitude towards him. Instead of hiding from God or forgetting God or taming God is a thirst for God, a passion, a love for God. Yet this thirst for God is not incompatible with suffering.

Today we move from heaven and our attitude towards God, to earth and our attitude towards our neighbour, towards others. If we are concerned in our Christian faith only with God we will probably end up in shallow mysticism or as modern monks. We need to have one foot in heaven, the right relationship with God, but as a natural result we need the right relationships with others, with our neighbour, so we need to have the other foot on earth. As I said, having the two feet in heaven is shallow mysticism but also having the two feet on earth is pure humanism and both extremes are wrong, so we need the balance. We care for our neighbour and we love God with great passion.

The book of Ruth contains many relevant things to say to our society, particularly about relationships and especially about family relationships. The emphasis I will give will be on two families, our own family and our Christian family, that is the church, because these are the two closest areas of relationships we have.

LESSONS FROM THE BOOK OF RUTH

Ruth is a very rich and contemporary book in a world afflicted by so many broken relationships. Ruth shows us how changes and changing attitudes and changing persons can have meaning in life.

ICMDA European Congress, Balatonoliga, Hungary, 1996. **Pablo Martinez.** *Clinical psychiatrist, church elder, Barcelona. Chairman of UME Spain.*

In Ruth we find three realities, three features in this ancient family which correspond to the three main events in their life story and it is the same for many families and people today. The first reality is *suffering*. This has to do with outward circumstances, especially the changing circumstances of their family life. (In psychology we would speak of the life events.) Secondly comes *love*, which has to do with the family's reaction towards these changed circumstances. Thirdly, *restoration*, which has to do with God's reaction to these changes and problems.

Suffering

The very first thing we find in Ruth is tears, pain and bitterness. Ruth is a story of relationships which revolves around suffering and love.

The circumstances which changed the life events and caused so much suffering are very contemporary.

Famine and exile (verse 1). They had to leave their home country and experience suffering due to social and financial problems, poverty, broken roots, emigration. Additional suffering was also caused in that family by the deaths firstly of the husband, Elimelech (verse 3), and then of the two sons, Mahlon and Chilion (verse 5).

Deep personal suffering is added to 'social suffering'. Here we find a broken family, totally disrupted, and their circumstances suddenly changed for the worse. We have a family in the dark night of crisis. Naomi had lost almost everything. Certainly she had lost the ones she loved most. She was a relatively young widow, quite lonely, in a foreign land, and the future seemed really threatening to her. Humanly speaking the changes in her life were for the worse. This is the reason why she reacted in a very human way (Ruth 1:12–13,20–21). 'My soul is bitter, I am embittered in my heart, I can't avoid complaining.'

Naomi's heart is obviously broken. Three times in that chapter she mentions the great pain in her heart. Is it wrong to complain to God? Is it wrong to have a protesting attitude? God, why? How long? By the end of the book we will notice that God was not disturbed by Naomi's reaction.

Now Naomi's suffering and this family's suffering show us two important points in relationship to family life, including our church life and our relationships in general. First, *suffering in family life or in church life or in any human relationship is not exceptional, but normal.* Tears, pain, losses, separation, divorce and embittered hearts are a constant feature in families, churches and human relationships throughout history, in fact throughout the Bible.

Once I was asked in my church to preach about family and what a family is like. For two weeks I tried to find a family in the Bible which could serve me as a model. I didn't find any. No family in the Bible is perfect. The reason why this is so is that the family became one of the main targets of the devil after the Fall. It is not by chance that the most painful problems for doctors in many countries come from family problems, not from their patients. More than half of American doctors' marriages end in divorce. How many problems with children, especially teenage children, result from this?

All the outstanding families in the Bible, such as Abraham, Jacob, and David, had at one time or another their portion of tears, pain and suffering. What a great failure David was as a father. Do you remember all the problems he had with Absalom? He was successful in every area of his life, a great king and statesman, a great poet, a fantastic musician, a great warrior struggling bravely; but he was a total failure as a head of a family. By the end of his life he recognised this. So, suffering in family life is not exceptional but normal and this applies also to our other family which is the church. We cannot idealise the church. The church in Jerusalem was beautiful but also had many problems which very soon started to emerge.

The second practical point is that a *romantic view of family life can kill or destroy the family.* Very often we Christians approach the subject of relationships within the family, within the church, etc, with wrong expectations. We have the idea that a happy family or a good church or a good relationship is one without problems, tears, stress or tension.

A practical word of caution here. Many Christian books, lectures and retreats on family and church life and relationships in general give us a picture which is neither realistic nor biblical. The model they present to us is a secularised one. What is a happy family, a good church, a mature relationship? The idea they give is that a happy family never quarrels; in a good church there are never tensions; in good relationships suffering has no place. A permanent smile seems to be the hallmark of these relationships. Then people go home from those retreats or lectures more frustrated than relieved, 'Oh, how far away I am from the perfect model they presented, what a disaster I am.' Yet they had been given as a model a replica of Disney World. We have to be very careful with Disney World theology or psychology. A romantic view of the family is not biblical and it can be very harmful. That applies to all our relationships.

Behind this romantic idea of relationships, there is a deep philosophy which is hedonistic in essence. Hedonism is affecting our concept of faithfulness, love, marriage and relationships in general. As soon as you have a problem or a tension in a relationship you must break it! Go for another person, look for another church, choose another partner! Then we find people going round and round seeking the perfect church or the right partner, which in psychology we call the Marco Polo syndrome; they spend their whole lives travelling around and find nothing. This is a secularised view on relationships.

As Christians we have to claim that the ideal relationship (that is the ideal family or church) is not a perfect family or church in the sense of blamelessness or impeccable behaviour with no problems. It is the family or the church or the relationship that is able to face such problems with dignity and maturity. I want to emphasise this concept. Problems and suffering can be fruitful.

This is the first feature that we find in the book of Ruth, but if we had to stop here it would be very gloomy. So let us move from the more negative to the positive.

Love
Now if the first feature of suffering had to do with changed circumstances, the second has to do with reactions, my reaction faced by these circumstances. How do I react? All the characters in Ruth have one feature in common and that is *love*. Love is the secret for any relationship, for any church or for any family when responding to problems and suffering and tension. Love within any community is the backbone that supports the whole body in difficult times. A mature and healthy family, a mature church, a mature relationship is the one where the members are able to love one another in spite of suffering and even through suffering. Now

I don't have time to go into details but I need to emphasise a couple of ideas which are important.

Love is not a feeling

Love is never a feeling according to the Bible; I refer to *agape* love. Love according to the New Testament teaching is not affection but a decision, an act of my will. I decide, I make up my mind that I will love you, regardless of my feelings. As a psychiatrist I have to love my patients with agape love, even those who hate me, even those who are very neurotic. I have to love them. Therefore love is not a feeling, a natural affection, or a spontaneous automatic reaction, but a decision to cultivate.

Why are there so many divorces amongst young people? I think one of the main problems is that they mix falling in love, the erotic idea of love, with actual love. Many, many married couples believe they are in love and love each other, when the amount of self-giving is pathetically poor. Now the same could be applied to our church relationships. Many people go to church with the idea that they have to be liked by others, or that they have to like others. Notice that the commandment given by Jesus never was, 'A new commandment I give unto you, that you will *like* one another', or '. . . that you will become friends with each other'. This is not the biblical idea. The word Jesus used was, 'You will love one another'. You give yourself, you serve one another, seeking the good of the other person.

Loving in the church does not mean agreeing with. Many times with my family or other church members we have had to arrive at a point which is very, very practical; we have to agree to disagree. This is vital and we have to learn it in all our relationships. Many people never learn to agree to disagree.

So the first observation on love is that it is not liking or agreeing, because it is not a feeling, but is serving and self giving.

Love can only come by being cultivated by the influence of the Holy Spirit

Love is a fruit of the Holy Spirit and is deeply connected with faith. This is where the difference between humanism and Christianity comes in. My love does not arise from a desire to have a better society, as Greenpeace members strive for. My desire comes from God's love within me, Christ in me. This is not natural but supernatural and we need to cultivate this love.

It is very sad to see the wrong concepts of love that we have in so many families and so many churches, and we need to review our practice of love. I don't have time to go into details but in the book of Ruth you will find love expressed in three ways. I will just mention them. You find love expressed in words, in attitudes and in decisions. The three must always go together, they cannot be isolated. I cannot contradict my attitudes by my actions. In other words, attitudes, decisions and actions underline our words. They should not be separated. I cannot call myself a Christian if I have very nice words when I am in church and then go home and start shouting like an animal.

Christian faith is not simply a matter of worshipping God, although of course it involves that. There should be changes in our family life and in friendships and relationships as a result of our thirst for God, otherwise our Christianity will be shallow.

There was an evangelistic meeting in one of the Latin American countries and by the end the speaker invited people to come to the front. When everyone had left a small suitcase was discovered on the floor. Nobody claimed it. It was picked up and opened and inside they found a machine gun with a note which said: 'Thank you, now I do not need it any more.' This happened to be a leader of one of the terrorist organisations in Latin America. That is real understanding of the gospel; forgiveness instead of resentment, peace-making instead of aggression, self control instead of explosion. Attitudes should change as a result of our encounter with the Lord. We have to review our attitudes.

Restoration

I would like to make a point here that the church is a therapeutic community. It has therapeutic potential, not in the sense that we perform some kind of specialised or non-specialised therapy within the church. I am not thinking primarily of healing within the church, but of the tremendous benefit for my identity that new relationships, tasks and gifts bring to life. We need to cultivate the church as a place for restoration and healing in all our relationships.

I don't have time to expound this third element in the book of Ruth: God's action in all these changes and circumstances. God is able to change the tragedies and dry deserts of our lives into fertile fields, dark tunnels into new situations. He did it with Naomi. God restored Naomi. God's reaction ultimately is a reaction of restoration. This is why we should not be afraid of tension and suffering, or of changes which seem to be outside our control.

'God watches over his people. He rules over all and brings blessings to those who trust him.' Ruth 2:12 is an excellent summary of your life, of your church, of your relationships. The Lord Jehovah, the God of the Covenant, richly rewarded Ruth. He rewarded Ruth and he will reward all those who trust him in their relationships.

Co-ordinating the child's needs with medical practice. Long ago, the relationship between a doctor and a child patient was one whose major concern was to keep the child cared for at home. Technology has now advanced so much that the child may literally be isolated in a tent or incubator, and family involvement discouraged . . . yet child abuse, when first recognised, was noted to occur most frequently in children who had been intensively nursed as neonates, but whose parents had not been allowed access.

We have also behaved very badly towards young siblings of very sick children by thinking that to allow them to visit would be upsetting . . . but alienation from a loved brother or sister is read as rejection . . .

If we remember in all our dealings with children that their prime need is for sustained, caring and personal relationships which in turn profoundly influence their physical and emotional development, then we shall make fewer mistakes. A fourteen-month old child, sent to child minders by his working parents, was sent into care because bruised and deprived, despite the paediatrician's plea that the parents be helped to do better, with their children still in the family. Eleven years, two foster homes and four children's homes later, that child is still longing to go home. If such mistakes are made by caring, informed professionals, there must be many more brought about by sheer ignorance.

JANET GOODALL

ICMDA Cancun, Mexico, 1986. **Janet Goodall.** *Consultant paediatrician, Stoke-on-Trent, UK.*

GOD AND SUFFERING

RONALD WINTON

IT'S happened right through the history of the world, philosophers great and small, religions great and small, people great and small — all have talked about suffering. It is one of the great conundrums of the universe.

Suffering

Perhaps we should look at what is the basic problem. It always puzzles me when I meet atheists who are puzzled about suffering. Why, if you don't believe there is a power behind the universe, good or bad, why should suffering be in any way a problem? It just is. And yet this unhappiness about suffering seems to go to the heart of all sorts of people. And let's not make any mistake about it, atheists are not always unkind people. A person may not believe in anything outside the world of man and the physical world we live in, but he can still feel compassion. He can still be concerned because his child is suffering. Don't let us ever think that, as Christians, we have the monopoly of compassion. If we are not compassionate then our Christianity is not worth much, for compassion is at the heart of our faith, but we are not the only people who care about other people. The real problem arises because the vast majority of people do believe in a God but wonder, if there is a God, is he a good God or a bad one? If God is bad there's no problem, because suffering is not then incompatible with him.

The challenge to Christians

The real challenge is to the Christian. The Christian says that we have a good God. The Christian goes further, and says that we have a God who is not just a loving God but who is Love. The essential nature of our God is love. Love is of God. We also believe that God is all-powerful. If the God who made the universe doesn't

ICCMS Bangalore, India, 1983. **Ronald R. Winton.** _Past editor_ Medical Journal of Australia _and formerly Chairman World Medical Association and WMA Committee for medical ethics. ICMDA Chairman 1980–86, Vice-President 1986–94._

control the universe, if he is not absolute, if he is not almighty, then he is no God. But we believe in a God who made the universe, who planned it, who watches over it and who gives it its life, and its very existence depends on him. One philosophical way of putting it is that the universe exists in the mind of God, and I don't think that's an unbiblical attitude. That if God ceases to think about us, then we wouldn't exist any more. All life is of God, in him we live and have our being. He is not, however, to be identified with his creation; don't let us get lost in the pantheistic view. No, his creation is the object of what he has done, it is not God himself. We have God, then, who is Love, we have God who is Almighty — and we have suffering.

A stumbling block to faith

This is a problem that puzzles many thoughtful people. There are many people who long to believe, who want to put their trust in God; many folk look at our Lord Jesus and say 'I'd like to be one of his people, but I can't get past this — Why? oh why? oh why? He says that God is Love. He says that God is the creator of all things — but, look at the suffering. Suffering is all around us.' All kinds of suffering. Physical pain is one. We know that pain is something to thank God for. Dr Paul Brand, as a leprologist, has spent his life helping people who can't feel pain to compensate for that fact. Yet physical pain can make people bitter. Physical pain can destroy. Physical pain can change people. An Australian poet refers to 'the rat pain that gnaws away at us'. Yes, physical pain can be destructive. All kinds of suffering can be destructive and make people bitter and drive them away from faith in Christ.

Many kinds of suffering

There are many forms of suffering, some physical, some mental, some spiritual. They range from depression, particularly the endogenous depression in which people just feel unutterably miserable for no reason at all. Depression of that kind can be a very intense kind of suffering. There is the suffering of grief and loss, and it's not only the loss of a person. The same kind of grief can follow the loss of a limb, or the loss of something that's very precious to us, and people can grieve for the full range of what grief means, over more than just the loss of a loved person. Grief is a very deep kind of suffering, and it's one of the kinds of suffering over which people puzzle most of all. A parent loses a much-loved child through an illness perhaps, or an accident. The child who showed great promise, the child whom the parent had loved very greatly, that kind of grief can be a very deep kind of suffering. Sheer poverty can be a form of suffering, the suffering of a parent who doesn't know where the next meal is coming from for his or her children. Relative poverty in an affluent society can be a cause of suffering which it wouldn't be in a poorer society. When it's not possible to do the things that other people do, that's not being jealous, it can be grieving to a parent to have to deny his children the things that other children quite reasonably have.

The world is full of all forms of suffering and people say 'Why doesn't God stop it?' That's the basic question, why doesn't God stop it? Why did God let a mad man in Germany take hold of the people of Germany and push them into a war which set half the world ablaze in 1939? Why did millions die as a result of that war? Why were thousands put to death in their own countries, and in occupied countries, during that time? Why, oh why, didn't God stop it? Why didn't he strike Adolf Hitler dead? If God struck Adolf Hitler dead because he did wrong, should he strike everybody else dead who did wrong? If he did, would there be anybody left alive? I wouldn't be.

Some answers to the problem

The fact remains that we say that God should be able to do something about it. To this there are a number of answers. Obviously, certain things are inevitable and the laws are there. If you climb up on the roof and jump over the edge and land on the ground and defy the law of gravity, you're going to get hurt. You can't argue about that for you know that that law is there and yet you break it. However, this does not answer the question, asked in the terms of the religious tradition of the day, 'Who sinned, this man or his parents, that he is blind?' (John 9:2). People don't like the subject and so they want to blame someone for it. If they don't blame God they blame the people. Now there is a lot of suffering that is the result of wrongdoing. A lot of disease is the result of wrongdoing or foolishness — carcinoma of the lung, for example, yet people will go on smoking. All forms of venereal disease, the result of the kind of thing that most people know is wrong, yet put that aside for what they think will be pleasurable. There is an awful lot of disease which is the result of wrongdoing. It may not always be what we call immoral wrongdoing, but it is still doing the wrong thing. Like jumping off the roof — the inevitability is there.

I get a little worried sometimes when people speak about God doing the impossible. We know that God can do all sorts of things that we can't do, and the things that seem impossible to us he can do, but God can't do what can't be done. To try and put it in a concrete form — God can't make anything absolutely black and absolutely white at the same time. I don't think that God can make anything go up and come down at the same time. There are lots of things that are mutually contradictory, so we must be very careful when we say that God can do the impossible. We have a great God, one who created everything and sustains the universe, and he does things for us which we don't deserve and when we least expect them, but don't expect God to do the thing which just can't be done by the nature of the world that he has made.

People ask questions of us who say that we trust God, and we've got to be prepared to give a response — which is not always the same thing as an answer. We must give a response because it has been well said that Christianity does not explain suffering, it tells us what to do about it. We must not try to answer all the questions. Some of the questions that are asked are silly, some of them are real, and some of them are questions that do tear at people's hearts.

Does God send suffering?
Another question that people ask is, 'Is suffering sent by God?' I think the answer is 'Yes' and 'No', depending on what we mean by it. I don't think for one minute that God wants people to suffer. He doesn't want to hurt. There is no joy in the heart of God to know that someone is suffering in a meaningless kind of way. But, the judgement of God is another matter. Read what Joel and Amos said to people who called themselves the people of God but were behaving in all sorts of ways that were against the ways of God, particularly where they were exploiting the poor and showing their greed and their lack of care for people, and their love of money and ease. Joel and Amos spoke of the judgement of God, of how terrible it would be when he visited their sins upon them. We have got to acknowledge quite simply that God does send judgement, and judgement usually means suffering.

Then there is the story of Job, the man who was righteous, but who suffered terribly. If you haven't read the book of Job I advise you to do so. Read from the first chapter, and you will see that those plagues came from Satan, by the permission of God. Satan taunted God that his man, Job, wouldn't be able to take suffering. Satan says that if Job suffers in this way and in that way, he'll curse God. But God knew his Job, and he let Satan visit these things on poor old Job. Believe me, he had a rough, rough time. Some of the roughest of the times he experienced were from his friends, who were trying to comfort him, and who just loaded him up with platitudes, then told him that what he was going through was because he had done wrong. You should read the book. A lot of the things which his friends said to him were true, but they just threw them at poor old Job. He wanted someone to help him. He even argued with God! He didn't argue with God because he didn't believe in God, but he argued with God because he knew God. He wanted to have it out with the God whom he knew and trusted. How wise of Job. It's not wrong to ask 'Why?', but it's wrong to ask it in a bitter way. In the end, God made it very clear to Job just who he was — God. And who Job was. Job finished up better than ever, having had it out with God, and having acknowledged God, and having come to terms with the fact that God was to be trusted — because God is to be trusted.

In knowing God we have understanding

An early saint of the Christian church said this: 'We who have heard the word of God can bear his silences.' There are times when God seems not to be there, when some troubles and suffering come and God doesn't seem to be there at all, and I think many of us have experienced times in our lives when it was like that. 'God, where are you? Have you left me?' The greatest and most poignant occasion when that happened was when the Son of God, suffering physical and unutterable spiritual agony, said, 'My God,' — he spoke to his Father from whom he had never been separated — 'My God, why has thou forsaken me?' The aloneness of that was beyond our imagining, but in many of our lives there have been times when we've said 'God, where are you? Are you really there?' And God is silent. This great saint said, 'He who has heard the word of God can bear his silences.'

C.S. Lewis experienced suffering, and in one of his books he emphasises the fact that when we are feeling well, and when things are going well, that is the time to consolidate our faith in God. Because when things go wrong, and we feel lost and hopeless, then we should be able to say, 'This has thrown me off my balance, but when my mind was sane and balanced, I did trust God. I did know that he was there, I am sure of it. OK. I'm not normal now, my problems, my suffering, have thrown me off balance, but let me look back to the time when I was thinking straight, and know that God is there.'

Miss Amy Carmichael, who spent most of her life in South India, spent a large amount of her life suffering physically. She says that when the suffering and pain come, and we look up at the suffering Christ, we can say, 'Love that loves like that can be trusted about this.' My body might be tormented by pain, my heart might be torn with pain, my mind might be baffled with problems, but I look at the Lord whose love took him to the cross to suffer the utmost of physical and spiritual pain, and I can say that love that loves like that can be trusted about this. As Job said of God, 'Though he slay me, yet will I trust him.'

May I finish with a very personal story, which I hope you won't think sentimental, but it has meant a lot to me. I had a small black dog, a good many years ago, and at that time it was not long since I had come back from the war. My father had died during the war, and I made a home for my mother. We were given this tiny black puppy and he completely attached himself to me. As he grew I was the centre of his world. The relationship between a man and his dog is, I think, almost unique. A dog can treat a person — man, woman, or child — with an extraordinary kind of affection, and if you haven't experienced it you may not know what I'm talking about. Many of you, though, will know what it is. To be sitting down, and have a dog there and looking up at you, with no other obvious focus of attention but you — one can only see it as a kind of adoration. It can be very humbling. It is the nearest thing I know, in relationships between created creatures, to our adoration of God. This was so, for when I was at home that little black dog never left me, my presence was all he wanted. I looked after him, I took him for a run in the morning, saw he was fed, and so on. His attachment to me was absolute, his trust in me was completely unquestioned.

Later I moved away to take charge of a students' hostel and my mother went into hospital and didn't ever come out. I had to take the little dog with me, but in the hostel it became impossible to control him. He had had distemper, which apparently caused some brain changes, and he was becoming aggressive instead of being a gentle, friendly little dog. He was aggressive with almost everyone except me. He bit the butcher — and this made me decide that it just couldn't go on. I didn't feel I could give him away, as no one could control a dog like that. So I went and talked to my friend the vet, and he said, 'Well, there's nothing we can do about it. The kindest thing to do is to put him down.' To which I said, 'Yes, I think so.' So I took him in — I can still remember what happened; I had the little dog on the lead, and he was jumping up at me with affection in his usual way. The vet took the lead, and led him away. After a while he came back, with the empty collar and lead. And I went away and cried. I couldn't help it. I had slain that little dog. He trusted me — absolutely, and I had his completely unqualified affection.

Now that taught me something, and I pass it along to you as I hope it will not be thought of as a sentimental story. This is just about as near as we can get to understanding something of our relationship with God. We may trust God absolutely and may say, 'Why, oh why, oh why?' If that little dog — and I don't believe that dogs have this capacity for conceptual thought — had known what I was going to do to him, and what I did do, how could he have said otherwise to me than, 'Why, oh why, oh why? I have given you all my affection, all my trust, and this is what you do to me, you kill me.' I then knew what Job meant when he said, 'Though he slay me, yet will I trust in him.' Because it could have been that that little dog would still (if he was capable of that kind of thought) have said 'Well, Boss, you know best.' I did for him what I believed with my limited wisdom was the best thing for him and I believe that I had the authority as well as the power to do that. I did what I did in love.

Forgive me if I've told you a fairly personal kind of story, but it taught me so much. How much more can we trust the God who made us, and who himself died to save us.

DISABILITY – A CHANGE OF VIEW

M. C. MATHEW

I SUFFERED from slavery to an incomplete vision of health for the early part of my career as a pediatrician. I only saw physical well-being as my idea of health. When I was a consultant at the Christian Medical Hospital, Vellore, a father brought his five-year-old son for consultation. The boy had Down's syndrome. The father sought help to train and educate his son. I pronounced him to be intellectually limited and cautioned the father against expecting much from him. On hearing this he burst into tears. I did not know how to handle the situation. The father kept asking me, 'Doctor, can't you do something for my son?'

I saw that boy as physically unwell because of his ventricular septal defect and his limited intellect. I saw him as a burden to his parents. I could not attribute any worthwhile role for him in his family or society. Medical technology could not help him sufficiently. I believed that no form of help would really restore health to him. However, I was disturbed by the emotional turmoil of the father. That kept the memory of that boy alive in my mind.

Then something happened to enable me to see things in a proper perspective. My wife and I had our second baby. She was born with an intellectual disability. For a while I could not accept her like any other child as I was guided by the criterion of physical well-being as the minimum requirement for health. During her life, which lasted only four months, my wife and I moved to the position of seeing her as a person, created in the image of God. We saw her as the focus of God's love. Her smile communicated God's love to us. Her warm response to her name being called, or to being cuddled, made me feel that she was fully alive even though physically not well. This brought me to a point of appreciating health as fullness of life (even in the absence of physical well-being). Health to me became an inner disposition.

My wife and I have been involved with the care of intellectually

ICMDA Cancun, Mexico, 1986. **M. C. Mathew.** *Director of ASHIRVAD, Children's Rehabilitation Centre, Madras, India.*

handicapped children for the last three years. Every contact with these children reminds us of the fact that health has a dimension well beyond the physical dimension. Some of these handicapped children demonstrate glimpses of this fullness of life even when they are seriously disabled. This illustrates how there is a treasure in our earthen vessel which can be quickened to affect all other areas of our life, thanks to the activity of God. It is this activity of God that we need to recognise and facilitate in every person.

As Christian members of the medical profession we are today looking afresh at our concept of health. Every person is in some form of need. The physical needs may be visible and striking so they receive our immediate attention. Other needs are identifiable only to the eyes that look for them. The often unspoken needs for friendship, love, identity and a purpose in life can be met through the experience of abundant life in Christ. This makes a person complete.

We have a responsibility to take health beyond the horizon of the physical and prepare people to enter into this abundant life experience. This alone is health in all its fullness. Anything short of this concept of health is a borrowed concept from the world around us. We would be guilty of being squeezed into its mould and its concept of health. We cannot afford to subscribe to a concept of health less than this.

ETHICS OF COUNSELLING THE SICK AND DYING

CHARLOTTE TAN

Introduction

AFTER I became a Christian during medical school in China, I wanted to be a medical missionary. Instead, the Lord put me to work at Memorial Sloan-Kettering Cancer Center, New York. One night, after the first three months there, I went to my knees in tears and told the Lord that I could not take it any longer. It was so cruel and agonising to watch the children die, one by one, no matter how hard the doctors tried to treat and save them. Then clearly the answer came, 'Who do you wish to take your place?' If this is the place God wants me to be, then my reward is not in what I see but in obediently doing whatever God enables me to do.

Sharing faith

I remember the struggle of my early days at Memorial Center. I knew I should share my faith in God with these patients and their families, but I did not know how. I used to look first at the patients' charts to find out what religion they were. If the chart was marked 'Protestant' I would then get up enough courage to talk to them.

Prayer

As one child was about to return home for the local doctor to follow his treatment, I talked to the parents in the chapel. Before they left, I asked them if they would mind if we prayed together. I prayed quietly for this child and his parents, asking God to strengthen their faith and hope in him. When I had finished I looked up and there was a Jewish patient with his family in the chapel. Much to my surprise, their eyes were filled with tears and the Jewish patient came over and asked if I could pray for him. This experience opened my eyes, in that we all need God, whether Jew, Catholic or Protestant. Often we are afraid to pray for patients for fear that they might resent this and become more fearful of

ICCP Singapore, 1975. **Charlotte Tan.** *Physician, Memorial Sloan-Kettering Cancer Center, New York, USA.*

their impending death. In reality, I have found that every time I pray with parents, whether believers or not, they always respond, 'I need this prayer more than anything else at this time.'

After many years of working in a cancer hospital, I am convinced that no one human being alone is strong enough to face the tragedy of a dying child. There is a saying that man's extremity is God's opportunity. My responsibility then is to help these parents back to the presence of God's mercy, so that their suffering will not be wasted and that they will allow God to work mightily among them.

Scripture verses

Despite knowing what my responsibility was, I still did not know how to share with these parents. I realised that my own human words must be so limited in their comfort, so I started to memorise Bible verses, such as 'God is love', 'All things work together for good to those who love God', and 'Call unto me and I will answer you'.

I will never forget a Jewish woman, 45 years of age, who had only one son and he was dying of a malignant tumour of the eye. She very angrily said to me, 'If God is love, he would not have allowed this to happen to me.' Another woman said, 'You tell me to call unto God and he will answer. I have called him a million times and he never answered me. My husband died of cancer two months ago and now my only son is dying of a brain tumour.' It took me a long time to realise that hearts can be too hurt to be comforted by words.

Tuning-in

God used my own personal experience to teach me. The day my husband was advised to have heart surgery I, as his wife and also a physician, thought of all the worst things that could happen and felt that the responsibility was all on my shoulders to decide about which hospital and which doctor. I tried to take hold of those well-memorised Bible verses. Somehow they all seemed too remote. The words were not helping me until I realised that I needed to commit my life and my husband's life totally into God's hands. It was no longer my responsibility but God's. Once this new commitment was made, the words came to me in a different and more meaningful way. The word of God is true, but we have to let ourselves go and let God in.

It is many years since my own personal battle ended and it now seems easier to counsel patients and their parents. I say easier, although death and dying have always been distasteful to man and probably always will be, especially when a child is involved. It is never easy and one can never get used to it, because the problems of each child and family are different.

Each time I have to tell parents that their child has leukaemia, or other type of cancer, I always assure them that we will do everything humanly possible to help the child, but our human efforts are limited. Together we will pray and let our almighty God have a chance to help us. I don't give easy answers anymore, or mere words. I put my arms round them and pray with them. In a desperate situation like this, if the physician can give just a little more time, compassion, kindness and understanding, it will go a long way.

Reactions to death and dying

In general, there are various stages in the reactions to death and dying. The first stage is usually *shock*. Once parents hear the diagnosis of cancer they can't hear anything else that the physician goes on to say. The next stage is *denial*. They do not believe the diagnosis and prefer to think that the doctors have made a mistake somewhere. As a result they want to shop around many consultations, hoping that one will agree with them. Then comes *anger*. They are angry with the physicians, residents, interns and nurses. No one seems to be right. No matter how often you try to explain to them what is going on with the child, they turn around and say no one ever talked to them about what is happening.

In these stages the doctor's understanding and compassion are most important. We should not take their anger or doubt personally, but realise that these are their natural reactions. Sometimes the husband and wife are angry with each other or even angry with the child. In almost every instance, if the relationship between the husband and wife is not right in the beginning, then at the time of stress the defence mechanism collapses, the problems between them come to the surface and the end is divorce. If the relationship between the parents is good, then the husband and wife help each other and the stress brings them closer to each other and to God.

The next stage is *bargaining*. They bargain with the doctor and they bargain with God. The child may bargain, too. One little girl asked permission to go out to her sister's wedding. When she came back to the hospital, the first thing she said was, 'Doctor, don't forget I have three other sisters who are going to be married soon.' *Depression* is scattered throughout the course but the hope is that at last they will all finally learn to *accept*. During all this time, it is important for the physician to be in touch with the family's feelings. Maybe all that is needed is a sympathetic ear. Families need to be reassured that we will leave no stone unturned. There is always hope of another remission, or the hope of some new research drug, yet at the same time they are not to have false hope. More important, they must be helped to keep up their hope in God.

Caring for the dying can be a rewarding experience rather than a confession of failure if the physician is in harmony with the patient and parents.

Mystery and suffering

Human suffering is a mystery. Many parents ask the question, 'Why?' We don't know why, nor do we understand. Even our Lord Jesus asked, 'Why?' (Mat. 27:46). His question was not answered, yet we know that he himself is the answer, for he says, 'I am the way, the truth and the life' (John 14:6).

After the death of her six-month-old baby, a Jewish mother said, 'A rose blooms beautifully for just a short while, then fades away, because it has accomplished what it was meant to accomplish.' Our time is in God's hands. Another man, who had very little education, said to me after the death of his twelve-year-old son, 'There are only two words I can say and they are "He does" [God does] because God is too wise to make a mistake.'

'For my thoughts are not your thoughts, neither are your ways my ways, saith the Lord' (Isa. 55:8).

A theologian recently asked me a question. 'When are you research scientists going to come up with a cure for cancer?' I said to him, 'When are you theologians going to give an explanation for the mystery of suffering?' The lack of human knowledge about how to deal either with a fatal disease or with the mystery of suffering may help to remind us of our finiteness and our limitations and to teach us that we are not created to be independent from God, but to be dependent on him. Our responsibility as Christian physicians is to attend to both the physical and spiritual healing of our patients and their families.

THE SICKNESS OF MAN

MARTYN LLOYD-JONES

'BUT GOD'

I SHOULD like to call your attention to the first two words found in Ephesians 2:4, 'But God'. To remind you of the context of this statement, let me read to you some of the verses of this chapter:

> 'And you hath he quickened, who were dead in trespasses and sins; wherein in time past ye walked according to the course of this world, according to the prince of the power of the air, the spirit that now worketh in the children of disobedience; among whom also we all had our conversation in times past in the lusts of our flesh, fulfilling the desires of the flesh and of the mind; and were by nature the children of wrath, even as others. *But God*, who is rich in mercy, for his great love wherewith he loved us, even when we were dead in sins, hath quickened us together with Christ, (by grace ye are saved;) and hath raised us up together, and made us sit together in heavenly places in Christ Jesus: that in the ages to come he might show the exceeding riches of his grace in his kindness toward us through Jesus Christ.'

These two words 'But God' come, as you notice, as the kind of junction between the alarming and terrifying things that the apostle has been saying about human nature as it is as the result of the Fall and the character and the nature of our glorious Christian salvation. He turns from the dark picture to the bright and glorious picture which results from the coming of the Gospel.

I want to suggest that these two words also remind us of what our duty is as Christian people in this world at this present time. The first great function of every Christian, whether he be a physician or whatever, is to confront the world with these two words: 'But God'. I mean by that, that as we share life with others, and mix with them, and as we suffer the same difficulties, the same

ICCP Oxford, UK, 1966. **Martyn Lloyd-Jones.** *Minister, Westminster Chapel; past chief clinical assistant to Lord Horder, King's physician, London, UK.*

tragedies in life, it is our business to listen to them and to allow them to speak. They are very ready to do so at the present time; they say, 'Have you read the paper? Have you heard the news? Isn't it terrible? What's going to happen?' They are always ready to talk about life and the whole condition of the world, and to indulge in their forebodings and prognostications. I suggest that your business and mine as Christian people is to listen to them, to allow them to speak. Then when they've finished recounting troubles and tragedies we can say: 'Yes, what you've been saying is perfectly right; it's perfectly true, but God . . .' And so we introduce the Gospel to them. In other words, man's extremity is God's opportunity.

What do these words represent? Let us examine this word 'but' and see what it tells us.

The implications of the words 'but God'

The word 'but' introduces a hope. In the first three verses Paul has been describing our condition and he goes down from bad to worse. We are dead in trespasses and sins. We walked according to the course of this world, governed by the prince of the power of the air, but suddenly the whole situation changes. There's hope after all. Things are not as the non-Christian would describe them. We have this purpose, there is something more to be said. That is the way in which the gospel comes in.

Now, the Gospel itself is introduced like that in the gospels. Remember, 'The people that sat in darkness have seen a great light' (Isa. 9:2). This is the only hope for the world. We have examined what the world has to offer, we have looked at its proposals, we have seen that they are totally inadequate. They must be, and for this good reason, that we are dealing with a state of death; but where there's life, there's hope. There's no hope when there's death, and we all by nature are dead in trespasses and in sin. Realise furthermore that we are concerned in a great fight against the prince of the power of the air, the spirit that now worketh in the children of disobedience. 'We wrestle not against flesh and blood'; that's not the problem. We are not fighting flesh and blood in ourselves, nor in other people. The problem is not just man. 'We wrestle not against flesh and blood, but against principalities, against powers, against rulers of the darkness of this world, against spiritual wickedness in high or in heavenly places'

(Eph. 6:12). What can man do against such a power? The world is as it is because man was defeated at the beginning by the devil, the power of Satan, and this has continued to be the problem ever since. However able men are, however erudite, they cannot match themselves against this terrible power which is second only to the power of God himself. The situation is completely hopeless, apart from this one thing: *But God.* Man can't, but with *God* nothing shall be impossible.

The word 'but' separates the natural from the supernatural. It introduces God. You pass from the natural to the supernatural. Here is something we need to remind ourselves of, constantly, and to assert, without failure ever at any time, that our gospel is frankly miraculous, supernatural, divine. A gospel which is not miraculous, supernatural, is no gospel. Why is it that mankind stumbles at this? There's nothing new about this. We tend to think, of course, that it is because of our scientific knowledge that we are in trouble with regard to this, but it isn't. It's a very old complaint. Let me illustrate what I mean.

We have the account of the announcement to Mary, the mother of our Lord, of his coming birth (Luke 1:26–35). 'Fear not, Mary, for thou hast found favour with God, and behold thou shalt conceive in thy womb and bring forth a son.' Then said Mary unto the angel: 'How shall this be, seeing I know not a man?' Mary stumbles at this glorious announcement. She stumbled at the supernatural, at the miraculous. She didn't understand this thing, so she can't take it. And the archangel has to enlighten her. 'The Holy Ghost shall come upon thee, and the power of the Highest shall overshadow thee. Therefore also that holy thing that shall be born of thee, shall be called the Son of God.' The archangel says in effect 'With God, nothing shall be impossible'. Now there, you see, is an illustration of this self-same tendency on our part to stumble at the miraculous and the supernatural and the divine, and we miss the glory of the gospel as we do so. Let's not be unfair to Mary; she is not the only one who stumbles at this.

There is that extraordinary account in John 3 of the interview between a man called Nicodemus and our blessed Lord. Here is a master of Israel, a learned man, a wise man, a teacher of Israel. He has been impressed by our Lord's miracles and by his teachings, so he goes at night to seek an interview with him, and says: 'Rabbi, we know that thou art a teacher come from God, and no man can do these miracles that thou doest, except God be with you', and our Lord interrupts him. Jesus answered and said unto him: 'Verily, verily, I say unto thee, except a man be born again, he cannot see the kingdom of God.' Do you remember Nicodemus' reaction to that? He stumbles at this in exactly the same way as Mary had done. Nicodemus saith unto him: 'How can a man be born when he's old? Can he enter the second time into his mother's womb, and be born? What are you talking about? Are you suggesting that a man like myself who is now old, that I can be born again?' He stumbles at the miraculous and the supernatural. Our Lord replies to him saying: 'Verily, verily, I say unto thee, except a man be born of the water and of the spirit, he cannot see the kingdom of God. That which is born of the flesh is the flesh, and that which is born of the Spirit is the spirit. Marvel not that I say unto thee ye *must* be born again.' 'Listen,' said our Lord to Nicodemus, 'the trouble with you is that you are thinking on the fleshly level. I wasn't talking about the birth in the flesh. I am talking about spiritual birth, it is the action of God.'

Here you see is still the difficulty. The world is prepared to accept the teaching of Jesus. It is prepared to laud and to praise him as a man, but it stumbles at his deity. It stumbles at the supernatural element, but if you take this out you've no gospel. You've nothing left in a sense but a good man amongst other good men. No, no, our gospel is frankly, gloriously miraculous, supernatural. It is divine, it is the action of the living God.

The Bible is full of this element of surprise and of astonishment and none, of course, expresses it more frequently than this very apostle Paul, who penned these words to the Ephesians. If ever a man was surprised at what happened to him in this world, it was Saul of Tarsus. He was a Pharisee, trained as a Pharisee. He held their views and ideas. He'd heard of Jesus of Nazareth; he didn't like what he'd heard. He was opposed to it all, and he was so zealous in his opposition that he went to the authorities at Jerusalem, and asked them to give him a commission to go down from Jerusalem to Damascus to exterminate what called itself a church (Acts 9). If there was one thing of which this man, Saul of Tarsus, was more certain than anything else as he went, it was that he would never be a Christian. If the whole world became Christian, he most certainly wouldn't. Somewhere round about noon he suddenly saw that light in the heaven, shining above the brightest shining of the sun at noonday, and there in the light a face such as he'd never seen before, a face filled with glory and love and passion, a divine face. And he cries out, saying, 'Who art thou, Lord?' and the answer that came back was the last thing that this man ever expected to hear — 'I am Jesus, whom thou persecutest.' What! Was it possible that Jesus of Nazareth, the carpenter, that fellow, that impostor, that blasphemer, could be the Lord of glory? But such is the truth and the apostle never recovered from this. He continues to be amazed, he writes to the Galatians, and he says: 'I have been crucified with Christ, nevertheless I live; yet not I, but Christ within'; because he has become a Christian, he is amazed at himself, he doesn't understand himself. He has become an enigma to himself. He seems to contradict himself. He says: 'I live, yet not I.' 'I'm alive, yet I'm not alive.' 'I'm Saul of Tarsus, yet I'm certainly not Saul of Tarsus.' Is there a better definition of a Christian than that? The Christian is a man who cannot understand himself because of what the grace of God has done to him. A Christian is a man who in order to try to understand himself has to call in the Lord Jesus Christ as the only explanation. 'I live, yet not I.' Christ liveth in me. The life I now live in the flesh, I live by the 'faith of the Son of God who loved me and gave himself for me' (Gal. 2:20).

Is this confined to apostles? No, no. This has been the feeling and sensation, the experience of the saints of the centuries. Let me give you but one instance. A man who once was a student here in Oxford, Charles Wesley, he knows exactly the same surprise as Saul of Tarsus knew when he became the apostle Paul. He puts it in his own language. This is how Charles Wesley puts it: 'And can it be that I should gain an interest in the Saviour's blood? Died he for me who caused his pain, for me who him to death pursued? Amazing love! And can it be that thou, my Lord, my God, hast died for me?' Charles Wesley couldn't get over this, he couldn't believe it, it's incredible. Yet he knows it's true.

My friends, I make no apology for asking you this question. Are you surprised at yourself? Do you understand yourself? Can you explain yourself and all you do? If you can, I suggest you are not a Christian. You can be a religious person and a very moral person. You can do a lot of good, but you know exactly what you're doing; you can explain it all. You are a self-contained person and you can explain yourself, but you are not a Christian. A Christian, by definition, is a man who is astounded at himself. 'Can it be that I should gain?', is it possible that *I* am a Christian, that *I* am a son, a child, of God? Impossible! And yet I know it's true with the 'but' of surprise and astonishment.

The word 'but' emphasises the eternal difference between God and ourselves. 'But God'. We are described in the first three verses of Ephesians 2. Now he is going to tell us about God. And what he tells us, and the word 'but' really suggests it all, is that God is eternally different from us. That is the explanation of our salvation. If God were like us, there would be no salvation. This little word 'but', you see, is the measure, the difference between us and God. And it introduces us to this amazing love — the love of God, that sends his only Son to the death and the shame of the cross, 'even the death of the cross' (Phil. 2:8), and the agony and the pain and the cry of dereliction. All that, so that you and I, who deserve nothing but the wrath of God, might be forgiven, might become the children of God. In the same way it reminds us of the power of God which, 'even when we are dead in sins, hath quickened us together with Christ. By grace ye are saved' (Eph. 2:5). It is only God who can do this, and that's why we should glory in the fact that he is eternally different.

Furthermore, have you ever noticed this amazing statement 'And hath raised us up together'? (Eph. 2:6). Beyond that he has made us sit together in heavenly places in Christ Jesus. The apostle is not saying that one day we *are* going to sit in the heavenly places in Christ Jesus. He says we are already there. We are *in* Christ. Not only quickened, not only resurrected, we have ascended, and we are seated in the heavenly places already. In Christ Jesus, the power of God has come to us, and has raised us from death, sin and the grave, and has lifted us up to the very heavens, and we are seated with Christ in the heavenly places at this present moment, if we are Christians at all.

The word 'but' introduces us to what is our only encouragement. We have met in congress. We have been considering some of the terrible appalling moral problems afflicting mankind at the present time, and it's very difficult not to lose hope. It's no longer a popular thing to be a Christian. It is a hard time for the Christian church. Is there any hope for the Christian church in this land and in other lands? If the future of the church depends upon man's power, well then I say we are already defeated. Thank God the future of the church is not in our hands, the church is the church of God, and there is no limit to the power of God. Isn't this the great history that we have behind us? There have been previous times in the long history of the Christian church when she seemed to be as powerless and as ineffective, and almost as moribund as she seems to be today, and the clever people of those ages were preparing their funeral orations at the burial of the Christian church. But God! God suddenly intervenes, in a mighty reformation or reawakening. When everything seems to be lost and the darkness is covering the minds even of God's own people, and everything is hopeless, God arises. The moribund church is renewed and reinvigorated and filled with life and goes forward to a mighty period of effectiveness in the world. Isn't that the story? And thank God, God is still the same.

Whatever the omens, whatever the signs, whatever the appearances, our confidence, my friends, is this, that God is still with us, and while God is with us who can be against us? Let us shake off any tendency to discouragement, to despair, or to hopelessness. Let us realise that we are still the people of the *living God,* and that in spite of men, in spite of hell, his work will go on.

This is not only encouragement for the church, it is encouragement for the individual also. Don't give in; don't stop praying — pray on. Hope on — with God nothing shall be impossible. Whatever the circumstances and conditions, in us or in others, the answer is always 'but God'.

Section 3

Ethical Principles

❋

Christian distinctiveness in a changing world

THE MASTER PHYSICIAN — HIS ETHOS AND ETHIC

BENJAMIN CHEW

Introduction

AS Christians, the partnership (koinonia) we have with one another is centred on our Lord Jesus Christ, the Master Physician. I have chosen for this reason the scripture portion in Luke 6:17–49 for our meditation.

The submissiveness of the disciple

This matchless ethical mandate of our Lord in all his sovereign authority was given primarily to his disciples. Luke, in his characteristic and careful manner, as a research historian and writer, inspired by God, gives us details of the speaker, venue and audience.

The Lord commenced his ministry in Galilee (Mat. 4:17 ff) by first proclaiming the gospel of the kingdom and healing every disease and malady. Great crowds from Judea, Jerusalem and the capital city, Decapolis, and beyond Jordan as well as Syria in the north followed him.

He went up the mountain with his disciples; Luke typically emphasises the fact that he went to pray (Luke 6:12) and spent the whole night in prayer to God. This emphasis on the prayer life of Christ is noteworthy. Seven of the nine prayers recorded are by Luke alone. He alone mentions the fact that Jesus prayed for Peter (22:31 ff) and for his enemies (23:34). The great parables on prayer, the importunate friend at midnight (11:5 ff), the unjust judge and the Pharisee and publican (ch. 18) are from Luke's pen.

For Jesus himself, his prayer was always, 'not my will but thine be done'. In Luke 6, in view of the momentous selection of his apostles and the very busy day ahead, he prayed the whole night.

What an eloquent testimony his prayer life is to the reality of his human nature! 'Though he were a son, yet learned he obedience by the things he suffered' (Heb. 5:8).

*ICCP Singapore, 1975. **Benjamin Chew**. General practitioner, church elder and Bible teacher, Singapore.*

When day came, he called his disciples. Luke described them as a large throng and from these the Lord chose twelve to be his apostles. These men would be his first missionaries.

He came down with them to 'a level place', a suitable plateau, which Luke noted as the venue for the large number of his disciples (6:17) and the great throng of people, who had come to hear him and to be healed (6:18).

I would like us to recognise him in our midst, just as he was among them, and ourselves, more than 600 of us like those disciples of old, as eager as they were to hear his word and to share with him, the Great Physician, in the same ministry of healing. We need to take to our hearts afresh the ethos, the character and life-style of Jesus, the Master Physician, in his perfect humanity; incarnate God, yet truly and completely man.

The partnership and fellowship which we share with one another, such as we seek to foster at this congress, must always be in the practical context of ordinary human relationships. Similarly, the practical communion we have with our Saviour, Master and Lord will depend upon our personal knowledge of him not only on the special occasion of this congress, but in the daily affairs and diverse activities of our lives and common profession.

To gain this intimate personal knowledge was the apostle Paul's single ambition. 'I am esteeming all things as loss for the excellency of the knowledge of Christ Jesus my Lord, on account of whom I suffered the loss of all things, esteeming them to be refuse, that I may win Christ and be found in him, not having my righteousness which is of the law [human ethical standards] but that which is through the faith of Christ, the righteousness of God based upon faith [his ethos and ethic], that I may know him and the power of his resurrection and the fellowship of his sufferings being made like him in his death' (Phil. 3:8–10).

We look again at the great multitude who had come. All were seeking to touch him, for power was coming from him and healing them (vv. 18–19). Shall we not also seek to know him and touch him in a new way at this congress? His touch still has its ancient power for healing, not only for us but, through us when we leave, for others in the far-flung countries from which we come.

They had come first to hear him and also to be healed. May we preserve this right priority in our deliberations. Luke, the physician, gives only two short verses to the healing ministry of our Lord on this occasion. Nevertheless let us note that as was always his practice, the Lord attended to the urgent physical needs of the multitude, healing their sick before he turned to the disciples and spoke to them.

We, as doctors, sympathise and deal with the immediate area of need of body and mind, but then as Christian doctors we must be always sensitive to the deepest need of the soul and spirit — the total person. (Bishop Taylor Smith: 'Man has a body but is a living soul.')

The Lord's discourse and ethic (vv. 20–26)

Luke has the physician's sharply defined outlook on desperate need on the one hand, and all the rich resources of heaven on the other, to meet the need. He sees the dreadful consequences of need unfelt and unmet.

He gives us four Beatitudes and his four corresponding Woes present a direct antithesis.

6:20 'And lifting up his eyes upon his disciples, he said:

- Blessed are the poor for yours is the kingdom of God . . .'
  6:24 — the first woe: 'But woe to you that are rich, for you are receiving your consolation in full'.
- 6:21 'Blessed are (ye) who hunger now, for you shall be filled'.
  6:25 'Woe to you who have been filled for ye shall hunger'.
- 6:21b 'Blessed are (ye) who weep now for you shall laugh'.
  6:25b 'Woe to you who laugh now for you shall mourn and weep'.
- 6:22–23 'Blessed are (ye) when men hate you and ostracise you, and heap insults upon you, and spurn your name as evil, for the sake of the Son of Man. Be glad in that day, and leap for joy, for behold your reward is great in heaven: for in the same way, their fathers used to treat the prophets'.
  6:26 'Woe to you when all men speak well of you, for in the same way their fathers used to treat the false prophets'.

The Beatitudes portray the ethos of Christ. In these paradoxical definitions, they are addressed to all his followers to form the basis of his supreme ethic. Luke's startling contrasts of 'Blessedness' and 'Woe' impress upon us that the ethic of Jesus is not something simply idealistic to be admired, but that which is intensely practical, to be implemented and lived out in living relationship to him, and in the enablement and direction of the Holy Spirit. It becomes gloriously possible of fulfilment only in the terms of the Gospel and the power of the Spirit.

The conditions of the Beatitudes leave us in no doubt as to the inwrought basis of Christian character. The single outstanding quality in the character of the disciple is *submissiveness*. For us, this does not primarily depend upon ethical codes and external rules but upon our vital relationship with the Lord himself.

The first Beatitude is foundational

'Blessed are the poor … for yours is the kingdom of God.' 'Blessed (*makarios,* happy, to be congratulated) are the poor (*ptochos,* totally destitute) for yours is the kingdom (the rule, reign with all the riches and resources) of God.'

The disciples were those directly addressed. They were the possessors of the kingdom, happy and to be congratulated, in their complete submission to the rule and reign of God, and their claim upon all his riches and resources. Otherwise they were totally bankrupt. True it was that discipleship in those days meant faithful following and submission to the rabbi. Disciples, like medical interns, could be identified by the mannerism of their teachers, which they had unconsciously imitated.

True happiness in any person's life begins at his conversion and new birth — the happiness of humility. In Matthew's account, the Lord spoke of the comfort given to the humble poor, who mourn. These are happy indeed in the comfort and strength, in cleansing and enablement, which they find as they mourn on account of their sins, and in sympathy with others.

As part of the kingdom of God and of heaven, there is the inheritance of the earth of the meek. Meekness, the only self-description of the Lord's character (Mat. 11:29) is inseparably linked with humility. It is the fruit of the Spirit (Gal. 5:23), a steadfast equanimity in the strength of the resources of God, expressing itself in unchanging gentleness.

Our Lord is the supreme example of true humility and submissiveness. 'You know the grace of our Lord Jesus Christ that though he was rich, yet for your sakes became poor (completely destitute), that you through his poverty might be rich' (2 Cor. 8:9).

In the incarnation he laid aside the authority and glory of the Godhead; and as a slave, he humbled himself and became obedient even to the death on the cross. We are to have this in mind as the pattern of humble submission.

Anything less would mean the intrusion of meritorious self-interest in some degree. Luke's woe (the word is not that of condemnation but that of compassion and sorrow) was a warning to the multitude but nevertheless had a lesson for the disciples. 'Woe to you, the rich, for you are receiving your consolation (your comfort in full).' They are like the member of the Laodicean church who said, 'I am rich and have become wealthy and have need of nothing' and who did not know that he was 'wretched, miserable, poor, blind and naked'.

You will remember Luke's story of the rich fool (Luke 12) who laid up treasure for himself and was not rich towards God. There is no place for complacency and self-satisfaction in the humble submissiveness of the disciple.

What we have received of possessions, powerful therapeutic weapons, professional skills, and high ethical standards (and we thank the giver for these) must be always held by us as responsible stewards for the Master's use, with a sense of our own inadequacy and our need of his constant enablement and grace.

There follows Luke's second Beatitude

'Blessed are you who hunger now, for you shall be filled.' The humble poor, spiritually destitute, are ever conscious of desperate need. As they hunger, Matthew states explicitly, and thirst after righteousness, they shall be satisfied. What a blessed satisfaction this is! What a glorious promise! For 'righteousness' sums up the Lord's ethos and ethic — the divine righteousness revealed in him. He is Jehovah Tsidkenu, the Lord our Righteousness (Jer. 23:6), Christ Jesus who is made unto us wisdom, even righteousness, sanctification and redemption (1 Cor. 1:30).

All human ideas of holiness and standards of morality, including even our most enlightened code of medical ethics, fall short of God's righteousness.

Here again are the gracious terms of the Gospel, the righteousness of God imputed and imparted to the believer in sovereign mercy at the cross, 'where mercy and truth are met together, righteousness and peace have kissed each other' (Ps. 85:10).

The disciples' submissiveness is in holiness. That it is inward and not superficial and external is seen in Matthew's sixth Beatitude, 'Blessed are the pure in heart, for they shall see God'.

In contrast is the 'woe' of those who are full, who are self-sufficient outside of Christ: they can manage without him.

Spiritual starvation and hopeless sorrow will be their portion.

Luke's third Beatitude

'Blessed are you who weep now, for you shall laugh.' The exact opposite — 'Woe to you who laugh now, for you shall mourn and weep.' Jesus wept with Mary and Martha in their sorrow and bereavement. He wept over Jerusalem in her rebellion and rejection of his love. The prophets of old wept over the sins, social injustice, corruption of the nations of the people of God. We can also weep if we have the same sensitivity, the same sympathy and sorrow — over the needs of men, women and children. We are more sensitive to physical social needs as doctors — how necessary this is, but the spiritual need of a lost world and lost individuals must be predominant.

Then only the triumph and joy of salvation will be ours. We are reminded of our Lord's words in the upper room to his disciples, 'Truly, truly I say to you that you will weep and lament, but the world will rejoice: you will be sorrowful but your sorrow will be turned to joy' (John 16:20). 'Weeping may last for the night but a shout of joy comes in the morning' (Ps. 30:5).

Submissiveness is often associated with suffering and sorrow. In these words of our Lord, he confirms the hope of eventual triumph and exultant joy: this note of certain triumph is sung again and again towards the consummation of our salvation, when he returns. Paul dismisses his sufferings thus: 'Our light affliction, which is but momentary, is producing for us an eternal weight of glory far beyond all comparison' (2 Cor. 4:17). Submissiveness is in this hope. But the laughter of insensitivity, callousness, and exulting and taking pleasure in earthly things, regardless of sorrow and need, brings inevitable sorrow and lamentation.

The fourth Beatitude

'Blessed are you when men hate you and ostracise you and heap insults upon you and spurn your name as evil for the sake of the Son of man. Be glad in that day and leap for joy ... for in the same way, their fathers used to treat the prophets.'

Then the final woe (v. 26) in contrast: 'Woe to you when all men speak well of you, in the same way their fathers used to treat false prophets.' Universal popularity with unbelievers — a warning!

Faithful prophets had always been persecuted: but on the other hand, false prophets had been universally popular. Happiness in the midst of implacable hatred and hostility! Yes, even jubilation, the testimony of history. Rejoice and leap for joy for behold, great is your reward in heaven!

Anti-Christian persecution is with us today throughout the world. Even in Singapore, many young Christians have to face bitter persecution in their homes. The killing of our two beloved nurses in southern Thailand by lawless men was basically anti-Christian. The withdrawals from Vietnam, Cambodia and Laos were because of Communist and essentially anti-Christian pressure. We have to prepare ourselves for persecution.

It would be impossible to honestly apply this Beatitude to the persecuted church in these lands, or to the young student in the non-Christian home, were it not that the Lord has spoken it and he makes it so.

The positive feature is revealed in Matthew's seventh Beatitude, 'Blessed are the peacemakers for they shall be called sons of God'. In their relationship and responsibility to the Father, they act as peacemakers, like their Lord.

They are reconcilers as we are, with the ministry and message of reconciliation. We have this peace with God (Rom. 5:1) and the peace of God, which garrisons our hearts in all circumstances, in times of persecution for his sake.

This is the submissiveness brought out to bring harmony through the message and life of Christ in his followers amidst hostility and hatred.

ONE SOURCE, GUIDE AND GOAL OF ALL THERE IS

ALAN JOHNSON

THIS theme has been taken from Romans 11:36 which in most editions reads: 'From him, and through him, and to him are all things.' Because English grammar is particularly difficult, and more difficult when translated from the Greek, we have used one of the modern translations — 'Source, Guide and Goal of all there is.' Paul is saying that everything we have comes from God in the first place; everything we do, we can only do because God allows it and in the end everything is moving towards him for his glory. In this article we are going to look at God's perspective on medical practice; we are going to look at ourselves and our studies and our future through *God's* eyes. As Paul reminds us in the preceding verses, it is not up to us to question *why* God has made things as they are; there is no reason why he should explain to us his reasons, but he has given us glimpses to enable us to see the right perspective — his perspective.

GOD, THE SOURCE OF ALL THAT IS

God, the source of all creation

One of the great problems of our age, particularly in science, is that we are afraid to use the word 'Creator'. Most of the educated population, in the West at least, thinks that science has disposed of such out-of-date ideas. Most see no conflict between science in the form of atheistic evolution and Christian creation because they think God is dead and isn't even to be reckoned with. However, the Christian must be sure of this ground if he is to declare to his fellow students and to the world who is the source of all creation. Some of you may have seen that lovely cartoon of a monkey in a cage, holding in one hand a Bible and, in the other hand, Darwin's

ICCMS Oxford, UK, 1980. **Alan G. Johnson.** *Professor of surgery, University of Sheffield, UK. ICMDA Chairman 1994–98.*

Origin of Species. He is saying to himself, 'Am I my brother's keeper or my keeper's brother?' To resolve this question we must know the difference between religious truth and scientific truth.

A very distinguished Fellow of the Royal Society recently wrote this: 'Scientists must never be tempted into mistaking the *necessity* of reason for the *sufficiency* of reason. Reason falls short of answering the many simple and childlike questions people like to ask, questions about origins and purposes. Those are questions that science cannot answer.' Another scientist said: 'Science is not at all incompatible with the concept of a benevolent God, who has, by the operation of natural law brought into existence man, who has genuine freedom to act and therefore to do good or evil to his fellow human beings.' He goes on to point out that science today is making just the same mistake theologians made a hundred years ago, by trying to pronounce on things that it cannot speak about. We must resist the common temptation of just believing in a 'God of the gaps' — a God in the gaps of natural science or a God who just fills in occasionally with the odd miraculous healing. Our God is the God of all truth and his word is a revelation to people of all ages, not just a privileged class of twentieth-century scientists. That is why it is not written in modern scientific language. Our whole attitude to animal and plant life, whether we are using animals for research or for food, must be the responsible one of realising that these too are part of God's creation. If we try to alter natural laws in our own way without acknowledging this, we do so at our peril.

God, the source of man's uniqueness

Man's unique position in nature is not just an accident, because he happens to have become more intelligent than cats or dogs. His place in nature is God-designed. It is not, therefore, arrogant for us to say that we are the pinnacle of creation. It is only pride if we think we have reached there by our own efforts; it is a truth to be received with humility and an aweful sense of responsibility.

Many of our ethical discussions come down to this basic question — is man just a mere animal or has he a spiritual nature? If we are not sure of that basic difference we can see why so often people now want to treat him just as an animal. It is man's spiritual nature that gives dignity to his body, a body that can be the temple of the Holy Spirit.

What finally convinces us that the human form and personality is something very special is that it was in this way that God chose to come into this world. He could have chosen all sorts of ways, but, 'He made himself nothing, taking the very nature of a servant, being made in human likeness' (Phil. 2:7). As a Christmas hymn puts it — 'Lo, within a manger lies he who built the starry skies.' How dare we not show honour and respect to the human body and human personality, when God has honoured it in this way? It also means that our whole search for what is *normal* in human experience, psychologically and physiologically, will have to take account of God's purpose. We may have to ask what is ideal for man, rather than what is normal for man. Why was man made? Man was made to worship God.

God, the source of the means of healing

This comes in three ways. First, the natural healing properties of the body, without which all medicine and surgery would fail. We don't heal patients, we just improve the conditions to encourage natural healing. As a surgeon, I don't join a wound together. My stitches merely hold the edges together while the natural processes do the healing. You have only to see the delayed healing that takes place in a patient on drugs that suppress these healing processes to realise its importance. We should constantly bear this in mind, otherwise we will become proud and arrogant and say how clever we are to heal these diseases. God has designed natural healing processes, and we must work with them, not against them.

Secondly, he is also the source of the drugs that we use for healing. We sometimes forget this when we synthesise a particular chemical. Many of our drugs are extracted from natural plants or moulds or adaptations of such. All man is doing is finding things, or finding chemicals, combining them and adjusting them for a specific action. Somebody has described morphine as one of God's greatest gifts to mankind. Perhaps we should receive our drug treatment and give it in this spirit.

Thirdly, of course, God is also the source of miraculous healing, from the serpent in the wilderness (Num. 21:9) to Jesus Christ's miracles.

To close this section, I find it quite fascinating that in the first disease to be eradicated completely in this world — smallpox — the healing mechanism was through a cow disease, plus the God-given insight of Jenner. Isn't that extraordinary! God is the source of all healing, but he leaves us to do the hard work, to find out the means and to apply it.

GOD, THE GUIDE OF ALL THERE IS

If he's the source of all there is, he's also the guide in our use of it. It is important to realise that God did not just start this world off, like winding up a clock, and then go away and leave it. That is how so many people think of God, but he is the guide of all there is. He is still involved in this world, he is keeping it going by his power. He has not left us to try and work out our own solutions and salvation. We must always remember that he is involved in our everyday management of every patient, not just in making remote principles.

There are three areas, amongst many others, where we must particularly acknowledge God as our guide.

God, the guide in our responsibilities

From all we have said, it follows that a Christian has a three-fold responsibility: to his patient, to his employers and society, and to his God. It is not enough just to satisfy our patient's demands or our employer's regulations, we are answerable to God and we must have a clear conscience in our methods. We have been given the authority to heal. People say to you, 'Why interfere? You doctors are intruding into natural processes. Why not leave people alone who are suffering enough already?' Now there are times when we should not interfere, when we should let things take their natural course. On the other hand, we have an authority from Christ to heal. It is not interference, it is obeying Christ's command. Because in some instances doctors have interfered too much, the public are reacting against it and saying that we should leave people alone and always let natural things take their course. The Christian cannot do this.

We must also act responsibly about our environment. Francis Bacon, one of our famous scientists, said this: 'We direct and domineer over nature. We will have it that all things are as we think in our folly they should be, not as seems fit to divine wisdom or not as they actually are. We clearly impress the stamp of our own image on the creatures and works of God instead of carefully examining and recognising in them the stamp of the Creator.

Wherefore, not undeservedly, our dominion over the creatures is a second time forfeited. We should approach with humility and veneration to unroll the volume of creation.' This leads on to:

God, the guide in research

I well remember one of my first visits to a research unit. It was run by a previous President of the Christian Medical Fellowship in England, and to my surprise the research meeting started with prayer. I should not have been surprised. What is more natural to the Christian than to pray about his research? After all, he is in God's world trying to unravel God's secrets to help God's people. Why not ask God's guidance in finding the answer? I like the poem that Dr Ross wrote just after discovering that mosquitoes were the carrier of malaria:

> This day relenting God hath placed within my hand
> A wondrous thing, and God be praised.
> At His command, seeking His secret deeds
> With tears and toiling breath I found
> Thy cunning seeds, O million murdering deaths.

This illustrates so well the recognition that God was the source, but that man had the toil and the tears to find it. There is a lot we will never understand and we are not meant to understand. It is not surprising that God should keep some secrets from us, but if we look at things with God's perspective we will follow his guidance.

God, the guide in relationships

Just as there is no conflict between the Creator and the findings of science, or between our responsibility to God and our research, so there should be no conflict between these and our relationships with others. There may be a grain of truth in the accusation that when doctors are fighting for the patient's life they are fighting each other. Even great discoveries are accompanied by difficult relationships, but it is not a *necessary* part of scientific discovery or medical treatment. You do not have to trample on others to succeed in medicine yourself.

There is far more teaching in the New Testament about relationships than about being successful in our jobs. We are called to be peacemakers in our hospitals and practices and we should not use our colleagues for our own ambitions. We will witness to Christ more by our relationships than by our achievements, and there is no conflict between showing Christian love to a colleague and being a scientist. The public image of the cool, calculating scientist with no feelings need not apply.

GOD, THE GOAL OF ALL THERE IS

The goal of our patients, the goal for our world, and the goal for ourselves. What are we aiming for? This needs asking at least once a year, if not more frequently!

God, the goal for our patients

Physical healing is only a part of our aim. Our medicine is always bound to fail, as death comes in the end, so it is most important that we do not make great claims for it. We will never produce a Utopia; we will never produce perfection in the human species, and frustration follows if we cannot see this. God never promised it. We can make things better, we can relieve much suffering, we can palliate; but that is all. Death is a spiritual battle, won by his Son alone, not by science.

There *is* a land where there will be no pain, or crying, but it is not on this earth, and we must work within these limited aims. The ideal for our patient is that they will find their goal in God. To heal their bodies is only partial success but, perhaps, one of the best things we can do is to heal them temporarily, to give them more time to come to know him.

God, the goal for our world

The Christian doctor may become involved in passionate campaigning for human rights, conservation or disease preven-tion, but he must do so within God's framework, God's timing and by God's strength. He must resist the temptation to think that there is one magic cure for the problems of our world.

One of the best illustrations of this is that of a tapestry — a picture made by stitching, which often used to be hung on the walls of houses. It has a beautiful picture on the front, but if you look at the back of a tapestry it is just a complete network of stitches and threads criss-crossing, with no apparent form at all. In this world we are looking at the back of the tapestry, and we find it very difficult to pick out where those threads are going and what sort of sense it is all making. God is looking at the other side of the tapestry, and he is designing the picture. All these apparently haphazard stitches are making a beautiful picture in God's plan, and one day we are going to have the privilege of going to the other side of the tapestry and seeing the picture that we helped to make.

God, the goal for ourselves

Now is the time to plan your aims and motives, not to wait till you have qualified. Your planning is not necessarily in detail, but in outline. You may not know whether you want to be a neuro-surgeon in London or a public health doctor in Peru, but you should know what your overall aim is.

Is your aim status, money, a secure job, international recognition or satisfaction? Unfortunately, Jesus made it quite clear that none of those was his goal and none led to real greatness. Greatness only lies in service. Jesus took upon him the form of a servant, he washed his disciples' feet. Why is it so important that we realise that God is the source, the guide, the goal of all there is? It is important because the greatest temptation to man is that of pride instead of gratitude.

Instead of boasting how clever we have been as a medical profession in the last 100 years, to conquer this and to operate on that, we should be on our knees in gratitude, thanking God for giving us these means of relief and for helping us to find them out. We must, again and again, change our attitude from that of pride to that of gratitude, and we can only have a spirit of gratitude if we really see God as the Source and Guide and Goal of all there is.

THE SICKNESS OF MAN

THE BASIS FOR DIAGNOSIS

MARTYN LLOYD-JONES

Introduction

I HAVE been asked to speak on the subject of 'The sickness of man'. I am not going to speak on man's sicknesses: the rest of the conference is doing that. I would speak on *the* sickness — of man. I am emphasising this because I believe that one of the greatest of all the dangers confronting us in a conference like this is to be so concerned about the particular sicknesses of mankind, that we forget *the* sickness of humanity. This is a congress of Christian doctors from different parts of the world. It is fitting that this subject should be given prominence.

There is a danger of confusion coming into the realm of medicine with medical men handling the soul. It is here that the doctor may misinterpret his exact function as a Christian doctor.

What do we mean by Christian?

Now, to reach a diagnosis the first thing we have to do is to define our word 'Christian'. Isn't this the most confusing subject of all at the present time? What is a Christian? I think it is not at all surprising that the masses of the people are outside the Christian church because they are given so many different teachings and so many different impressions as to what it is that constitutes a Christian. We must be perfectly clear about this and we must be very dogmatic about it; there are no special types of Christian. A man is either a Christian or else he isn't. Sometimes we will almost be given the impression that there are special types of Christian of whom you might not expect as much as you would expect of an ordinary Christian. There are some people who think that the doctors are special types of Christian, that you let him off at certain points where you would not let off an ordinary Christian! I have

ICCP Oxford, UK, 1966. **Martyn Lloyd-Jones.** *Minister, Westminster Chapel; past chief clinical assistant to Lord Horder, King's physician, London, UK.*

also noticed a tendency to laud and magnify certain men as *great* Christians who quite literally deny the very essence of the Christian faith. They are regarded as great Christians because of the work they have done, because of the sacrifices they have made. Well, that you see is nothing but sheer confusion. If, as Christian doctors, we are to play our part in the modern world, then I say we must get our definitions perfectly clear.

The need for authority

Now, how do we diagnose the sickness of man? How do you arrive at a medical diagnosis? You must have some standing; you must have some authority. We don't do these things intuitively. You do not act in terms of your emotions or your feelings or sensibilities. Pathology and other subjects have to be studied. Now, as we seek the diagnosis of the sin of mankind in this realm, the great problem facing us is the question of our authority. If the Christian doctor is to act as a pastor and as a spiritual counsellor (and I think every Christian doctor will have to do that increasingly), it is not enough that he is a nice man and a good man, a sympathetic man. If he is to counter this disease, he must be clear in his diagnosis and in his understanding of the situation.

In other words, we are back to the whole question of our ultimate authority, the Word of God. We have got to fight this battle over and over again.

The authority of the Bible

We arrive at our diagnosis of the sickness of man solely on the basis of the teaching of this Book. It is revelation from God. The Christian by definition is a man who is in his position because he is bound by this teaching which he regards as a revelation from God. This was put once and for ever very perfectly by the apostle Paul when he visited Athens, when he saw the place cluttered with temples and especially that one temple inscribed 'To the unknown God'. He turned to the people and he said 'Whom you ignorantly worship, him declare I unto you' (Acts 17:23).

Revelation

Now, this is authority to you. This is based on revelation. Paul does not say 'Well, now, you have been searching for this unknown god and I also have been engaged in this quest. Your ideas are all right as far as they go. I think I can add a little to them but I want to join you in the research team — in the research and search for this unknown god.' No, no, that is not Christianity. 'Him *declare* I unto you.' *Revelation!* Or take the way in which our Lord himself puts it, when he turned to his Father and said in prayer: 'I thank thee, O Father, Lord of heaven and earth, that thou hast hid these things from the wise and prudent, and hast *revealed* them unto babes. Even so, Father, for so it seemed good in thy sight.'

We must be clear about this. We must get rid of this notion that we are seekers after truth. This is the danger at the moment. It is a scientific age; it is the age of investigation and of searching. It is an age in which what was regarded as true has proved to be no longer true. You have had it in the realm of physics, you have had it in the realm of medicine. People are tending to say that such investigation must be true in every realm, including Christianity, but here is the grand exception. This is the truth, once and for ever, given to the saints. It is revelation. It is not man seeking, it is God showing.

Now, the Bible is full of this teaching. You have got the marvellous summary of Paul's where he points out how the great men of the world did not know our Lord, for had they known him they would not have crucified the Lord of glory. 'Eye hath not seen, nor ear heard, neither have entered the heart of men, the things which God has prepared for them that love him' (1 Cor. 2:8–10). But he says God hath revealed them unto us by his Spirit, so the Christian, by definition, is a man whose whole thinking is governed and controlled exclusively by the teaching of this Book, the revelation of God. That involves the doctrine of inspiration also. All Scripture is given by the inspiration of God. God speaking. It is profitable for doctrine, proof, instruction in righteousness and so on. Holy men of God spake as they were moved by the Holy Ghost. No prophecy in ancient time came by the will of men. No prophecy is of any private interpretation. It is all given by God.

Now, I have to establish this because I must be sure of the grounds for my diagnosis of the sickness of men. It is a peculiar diagnosis; it is an unpopular one. So we must be absolutely certain of our authority if we are to make the contribution that we alone can make in this tragic age of confusion in which we find ourselves.

Biblical doctrine

Let us be clear about this further. There are those with a supposedly scientific approach to the Scriptures who say that they are only meant to be man's experience. That is not true. All Scripture is given by inspiration of God and is profitable for doctrine. What does the doctrine include?

Well, it includes the doctrine of God the Creator; it includes the doctrine of creation; it includes the doctrine of man. All of these doctrines are tied together; all intimately involved in each other. You can't isolate man's experience. The Bible claims that it is a complete view of life. Before you can understand man's sickness you must know what man is and you must know what the world is in which man finds himself. And you must know where the world came from. You can't say 'Ah! but that is science', because it is all part of the biblical doctrine. Biblical doctrine does not start with the Lord Jesus Christ. Biblical doctrine does not start with the doctrine of salvation. Biblical doctrine starts with the doctrine of God. God the creator, God the ruler of the universe, and so on. In saying that the Scriptures are only concerned about man's experience, we are denying the very doctrine of the Bible itself. So ultimately we shall be losing the entire case for our diagnosis of the sickness of men and our assertion about the only cure for the sickness of men. We must therefore stand firmly on our authority.

We are examining the sickness of man in the light of the biblical teaching. We must not only believe that it is the Word of God but that it is the identifiable Word of God — it is definable.

The truth, the whole truth

So, we start then with the Bible and we regard it as a book that contains the whole counsel of God. If we are to be of any value to our fellow citizens in this terrible age in which we live, we must be familiar with the whole counsel of God. We must not try to add to it. We must never give the impression, and I am saying this in a scientific congress — we must never give the impression that because we happen to live in the twentieth century we know more about these matters than men did in the first century. If you say that, you are denying the whole category of revelation. We don't add to it; we have got nothing *to* add. But we mustn't subtract from it either. There are branches of the church that have added many things to the teaching of this book, and there are others who are detracting, taking out of it. They say that modern man has become the arbiter in the matter. The pew decides what the pulpit is to preach. That is as bad as allowing the patient to dictate the treatment to the doctor.

We have no choice in the matter; we mustn't add, we mustn't subtract. We are to preach the whole counsel of God. We are not to trim our message in order to make it fit modern philosophy. We are not to trim it, either, in order to fit into modern psychology. This is a word, this is a power, this is a gospel, that has been dealing with the sickness of men throughout the running centuries and it, and it alone, can do so in this present age and generation.

Very well, taking that as our basis and our authority for diagnosis, what do we find? What are the outstanding symptoms of this sickness of men at this present hour? I suggest that there are three main symptoms.

THREE SYMPTOMS OF THE SICKNESS OF MAN

The first is his complete misunderstanding of law, secondly his misunderstanding of the nature of man, and thirdly his misunderstanding of God.

The misunderstanding of law

We are living in a lawless age. Our newspapers and news bulletins are full of crime, vandalism, theft, robbery, the results of promiscuity, and the horrors of modern life — all the result of misunderstanding the law. Paul in Romans 1 says that he is not ashamed of the gospel of Christ for it is the power of God unto salvation to everyone that believeth. Why? Well, for this reason: for, he says, 'the wrath of God from heaven is revealed against all ungodliness and unrighteousness of men, who hold the truth in unrighteousness; because that which may be known of God is manifest in them; for God hath shewed it unto them. For the invisible things of him from the creation of the world are clearly seen.' This is the argument from creation, you see, 'being understood by the things that are made, even his eternal power and Godhead; so that they are without excuse: because that, when they knew God, they glorified him not as God, neither were thankful; but became vain in their imaginations, and their foolish heart was darkened. Professing themselves to be wise, they became fools.' What a description of the whole century! 'And changed the glory of the incorruptible God into an image made like to corruptible man (humanists), and to birds, and fourfooted beasts, and creeping things. Wherefore God also gave them up to uncleanness through the lusts of their own hearts, to dishonour their own bodies between themselves, who changed the truth of God into a lie, and worshipped and served the creature more than the Creator, who is blessed for ever.' That's the diagnosis. But you notice what Paul is emphasising. He is emphasising that mankind has developed an entirely false and wrong view of law. Isn't this the main symptom of the disease of man at the present time? This perverse attitude towards law is shown in three ways.

Modern man regards law as being opposed to happiness. Happiness is the great idea, and he thinks of law as something that makes us miserable, something that robs us of joy and that Christianity is a life of misery because it is a life of discipline. Isn't this the most tragic fallacy of all? What is happiness? Well, according to the modern theories, happiness is experience only, the present moment. It does not think of consequences. It does not think of how you feel about the pleasure of the moment in a year's time, still more in fifty years' time. No, it is the pleasure of the moment that is their view of happiness.

Yet the very story of the modern world proves how fallacious this is. This is all due to the idea that law and discipline are opposed to happiness, but it's quite wrong. The moment you ignore law, you are increasing your unhappiness. The world is really proving that. These people are rushing off to pleasures, to drink and drugs, because of their misery. It's an escape mechanism in order to try to forget their lostness. The Bible says, 'The way of the transgressor is hard.'

The law is regarded as being the opposite of liberty, but what is liberty? We have to ask this question. The modern view, of course, really regards liberty as licence; if I want a thing I am entitled to it. Every man is doing that which is right in his own eyes.

Again, we must challenge the modern world and ask: Does your view of law and liberty really lead you to freedom? The answer is again that it doesn't. Our Lord has put this once and for ever: 'Whosoever committeth sin' (by which he means whosoever goes on committing sin) 'is the servant or the slave of sin'. It's no use talking about freedom or claiming that you are free if you are a slave to certain habits. And in any case, if you regard liberty as licence, you'll not only find that you are not free yourself, you'll be bringing others into bondage with you. You can have discipline without liberty, but you cannot have liberty without discipline. The modern generation doesn't realise that. Perfect freedom is alone found when a man is in the service of *God*, or, if you like, is the slave of God.

Law is regarded as the opposite of love. The people who are guilty of this are the ones who are always contrasting our Lord with the apostle Paul. Paul the legalist, the Pharisee, they said, who came and foisted his legalistic notions on the delightfully simple gospel of Jesus of Nazareth, namely, the gospel of love. But what is love? Again, a characteristic of the modern view of love is that it is vague and involves sheer lust. The modern man's idea of love is gained from the television screen or from films, and it's nothing but lust, it has nothing to do with biblical love at all. Again, the apostle has put this: 'Love is the fulfilling of the law.' No man knows anything about love until he has fulfilled the law.

Misunderstanding of the nature of man himself
We are living in an age in which man has set himself up as his own authority in all matters. It is an age which glories in what it calls self-expression. But what is modern man's view of himself? We haven't time to deal with all these. You're familiar with many of them; the purely biological view of men, a purely economic view of men, the Marxist view, and at present the existentialist view of men. We have got to be familiar with this in order that we may expose its fallacy.

What is the existentialist view of man? Here are some of the definitions: 'a bundle of sensations'; 'there is no such thing as Me'; 'I don't exist'; 'we are what we are, momentarily'. Or, 'he is a mere nucleus of conscious experience in the space time's stream'. I hope you recognise yourselves!

Sartre, the French philosopher, atheist and thinker, the most famous of all these existentialists, says: 'Man must make his vital choices without any sure premises from which to reason.' Now this is man's modern view of himself — and remember it is your view of man that is going to determine your diagnosis as to the sickness of men. Sartre also says: 'You must take your decisions, you must make your vital choices without any sure premises from which to reason. We are thrown into the world, we know not how, and left free to make ourselves by our own choices. We make ourselves, and we make ourselves by our own choices.' He naturally goes on to say that this must end in despair.

Well now, with such views which are taken by modern men, it's not surprising that the world is as it is, is it? It's not surprising that you've got this mounting moral problem in every country. It's not surprising that family life and the sanctities are breaking down; it's because of this view of men. Then, in spite of all this they believe that man is capable of deciding what is best for him. Again, the facts of life give the direct lie to this. Opinions differ and contradict one another. Hence we have wars. 'They have come', James says, 'from the lusts that are warring in you' (James 4:1). If you regard the facts of life as but bundles of sensations, if you live only by these desires, without any bases or principles from which to reason and build up your case, it is inevitable that you should have conflict. Man becomes selfish, self-centred, self-justifying, and concerned with nothing but to satisfy himself. He is controlled solely by desire. The apostle Paul has dealt with this eternal conflict: 'In my mind I know that the Lord God is right, but in my members I find another law. I desire to be right, but I find that I do that which is wrong. O wretched man that I am ...' (Rom. 7:22–23).

This has been the story of mankind from the beginning. That is why, throughout the long history of the race, even primitive societies have recognised that man is not capable of managing himself and his own affairs. The primitive tribes have their laws, taboos and customs. In spite of all that has been said by the intellectuals of today, man experimenting and experiencing has always found that there is need of law, discipline and restraint.

Man's misunderstanding of God

The sickness of mankind at the present time is due to an entirely wrong attitude towards law, an entirely wrong attitude towards himself, and above all, of course, his entirely wrong view of God. He doesn't believe in God. There's nothing new in that and today he thinks this is scientific, but the 14th Psalm starts off by saying 'The fool hath said in his heart "There is no God".' That was said a thousand years at least before the birth of our Lord and Saviour. Others do believe in some sort of God, but they hate him, and regard him as a monster. Others have nothing but a sentimental projection of their own thoughts and their own desires.

WHAT IS THE DIAGNOSIS?

After all that, is there any difficulty about the differential diagnosis? Surely, to any man who knows his Bible, there is no difficulty. You don't need a congress of world faiths. You don't need to call in the help of Hinduism, Confucianism, or Buddhism, or any other 'ism', to help you to arrive at a diagnosis. Indeed to do so is to confuse the issue. There is only one way to the diagnosis and it is to understand this. *Man is a creature who has been made in the image of God.*

You start with God. In the beginning — *God.* The universe is not an accident; it's incredible that it should be with its order, arrangement, balance and delicacy. God, the great eternal mind, God the everlasting creator, made man in his own image. Man is not a mere bundle of sensations. Man is not merely what he feels at the moment. Man as man is a responsible being. He has a mind, he has an understanding. He can criticise himself, he can evaluate himself. He has a conscience, he has a sense of right and wrong. He is made in the image of God and he was made *for* God. He was meant to be the companion of God. He was meant to enjoy God. What's the matter with man? What then is the matter with the world? It is sin.

The consequences of sin

Sin is not merely sickness. Sin *is* sickness. Sin does lead to unhappiness, into many other troubles, but that is not the essence of sin.

The essence of sin is rebellion against God

Man is as he is because he has rebelled against God. God has put certain laws into men, and man can only be happy as long as he responds to them, and as long as he lives according to them. He can't help himself, and the more man begins to defy these laws he creates a civil war within himself. The main trouble with him is that he has fallen, and that he is a rebel against God. And the result of this fall is historical, 'In Adam all men die' (1 Cor. 15:22).

Man is born spiritually dead

He doesn't understand himself, he doesn't understand life, he knows nothing about his origin, he knows nothing about that for which he was meant. Man, furthermore, is the slave of sin. He is governed, 'by the god of this world, the spirit of the age, the spirit that is the prince, the power of the law, the spirit that worketh in the children of disobedience' (Eph. 2:2). This is the sickness of men and this the sickness of the modern world.

The reprobate mind

Why is our world as it is? In Romans 1 Paul says God gave them up to a reprobate mind. The apostle there deals not only with immorality but also with amorality. He deals with sexual perversions. Where have they come from? Why do people do these things? The apostle's answer is this: that men and women, having refused the overtures of God, having rejected the law of God, set themselves up, saying they are capable of ordering themselves and their affairs apart from God. So God has abandoned them for the time being, has handed them over to a reprobate mind, and the result is that they become utterly confused, men with men working that which is unseemly and women doing exactly the same. This is the diagnosis of the sickness of men, and the resulting sicknesses of our world, as stated by our authority:

> 'Being filled with all unrighteousness, fornication, wickedness, covetousness, maliciousness, full of envy, murder, debate, deceit, malignity, whisperers, backbiters, haters of God, despiteful, proud, boasters, inventors of evil things, disobedient to parents, without understanding, covenant-breakers, without natural affection, implacable, unmerciful, who know the judgment of God, that they which commit such things are worthy of death, not only do these things, but have pleasure in them that do them' (Rom. 1:29–32).

The wrath of God

That, my friends, is what you and I are confronted with. It's not surprising that mankind is turning to drugs and to drink and to a pleasure-mania and to perversion. People are defying not only the law of their own being, they are defying the living God, and the wrath of God is upon us. To me, it is the only adequate explanation of this twentieth century in which we live. God is punishing us, exposing us to touches of his wrath in order to reveal our folly to us, and in order to turn us to a consideration of the remedy which he himself has provided for us.

GOD AS PHYSICIAN

HADDON ROBINSON

A FEW years ago my father faced a crisis in his faith. At 82 years of age he began to develop a hernia and he wasn't quite sure what it was. Being a man of faith he did a very normal thing: he began to pray. I'm sure that he hoped he would go to sleep one night with the hernia quite evident, and that during the night God would touch him and the next morning he would wake up healed. However, that did not occur. When he contacted me I discovered that he was disturbed about his physical condition, of course, but also the fact that he had taken this to God in earnest prayer and God had not healed him. I arranged for a friend of ours, a surgeon, to operate on him; and the hernia was corrected. However, when I told my father that he was healed, that the surgeon had restored him to health, he could not see that this was really an answer to prayer. Even though he was now well physically, his faith was disturbed. You see, he had expected God to act directly through a miracle, and it had not occurred.

Now my father is not opposed to physicians. During the first world war he was wounded in France and spent several months in the hospital. In the thirties he was involved in an automobile accident. On both occasions physicians helped restore him to health. But this was different: he wanted God to work directly in his life, and God had not obliged. Now, you may feel sorry for an old man who is growing senile. And yet I suspect that you have often made the very same mistake he made.

You are becoming physicians; you will have numerous skills and assorted medicines which you will use when people come to you. Usually these remedies will work, and even though at times you may acknowledge God as the healer, you really begin to think about God only when things do go wrong, when the injection fails, when the bone will not heal, when the simple cold turns into a raging fever. At a time like that you would like to have God as a consultant who will hopefully intervene in a miraculous way.

ICCP Toronto, Canada, 1972. **Haddon W. Robinson.** *Associate professor of practical theology, Dallas Theological Seminary. General Director of CMS, USA.*

Many people are enamoured with 'divine healing' today because, in an age which has lost its sense of God, we would like to believe that God is still at work in the world. And often, because we so deeply want to believe that God is a physician, we who are very critical and analytical about other things hear reports of divine healing and accept them almost without question, even at times overlooking obvious evidence to the contrary, in order to believe that God has performed a miracle.

No distinctions between supernatural and natural

Now I submit to you that the distinction that we make between the supernatural and the natural, between the spectacular and the ordinary, is not found in the Scriptures, but has come to us out of the period of the Enlightenment. During that time there came a division of labour between the scientists who began to be concerned about immediate causes, and the theologians whose concern was for ultimate causes. And so the two of them began to operate in their own areas in relation to man. The scientist would be concerned about the body and healing, and the church and theology would be concerned about salvation and the soul. The church would concentrate on miracles and mystery, while the scientist would study boils and sickness. However, as long as the church was in charge of mystery it was always vulnerable when the mystery was moved back. Our forefathers prayed for rain and thought that God formed clouds and the clouds got heavy. Now we see the clouds and watch the progress of the storm on the six o'clock news. At one time, when a man had a raging fever, we prayed for him beside his bed. Now we give him an injection of penicillin. Once we turned to the priest for counsel; today we turn to the psychiatrist. Bonhoeffer said that in our day our problem is to live 'with God without God'. What he meant was that as long as God is reserved only for the mysterious and the unexplainable, every time something is explained, God's domain is made smaller and smaller.

Now this distinction between the supernatural and the natural, between the miraculous and the normal, is not a distinction that is laid out in the Scriptures. The writers of the Bible saw all of life as being under the hand of God. It is interesting to note that throughout the Old Testament there are only six or seven miraculous healings. They include the healing of Miriam from leprosy in

Numbers 12; the healing of the Israelites bitten by the serpents in Numbers 21; the raising of the widow's son by Elijah in 1 Kings 17; the raising of the Shunammite's son in 2 Kings 4; the healing of Naaman of leprosy in 2 Kings 5; the giving of fifteen years to Hezekiah in Isaiah 38. You do not find that there were healings every Saturday night; however, you do find that God's people were very well aware that God acted as a physician. In the psalms these men made supplications and gave thanks for physical healing. There is no intimation that they thought God did it in a dramatic way, that a prophet had to touch them and suddenly they would be healed. In the ordinary course of life they saw the hand of God working.

In the New Testament, where there are a great many of the more spectacular healings recounted, you discover that they do not occur merely to make people well. In fact, the miracles in the gospels are given as signs to demonstrate who Jesus Christ was — that's the whole argument of the book of John. You find that in the life of the apostles the miracles that they performed authenticated their ministry. Hebrews 2:4 says very clearly that these men have witness borne to them 'by signs and wonders and mighty works'. And Paul refers to this as the evidence of his apostleship in 2 Corinthians 12:12. There were many folk who did not get healed in the New Testament. At the pool of Siloam, Jesus chose one man but did not heal the others. When Paul wrote to Timothy he told him to take a little wine for the sake of his stomach (1 Tim. 5:23). He also says, 'Trophimus I left ill at Miletus' (2 Tim. 4:20). The apostle was not able to deal with him. And in his own life Paul had a thorn in the flesh which he besought God three times to remove. Thus, the Bible indicates that God uses what we call the miraculous only in special circumstances. But there is also in the Bible the recognition that whenever a person is healed, God does it; that the physician of all men is God himself and that, whether you are healed in a spectacular way or in an ordinary way, God is the physician.

Healing comes from the Most High

Our tendency as a reaction to the Enlightenment is to say that God is *only* a miracle-working God, and so to reserve him for special occasions. Over the entrance to the Presbyterian Hospital in the city of New York there is chiselled the phrase 'Healing comes from the Most High', and that belongs there.

Healing is not God's *salvation* work (that which he does for his own people); it is his *creation* work (that which he does for all men). When the Christian prays, 'Give us this day our daily bread', he does not expect to have bread while his neighbor starves. Instead, he recognizes that God, as the creator, is providing the food for his table *and* his neighbor's table. The difference is that the Christian recognizes the source of the bread while the ungodly man simply fills his hunger. Similarly, the godly man responds to God the physician who has healed him, and is grateful. He is not simply healed but, in the midst of that difficult tortuous experience, he encounters God, and God uses that experience, not only to restore him to health, but to bring him to a whole new way of life. The ungodly man is healed, spared from death, but, from the view-point of the man of the Bible he suffers in many ways. That is, when he is sick, he is physically ill, but in addition he sees no purpose in it. It is like half-time at the football game; a wasted episode which he waits out until life starts again. But for the man of God it is actually a time when God encounters and renews him.

There is only one passage in the New Testament that deals explicitly with healing in the early church, telling us what went on in the apostolic church as an ordinary affair. The miracles in the book of Acts do not occur again and again. In turning to Scripture I seek to answer this question, 'If God is the Great Physician and I am a man of God, then how should I behave as a physician in his service?' A study of James 5:13–18 is helpful in shedding some light on this problem.

One of the major themes of the book of James is how to deal with trials. In this particular passage he discusses sickness. However, the theme of this passage is not sickness or trouble, but prayer. In verse 13 he says that all of life's experiences should drive us to God. 'Is any among you suffering? Let him pray.' If you, as a believer, experience misfortune — *pray*. When life crumbles in — *pray*. Pray continually, don't reach for pills first, turn to the Lord. On the other hand, 'Is any cheerful? Let him sing praises.' When things go well for you, when your heart is singing, when the sun is shining brightly, that ought to be a time for praise and rejoicing. All situations of life should call you back to God.

Then he says, 'Is any among you sick? Let him call for the elders of the church and let them pray over him, anointing him with oil in the name of the Lord.' The word used for sickness speaks of sickness that makes a person weak; perhaps he is saying that when you reach that state you may need others to pray for you. Now, the distinguishing feature of the elder in the early church was that he was a godly man. Essentially, James is saying, 'Call the *spiritual leaders* of the church and let them pray.' Notice that this is the normal habit of the early church. He isn't saying to call in the minister to pull him through after medicine has failed and the man is dying. Nor is he saying this to prepare him for burial. Rather, the normal course of events when a person was sick was to call for the elders of the church.

The emphasis of the early church fell on the spiritual because they had so little technical knowledge. If James were writing this today he might say, 'Call a spiritual physician; call a doctor who is a godly man.' Or, putting it another way, I think this is a kind of ministry that you as Christian physicians will have in the name of Christ, to those who are sick. I often have people who ask me to recommend a Christian physician. When a person does this I think he is recognizing that illness is not merely something physical, but there are emotional, psychological and spiritual overtones involved in it, and he would like a man who works to heal him to be a man who recognizes Jesus.

What spiritual leaders do for the sick

Referring back to James there are three things the spiritual leaders are to do for the sick man. *They are to anoint him with oil.* The word 'oil' simply means olive oil, a very common remedy in the ancient world. Galen, a Roman physician who wrote about AD 160, called olive oil a universal remedy. In the story of the Good Samaritan, when the traveller was mugged by the side of the highway, the Samaritan poured in oil and wine to dress his wounds. It was used to reduce fever and ease the pain. Now, look at the word 'anoint' — that's a kind of holy word. There are two words that are translated anoint in the Scriptures. The first, found in 1 John 2:20, has a symbolic meaning; we are said to be anointed with the Holy Spirit. But the word which James used is the ordinary word meaning the rubbing down. It appears eight other times in the New Testament, and in seven of these it refers to the toilet or grooming. In Matthew 6:17 Jesus says, 'If a man is fasting, let him anoint himself with oil.' That is, 'Let him go out with shaving lotion on, not looking like he is fasting.' In Luke 7:38 Jesus had been invited to Simon's house.

He came, weary from the road, and Simon should have anointed him with oil to cool him off, but didn't. A woman of the streets used precious ointment to anoint Jesus's feet, to rub his feet. Thus, the word used by James means just to rub, to rub in with oil. What he is saying to these elders then is, 'Give him his medicine in the name of the Lord.' When he said, 'in the name of the Lord' I am sure what he didn't mean was just to say the words 'I give you this in the name of the Lord'. I think he was saying to give him his medicine in the will of God. For example you can pray, 'Give us this day our daily bread' and a diabetic could pray, 'Give me this day my insulin', for ultimately that is part of God's provision for his people.

The second function of the elder for the sick man is a spiritual interaction — 'Confess your sins to one another and pray for one another that you may be healed' (James 5:16). Confessing is not a gimmick — it is a confrontation of souls. Dr Paul Tournier said that there are really only two diagnoses a Christian physician must make. One is to decide what the man has, and in that case the person is obviously passive and you ask the questions. The other is to determine why he has it. Now you are exploring things with him, and out of that there may come the confession of sin and the recognition of a need to restore relationship with God.

The tendency for us is not to look at sin, or if we talk about it we talk about colossal sins — the ones everybody else commits. But when a man faces up to life, truly what it is, he confesses his sin, and through interaction, he sees himself. This is not given as a basis of judgment (you are sick, therefore you've sinned); it is the exploring of life that often occurs when people are ill. Nevertheless I think there is a direct relationship between sin and sickness. When people will not submit to the sovereignty of God they live their lives with ego and are constantly frustrated with life around them. That can lead to sickness.

The third task the elders have for the sick man is to pray for him. What James is emphasizing is this: 'I understand this man's sickness and I've been physically involved with him — I've rubbed him down with oil. I have also been involved with him at a deeper level. Now I pray for him.' James says a prayer of faith will save the sick man. The word 'save' in James 5:15 is a very general word which can mean either physical deliverance or spiritual deliverance. James is saying that God answers prayer and will meet this man's need.

Now the obvious question is, 'Are you saying that God heals all people who are ill?' And I think that James would say 'No', I think he limits his meaning by saying, 'The Lord will raise him up.' God has purposes in sickness not understood by us, but for his glory. But we are to know that if or when that man is raised up, God raised him up. And we will be conscious that God has worked because we are closer in a spiritual way. The implication of this passage is that there is a way of coming to the whole man and dealing with him that restores him to health and leads to forgiveness of sins. When God moves to heal that brother, he will be restored not only physically but spiritually, and the broken relationship with his neighbor and with his God will be healed.

Then James says that the prayer of a righteous man has great power to intercede, that God is really there and he is really concerned. I enter into this ministry of healing under the hand of the Great Physician, and what I must be aware of is that God does answer prayer. It ought to be a part of my practice in life to commit these things to the Lord.

Then, in the last two verses, he gives the example of a righteous man. Elijah, he says, was just like you — same passions, same questions, same doubts — and he prayed and it didn't rain, and he prayed again and the rain came. Now that was pretty natural, wasn't it? I think the ungodly man would have said, 'We've had famines before, we've had droughts before, we've had rain before: the whole thing is just a coincidence.' But to the godly man, God was at work to bring healing to that nation, to bring the nation back to himself.

Healing today

We have a friend who, when we first met her, was an atheist (or so she said). Over the years I spoke to her as best I could about Christ. Then, about two years ago she developed cancer of the breast. I went to the hospital to see her and I talked to her and she talked to me. Despite her professed atheism, every day she requested that I pray for her, and I did. I also spoke to her of Christ. Ruth had the operation; she came through it well. But through that experience of sickness she gained a personal faith in Jesus Christ and her life has been changed. All of her friends notice it; she just can't keep from talking about how good the Lord is. The other day, while we were chatting she said, 'You know the time in the hospital really was a wonderful time. I never expected it when I went in, but that's where I met God.' She put it in the jargon of our times, but it sounded just like the psalmist. She was ill and she was restored to health. Ruth saw in that healing the hand of God, but more than that, in the suffering and the healing she met God personally, for when God acts as a physician he not only heals sickness, he heals people. And as physicians under the Great Physician we need to keep that in mind.

Artificial prolongation of life. Intensive care and resuscitation may achieve prolongation of life in a dying patient. In that respect they are a substantial advance in modern medicine. In some cases, however, results are very unsatisfactory, even though proper indications were observed. This has caused much confusion in the profession and some even feel that a new code of medical ethics should be devised to meet some of the sorry issues of this treatment. It will be shown that careful evaluation of these cases will make it quite clear what line of action, if any, should be followed, without reason for conflicts in the ethical field. When all efforts directed at prolongation of life fall short and achieve nothing but prolonged dying, without a real chance of ultimate cure, these efforts should be stopped. Suspension of treatment should be a positive medical act, based on clinical experience and a thorough understanding of the pathophysiology of the case at hand, cleanly marking the point where (other than palliative) medical treatment becomes irrelevant to the patient.

DEN OTTER

ICCP Amsterdam, Netherlands, 1963. **G. Den Otter.** *Professor of surgery, Free University of Amsterdam, The Netherlands.*

MEDICAL ETHICS — CAN THEY BE DISTINCTIVELY CHRISTIAN?

WILLIAM KIESEWETTER

Introduction

MEDICINE and religion have always been intertwined since earliest times, when ideas of supernatural forces and demonology existed and the role of the witch doctor came into being.

For the sake of clarity, it might be well to define one or two terms. By religion I mean the personal credo, that internal force which drives someone on. It is the spiritual dynamic of life, or, if you will, the essence of character. The term medical etiquette is primarily concerned with the conduct of physicians toward one another, and embodies the tenets of professional courtesy. Medical ethics, on the other hand, indicates concern over the doctor-patient relationship or, in the broadest sense, relations with society and the State as a whole.

Historical perspective

The opening chapter in the story of medical ethics takes place in Babylon about 2700 BC when a treatise was published dealing with the regulation of the conduct of a physician. The celebrated Babylonian Code, written by Hammurabi, appeared about 2250 BC. This contained the idea of the responsibility of a physician. The principle of Lex Talionis (an eye for an eye) was laid down. The imposition of penalties (up to the death penalty) for unsuccessful treatment must have checked, to some degree, the progress of medicine.

Not until the Hellenic period did medical practitioners really get away from having such a strict legal code. Greek physicians were guided more by their desire to help suffering humanity. It is to the much venerated Hippocrates that we owe the fullest concept of the responsibilities devolving upon medical practitioners. His simple

ICCP Oslo, Norway, 1969. **William B. Kiesewetter.** *Chief of surgical services, Children's Hospital, Pittsburgh, USA.*

criteria of professional dignity and duty became the ideals of medicine for the succeeding 2,500 years and constitute the foundation on which our modern codes have been built.

The Romans delayed the legal control of medical conduct until it became necessary to protect the public. After the fall of Rome, Lex Talionis was once again introduced.

On the Continent, the close relationship of the medieval church and medicine let the former set the standards of conduct. It was not until the severance of the medical profession from its connection with the church that doctors acquired a pecuniary interest in the continuance of the ills of humanity, despite their ideal of eliminating those ills.

The beginning of the nineteenth century saw the appearance of Thomas Percival's publication, *Code of medical ethics,* which became a prominent landmark in the progress and evolution of medical ethics as he emphasized the need for combining tenderness with steadiness, and condescension with authority, in the management of hospital and charity cases. The impact of Percival's work cannot be underestimated, because it has been the undergirding of medical ethics in the English-speaking world for the past 150 years.

Limitations on ethical codes

No ethical code can be at one and the same time rigid enough to be a guideline to live by and elastic enough to meet all situations. At best, an ethical code is a set of principles and a rough guide rather than a series of inflexible rules. Thus, a young teenager might be found in labor by a general practitioner who is called in for the first time. On superficial questioning, he finds that this girl is unmarried, and the child is therefore going to be born out of wedlock. It is conceivable that a completely ethical, but rigid, physician might abandon the girl, with the suggestion that she call in someone else. An obstetrician comes and handles the case successfully. He is then faced with the dilemma of what his responsibility is in reporting the incident involving the general practitioner. Was the first practitioner right to stand by his principles, or was there some other way out of the situation?

In the second place, any ethical code fails to take into account the motivation behind a given act. The action may be motivated by the highest of ethical principles but have improper consequences.

As someone once said, 'A good motive should not become bad law.'

Thirdly, it is certainly true that today's codes may be at variance with tomorrow's practice. Hippocrates, for example, advised practitioners to share their income with their professors and, if necessary, to adopt the sons of their teachers. This may have been possible in the communal society of five centuries before Christ, but it is certainly unrealistic today.

The distinctive Christian ethic

What it is not. The ethic by which a follower of Jesus Christ practises medicine is not, and should not be, a set of rules — a sort of decalogue for Christian physicians. There are no easy, specific answers to our puzzling professional problems. To attempt to codify every aspect of them would build in a rigidity that would result in harsh attitudes and actions, or the constant frustration of compromise. There is not always a morally good versus a morally evil choice involved in an ethical decision.

What it is. The Christian ethic, of course, is embodied in the life of Jesus Christ. It is often referred to as the Law of Love. In Biblical terms, the Christian ethic is expressed in the words of Jesus Christ when he told men that they should love God with their whole being and their neighbor as themselves.

Natural and Christian ethics contrasted
Natural ethics are basically rooted in human intuition, conscience, reason or tradition. While it must be admitted that Christian ethics have some element of all of these, they are fundamentally based on the character of God. What a vast difference there is between our human frailties, as expressed in our traditions, and the unquenchable greatness of divine characteristics. To follow one is to become a slave to man's past and its failings and to be enveloped in the pursuit of expediency. To follow the other is to enter the limitless possibilities of a God-inspired existence.

Natural ethics always seem to have some self-interest in them. Any human action, analyzed to the ultimate degree, can appear to be thus tainted. However, the roots from which ethics spring should be, and generally are, unselfish and oriented to the other person.

Natural ethics must, of necessity, deal with the principles of conduct, and these may vary in rigidity. The distinctive Christian ethic is concerned with relationships between people. In John 8, our Lord contrasts the attitude of the Pharisees toward the woman found guilty of adultery and his own kindly but realistic forgiveness of her, with the admonition not to be guilty of this again.

Finally, natural ethics deal essentially with actions and the judgement of those actions. The distinctive Christian ethic is primarily concerned with motivation. Although good motivations can result in poor actions, the proper judgement of an action must include consideration of its motive. This interrelationship of motive and action is well seen in the dialogue between Jesus and the rich young man (Mat. 19:16–22). The man's actions lived up to the ethical demands of the day, but he fell far short when asked about the motivation of his actions.

Applications of the Christian ethic

Two illustrations point out the distinctiveness of the Christian approach. One is in the field of etiquette as between two physicians, the other is in the field of ethics where relationships between the doctor, the patient, and the State are involved.

If one doctor believes that another practitioner has treated a patient inappropriately, it would be natural to wish to expose him and perhaps to gain from such exposure. The Christian doctor should remember that he is not in possession of all the facts of the case, and be charitable within the limits of honesty. It would be more in accordance with the law of love to deal directly with the other physician, rather than to expose the problem to the patient and avoid contact with the one who caused it.

Of the many ethical situations from which one could derive examples, euthanasia perhaps gives the best medium for comment, because the scientific advances of recent decades mean that the prolongation of life is possible to a degree never before known.

From the naturalistic standpoint, euthanasia has always had its advocates. The case sounds plausible, with the arguments for compassion, freedom of choice for the sick individual and a more progressive method of reducing suffering. However, in the Christian context, let us briefly consider each of these arguments and see if there is not a rebuttal to each.

Compassion. The argument that euthanasia is a compassionate relief of suffering leaves out at least three considerations: there is a moral content to personality which should not be violated; the Christian recognizes the fact of the immortality of the soul; we have a responsibility to God who gave us this life to let him decide when to withdraw it.

The compassionate plea of the naturalist seems to me to be a selfish argument. It relieves the physician of his burden, but transfers it instead to the family. They may live to regret having given permission for euthanasia and feel guilty. It also puts the doctor in the untenable position of not seeming to do all that can be done. It is not always possible to be sure that someone is incurable.

Free choice. If we argue, from the natural point of view, that euthanasia should be the free choice of the sick man or his family, it seems to me that we are unrealistic. We assume that a patient is a free agent and capable of rational choice, but a sick man has friends and relatives who influence him. Under these circumstances, such an individual is not always competent to make a rational choice when offered an end to life.

Christians would subscribe generally to the fact that suffering does have meaning. To take life and death into one's own hands might be to abrogate a higher will. Obviously, this would not be carried to ridiculous extremes, yet to open the floodgates to this possibility seems to be basically unthinkable from a Christian standpoint.

Progress. Finally, if progress is indicated by adopting euthanasia as a way out, this would suggest that any other point of view is simply reactionary. I submit that, with the analgesia and methods of pain relief available to us today, as well as the prospect of cure tomorrow for the incurable of today, we should look seriously at whether euthanasia is in truth progress.

Conclusions

Some say that Jesus Christ came into the world with new ethical insights and a new power of life, but that there is no necessary distinction between the actions taken by Christians and by other men. I would equally strongly say that there can be and should be a distinctively Christian approach to our ethical problems. If one views ethics as a horizontal expression to others of one's concern for them, there is a dimension left out of the naturalistic approach to ethical problems. There is very little motivation or enablement to be found without the empowering presence of God in life. Christianity, therefore, adds a vertical dimension which is all-important.

Ethics, taken alone, become Pharisaical, rigid and sterile. Christianity alone becomes theoretical and evades the issues of life. These two must be joined. The element of love and concern for the welfare of the other person must bring the two together in full fruitfulness. This Christian law of love and concern can best be offered to fellow human beings by a Christian physician whose ability to live it out is rooted in a vital relationship with his Creator.

The so-called **Hippocratic Oath,** which was formulated probably not by Hippocrates himself but by the Pythagoreans about 400 BC, emphasised four major principles. First of all was the principle of ethics with regard to the patients and to life: Never injure but always preserve life! The three other principles were more concerned with etiquette. The physician should be more interested in the advancement of the profession than in the promotion of his own individual practice. He should respect his colleagues and consult them whenever necessary. Delicate information should be handled with confidentiality and not be abused, and in all respects the doctor should remain free of intentional injustice, of all mischief and in particular of sexual relations with patients. If the physician fulfilled this oath, it might be granted to him to enjoy life and art, being honoured with fame among all men for all time to come.

KARL METTINGER

ICCP Bangalore, India, 1982. **Karl L. Mettinger.** *Clinical neurologist, Karolinska Hospital, Stockholm, Sweden.*

OUR ETHICAL DISTINCTIVENESS

JOHN STOTT

THE Christian has different moral or ethical standards from the non-Christian world. The great majority of human beings don't like to be different. We like to be much the same as everybody else. It is true there are a few exhibitionists around, who thrive on drawing attention to themselves and advertising themselves, but most people don't like being conspicuous. We prefer the homogeneity of our own cultural background into which we can merge without seeming to be different from anybody else. We feel safer that way and for this reason most of us resent an alien in our midst. We don't like non-conformists; conformity is a human characteristic and therefore the commands of God are very difficult for us, because he calls us to be different. In Romans 12:2 we are commanded not to be conformed to this world; we are to be *transformed* by the renewing of our mind. It's a call to be different.

I don't know if you realise that this is a theme that runs right through the Bible from beginning to end, or at least — to be slightly more accurate — from Genesis 12 to the end. At the beginning of Genesis 12 God called Abraham, 4,000 years or so ago, called him to leave his home, to leave his country, to leave his kindred and in leaving them to leave their idolatry, and come to a land that he would be given and there to worship the true and the living God. God said to him 'I will be your God and you and your descendants will be my people', and he entered into this covenant with them so that they should be different from everybody else. The Old Testament is the story of this holy people of God. If you don't like the word 'holy' try the word 'different', because that's what it means.

To be the holy people of God is to be the distinct people of God, set apart from the rest of mankind. I remember how strongly I was struck when I first noticed the verses at the beginning of Leviticus 18 where God says to Moses, as part of the law, 'You shall not do as they do in the land of Canaan to which I am bringing you. You

ICCMS Oxford, UK, 1980. **John Stott.** *Rector Emeritus, All Souls Church, London, UK.*

shall not follow their ordinances. You shall obey my statutes and my ordinances for I am the Lord your God.' That is a tremendously strong statement, isn't it, 'You shall not do what they do all around you.' You are to be distinctive, you are to be my holy people.

In the Sermon on the Mount, Jesus calls us to be different. I want to take you to that sermon and seek to draw from it the essence of the message of Jesus in it. The dominant thought of the sermon is in Matthew 6:8. Here are five words, each of which is a mono-syllable, each is very simple to say and very simple to understand, but of profound significance in our Christian lives: 'DO NOT BE LIKE THEM.' It is just as in Leviticus 18, 'You shall not do what they do in the land of Egypt in which you dwelt. You shall not do what they do in the land of Canaan to which I bring you.' Jesus says exactly the same thing — 'do not be like them'. You are surrounded by people of different kinds — pagan people, religious people, but do not be like them. I call you to be different.

Salt and light

Consider the salt and light metaphors. Matthew 5:13–16 says, 'You are the salt of the earth, but if the salt has lost its taste how shall its saltness be restored? It's no good for anything except to be thrown out and trodden underfoot by men. You are the light of the world. A city set on a hill cannot be hid. Nor do men light a lamp and put it under a bucket but on a stand and it gives light to all in the house. Let your light shine before men that they may see your good works and give glory to your Father who is in heaven.'

Probably we are all familiar with the salt and light metaphors. Salt and light were, and still are, universal commodities. In Jesus's own day in Palestine they were in everyday use in every home. So he uses these two metaphors of salt and light to illustrate the influence or the impact which he wanted his followers to make on society. They were only twelve men he was talking to, yet they were to be the salt of the world, and they were to be the light of the world. It is extraordinary what confidence he has in the power of a minority when it is following Christ and filled with the Holy Spirit. If you are a small minority in your country or in your university or medical school you can be the salt of that society and the light of that community if you are following Jesus with all your heart. From the salt and light metaphors we need to learn three very important lessons.

First, *there is a fundamental difference between Christians and non-Christians.* These metaphors, salt and light, set the two communities, the Christian community and the non-Christian community, apart from one another. They stand in contrast to one another. On the one hand there is the world. It is like a dark, dark night, the night of sin, the night of evil, the night of tragedy, the night of sorrow, the night of alienation. And you are to be the dark world's light. Then again, the world is a rotten and decaying place. It is a society that is like meat that is putrefying and going bad. You, in distinction from the world, are to be the world's salt.

Both these metaphors teach that there is a fundamental difference between Christians and non-Christians. But, secondly, both metaphors teach that *Christians must penetrate the non-Christian world,* the non-Christian community. Let your light *shine* into the darkness. If you have a lamp, you don't put it under a bed, you don't hide it under a bucket, you put it on a lamp-stand. The purpose of the light is to illumine the house, and so you must let your light shine. Similarly, the purpose of salt is to be rubbed into the meat, so that it soaks into the meat, in order to arrest, or at least hinder, the process of bacterial decay. Salt does no good if it's left in the salt cellar. So we must be rubbed into society, we must penetrate non-Christian society, and not stay in our elegant little ecclesiastical salt cellars.

The effect of salt is negative — it prevents decay. the effect of light is positive — it illumines the darkness. The one seems to emphasise particularly our social responsibility, like salt stopping society going bad, the other our evangelistic responsibility, spreading the light of Jesus. As Christians we cannot be either socially or evangelistically responsible unless we penetrate the community into which Jesus sends us. So first, there is a fundamental difference between the communities, Christian and non-Christian, and second, the one must penetrate the other.

Thirdly, *Christians must retain their distinctiveness,* even when they penetrate the non-Christian community. Penetration without distinctiveness is of no value, any more than distinctiveness without penetration is of value. Salt must penetrate the meat but it must retain its saltness, otherwise it becomes useless, it is good for nothing. You can't even throw it on the compost heap. It's useless for anything except to be trodden under foot and become material for footpaths. And if the salt must retain its saltness, the light must retain its lightness, and *shine,* brilliantly, otherwise it does no good. As we Christians seek to penetrate the non-Christian community, we must retain our Christian distinctiveness. Penetration is not a synonym for assimilation. We penetrate without becoming assimilated, without becoming conformed. We retain our ethical distinctiveness. We identify with people in their need without losing our own identity. Identification without loss of identity is a summary of the message of these metaphors. So as we go into the world for Christ, as we seek to make friends with non-Christians, as we penetrate the non-Christian society, we must not lose our Christian convictions, our Christian ethical standards, our Christian value system. We maintain them as we seek to go into the world for Christ.

What is it that makes Christians distinctive? What is the lightness of the light, what is the saltness of the salt? I want to give you four answers — and I am now selecting from the rest of the Sermon on the Mount.

Jesus calls us to a greater righteousness

This righteousness is greater than the righteousness of the non-Christian world or even the religious world that is non-Christian. In Matthew 5:20, Jesus says, 'I tell you that unless your righteousness exceeds the righteousness of the scribes and Pharisees you'll never enter the kingdom of heaven.' It's difficult for us to understand, I think, how utterly astonished the disciples would have been when they heard Jesus say that. They must have thought that he had lost his reason, because the scribes and the Pharisees were the most righteous people on earth. They studied the Old Testament. They knew the commandments of God by heart. They calculated that there were 248 commandments and 365 prohibitions in the Old Testament, making 613 ordinances of God altogether, and they claimed that they kept the lot. And now Jesus says, unless your righteousness is greater than that, you won't even *enter* the kingdom, let alone be great in it. What did Jesus mean?

What Jesus meant is that Christian righteousness is greater than Pharisaic righteousness because it is deeper. It is a righteousness of the heart, an inward righteousness of thoughts and motives. Already Jesus has said in the Beatitudes, 'Blessed are the pure in heart, they shall see God.' The scribes and the Pharisees were pure in external righteousness. They may have kept these 613 commandments externally, in word and deed, but they knew very little of the purity of the heart.

Now, inward integrity, wholeness as a Christian, is what we are discussing, and we cannot be righteous according to the righteous demands of Jesus until we have been born again. The Christian life is not just struggling to obey the Sermon on the Mount by our own effort. It's impossible to do that. We cannot change our hearts, or make our hearts pure, or develop a righteousness of the heart. We need a new heart. Jesus has said, 'Out of the heart of man proceed evil thoughts, adulteries, fornications, murder, jealousy and covetousness' (Mark 7:21–22). These things come from the evil heart of man so how can we be righteous in heart? Only by a new birth. And of course the whole Sermon on the Mount presupposes the new birth. This is the new righteousness of the new-born, and without new birth there is no new life and there is no new righteousness, and all that is implicit in the teaching of Jesus.

The Ten Commandments say very clearly 'You shall not commit murder' and 'You shall not commit adultery', and the Pharisees said, 'Fine, we haven't committed either.' Nor had they, as in external righteousness they were not murderers and they were not adulterers. But Jesus said that unjustified anger is tantamount to murder and that lustful looks and lustful fantasies are tantamount to adultery in the reckoning of God. His meaning is clear in Matthew 5:22, 'But I say to you that everyone who is angry with his brother' (and whether or not the phrase 'without a cause' should be added, that is obviously its meaning), 'shall be liable to judgement', and again in verse 27, 'You've heard that it was said "you shall not commit adultery" but I say to you "everyone who looks at a woman lustfully has already committed adultery with her *in his heart*".'

Do you see again the reference to the heart? The righteousness of Jesus is a righteousness of the heart. And he is concerned that we shouldn't be angry in our heart, even if this inward anger never breaks out into murder. Again, he's concerned about the lustful fantasies of our heart, even if they never break out into acts of adultery. And we have to say, 'But who is sufficient for these things?' We must be born again, we must seek the fullness of the Holy Spirit and the constant inward purification that is possible only to those whom Jesus Christ has mastered. Christian righteousness is an inward righteousness of the heart. It includes those deep and secret places which nobody sees but God only and which are usually the last fortress to surrender to the Lord Christ. He calls us to a greater righteousness.

Jesus calls us to a wider love

A love that takes in everybody, so wide it is in its embrace. Here we look at Matthew 5:43. What is the point of the parable of the Good Samaritan? It isn't just that if we love we will serve people in their need. It is that a Samaritan did to that victim of the robbers what no Jew would ever have dreamed of doing, he gave a cross-cultural kind of service. This was the emphasis of Jesus. Your neighbour is a person in need whatever his racial or religious background may be. If a human being is in need we are called to serve him, irrespective of culture, race, nation, religion or anything else. So Jesus goes on, verse 44, 'I say to you,' (and this is the true interpretation of the law's demand that we should love our neighbours) 'love your enemies, and pray for them that persecute you, and do good to those who hate you.' This, then, is the higher demand of Jesus. It is only as we obey this command, that we prove ourselves to be authentic children of God: 'You shall be sons and daughters of your Father in heaven' (verse 45).

God's love is indiscriminate. 'He makes his sun to rise on the evil and on the good. He sends rain on the just and on the unjust.' The embrace of his love is universal and our love must be like his love, not like that of the world outside. So Jesus goes on in verse 46, 'If you only love those who love you, what reward do you have? Even tax collectors [despised tax collectors] can do that.' Or as Luke's version of the sermon puts it, 'Even sinners love those who love them; even sinners lend to sinners.'

Love is not restricted to the Christian community; there is love outside it as Jesus clearly says here. Sinners can love. Those who have never been born again can love. In the world a boy can love a girl, a girl can love a boy, parents love their children and children their parents, husbands love their wives and wives love their husbands, friends love each other; that is the way of the world — reciprocal love. You do me a good turn, I'll do you a good turn. You scratch my back, I'll scratch your back. And that is the highest that the world can reach, but it's not high enough for the kingdom of God. If you only love those who love you, Jesus says, what *more* are you doing than the rest of mankind. Have you ever noticed that phrase, 'What more are you doing than others?' (verse 47). Sinners love sinners, they love each other, but we've got to love those who hate us, even our enemies. We must not copy the world. We must copy God, then we shall be his children. We are to 'Be perfect as your heavenly Father is perfect' (verse 48), and that in the context means, of course, the perfection of love. The equivalent in Luke is, 'Be merciful as your heavenly Father is merciful.' He's speaking of the perfect embrace, the broad embrace of God's love, including our enemies.

Now let me ask you, as I ask myself, have we accepted that standard of Jesus? I think we have to admit that many churches are not always communities of love.

Jesus calls us to a deeper devotion

This is in chapter 6 of Matthew, verses 1–18, when Jesus talks about religion, or piety, and in particular those three common practices of religious people — almsgiving, prayer and fasting. Such practices are done almost throughout the world, by everybody who claims to be religious, whether Christian or non-Christian.

We will concern ourselves with prayer — just one of the three. Jesus quarrelled with two groups of mankind, the religious and the irreligious, the Pharisees and the pagans. They both pray and, says Jesus, you're not to be like either of them. The Pharisees were hypocritical — they were the exhibitionists. They didn't pray in order to commune with God, which is the purpose of prayer, they prayed in order to be seen and applauded by men. Do not be like them, says Jesus.

Then he comes on to the pagans. They, too, pray, but their prayer is mechanical for they use empty phrases (chapter 6 verse 7). And they keep repeating them, endlessly supposing they will be heard for the volume of their speech. Or they turn the prayer-wheel and go on and on, thinking that the volume is the thing that matters.

Jesus said, you're not to be mechanical in your praying, neither hypocritical like the Pharisees nor mechanical like the pagans, but real, like little children coming to their heavenly Father. 'Go into your room and shut the door' (verse 6), that is, don't hope that people are watching you in order to applaud, and pray to your Father who is in that secret place. And there, as you draw near to him, he will draw near to you, and you will have sweet fellowship as a child with your heavenly Father.

Private prayer is not the only form of prayer. There is a place for public prayer, as is clear when Jesus continues in verse 9, 'When you pray say *our* Father', in the plural: that you can't say when you're praying alone, so there is a place for corporate prayer. We come to him as little children and say, 'Dear Father, *our* Father, our loving Father in heaven, may your name be honoured, and your kingdom come, and your will be done. Give us our daily bread, and forgive us our sins and deliver us from evil.' In those six petitions is encompassed the whole range of worship and prayer.

Jesus calls us to a nobler ambition

All human beings are ambitious, just as all are religious. Everybody is ambitious. Jesus contrasts two ambitions: chapter 6 verse 32, 'The Gentiles seek all these things', but, verse 33, you are to seek first something else. Our ambition is what we set before us as the supreme good and to which we devote our lives. What do we want to achieve in life? To what are we committing ourselves? What is our goal?

Jesus says in the end there are only two possibilities. Either we are concerned with ourselves and our own material comforts, and that explains our hunger for wealth and power and fame, or we are concerned for God and his righteous rule in the world, his kingdom and his righteousness. So Jesus sets these two over against each other. First, he says of the Gentiles, the pagans, they are always asking, 'What shall we drink, what shall we eat, what shall we wear?' They are concerned with the body and its material comfort. It is a hopelessly inadequate goal for human endeavour.

Now don't misunderstand that. Christians don't despise the body. There is a sense in which Christianity is a very material religion. We believe in the material created order, we believe in the resurrection of the body, and in the regeneration of the universe, and we have bread and wine in communion and water in baptism, so in this way Christianity is a very material religion. In addition, Jesus, in the Lord's Prayer, said that our first request is, 'Give us our daily bread'.

So when Jesus goes on to say, 'Don't seek what ye shall eat and drink and wear', he isn't despising the body, he is simply telling us to get our priorities right. And the Lord's Prayer begins, 'Father, your name be hallowed, your kingdom come, your will be done'

— but goes on 'and by the way, don't forget I've got a body and need some food'. But material need comes, you see, at the bottom of the list. Our preoccupation and prayer should be with God and his kingdom, and his name and will. Verse 33 says, 'Seek first', that is, make the rule and the righteousness of God in the world the priority to which you devote your life. So I wish more Christians were ambitious. There's nothing wrong with ambition if it's the right ambition, but let's be ambitious for God, and let's not be ambitious for ourselves. Let's be ambitious to get on in medicine, but in order to stand where we are on the medical ladder for Jesus Christ, for the kingdom of God, for the righteousness of God. That ultimately is your concern — a nobler ambition.

So I conclude. Here is the call of Jesus, to us today as much as it was to the disciples of Christ centuries ago. 'Do not be like them.' We are to be different from the world around us. He calls us to a greater righteousness which is the righteousness of the heart. He calls us to a wider love which embraces our enemies. He calls us to a deeper devotion which is real communion with God. He calls us to a nobler ambition that is God's rule and righteousness. So Jesus sets over against each other the way of the world and his way.

He ends the Sermon on the Mount with the parables of the two house-builders, one who built his house on a foundation of rock that withstood the storms of life and of the judgement day, the other who built his house on sand which, when the storms of adversity and judgement arose, inevitably collapsed into irreparable ruin. And what is the difference between the rock house and the sand house? It is whether, said Jesus, you listen to my teaching and obey it or you listen to my teaching and disobey it. If you listen to my teaching and you don't obey it you're a fool, building your house on sand; it will not survive. If you listen to my teaching and you obey it, you are a wise man, building the house of your life on rock, and no adversity, not even the day of judgement, will cause that house to fall.

So Jesus compels us to choose; we cannot escape this choice. 'Nobody can serve two masters, either he will hate the one and love the other, or he will be loyal to the one and despise the other. You cannot serve God and money' (Mat. 6:24). We cannot serve God and anything else. We cannot share God with any idol. He demands our exclusive allegiance. It's only if we put him first, as he deserves, and accept his higher standards, that our salt will retain its saltiness, our light will retain its lightness, and we will have a testimony and an influence in the world. But first we have to choose the narrow way, the way of Christ.

So I want to beg you this morning, give up your safe compromises, turn from your half-heartedness, put Jesus Christ first in your life, make him your Lord, follow his standards, then your salt will be salty, then your light will shine, and non-Christians will 'see your good works and give glory to your Father who is in heaven' (Mat. 5:16).

❈

The changing face of medical ethics. The discovery of new drugs and safer anaesthetics with the devising and perfecting of surgical techniques bring their own train of problems. The doctor is sometimes faced with the grave decision of when *not* to treat, when to do so would be to prolong misery rather than to bring relief of suffering. Then there are the problems surrounding sex, including contraception, abortion and artificial insemination.

Medical research may involve some form of human experimentation and raises its own peculiar ethical problems. These and other applications of the principles of medical ethics are constantly changing. In a world of changing moral values it is important for us to look to the principles again and to ensure that, as much as lies within our power, they are based and maintained on the best and surest Christian foundations.

VINCENT EDMUNDS

ICCP Amsterdam, Netherlands, 1963. **Vincent Edmunds.** *Consultant physician, Mount Vernon Hospital, Northwood and Mildmay Mission Hospital, London, UK. Co-editor* Ideals in medicine *etc.*

❈

CHRISTIAN ETHICS IN MEDICINE — DEFINITION AND APPLICATION

GORDON SCORER

Introduction

ETHICS comes in when my treatment of the patient affects his relationship with others, including God and the natural world around. Ethics covers the background of medical practice, but it intrudes at many points among our daily decisions. Ethics has to do with living and behaviour, with dying and death, with marriage and family, with work and the way it is done, with the use of resources, with leisure and how we spend it, with individual freedom and social pressures, with the State, the law, professional regulations and the media. All our medical practice is carried out against a background of individual and social customs which are variable and changing. The rights and wrongs of human behaviour influence a doctor's decisions. This is where ethics comes in.

The importance of ethics today

When I was a medical student we had scarcely heard of ethics. Nobody ever mentioned the word and it did not seem to concern us. We might have heard of Hippocrates, but we certainly did not know what he had said. Why was this? Possibly the main reason was because at that time most people in our country, and in Western Europe, thought alike. We had a Christian heritage and a similar historical development so we had the same ideas on medical, social and personal issues. The divorce laws were relatively tight and we regarded marriage as something which took place for life. We did not destroy life, we protected it. Medical practice was not as powerful then as it is now, and we had not developed the technology which we have today and the ability to sustain life and alter bodily function. Moreover, there was no State medical service in those days. The kind of ethical problems which we now discuss did not then exist. There were one or two matters

ICCMS Oxford, UK, 1980. **C. Gordon Scorer.** *Late consultant surgeon, Hillingdon Hospital, UK. Co-editor* Decision making in medicine, *etc.*

like advertising, fee-splitting between general practitioner and consultant, and preserving high moral standards, which were discussed, but by and large ethics was not of great interest, and there were no lectures on it or books to be read.

Why has there been this great change? There are three good reasons: the first is because *medical technology has become so powerful.* Support systems have been introduced and we can do much more to preserve bodily function than we ever used to. Recently pharmacology has advanced enormously. We have got a very wide range of drugs which we can use, some of them affecting human moods, some of them healing diseases, all of them modifying function and producing side effects which may be serious. These advances have led to a rapid rise in the cost of medical treatment so we now have to discriminate with regard to whom we can treat. The cost of care is itself an ethical problem. The science of genetics has increased our understanding, and what we can do to influence the development of the human body also raises ethical issues. So medical technology and its very powerful influence in medicine today is one reason why ethics has become important.

A second reason is the *participation of the State in medical practice.* This is happening in all countries to a certain extent. The State now controls medical practice in a way which it never used to before. In the old days it was just one doctor working with one patient. Now the State is interested in how the work is done and the State is the paymaster of most of our doctors in this country. We have no ethical rules about how we should regard the State. Of course we should obey the laws of the land, but how far the State should go in seeking to control clinical practice is an area of ethics which has not yet been fully explored.

My third reason why ethics has become important is because in Western Europe *we are increasingly living in a pluralistic society.* We used to recognise a Western Christian tradition and the laws of the land were based upon it, but gradually over the last thirty years we have dismantled many of those laws. We are producing a permissive society. We are no longer supporting our Christian beliefs by our legislation. The basis for our living is more and more becoming a secular and materialistic humanism, a Godless humanism. Man's appetites and man's evolution have become our prime interest. In addition, since the last war we have admitted to our country a great many people from other continents. In the area where I practise, which has a population of about a quarter of a million, we have at least 50,000 from India and Pakistan. We have more than 10,000 from the West Indies. This change in the pattern of society is altering the way we practise medicine and therefore has to do with medical ethics.

Society is changing, medical skills are becoming more powerful, the State's concern with medical practice is increasing, it is no wonder that medical ethics has become an important subject for discussion.

WORKING OUT A SYSTEM OF ETHICS

When it comes to making an ethical decision, what is our basis for doing it? We must work out our ethics on some basis, that is what the word 'ethics' means. *Ethics is a systematic study of what men and women consider the right way to act.*

Morals concern individual actions. You have a morality, I have a morality. There are as many moralists as there are individuals. Of course, within any country there is usually a broad agreement on what is morally right and morally wrong. Ethics classifies morality and puts it on a basis which is both consistent and comprehensive. By doing this we can each understand what the other is talking about, why we do certain things and why we do not do certain other things. For example:–

The doctor should do what the patient wants

The patient comes to the doctor asking for a particular drug or operation or service. The doctor may well say, 'Well, I don't think that is very wise, I wouldn't do that', or he may say, 'You ought to look at your problem in a different way'. But the patient persists in his request and the doctor gives way. The doctor does what the patient wants. In other words, where there is an ethical decision to be made the patient should be free to make his own decision and the doctor should accede to the patient's request.

This is called the patient or person-centred ethic and was popularised by the writings of Joseph Fletcher in a book called *Morals and Medicine* published twenty years ago. The emphasis in the book is on the patient's rights. The patient has the right to request from his doctor what he wants. Here we have moral flexibility. Do not let us talk about what is right and what is wrong;

what the patient wants is right. It adds to human freedom. Freedom of choice should always be given first consideration. By implication, we must make sure that the patient is well-informed about all possible courses of actions *and their consequences.*

The doctor should abide by the rules

Traditionally we have been guided by unwritten rules and controlled by laws. But some say let's have more laws and regulations to tell us exactly what we may do and what we may not do. That would make it easier for everyone. Making decisions is difficult; the doctor, therefore, needs to be told by Parliament what he should do and what he should not do. Some religions support this kind of leading and give official pronouncements and personal directions to doctors with regard to their practice. But is this a good basis for medical ethics?

The trouble about rules and laws is that they are rigid and often inappropriate. It is very difficult to put into words what a doctor should do with any particular patient at any particular time. Laws can be very easily misinterpreted. The 1967 Abortion Act was introduced with such loose wording that it eventually led to abortion virtually on demand.

The doctor should be guided by consensus opinion

The idea of consensus is that we get together, sit round a table and discuss the pros and cons of what can be done and what cannot be done, and then we agree on what is the right thing to do. In other words, we identify a current problem, we present factual information to one another and we then clarify our different moral assumptions. Unfortunately, each person sitting round the table will probably have a different point of view. Nevertheless, out of it we hope will come an agreed opinion, a consensus on what is the right way to act. It sounds attractive and plausible.

Clearly there are great advantages in general agreement and united action. The only trouble is that doctors, like many others in society, have sharply conflicting ethical views on many important subjects. In addition, they often change their opinions, and move from what is cast-iron in one generation to something almost diametrically opposed in the next generation. This happens, of course, in clinical medicine and this may be right because it encourages progress. Ethics, however, deal with the nature of man and his relations with his fellow men and the world around him and these things do not change. Ethics cannot become subordinate to changing opinions and pressures.

A CHRISTIAN FRAMEWORK FOR MEDICAL ETHICS

What is then the Christian basis and understanding of medical ethics? May I try to summarise it in a simple phrase: *The Christian doctor serves his patient by love, in righteousness, for God.* Such a basis is not patient-centred, although it includes that; it is not rule-centred, although it has some valuable rules; it is not a consensus of medical views because they vary from one decade to the next. We serve by love in righteousness for God.

Love. It is a compassionate identification with the patient in his need. Our genuineness and transparency are shown to him by recognising him as a unique person, by exhibiting a sensitive ability to see his world and himself as he sees them, and trying to understand the true nature of his illness. We move alongside him in order to help him and lead him out into what is the best solution for his problem.

But *righteousness* is also important. It is not enough to say we have compassion for our patient because such a kind of love may easily end up in sentimentality. We are then led to take the easy option. No, our actions must be in righteousness, that is, applying true values to the patient's need.

But how do we know what is right as Christians? First, God has created us men and women in a certain pattern. There is a natural order and by observance of this order we find our freedom, our fulfilment and our health. Secondly, God has given us a moral code. It is broadly stated in the Ten Commandments and their moral depth comes to us in the teaching of Jesus Christ, that true righteousness is heart righteousness. Thirdly, to be righteous is not merely to maintain standards of right and wrong but to promote righteousness through our own activities. This can be done through proclamation of the gospel, through education of the young, through service to others and through the promotion of wise legislation. A Christian doctor can serve in all these areas. He is not only himself a righteous man, he tries to promote righteousness in the society in which he lives.

A Christian basis for medical ethics suggests that we serve our patients by love, in righteousness, *for God*. As Christians we know we are accountable to God for all we do. Our knowledge and our gifts — such as they are — come from him. Our patients are our equals before God; we all — doctor and patient alike — share the common frailties of humanity and need his help. Our calling is to bring honour to his name in the work we do.

The future of Christian medicine. In a scientific sense there can be no particular Christian medicine. We cannot, however, do without a medicine inspired by Christ himself. In a world, in our own native countries as well as in foreign fields, where rigorous judgements are passed; in a world where man is relying on his own strength and power; in a world which appears to be without meaning and purpose; in a world where the individual is given less and less attention; in a world where mercilessness is reigning, the Christian viewpoint and vision are intensely needed today, and perhaps will be still more needed in the future. They are very important in the presence of disease, ageing and death.

R. EEG-OLOFSSON

ICCP Amsterdam, Netherlands, 1963. **R. Eeg-Olofsson.** *Physician, Sweden.*

CHRISTIAN ETHICS IN HEALING AND ORIENTAL PERSPECTIVES

MYUNG SOO LEE

Introduction

ETHICS has to do with the way people behave. The term 'ethics' is derived from the Greek word 'ethos', meaning 'custom'; its equivalent, 'moral', comes from the equivalent Latin word 'mos' with the same meaning. The concern of ethics or morals is not merely the behaviour that is customary in society but rather behaviour which ought to be customary in society. Ethics is prescriptive, not simply descriptive. Its domain is that of duty and obligation and it seeks to define the distinction between right and wrong, between good and evil, between justice and injustice and between responsibility and irresponsibility. Because human conduct is all too seldom what it ought to be (as the annals of mankind amply testify) the study of ethics is a discipline of perennial importance in order for life to be lived in harmony with other people, with nature and with God.

The objects of a healing ministry

Healing should be directed towards individuals and to the society in which they live. (The term 'society' here includes the corporate body of humanity, the environment and nature.) Disease, ignorance and poverty are always interrelated and form a vicious circle, so one cannot expect complete healing unless all aspects of human life are dealt with together and simultaneously. Because resources are so limited, it would be most effective to focus concern where this interrelationship is most obvious. Our Lord's own expressed priorities were to bring good news to the poor and healing to the brokenhearted, deliverance to captives and liberty to the bruised and abused, as well as the offer of sight to the blind (Isa. 61:1–2; Luke 4:18–19).

Since the prime object of a healing ministry is a human being, one cannot expect effective healing without a deep understanding

ICMDA Seoul, Korea, 1990. **Myung Soo Lee**. *Director and professor of the Institute of Healing Ministry, ACTS, Seoul, Korea. ICMDA Vice-President 1990–94.*

of human beings. This raises questions such as 'What is man?', 'What are the components of man?', 'What is the nature of man?'. Such questions are important for healers as well as for theologians and philosophers.

Oriental culture is related to Oriental religions, so it is necessary to reflect on these to understand ideas relevant to the healing ministry.

ANTHROPOLOGIES AND ETHICS IN ORIENTAL RELIGION

Buddhism: Buddha (563–483 BC)

Buddhism does not speak about the origin of man. It simply explains the state of human existence as a cycle of birth and death with only suffering in between. Buddhism tries to find a way to overcome this perpetual cycle of suffering, namely by entering into the world of Nirvana, the ultimate goal. The Buddhist view of man is that everyone possesses the nature of Buddha, so the one who attains the state of Nirvana is regarded as Buddha, the enlightened one.

To reach Nirvana involves giving up the desires which are the cause of suffering and instead treading the 'Eightfold Path', marked out by eight ethical principles. Four of these apply to good behaviour, with right understanding, right aspiration, right speech and right conduct. The other four relate to the purification of the mind by right vocation, right effort, right mindfulness and right concentration. Buddhist ethics thus apply both to outward behaviour and internal thought.

Confucianism: Confucius (K'ung Fu-tzu, 551–479 BC)

Chinese traditions have tried to achieve and maintain harmony with the forces of the cosmos. Confucius did not pose questions about the origin or end of man, or about a world after death. His aim was to achieve public welfare and a stable society, based on harmonious human relations. In this respect, Confucianism is more like social ethics or politics than religion.

To achieve harmony with the universe through human relations, Confucius emphasised internal and external qualities which, he believed, contribute to moral life.

Internal qualities:

Jen is the supreme virtue in Confucius' catalogue of values. As the symbol of Chinese humanism the term embraces a wide range of meaning, including humanity, love, benevolence and goodness, all reflecting the importance of human relations. Essentially, jen is what one does when most truly human and implies that being human is a task and an achievement.

Chung is conscientiousness or loyalty, so represents the development of one's mind on behalf of others.

Shu is reciprocity or altruism, these extending the mind towards others. Chung and shu both come from jen.

Hsueh is learning or study, not merely to find instruction or information, but in order to build moral character.

External qualities:

Li This covers the whole range of human activities, from performance of religious rituals to choice of dress, or personal manners and decorum amongst family and friends. Li accompanies jen and is a means of maintaining harmony.

Hsiao is filial piety, which Confucius saw as a test of an individual's moral character.

Confucius understood that man was the most spiritual being of all creation. He described the one who possessed these internal and external qualities as *chun-tzu,* the ideal person or perfect gentleman. The aim of his teaching may thus be said to be the practice of the ethical way in order to become chun-tzu.

It was **Mencius** who systematised Confucius' thoughts and made clear what was unclear in his understanding of human nature. Mencius considered this to be essentially good. He found four 'beginnings' in man which distinguished mankind from animals, namely: a sense of compassion, marking the beginning of becoming man-at-his-best; a sense of shame, marking the beginning of propriety; submissiveness, marking the beginning of a sense of ceremony; and a sense of right and wrong, marking the beginning of wisdom. Every human being possesses these four beginnings just as he possesses four limbs.

Mencius argued that the four beginnings give rise to four ethical principles: *jen, i, li* and *chih.* Through these he tried to set up right relations and to realise these politically.

Chun Doism: started in Korea by Choi Soo Wooni (1824–1864)

Chun Do Kyo is a religion whose key doctrine is *'in-nae-chun'*, meaning 'man is heaven'. According to this doctrine, the truth is not that which may be realised through enlightenment, but heaven is the transcendent, which everyone has within him. This is the idea of *'si-chun-ju'* and serves as a basis for the doctrine of *in-nae-chun.* Because everyone has heaven within himself, man is heaven itself and so there is no distinction between persons.

Chun Do Kyo does not offer concrete ethical principles, but by perceiving heaven to exist within man it urges behaviour which accords with this perception.

Christianity

The Christian understanding of man is that he is a whole being, composed of body, soul and spirit (1 Thes. 5:23; Heb. 4:12) and created in the image of God (Gen. 1:27), a living soul (Gen. 2:7) and a temple of God (1 Cor. 3:16; 2 Cor. 6:16).

Bearing God's image before the Fall, man presumably had the same attributes as God himself. What, then, are the attributes of God? God is love (1 Jn. 4:8). He is also merciful (Luke 6:36), righteous (Col. 4:1), holy (1 Pet. 1:15) and perfect (Mat. 5:48). Made in this image, man cannot be merely a collection of cells or a mass of substances, as seen by a materialist or biologist, but is the most precious being, who cannot be exchanged even for the whole world (Mat. 16:26). The Christian concern for a man's soul and spirit over-rides that for his body alone. The spirit is seen as the essence of life — life everlasting (John 6:35). Since Christians believe that physical death involves the separation of soul and spirit from the body, a dying patient should not be referred to as 'terminal' but as being 'in transition'.

If a healer views man simply as a materialistic being, then a wholly materialistic medicine will be practised. If he views man as a biological being, then biological medicine will result. Only as a healer understands man to be a whole being can there be the practise of the medicine of the whole person.

Essential differences between the ethical systems

Buddhism: 'Hurt not others in ways that you yourself would feel hurt' (Udan-Varga 5:18).

Confucianism: 'Surely it is the maxim of loving-kindness; Do not

do unto others that which you would not have them do unto you'
(Analects 15:23).
Chun Doism: 'Respect heaven, love your neighbours'.
Christianity: 'All things whatsoever ye would that men should do
to you, do ye even so to them; for this is the law and the prophets'
(Mat. 7:12).

The value system and the ethical standards of a healing ministry
should be based on the premise that man was created in the image
of God and one soul is more precious than the whole world. So
many perplexing practical problems, ranging through the various
methods of population control and other matters of life and death,
including environmental issues, need re-examination in this light.
Particular attention needs to be given to the problems of those who
are poor, ignorant, sick, handicapped, aged, dying or alienated.

SOME ASSUMPTIONS ABOUT HEALTH, DISEASE AND HEALING
A Christian views mankind from the perspective of the Creation,
the Fall and the Restoration. Similarly, a Christian healer tries to
understand health, disease and healing from the same perspective.

Concept of health
The Creation: 'And God saw everything that he had made, and,
behold, it was very good' (Gen. 1:31).

'Health is a state of physical, mental and emotional soundness.
It is not merely the absence of disease and infirmities, neither is it
dependent upon the absence of disability' (WHO).

Health is a state of harmony between cognition, emotion and
will *mentally,* between soma, psyche and spirit *personally* and
between people, the environment and nature *socially.* The word
'harmony' denotes relationship, which means 'withism', or
togetherness, for good. If the mind is in a state of harmony then it
can maintain tranquillity and peace. If man is in a state of harmony
then he is a whole being, functioning normally. When society is in a
state of harmony then there will prevail freedom in truth (John
14:16–17), equality in justice (Col. 4:1) and peace in love (1 Jn. 4:8).
Mankind may then enjoy life with joy and shalom under the
sovereignty of God, the Creator. Such a state can be perceived as the
coming of the kingdom of God on earth (Luke 17:21; Rom. 14:17) as

it is in heaven (Mat. 6:9–11), since the attributes of God are truth, righteousness and love.

The Christian view of health is not a static one, but a dynamic, continual and victorious encounter against evil (Satan) to establish the kingdom of God. Such a positive state of health will be the goal of the healing ministry.

Concept of disease

The Fall: 'Then when lust hath conceived, it bringeth forth sin: and sin, when it is finished, bringeth forth death' (James 1:15).

Diseases arise from the interplay between inherited and environmental factors. They also follow disobedience to God's law, which includes natural law. Diseases arise when mental integrity is disrupted by factors like lust, anger or hatred, or when the body is damaged, for example by infection, intoxication or poverty and when society is disintegrated by immorality, injustice, etc.

'For we know that the whole creation groaneth and travaileth in pain together until now. And not only they, but ourselves also, which have the first-fruits of the Spirit, even we ourselves groan within ourselves, waiting for the adoption, to wit, the redemption of our body' (Rom. 8:22–23).

One dictionary definition of disease is 'the state of being deficient in tranquillity or experiencing disorder of health' (Webster). Impaired tranquillity is usually taken to refer to a disturbed mental state (an experience of anxiety, fear, despair, anger, etc) whilst a disorder of health usually suggests a physical problem, stemming from imbalance between vitality and infirmity and causing specific symptoms and signs.

Yet disease is not only a state of disharmony between an individual's body, mind and spirit. It also damages the whole society when there is deviation from the normal patterns of physical, mental, spiritual and social order. Thus, disease means a state of disharmony within the self and with others, the environment and God.

Concept of healing

Restoration: 'God was in Christ, reconciling the world unto himself, not imputing their trespasses unto them; and he hath committed unto us the word of reconciliation' (2 Cor. 5:19).

Healing can be understood as the on-going process of restoration from a pathological state to a physiological one. It is the whole restoration from disease, whether physical, mental, spiritual or social, to normality; from a disintegrated, disharmonised, disordered and alienated state to one which is integrated, harmonised, ordered and reconciled. Such healing not only moves individuals towards wholeness and holiness but restores society towards the Creator's intended order.

Calvin suggested that human healing is fully realised as human salvation, comparing this to the right hand of God's kingdom. A healed society means social salvation, which he compared to the kingdom's left hand. As the two hands come together, they will bring God's kingdom on earth, as it is in heaven. Health and salvation are like two sides of a coin. To bring them together is the ultimate goal of the healing ministry.

> 'And I saw a new heaven and a new earth: for the first heaven and the first earth were passed away; and there was no more sea. And I John saw the holy city, new Jerusalem, coming down from God out of heaven, prepared as a bride for her husband. And I heard a great voice out of heaven saying, Behold, the tabernacle of God is with men, and he will dwell with them and they shall be his people, and God himself shall be with them, and be their God. And God shall wipe away all tears from their eyes; and there shall be no more death, neither sorrow nor crying, neither shall there be any more pain: for the former things are passed away' (Rev. 21:1–4).

MEDICINE OR PATIENTS?

KARL METTINGER

Introduction

TODAY, we find ourselves involved in three overwhelming processes. Firstly, we have the technological revolution, where the machine rather than the patient tends to become the centre of the medical universe. Secondly, we live in the middle of a secularised society, where the old morals are being replaced, for example by situational ethics. Thirdly, we are all more or less frustrated by the continuous but perhaps necessary reorganisation of health care. We have ended up in a turmoil of ultra-specialisation, bureaucracy and labour unions.

Perhaps never before, as Christian doctors, have we been so much challenged to reconsider our responsibility and motivation. It is far too easy to conform to generally accepted concepts. We need one another, to challenge our shallowness and shortsighted-ness, to rebuke our selfishness and to provoke one another to good works. As Christians, we advocate concepts which are in keeping with God's plan for men. We have to ask ourselves: Is this mere talk, or does it really matter in our daily activities that we are repre-sentatives here and now of him who is referred to as the source, the guide and the goal of all that is?

The development of medical ethics

My task is to review briefly some important aspects of the potential conflict between the interests of medicine and/or doctors on the one hand and patients on the other. From time to time, this conflict becomes overt, acting as the very stimulus needed to codify medical ethics.

I should like to make three observations on the history of medical ethics and etiquette.

Firstly, ethics is not primarily a Christian invention (witness the so-called Hippocratic oath of about 400 BC), but it is rather a

ICCP Bangalore, India, 1982. **Karl L. Mettinger.** *Clinical neurologist, Karolinska Hospital, Stockholm, Sweden.*

necessity for the survival of the human race. Anthropologists try to convince that altruism in the human species can be traced for some 60,000 years. An ethical baseline in various cultures has been the Golden Rule of mutual respect, suggesting to us to do or not to do what we expect or do not expect from others. No version is as free of compromise as that of the New Testament: Love your neighbour as you love yourself.

Secondly, in a so-called Christian society, the ethics and etiquette of medical practice now and again fall to the lowest level. This is what happened in the early 19th century to British society, when Thomas Percival felt urged to formulate his *Codex of medical ethics.*

Thirdly, after periods of flagrant abuse of (and by) the medical profession, there often follows a period when the need for professional standards is recognised. This is what happened within the World Medical Association after World War II, as manifested by a series of Declarations.

However, no ethical code can be at the same time rigid enough to live by and elastic enough to meet all situations. At best, an ethical code is a set of principles or a rough guide. Furthermore, most ethical codes neglect to take into account the motivation behind a given act. Finally, it is most likely that there will be a discrepancy between the codified ethics of today and the medical practice of tomorrow.

Differences between Christian and natural ethics

The pertinent question is whether distinctive Christian ethics exist. Certainly, if they do, they are not a set of rules. Yet Christian ethics do exist, often being referred to as the Law of Love and exemplified by the life of Christ. They differ from natural ethics in three important aspects:

- Natural ethics are basically rooted in human intuition, reason or tradition, whereas Christian ethics are fundamentally based on the character of God.
- Natural ethics deal with principles of conduct, whereas distinctively Christian ethics deal with one's relations with people.
- Natural ethics deal primarily with actions, whereas distinctively Christian ethics deal essentially with motivation.

Motives for the practice of medicine

If we analyse for a moment why each of us has chosen a medical career, we would probably come up with several different answers. Only a few of us may be able to trace an explicit vocation, when God pointed out the route to be chosen in life. I can still remember a particular Sunday evening nineteen years ago when the idea of studying medicine came to me for the first time. It was unique in that the idea had never entered my head before. It may have been generated by my cerebral computer, coming up with an unexpected answer to the prevailing question of what to do with my life, or it might have been my personal call. There was nothing dramatic or supernatural to report, but I am convinced that God usually prefers to work with us in the natural realm. The significant thing was that a new purpose was growing within me.

As a young medical student, I took a term off to study the work of medical missions in East Africa and for some time it could have seemed that I was heading for medical missionary work. Who would have thought that I would end up as a clinical neurologist, conducting research into stroke, at Karolinska Hospital, Stockholm! Yet I have never doubted that God has been with me all the way along.

I have been dwelling intentionally on the concept of *vocation*, as this has been a controversial subject in many Christian circles. There has been a great overemphasis on standardised patterns, but this is to diminish God. He certainly expects us to use our common sense and, being his partners, make mature decisions for the future. If we set out on the wrong track he is fully able and gracious enough to let us know in one way or another.

So if vocation is not our personal experience, what are the motives for our involvement in the medical profession? About 30% of the students in our hospital have had various other professional backgrounds before turning to medicine and I have repeatedly put this question to them. Many of them seem to hold beautiful, humanitarian ideas, wanting to spend time talking to patients, a concept so often neglected in modern health care. The great majority report that they want to get more out of life and attain further advancement. This could be the expression of *stewardship* or *self-realisation*, or there might be a certain contamination with *secondary motives*, such as prestige, power or financial reward. However, I believe that very few medical students today, at least in my own country, choose a medical career for purely egoistic reasons. The prestige of the profession is falling in many parts of the world, whilst in others looms the threat of reduced income or unemployment.

A readjusted service

As far as the idealism of medical students is concerned the future outlook is promising, but what happens later? Let us try to visualise the natural life cycle of many Christian as well as non-Christian doctors. Most of us pass through a *stage of idealism* during our pre-clinical years. How then do we explain the frequent changeover to a predominantly professional attitude and lifestyle during the clinical years and the first years after qualification? The answer cannot be that this is simply due to the enjoyment of professional and financial achievement after an impoverished and prolonged period of study. Could it be that the values which senior doctors transmit to younger colleagues have such a ruinous effect? Here, we must scrutinise ourselves. Is there a discrepancy between the values we advocate and our lifestyles in professional and social life? One of the main concerns of the Christian medical societies in various countries is to help us analyse such questions. It is to be hoped that all of us will have an attitude to life in which our values are recognisable in our daily activities. To move from a *stage of pure professionalism* to a *stage of readjusted service* means tuning in to God's will for us and our fellow men.

Motives for medical research

Most pre-clinical students who become attached to basic science and start some research project may, in the first place, do so out of pure curiosity, or as a way of earning a small income. The motives might be more complex for those who take up long-term projects. The major incentive might be expected to be the advancement of medical science, but how many articles published in our medical journals honestly meet such criteria? This can be particularly true of clinical research, which is often so badly designed. Thus, human studies often lack valid conclusions because patients are drawn from an already selected group, or because the control series is inadequately defined.

Another confounding factor in many countries is that the quantity rather than the quality of published articles has become the basis for allocating research grants. It is obvious that competition and the hunt for power and prestige have become highly acceptable tools for any so-called advancement in medical science. Surely there is a great need for different concepts and standards.

Happily, in most hospitals which conduct research, patients have recently had their interests protected by the establishment of ethical committees. This is largely a direct outcome of the Declaration of Helsinki, 1964, which states that the consent of an informed patient is a prerequisite for involvement in a clinical study. Many respectable medical journals also require a statement about the ethical status of a project before an article about it is considered for publication.

Christian commitment in medicine

There should be three distinctive features of Christian commitment in medicine:

Our attitude should be that of a minister — and that means a servant. This does not necessarily mean lack of dignity. To follow Christ's example proves his own teaching: 'Greatest is the one who serves. I am among you as a servant' (Luke 22:26–27). At the same time, this is an efficient antidote to arrogance. To reach beyond the limits of the ego is likely to start a process of personal growth, often hindered before by preoccupation with self. This is the *paradox of service,* whereby ministry to others naturally becomes a channel of love, showing compassion and grace. The wisdom of Trudeau taught us 'to cure sometimes, to relieve often and to comfort always'. Christian commitment goes further still.

We should expose destructive lifestyles. Much physical illness may have a psychological origin, forming a large group of patients who come to our medical centres time after time, without being relieved. It is a special challenge for us to try to communicate appropriate health care by caring for the whole person. A word of truth may penetrate to the root of the problem. So much human activity seems to be dictated by ideas, good or bad, transmitted by parents and which still prevail. Reaction patterns from early childhood may also occupy the mind. Yet we are called to set people free, encouraging them to stand tall and finally start to live a mature life, taking full responsibility for themselves. I believe that it is our responsibility to indicate, without condemnation or moralising, that some disease is self-inflicted, caused by a destructive lifestyle.

We should promote development and stability. Here I should like to emphasise the distinctive Christian way of living, so often referred to as a pilgrimage. As human beings, we are expected to find a decent niche in life where we can be creative and find security. Many of us are in the fortunate position of being materially well off. Some criticise this today, but what matters most is our attitude to what we have gained, probably through hard work. At the same time, we must never be emotionally bound to these things, but always be prepared to move on to pastures new, when the time is right and should this be required of us.

François Mauriac once summarised his aim in life thus: 'I am a Christian, first and last.' Let us be aware that we are put here to play a significant role among our fellow men. We are challenged not to conform to the current ordering of priorities in health care. Yet we are not called to be supermen, all the time trying to compete with the best of our colleagues, neglecting our own health and also our families. Although many colleagues may attain higher standards than ours, we may still glorify God in doing our work to the best of our abilities.

Let us remember that one day, when our lives will be open to judgement, we may have to recognise that many of our ambitions and achievements were insignificant, like the grass that withers away in the sun. The only thing to matter then may be that what was done was done in love.

THE NATURE OF MAN IN THE LIGHT OF MODERN SCIENTIFIC ADVANCES AND OF THE BIBLE

MALCOLM JEEVES

Introduction

For most Christians in the West, as well as friends who may not share their Christian convictions, it is perfectly natural to think about our human nature in terms of some sort of dualism. It fits our common experience to think of the mind and brain or the soul and the body as distinct entities, possibly as separate substances. True, they interact in a very intimate and mysterious way but their separate existence seems intuitively very convincing. Today there are also many who, whilst not sharing our Christian beliefs, wish to champion some form of dualism. They quite often appeal to experiences of the occult, or the new age movement, or are impressed by reports of near-death experiences which they believe support a dualist view of human nature. What is more, it seems obvious to interpret many passages of the Bible in dualistic terms. It seems natural to give a concrete existence to some of the aspects of our make-up as human beings that are referred to in the Bible. Terms like 'mind', 'body', 'soul', 'spirit', 'heart' and so on, all seem ready candidates for building a composite picture of human nature.

Before too readily concluding that some sort of model of man in terms of a dualism of substance is the obvious biblical one, we should pause and check that we are not repeating, in our generation, some of the past ways of interpreting the Bible which have led to unnecessary conflicts with developments in science. We are familiar with the problems that arose in earlier centuries when, for example, passages of the psalms, which we can today clearly see as figurative or poetic, were used to challenge cosmo-logical theories. The most obvious is the statement found several times in the psalms that 'the earth is fixed, that it cannot be moved'. This, together with similar statements, was given as the biblical ground

ICMDA Seoul, Korea, 1990. **Malcolm Jeeves.** *Professor of psychology, University of St Andrews, UK.*

for refuting any theory of the movement of the earth about its own axis or in space, such as that proposed by Copernicus. In like manner there are 'obvious' meanings that we can attribute to familiar passages of the Bible which refer to man, but we would do well to pause and ponder over them before we assume that they are the only possible or indeed the necessary and primary meaning of what we read. Scripture is inspired, not our interpretation of it.

The changing scientific picture

The last two decades have seen some of the most exciting developments we have ever witnessed in neuroscience and neuropsychology. It could be argued that together they are converging on a view of man which points to a model not of a dualistic kind but essentially of a monistic kind. Every advance in neuroscience seems to tighten the link between mind and brain. Let us briefly review the main features of these converging lines of scientific evidence and ask how we can best interpret them. What sort of an emerging picture of man do they suggest and how do we relate this to the salient features of a biblical or Hebrew–Christian view of man? All truth is one and we wish to try and integrate scientific and biblical truth honestly in order to gain as accurate a picture of man as we can.

Converging lines of scientific evidence

For the great anatomists Gall and Spurzheim it was scientifically respectable to attribute differences in abilities and personality to variations in the size of the convolutions of the brain. 'Phrenology' was a respectable scientific discipline. It was not long, however, before it fell into disrepute, and for good reasons. Experiments with animals seeking to localise particular mental functions to particular parts of the brain were unsuccessful.

This century has seen a re-emergence of attempts to understand the link between mental activity and brain structure and function. Today we are intensively engaged in trying to gain a better under-standing of, for example, the psychopathology of Alzheimer's disease and of Parkinson's disease. Such attempts focus on links between the disordered state of the minds of some Parkinson's and Alzheimer's patients and how these may link to what we already know of changes in the structure and biochemistry of parts of their brains, such as the nigrostriatal pathways.

In the last thirty years the specialised functions of the two cerebral hemispheres have become well documented. The commissurotomy patients studied by Sperry and his colleagues afforded a new way of looking at the distinct abilities of each disconnected cerebral hemisphere. Accumulating evidence of the different effects of pathology on the two cerebral hemispheres, as well as studies of how the two sides of the brain process information in normal intact people, have also built up an impressive picture of localisation of function within the brain. Such localisation is not confined to particular areas of the brain but also to particular cells or columns and cells within particular areas. Evidence for specificity of localisation has steadily increased. So today when a patient presents with failure to recognise faces we not only have a good idea of which parts of the cerebral cortex have been affected; we know, from controlled studies of single cell recording in alert and awake monkeys, which particular columns of cells are likely to be involved in the processing of facial material. Similarly in some of the very recent and exciting reports by Galaburda and his colleagues in Boston we are now beginning to tie down certain forms of dyslexia to very small and circumscribed lesions in the brains of people suffering from that disability.

The link between mind and brain can be taken to another level by reminding ourselves of the intimate connection between disordered brain chemistry and behaviour and the activity of the mind. The example that comes readily to mind here is the so-called dopamine hypothesis of the basis of some forms of schizophrenia.

The point of giving these few examples is to indicate the flavour of a massive amount of research in neuroscience and neuropsychology which I believe points increasingly to the tightening link between mind and brain. When something goes wrong with the brain there is a very high probability that using sufficiently sensitive techniques we shall be able to detect abnormalities of mental function. Conversely there is increasing evidence that what is happening in the mind for a sustained period of time will be accompanied by changes in the functioning of the brain; it is certainly not just a one-way relationship. Mind and brain are mysteriously but intimately linked. But what does this all imply?

Some differing interpretations

The accumulating evidence of the ever tightening link between mind and brain does not carry with it a simple and straightforward interpretation of what it all means. Equally distinguished, equally knowledgeable brain scientists take different views on how to interpret the evidence. Sir John Eccles for example, a Nobel Laureate in brain physiology, seems to hold some dualist form of the relation between what he would call the soul and the brain. Another Nobel Laureate, Roger Sperry, already mentioned because of his work on split brains, holds a somewhat different view of the relation between mind and brain. His view seems more of a monist view and yet he emphasises repeatedly that this does not mean that the mind is any less important than the brain. These are for him two crucial and important aspects of the one unity, the mind–brain.

There seems to me to be emerging agreement that some form of *dualism of aspect* is essential to do justice to the accumulating evidence. But disagreement remains whether *dualism of aspect* has to be translated into *dualism of substance.* Here views diverge. My own view would be a monistic view of substance but one that asserts that *both aspects of the one set of events,* namely *the mental aspect and the physical aspect, are equally essential if one is to do full justice to the totality of what one is observing.*

In common with several of my colleagues, I find the computer analogy helpful in trying to make sense of the intimate and mysterious relationship between mind and brain. Thus, if we regard the mind as the software, the programme of our computer, and the brain as hardware, the electronic components, certain things follow which, I believe, help our thinking. It would be patent nonsense to pretend that by giving a full account of the *physical activities* of a computer we were saying anything profound about the *programme* that was running in the computer. Though for the programme to run at all it does depend upon the intactness of the computer. A mathematician solving an equation using the computer would regard it as arrant nonsense to pretend that an account in terms of the physical activity of the computer would say anything of any consequence about *the mathematics of the programme being solved.* In some analogous sense I believe that the mind is to the brain as the software is to the hardware of the computer. We shall return to this later as we reflect upon the biblical picture of man and what it may tell us about, for example, life after physical death.

The Hebrew–Christian picture of man

There are certain key features of what the Bible says about man which we need to keep in mind whilst trying to understand what we are given there.

- It is a timeless view; it has made sense to people long before science ever appeared. It conveyed important truths in pre-scientific times. That should warn us of the dangers of misconstruing biblical terms and endowing them with a precision never intended.

- The Bible's emphasis is primarily on what God has to say about man, not what one man has to say about another man and certainly it is not about one man's view of another man's physical make-up. It is, then, a God-centred view; more concerned with the relationship of God to man than with man to man.

- It is a picture given to help us to live each day to God's glory. It is not given to help construct scientific models of man or design experiments on man.

- The language of the Bible is not the language of any particular contemporary experimental science. It doesn't talk about species but about people; it is not biological but biographical. It isn't concerned with the properties of human beings, whether physiological, biochemical or psychological (in a precise scientific sense), but with the actions of men in history.

- The Bible contains a library of books. A great variety of different words are used to describe man. They amplify and extend the overall picture of man. By using so many different words in so many different ways the whole is enriched, but equally the whole is very difficult to summarise concisely.

The emerging biblical picture

From the opening chapters the Bible holds two themes in delicate balance. On the one hand, there is something very special about man; in some profound sense man is created in the image of God — something said of no other part of creation. At the same time man is firmly reminded of his creatureliness. He is made from the dust of the ground, like the other animals he has 'become a living creature' and to dust he will return. Thus the word 'nephesh' (used *both* of the animals and of man in the early chapters of Genesis) simply means to become physically alive as a tangible material being. Whilst it is frequently translated as 'soul' it is equally often translated as *life* or *creature* or *body* or indeed on one occasion as *dead body*.

The picture that we are given in the Old Testament is of man in some mysterious sense created in God's image, given custody of and lordship over the rest of creation, surrounded completely by God's providential goodness and yet incomprehensively denying God his obedience and rebelling against him. Instead of subduing the creation he failed even to subdue himself. Thus, through disobedience, the divine image was spoiled and man's dominion was largely lost.

As one moves to the New Testament it soon becomes evident that man and his nature there receive a much more extensive and detailed treatment. To put together a coherent synthesis requires a detailed study, not only of differences in the use of the same words by different authors, but also a sensitivity to the different cultures of the readers and in the case of the apostle Paul's letters the partic-ular purposes for writing. Despite all this diversity we can detect one or two salient features about the picture that emerges. First, the New Testament, like the Old, records man as a unity, a psychophysical or psychosomatic unity. He is a unity, both in this present earthly life and in a new form to which he looks forward in the new heavens and the new earth. Second, although man is a unity, nevertheless it is possible to make useful distinctions between different aspects of his functioning, such as the physical and psychological. The New Testament uses terms such as heart, mind, soul, spirit, body, not to identify separate substances but to draw attention to vital aspects of our total make-up. In paying attention to these distinctions we can learn a good deal about our nature.

As we bring together the Old and New Testament pictures what do we find? First we find a message for every generation, not one tied to a passing late twentieth-century psychological model. It tells man what is his calling, his nature and his destiny. He is encouraged to recognise the many-sidedness of his nature. He must hold in delicate balance several aspects of his nature highlighted by Old and New Testament writers alike. First, he must remember his physical make-up: he is of the earth, earthy. Second, he has a capacity for mental life: what he does with that, what he fills it with, where he focuses and directs it, will tell us about his spiritual dimension. Third, he has a capacity for making moral decisions, including an appreciation, by means of his mental faculties, of the spiritual dimension to life. When these different aspects work harmoniously together they enable him to maintain a personal relationship with God and other men.

The relationship with God is given to him and is an enduring one. It continues through the transition of physical death. For the true believer it is a relationship that guarantees an identifiable embodiment in a glorified body, whatever that means. Today we know ourselves and each other through our psychophysical embodiment; in some mysterious yet profound sense we shall, so our Christian hope assures us, continue to know and be known in our new embodiment.

How do we relate the scientific and Christian views of man?

Within science we have long since learned that even to begin to disentangle the incredible complexity of man we need to investigate and analyse him simultaneously at several different levels. We need to look at him at the biophysical level, the biochemical level, the physiological and the psychological, to name but a few. Ultimately none of these levels can be disregarded without missing some salient and important feature of the nature of man. The science of man thus provides us with a spectrum of different accounts, each framed in its own particular categories. The key question is how these different scientific 'spectator' accounts relate to one another and to our personal experience as human beings, as 'actors'.

One could, as some do, take a reductionist approach. If one did that one would say that, at the end of the day, the only acceptable explanation is to be found in terms of physical forces between molecules. That would rule out the possibility of an account given by a physiologist in terms of nerve impulses, or by a psychologist, and certainly any account by a theologian. Whatever these other interested parties would say would, on the reductionist view, be at best a temporary account until a full account is available at the molecular level. Everything else, it would be said, would be superfluous.

My understanding is that this kind of approach, together with its underlying presuppositions, is widely recognised as fallacious by most scientists and philosophers. Philosophers have pointed out that purely physical explanations, in terms of molecules, do not even have any concepts for the functions of the parts being described. To return to our earlier example of the computer solving a mathematical problem, it is possible to describe the computer in terms of molecules, physical motions or electronic components but the mathematician wishes to argue that such accounts cannot convey his understanding of the computer's activity.

The point is that it is possible, in some cases at least, for an explanation to be complete in its own terms, but not thereby to render superfluous or exclude another explanation given at a different level. We have certainly learned within neuroscience and neuropsychology that we need a hierarchy of levels, together with their different categories of explanation, to even begin to do justice to the richness of what we are trying to study. We certainly don't spend our time trying to find gaps in explanations at one level to fit in explanations from another level.

The way to an integrated understanding of man is not to hunt for gaps at any particular level of the scientific picture so that we can fit in other entities. The same applies to the relationship between scientific accounts in general and accounts given in non-scientific terms. We certainly don't look for gaps in the scientific picture so that we can fit in the concept of the soul. It is not even that we translate what is happening at one level to what is happening at another. The two descriptions we might give are neither identical nor independent, they are complementary.

Some have argued in the past that if we could only show that a particular prevailing scientific model of man fits what, at the time, is presumed to be the biblical model then that would give added support to Christian belief as a whole. Whilst the motive behind such thinking is understandable, I think that the endeavour is, for a number of reasons, mistaken. Primarily, it is to misunderstand the nature of scientific models. These are models made by man to make sense of the data available at the time from his empirical studies. By their nature they will change as more data come to light. We refine them, in some cases reject them, and then replace them by new ones. The problem is that, as happened in the past with some people interested in making the Freudian model of man fit the Christian model of man, just when they seem to have succeeded they discover that the great majority of psychologists have now abandoned the Freudian model as essentially flawed and wrong. The question then arises of what now becomes of the Christian model that they have so laboriously made to fit with what they believed was the correct psychological model of man, the Freudian one.

The biblical pictures are not just for one particular age, they embody truths about man which endure. They are as relevant and important in scientific as in pre-scientific times. They make sense of the common experience of life in every age. They talk about good and evil, sin, redemption and eternal life — themes that are essential to the Christian view of man but are totally irrelevant to the building of scientific models of man. To try and fit scientific models of man with Christian pictures of man is to misunderstand what the scientific models are all about and to misunderstand the Bible's concern with what it is telling us about man.

TOWARDS A CHRISTIAN ANTHROPOLOGY

PAUL TOURNIER

LEARNING is not enough to understand man. It only grasps the animal side in him. There are two sources of knowledge: revelation and learning. Through learning man studies himself from outside, as an object. Face to face with God he discovers himself from inside, such as he is, as a responsible subject. 'Outside Jesus Christ we do not know what is either our life, or our death, or God or ourselves' (Pascal).

The story of the creation reveals to us that man is not merely the most perfected animal, and neither is he a fallen angel. It confirms his fundamental unity as a person. Man is the creature God speaks to, who must answer, with whom he has a dialogue. He asks himself questions on the sense of things and events and this marks him out as a religious being. Like God, he needs action and the adventure of creating.

The story of the Fall reveals to us that man previously enjoyed perfect health. He is now mortal as a creature of flesh and blood because of the Fall. But God's image in him is not entirely lost and he still has ideal aspirations which conflict with his sinful impulses. His efforts to save himself from this tragic conflict continue to increase his sufferings. But God comes to his creature's help and grants him prolongation of life. Medicine is God's gift and assures prolongation of man's life in order to enable him to meet Jesus Christ.

Salvation is to be found in the person of Jesus Christ who restores both a perfect relation with God and a perfect relation between men. In this fellowship man experiences God's mercy and however limited these experiences, they are a foretaste of the forthcoming glory.

This truth about man, which we who believe in God gather from the revelation, is valid for all men. All suffer from the consequences of the Fall, all enjoy the benefit of Jesus Christ's sacrifice. So we must try to put this truth into words in such a way as to be easily understood by all men, even by those who do not believe in God.

ICCP Amsterdam, Netherlands, 1963. **Paul Tournier.** *General physician and psychiatrist, Geneva, Switzerland. Author* The doctor's case book in the light of the Bible, *etc.*

ILLNESS AND SIN

BERNARD HARNIK

THE human mind is prone to seek a causal connection between illness and sin. In Antiquity and the Middle Ages the causes of disease were regarded as being in the spiritual arena, although even then there were doctors who were scientific thinkers, e.g. Hippocrates. Only with the Renaissance and the development of science were the causes of illness found to be more immediate.

The doctor who has trained scientifically without any Christian convictions will deny that there is any connection between illness and sin, whereas the theologian without medical training welcomes the idea of a spiritual basis of illness. The problem is not so easily solved, since psychotherapeutic scientists have discovered that there are connections between feelings of guilt and its complexes and the origins of neuroses. Does what is valid for the sick soul apply also to somatic illness? Psychosomatic specialists say: yes. Yet in everyday practice there is very general doubt as to the relation of illness and sin, for the following reasons:

- The connection between objective sin and the subjective feeling of guilt is very complicated. The Bible does not solve this problem because it regards everyone as under sin, whether with or without feelings of guilt. The question whether feelings of guilt proceed from actual or imaginary guilt is a psychological one and not a theological one.
- A patient often regards his illness as expiation and thereby blocks the way to recognition of sin, as is the case with criminals under detention.
- To speak of sin is not as popular today as it was in Biblical times.

In practice it is difficult to penetrate to the deep-set recognition of personal guilt and its relation to illness.

We are still without a scientific explanation of the relation between illness and sin. There is, however, some enlightenment

*ICCP Amsterdam, Netherlands, 1963. **Bernard Harnik.** Psychologist, child and family psychotherapist, Zurich, Switzerland. ICMDA Vice-President 1978–94.*

upon the problem in the Bible. In the Old Testament only a few passages confirm a causal connection between sin and illness. In the New Testament there are even fewer. The majority of these passages point in another direction: illness betokens apocalyptic decay in the kingdom of God, even as do other forms of human distress, and the conquest of illness signifies symbolically the restoration of the divine order and points to the future perfection of Revelation 21:1 ff. Those who effected healing miracles (Jesus, the apostles) showed by this that they were sent by God. Here is to be found the idea of an ultimate sense of relationship between illness and sin.

The task of the Christian doctor consists first of all in being a Christian, that is, in working by the power of the Holy Spirit. To this end he must ever seek the sanctification of his own life so that he may be God's instrument as the counsellor, helper, prophet or priest of his patients. Moreover he must be an active member of a Christian community. His missionary activity among unbelieving patients can only be fruitful as he is led by the Holy Spirit.

What is faith according to the Bible? It is reasoning trust. It is a trust based upon the reasonable revelation of himself that God has given us in his Word and this trust is reasonable because the Person we trust is trustworthy. It is always reasonable to trust the trustworthy and he is trustworthy because of his character and because of his promises. So you see we need to use our mind if we want our faith to grow. I don't know if you know that thought in Psalm 9:10 which says, 'Those who know your name put their trust in you.' In other words they put their trust in you because they know what kind of a God you are. They know that you are trustworthy and because they know they trust. This is faith based on knowledge. If you want to grow in faith, you have got to grow in knowledge and meditate on the character of God and on the promises of God. (See Exodus 34:5-7 to know how God describes himself.)

JOHN STOTT

ICCMS Oxford, UK, 1980. **John Stott.** *Rector Emeritus, All Souls Church, London, UK.*

ETHICAL PRINCIPLES IN CLINICAL RESEARCH

G.A. LINDEBOOM

Introduction

IN dealing with this subject, I presuppose that in clinical research we must not rely solely on our consciences. At the very least we must search for principles to govern our actions whenever we cannot clearly see our duty. The decisions which we have to take in this field often touch upon so many important human values that their ethical implications are of the highest importance. It is not sufficient that we try to be controlled by one main principle — for example, love for humanity, love of scientific truth, or service to Christ. In that way we should soon find ourselves in the position of a 'situational ethic', in which each case has to be considered separately, according to conditions prevailing at the time. This may prove as dangerous for our patients as, in another way, it may be for ourselves.

Looking for guidance

In quiet moments and for any meaningful discussion, we must reflect upon our duty towards the sick people we have to treat in all kinds of circumstances. We must try to find some clear directives to guide our actions. We should not, however, expect to find clearcut rules which, on application, automatically result in an unmistakeable conclusion. Sir Austin Bradford Hill, who is not medically qualified, when discussing the relation of medical ethics and controlled trials, said that in his experience of collaboration with doctors, the problem calls for close and careful consideration *in the specific circumstance of each proposed trial*. Whilst agreeing that it is possible to enunciate some very broad principles which are an intrinsic part of the doctor's training, he did not believe it possible to go very much beyond that, or to reduce the broad principles to precise rules to be applied in all circumstances. A close and careful consideration of each proposed trial in itself suggests a valuable principle.

ICCP Oxford, UK, 1966. **G. A. Lindeboom.** *Professor of internal medicine, Academic Hospital of the Free University, Amsterdam, Netherlands. ICMDA Chairman 1963–69, Vice-President 1975–94.*

Ethical background to clinical research

Medicine itself originally sprang from an ethical source — the impulse and duty to help one's fellow men in sickness and distress. Medicine is thus an ethical duty in relation to humanity as a whole. It is also a duty which may be undertaken with a sense of personal vocation.

Yet, without science, medical practice would remain empirical and as a result, many, perhaps most, patients would remain unhealed, would die, or would be unnecessarily distressed. Medical science aims at and is responsible for expanding the possibilities of successful treatment throughout medical practice. The promotion of scientific and medical advance is a duty for all those who have an opportunity and the intellectual equipment to pursue it. Christians should not praise God for this gift but then leave the difficult and hazardous work of medical science to others. On the contrary, they should feel a sense of divine calling to engage themselves in laborious research tasks, including work on the frontline.

However, as Pascal said: 'Science sans conscience n'est que ruine de l'âme' — science without conscience is mere ruin for the soul. Medical science is essentially a practical and an applied science. It is not an object of study in itself, to be pursued from an ivory tower. Its purpose is to increase the welfare of mankind. To a young research worker it too often seems only an aid to his ardent ambition, through which he can gain recognition and furtherance of an academic career. It is true that few men can reach senior academic office without the driving force of ambition. Ill-concealed ambition is all too human and high idealism may be hard to find. The impulse and motives, however, should be as pure as possible, for the distinctive Christian ethic is primarily concerned with motives.

This means that the Christian research worker should always strive to deepen his self-knowledge, to exercise self-criticism and unselfishness by weighing his motives and accepting the bridle of ethical principles. No medical man is more dangerous for sick people than one who is devoid of self-criticism and all too convinced of his own competence.

Twin goals of research

The clinician, aware of his duty to science, continually keeps before him two aims — the care of his patient and the advance of scientific medical knowledge. This dualism is the cause of both his elation and despair. Time and again he feels handicapped by the one or the other. Either science offers no help to his patient, or the patient's condition does not permit the use of procedures which could have increased knowledge and been useful for others.

At this point, however, let us remind ourselves that burdensome diagnostic procedures or therapeutic trials are not always necessary when contributing to the body of scientific data. They may sometimes even hinder. Patient history-taking, careful and scrupulously accurate observation over a long period and laborious note-taking may sometimes lead to a valuable insight which may be worth sharing, including by publication.

Risks to the patient
How far should a doctor cause the patient to submit to diagnostic examinations, which often leave discomfort, pain and sometimes even a risk to his safety? There are certain clinics in which all patients who come with a particular disease, for example lung cancer, are made to pass through the whole diagnostic mill of bronchography, bronchoscopy, mediastinoscopy, and so on. In this way a complete table of statistics may be obtained. If, from the outset, the case is clearly hopeless and inoperable, then, as a general rule, uncomfortable diagnostic procedures should be omitted. It is possible that in special circumstances, for example in the case of a colleague, a complete examination, although not strictly necessary, may be carried out for psychological reasons. There is no doubt that as a general rule all unnecessary, uncomfortable and exacting procedures should be avoided, even though they might clarify some interesting point. Most procedures carry with them some degree of risk. However small it may be, if it is a risk of mortality, then it is 100% for the patient upon whom it falls.

Therapeutic trials
Often the clinician feels inclined to undertake a therapeutic trial. The outcome may be uncertain and it may even carry a risk of harm. He is undertaking an experiment on a human being. We must not be afraid of that word, for everyday medical practice is full of therapeutic experiments on human beings. The practitioner who does not continually study and does not endeavour to keep himself informed about the progress of science will, after some ten years, degenerate into a dangerous experimenter who is probably

responsible for many more victims than a reckless research worker. In the one case there are sins of omission, in the other sins of commission: which is the more serious?

Therapeutic trials may be confined to a single case in which the patient is suffering from a disease which defies current therapy and the cooperation of a physician is required to evaluate a new drug. The usual practice is to treat one patient, afflicted by a certain disease, with the specific drug to be tested and another patient with a placebo. A series of paired patients becomes a controlled trial conducted in a way which will to some extent meet scientific standards.

It is necessary, however, to consider the question of placebos. Though I cannot say that I have never used them, it cannot be denied that their use implies an element of dishonesty. Only in ailments where there is no risk to life and in which no specific treatment is already recognised would there seem to be little objection. Once the physician is convinced of the value of a new drug in the case of serious illness, he is morally no longer entitled to withhold it from patients, who rest their confidence in him. Similarly, a new drug, whose value is still in doubt, should not be prescribed in cases of an illness for which there already exists a reliable treatment of proven effectiveness.

To many, the double blind trial seems to be the acme of clinical therapeutic trials. There are, however, so many factors which restrict its use that a critical evaluation of its place in medical practice exposes its feet of clay. Moreover, the position of the physician who treats one half of his patients with a placebo, known to be useless, is reduced to the simple experimentation of the research worker. He must feel unhappy in the presence of a patient who is relying upon his personal integrity to be treated as effectively as he can. His self-respect may be seriously undermined. He does not even know to which of his patients he is failing to provide a recognised and possibly effective treatment. The double blind trial essentially undermines the bond of confidence between physician and patient. If the position be accepted, the physician is relieved from something that he ought not to be relieved from — his personal responsibility.

Do ends justify means?

It must be admitted that medicine has sometimes derived invaluable new knowledge from experiments which in themselves were unethical. The inoculation against smallpox of seven imprisoned criminals by Robert Mead may have taken place as a result of an ethical impulse seeking good for others. Jenner's experiments, in which he infected some persons with smallpox after he had previously vaccinated them, secured invaluable evidence. Yet it is open to doubt whether these experiments were, from the individual patient's viewpoint, ethically justified. When unethical clinical experiments make contributions to medical progress, the conscience of the research worker is not thereby exonerated by the fortunate result, even though it may enhance his reputation.

The promotion of medical progress and the desire to help others do not justify unethical conduct. Even though the ultimate aim be praiseworthy, one should have the courage to say 'No'. If both kidneys of an unconscious patient, whose breathing is artificially maintained with a ventilator, were removed for transplantation, many people would feel that a major ethical principle, as well as the doctor–patient relationship, had been violated.

Experiments on the human patient, with the sole aim of acquiring new medical knowledge, are very rarely justified. It may be objected that the consent of the patient has been obtained, but what is this usually worth? Who can explain to a sick person, who has no medical training, the real and complete significance of the experiment, its hazards, its pros and cons? When conflict arises between medical research and the welfare of the individual sick person, research should unhesitatingly give way. An old but still trustworthy dictum states that nothing should be done to a sick person which the investigator would not permit in similar circumstances to be done to himself or to his wife or child.

It may seem that such rigid ethical standards may prove to be a serious handicap to medical research and progress. Yet the smallest deviations of this kind may lead on to greater and more serious ones in the future. One must constantly pause and reflect at every new step. The weighing up of the issues, essential in the ethics of clinical research, is a serious matter for the conscience. It must be undertaken in a sincere spirit and under God's guidance. In seeking to overcome the conflict between the care of the individual patient and the ambition to advance medical knowledge for the good of mankind, the physician should always accept that his primary task is to give personal assistance to those who are, in Christ, his sick brethren. The ultimate issues he may leave to him who rules the world.

THE CHRISTIAN HERITAGE IN MEDICINE

PAUL BRAND

LET us look at our Christian heritage in health and healing at four levels of time.

The first is our *heritage from God in creation.*
The second is our *heritage in the written word of God.*
The third is our *heritage from Christian doctors in the past.*
The last is the *heritage we must pass on to the future.*

Our heritage of health from God in creation

As physicians and dentists we are trained to think about what we can do to heal sick people. When patients recover, we expect them to be grateful to us and perhaps to acknowledge that without our timely help they might have died. The implication is that the doctor is the source of health and healing. It is not very different when a pastor prays for healing. When the patient recovers he likes to assume that it was the prayer which made it happen. We easily forget that recovery follows after most diseases, and that healing is the expected result when there has been a wound. Both medical care and prayer often make a difference, and in some cases either or both may be critical to recovery, but the truth is that all of us have within us a system of healing and health that is better than anything that has ever been devised by science.

The great triumphs of health care today, such as the eradication of smallpox, and the vaccines that save us from polio are mostly due to our finding ways to activate the normal immune system of the body a little early, to give it a start on the invading organisms. We still have never discovered a medicine which will cure either smallpox or polio. We have to depend on the cells and antibodies of the immune system. We still cannot prevent a person bleeding to death from any and every wound if that person lacks the amazing built-in system by which blood clots as soon as a vessel is wounded, but is prevented from clotting while it flows, year after

ICMDA Cancun, Mexico, 1986. **Paul Brand.** *Chief of Public Health Services, Carville, USA. Past director Christian Medical College, Vellore and Karigiri leprosy centre, India. ICMDA President 1986–90, Vice-President 1982–86, 1990–94.*

year, through the blood stream, where a clot might destroy life. If we want to save a hemophiliac from bleeding to death we still have to borrow natural blood from somebody who was born with the complete outfit designed by God for all of us.

Our life and health and our inbuilt equipment for healing are an inheritance from God. We who are Christian physicians and dentists have the special privilege of knowing and serving the author of life, and we should lose no opportunity of acknowledging our servant role.

Here in this congress we celebrate this common faith that unites us with each other, and that identifies us as different from others of the same profession. They also depend upon the same God-given mechanisms of health, but we return to give thanks.

I sometimes wonder about the nature of the *Word of God* in creation. When God said 'Let there be light', who was he talking to? What language was he using? And who or what could understand it and obey the command? When God said, 'Let the earth bring forth grass', who was listening? And what was the form of his command? We can never know these mysteries, but can only speculate that when God talked to the water and the earth he was using the language of physics and chemistry. His words must have been invoking his own laws of gravity and of thermodynamics; of kinetics and wave motion. He locked great forces into the tiny compass of the atom, and ordained that the basic spinning that was set in motion in atoms and in the solar system should continue with precision for all time, so that it could become the basis for stable combinations of elements, producing substances of infinite use and variety.

When it came to the creation of grass and of fish and of all life, however, we have less need to speculate about words and language. In recent years scientists have been able to decipher and read some of the wonderful instructions that control all of life. Watson and Crick did not invent the code of DNA. We give them honor for uncovering it and helping us to begin decoding the orders that are written there. It was God who wrote it. Perhaps he spoke it first, but when written down in the amazing replicating language of life, the alphabet letters of God's Word were not A B C or Alpha Beta Gamma Delta, but were what today we call Adenine, Guanine, Cytosine and Uracil. Human DNA in reality is the word of God which called up the amino acids and used them to build human flesh. The same word remained in every cell and in a literal sense it became flesh in the last days of creation. Instructions for the building and maintenance of every tissue and every organ, including the lymphocytes of the immune system and the nerve cells of the brain were all written down and have been copied by mitosis in every generation until now. When the Word of God became flesh in Jesus Christ, it was the same DNA from Mary his mother which combined with a fresh spiral of instructions from God to make the DNA which orchestrated the growth of the Son of Man who was also the Son of God.

We wonder at the skill with which scientists have manipulated the DNA of bacteria and of tumors and have spliced in fragments of normal DNA so that human insulin and other hormones and enzymes may be made available for men and women who are sick. At the same time we need to be cautious that we do not permit tampering with the authentic words by which God created and now sustains the human race. It is hard to be against efforts to identify and perhaps correct genetic errors that have occurred by accidental mutation long ago, and that have persisted by replication in generations of those who inherit hemophilia or sickle cell anemia.

I earnestly hope that it never becomes practical to introduce changes into basic normal human DNA, but I am afraid. The present eager teams of scientists who are racing with each other to be the first to achieve breakthroughs in this field are motivated less by a sense of wonder and respect for the work of God than by economic rewards and the achievement of personal fame. The companies that are funding research are expecting to patent the enzymes and hormones and other products of transferable segments of DNA. These patents will be enormously lucrative, and it is hard to see how the products will be denied to any who may bid enough money for them. It may be good to make growth hormone available to a child who is a dwarf, but what is to prevent the production of a team of ten-foot-tall players for international basketball championships? Or of whole races of uncomplaining people designed for industrial assembly lines? These nightmares seemed improbable when Aldous Huxley warned us about them in *Brave New World.* They look much closer and more likely today.

Heritage in the written word of God

The second inheritance is that which is our birthright in the written word of God, the Bible. It is there we learn some of the laws and principles of health laid down by God, the Creator, after he had seen his most loved creation begin to destroy itself by rebellion and by sin; followed often by plagues and by sickness and death. When God chose a family and then a nation to bear his name, he gave them laws to live by. Many of these laws were rules of health. In Exodus 15:26, the Lord lays down for Israel a clear connection between a healthy life and obedience to the moral law. As we examine these rules today we see that most of them promote a way of life that would result in peace and justice and health, including concern for the earth and its crops. Disobedience led to exile and ruin for the chosen nation, until at last Jesus Christ came in the flesh to demonstrate an acceptable way to live in a human body, and then to give his own life for us.

It is in the account of the life of Jesus on earth and in the writings of the apostles that we get the clearest understanding of the relationship between the Spirit and the flesh; between the moral law and the laws of health. It is here also that we get the clearest mandate for a close relationship between the work of physical healing and a ministry to the spirit and soul of those who are sick.

In Romans 8 we see God's design for all of us, that the flesh and the spirit should live together in the same body, and that the spirit should be in control. It is not that the flesh is bad of itself, it is only bad if it is out of control. God planned and designed all of the appetites that we often blame for leading us into sin. He invented all the best pleasures. But he never intended that our appetites should be unrestrained. They are good when they are subject to the spirit which is our interface with the Holy Spirit of God. True freedom and joy are inseparable from discipline. It is also clear from the same chapter that faithfulness to God does not ensure freedom from sickness or physical disaster. The chapter closes with an account of some of the sufferings we may expect in our mortal life and exclaims that '*in* all these things we are more than conquerors through him that loved us.' Our Lord saves us *in* all these trials, and *through* them rather than *out* of them.

Thus we should never assume that sickness and disaster in any individual is due to the wrongdoing of that person or that failure to recover is due to his or her lack of faith. We are not to be judges but servants and ministers of God's grace and of all the means of health that we have at our disposal. Part of our responsibility, however, is to teach from God's Word that his laws are also rules of health, and that it is the denial of them that is responsible for many of the problems of ill health that plague the human race. Today in the West the focus of concern in public health has turned from infections to such things as drug abuse, alcoholism, AIDS, tobacco-induced cancer, and other health problems that are directly related to the way we have chosen to live. Some life insurance corporations are offering premiums to members of Christian sects who keep to the strict practice of Biblical laws. *God's word is a heritage of health.* When we treat our patients in a spirit of love we are being a witness to our faith in the God of love who is the author of health.

Our heritage in Christian example and tradition

We now move on to thank God for all his servants down the centuries who have accepted as a privilege the task of ministering in his name to the needs of men and women who are stricken with sickness and the fear of death. First, I think we should pause to remember the fact that for most of these centuries there has been very little that physicians could actually do to heal sickness, although symptoms could sometimes be alleviated.

In my own field of leprosy, I have often recognized how much of my own encouragement to continue my work was based on the feeling that I was able to correct a deformity or cure a disease, and I have thought back to the pioneers who worked through a life-time, patiently dressing progressive ulcerations, unable to relieve the choking stenosis of the larynx, and maintaining courage and cheerfulness whilst one after another were dying around them. Thank God for these servants, and never let us think we have a higher credit rating because we have more powerful tools to work with. On the contrary, let us be alert to the danger that we may rely on our techniques and tools and forget that the hallmark of our profession as Christian physicians and dentists is that we are as much concerned with the person of our patients as with the disease they happen to have.

In the heritage of Christian medicine and dentistry there is no ranking that distinguishes between those who have made scientific advances and those who have served with devotion with little opportunity to break new ground. Nor between those who work in the atmosphere of hope and new life, and those who are called to devote themselves to the care of the terminally ill and the dying. We just need to be thankful that we have examples in abundance of those who have heard the Master's call, and have responded in a spirit of service. I pray that there will be a continuing stream of men and women who will be called of God to enter our professions with the challenge of service to needy human beings, in the Spirit of Christ, to sustain them against the urge to join those who are in it only for money or fame.

The Christian heritage in medicine for the future
Finally we need to think about the heritage that we shall pass on to new generations of Christian physicians and dentists yet to come. It is not enough that we follow in the train of those who have led the way in the past. We need to be led by the same Spirit, but we may need to move in new directions to meet new challenges, or at least we may need to have a changing emphasis.

Changes in priorities
During my first years in India, I wanted nothing so much as to make available in India all the very best of all medical advances that were available to the affluent nations of the West. It took some years for me to realize that there was another side to many of these advances.

Firstly they were often too costly to be within the means either of the sick people in India, or of the charity of donor countries and missions. I am glad that these advanced facilities are still available at Christian medical colleges in India and elsewhere, and that research goes on in frontiers of medicine that may lead to simpler and more fundamental ways to control disease. However, we cannot escape the deeper problem. Any treatment that raises the cost of medical care far above the earning capacity of most people in a country shifts the focus and emphasis away from the poor, and makes basic care more difficult to obtain. As in the West, the need to support the very highest levels of care actually puts simple care further out of reach of the poor. On the other hand Christian physicians have been at the forefront of movements in India and Africa to bring very simple medical care and prevention to the village, using local helpers who have minimal education and accepting the absence of most facilities on which most physicians have become dependent. By these means millions of people who had no medical care are now able to have advice and help within their means.

The second change in priorities that I have noted in my own thinking has taken me even further back in the sequence of causation of disease. It is not enough to recognize that where the poor live they are subject to infection and lack of primary health care. We must recognize that in many parts of the world it is *becoming impossible to obtain the basic nourishment* on which all health finally depends. Doctors who work in rural areas and in slums are waging a losing war unless they are able to help their patients to have access to water and to food. It may be good to send airlifted food supplies to areas of acute famine, but it is far better to undertake campaigns to halt soil erosion, to plant trees, and to encourage the use of land for production of good food for local consumption by the family rather than for the cash crops demanded by money-oriented economy. I am not really suggesting that physicians and dentists should exchange their syringe and scalpel for a spade and plow. But I am saying, with all the emphasis I can muster, that great changes for the better have almost always been spearheaded by those who, having seen and felt a great need, then involve themselves passionately in the advocacy of reform.

In years to come far more people will die of starvation and of diseases related to malnutrition than from any lack of drugs or surgical operations. Our responsibility is not only to work for better use of soil and water, but also to encourage the planning of families, and to bring more urgency into programs for the limitation of population growth. (Lest the North Americans among us feel that concerns about soil erosion and loss of farmland are only for countries of the third world, let me just comment that the highly mechanized and energy-dependent farming methods in the USA are resulting in greater loss of soil than has ever been known before. Pressures for fast financial gain are taking precedence over concern for the future.)

The third area of health concern which is new, and which affects the heritage we pass on for the future is related to *the spread of poisons in land and sea.* This menace to health in America and in Europe is growing faster than we realize. Modern manufacturing produces many toxic by-products of a nature that we have not known before. Toxic chemicals used as pesticides in farming run off into streams and rivers. Nuclear wastes and poisons which remain active for thousands of years lie in corroding barrels all over our land. Many of them leak and then the contents get carried into deep aquifers and ground water supplies.

The WHO has been worried about bacterial contamination of water, resulting in dysentery and cholera. The contamination that I am talking about is far more dangerous than that. Old fashioned contamination could be handled by filtration or simply by boiling a pot of water. It became safe. The new contamination is not healed by boiling or filtration or chlorination. It does not give warning by its appearance or by a bad smell. Its effects may not be noticed until many spontaneous abortions occur or babies are born deformed or when the rate of cancer rises in the population.

Responsibilities of Christians in health care

There is a reason why it is especially appropriate that an organization of Christian physicians and dentists should take strong initiatives to insist on urgent action to control these poisons. It is that most of these new threats to health are directly the result of a breakdown of public morality and of corporate and individual sin. It is easy to be angry at companies that make fast money by the illegal dumping of poisons. It is not so easy to admit that we, as members of a western society, have come to live by a money ethic which says that nothing can be bad if it pays good dividends and if it increases the Gross National Product. We have accepted the rule of management by objectives, where the objective is wealth, so that anything that promotes wealth is seen as good. Our society is dominated by greed. All our advertising tells us that we deserve more and more of whatever we desire. It matters not if our wealth comes at the cost of poisoning the water our children must drink, or of the killing by acid rain of the forests which our grandchildren will never be able to enjoy. We want more and we want it *now*.

In the same way that Christian doctors have come forward to bring basic medical care to the poor, and to help in the provision of a protected water supply for them, so in the face of multiplying nuclear weapons and other new and terrible threats to the health of the world, we need to be in the forefront of those who will stand up and cry 'Halt!'

There are two things that need to be done. The first is to use our influence to *clamp down on the spread of poisons,* and to clean up the threatening dumps. Let us not minimize the influence of a Christian physician. Every politician has his own doctor, and every administrator his dentist. We speak as experts in the field of health, and we must not be silent.

The second thing is to *state the conviction that we do not need and will not support the extravagant and opulent way of life* which is at the root of the high demand and therefore the root of its waste products.

The massive accumulation of waste products is due to a massive increase in manufacturing. Companies manufacture things because people buy them. People buy things that they do not need largely because they see others setting a 'higher' standard of living. Doctors tend to come high on the list, so that when a physician deliberately adopts a simple lifestyle, it will quickly be noticed. That will give him or her a wonderful opportunity to talk about the evil side of overconsumption of goods and also about the joys of deliberate simplicity of lifestyles. It opens the way for us to explain how true health stems from the harmony of body, mind and spirit, and that this becomes possible when the Spirit of God controls our lives. As Christian physicians and dentists we need to be concerned at least as much with the way we represent Christ in our personal lives as we do in our professional practice.

Finally, we need this reminder, that the *real heritage of Christian doctors and dentists is Christ himself.* With all the changes in knowledge and in methods of practice, with the changes in disease patterns and dangers to humanity, the one unchangeable reality that must define our life and profession is the life of Christ within each one of us, controlling and inspiring all that we do. We are members of each other. Our head is Christ. Our patients hear the words we speak, but more than that, they perceive our *body language* — the language that must tell them that we are part of the body of Christ. We must be constantly responsive to our Head, who makes us sensitive to each other, to our families and to our patients, as well as to the issues of today. Let us renew our commitment now, so that the world may see our love, and believe in our Lord.

WHAT OF THE FUTURE?

GARETH JONES

Introduction

IT is not my intention in this paper to debate whether scientific advance in general, or medical advance in particular, has been of value. I accept that it has and that the numerous revolutionary changes brought about by it have, on the whole, served human welfare. As such, they have been blessings from God. Yet scientific and medical advances are capable of destroying as well as benefiting human aspirations. Therefore, in order to serve human welfare, they require direction and are to be subject to wise control. Herein lie a myriad pitfalls, and herein lies the crucial significance of an ethical perspective.

A theological perspective

Evangelical Christians look to the Bible for direction on ethical matters but we delude ourselves if we expect the biblical writers to provide precise guidance on a host of scientific issues raised by medical advances. What we do find are broad principles. Of these, the one that stands out as crucial is the central theological truth that human beings are made in the image and likeness of God. This implies that as God looks on human beings, he recognises that human creatures are icons of himself, since in them God finds his own perfections mirrored back to himself. Consequently, when we see another human being we see another creature who delights God by mirroring him. This principle has within it a number of themes which, in turn, have profound repercussions.

The first theme. Like God, we are *capable of understanding.* Therefore, the more we understand, the more like him we become. A capacity for understanding is the pivotal mark of human existence, and all humans have something of this capacity, either actual or potential (with the exception perhaps of those with

ICMDA Seoul, Korea, 1990. **Gareth Jones.** *Professor of anatomy and structural biology, University of Otago, New Zealand.*

extremely severe brain damage). It is this longing for understanding that is the mainspring of science, human culture, artistic and other endeavour. In essence, these are not the marks of arrogance, but of the outworking of our God-likeness. In these terms, modern medicine is both to be welcomed and whole-heartedly forwarded by Christians.

The second theme. This follows on from the first, and is that of *control*. God has placed humans in control of themselves and their world, which in turn is control of God's world. The opposite of human control is not, as some think, divine control but anarchy and chaos. In the health sphere this signifies uncontrolled pain, rampant disease, and premature death.

The third theme. This is the theme of responsibility, incorporating *responsibility* for other human beings, for human welfare in general, and for all facets of the environment. Responsibility is essential if the control bestowed upon human beings is to be harnessed to good ends. Such responsibility is not because humans are acting as autonomous human beings against God, but is an integral part of our creation in the likeness of God. To 'be human' is to act responsibly, take decisions, be creative and seek new solutions to old problems.

The fourth theme. This is that of our *dependence upon each other* within the human community. As we are confronted by other human beings we are in the presence of those who, being icons of God, make claims on us. We are dependent upon them, and they are dependent upon us, because of our likeness to each other, and our mutual likeness to God. Human beings therefore have obligations towards each other which stem from our joint mirror-ing of God.

The fifth theme. This theme is a negative one, and it is that *human beings misuse their many abilities.* Although human beings are capable of understanding, control and exercising responsibility, they are prone to debase their understanding, to exercise control selfishly, and to act irresponsibly. This tendency lies at the heart of many of our problems. It gives rise to strife, enmity, and the domination of one individual or group by another. It leads to selfish excesses, inequality, and injustice. But it also stirs a response in those who fear the abuse of human power and wish to restrict it. Although humans cannot live with unrestricted freedom, neither is their freedom to be curtailed unnecessarily.

The sixth theme. This is that our likeness to God has *implications for our understanding of suffering.* God's suffering and human suffering are inextricably linked. The suffering of a human being means that one of God's icons is being hurt. In a sense, therefore, God is himself violated when a human being is injured or destroyed. Similarly, when one human being injures another human being, God himself is wounded, and illness and injustice bring sorrow to God. The relief of illness and the pursuit of justice are important means of helping us to assuage God's suffering, as well as relieving human suffering.

These six themes, emanating from the central theological teaching that humans are fashioned in the image of God, point to the power and control entrusted to human beings by God. They justify, in broad terms, the approaches of modern medicine and contemporary biomedical research which thus legitimately come within the range of human initiative and creativity. Such control can be used to good effect; it can also go abysmally wrong. Finite creatures make mistakes; rebellious creatures sometimes put arrogance ahead of the service of others. There are also genuine ethical conundrums where it is far from clear which course of action is the most appropriate. The ethical difficulties in modern medicine have to be approached within a framework of human responsibility and service, advancing human welfare and upholding human relationships, and always asking what is pleasing to God.

Placing medical technology in perspective

Many perceive the power of medical technology to be fearsome and frightening. The popular media reacts to medical developments with a mixture of awe and terror, congratulation and condemnation, viewing medical scientists as gods but — if anything goes wrong — as devils. The theological perspective I have just developed helps in a number of ways at this point.

In the first place, it *imparts meaning to human existence.* For instance, it helps us to appreciate the meaning and even the role of suffering and death, since it places them within the overarching perspective of our relation to God and his relation to us. It helps us to see them within a world brought into being by a purposeful and personal God. Its major contribution is to provide reasons why human beings are important and why, as a principle, they are to be valued and treated with the utmost respect. This is the context within which medical technology is to be approached.

In the second place, *limits have to be placed on scientific technique.* A theological perspective questions the value of science for its own sake. Science is a gift from God, essential to the well-being of society and of individuals within society. Danger looms when technology itself tends to become more important than the human beings it was designed to serve. Consequently, constant vigilance is required.

A third consideration is that a theological perspective throws light on the *power and control engendered by biomedical technology.* Choices have to be made, often in realms where choices were previously not required. These include choices between the patients to be treated or not treated, and sometimes the choices are invidious. Who has the 'right' to make them? Does the making of these choices imply that human beings are arrogant and are seeking a degree of control that rightfully belongs only to God?

Such questions stem from the fundamental premise that once a scientific understanding of the cause of something (including disease processes) has been discovered, this leads to power over that cause. Power can be wielded for human good or it can lead to human degradation. This is where the choices made become so crucial. Without understanding, there is no power and without power, no choices have to be made. Medical technology, powerful as it is, fails to provide any clues — let alone guidelines — as to how control might best be exercised.

This is the realm of biomedical ethics. The theological perspective I have mapped suggests that such control is legitimate if, in learning to exercise it, we seek to do so in cooperation with God. We have been given responsibility for other human beings, and it is in this onerous responsibility that we begin to experience what the freedom of being human actually entails. This is a deeply Christian emphasis, since it brings us face to face with sin, failure, self-centredness and errors of judgement, but also with forgiveness, grace, mercy, and love.

An illustration

In Western medicine the power of medical technology is no better demonstrated than in approaches to infertility. The advent of the new reproductive technologies (NRT) has brought into prominence techniques revolving around, and stemming from, *in vitro* fertilisation. These raise numerous specific ethical issues, as well as a far more basic one, namely the right to reproduce. How should this be approached in the light of the abilities of medical science and also the perspective to which I have alluded?

The right to reproduce stems from a basic ethical principle, namely the freedom and autonomy of human persons, according to which people should be free to make voluntary choices based on certain generally accepted principles and values. In the reproductive area, this leads to couples being free to act in accordance with the desire to have children and create a family. This desire is generally regarded both as a natural expression of sexual and generative urges and as an outworking of basic commitments to religious and family values (including specific Christian ones). Looked at in this way the right to reproduce is a *liberty right,* since its only demand is that others refrain from interfering. As such it is a straightforward and relatively non-controversial claim by couples wishing to exercise this right and have children of their own. This fits in with Christian perceptions, with the proviso that couples be married.

In the case of infertile couples, however, the situation is less clear-cut. This is because, to bear children, they need the assistance of others. If they are to get such assistance they have to exercise a second right, a *welfare right.* To varying extents, infertile couples make claims on the expertise, services and actions of others within society, as well as on technology, some of which may be sophisticated and expensive. Under these circumstances the right to reproduce becomes less clear, since the resources required by the infertile to reproduce may come into conflict with the resources required by others in the health-care sector, let alone in other areas of society altogether. As the technology available to circumvent infertility becomes more sophisticated the competition for limited funds becomes more severe. The right to reproduce as a simple liberty right becomes tempered by the need to depend on welfare assistance.

In terms of the theological perspective I have developed, I would argue that since infertility appears to be a medical and social problem of some significance, individuals from all economic backgrounds should have access to the reproductive technologies available. To deny them such access is to perpetuate injustice within society, since the infertile community is being discriminated against. Far too often, however, the question of injustice is avoided by suggesting that infertility is not a medical problem and therefore almost by definition any technological approaches to circumventing it fall into the luxury category. I would suggest that this is an appalling confusion of categories, that ignores completely the needs of the infertile as those whose completeness as male and female in marriage is seriously hampered. Indeed, the relevance to infertile couples of reproductive technology is best appreciated by reference to all six theological themes outlined previously.

Unfortunately, even when this confusion is recognised, there are no ethical grounds for arguing that unlimited resources are to be made available to provide children for the infertile. Their right to reproduce is limited by numerous factors within any particular society, ranging from health-related priorities through to theological and social ones. They include the acceptance or otherwise of artificial means of procreation, including the use of donor gametes from a third party; the degree to which infertility is seen to fall within the medical domain and therefore a legitimate recipient of health budget expenditure; and the extent to which resources are directed towards treatment utilising the NRTs. Each one of these factors needs to be assessed alongside the needs of infertile couples as icons of God. If this is not done, subordinate issues will be elevated above the benefits that might be bestowed by medical technology upon human beings in need of wholeness and fulfilment.

In ethical terms one important proviso has to be made. This is that the right to procreate on the part of an infertile couple must not compromise the freedom or moral interests of a third party. This proviso ensures that no third party is placed under duress to donate gametes or embryos or, in the case of health professionals, to participate in any procedure against their own value systems. It also ensures that no third party is exploited, for instance in commercial surrogate arrangements.

Another third party of concern to many people is the embryo. This third party inevitably differs from the others, since it is unable to consent to any procedures to which it is subjected. Hence, it is far more difficult to decide what its moral interests may be. It does not have value systems or freedom. How should such a third party's interests be weighed against the interests of a particular infertile couple now undergoing treatment, or against the interests of future infertile couples when considering the use of embryos in research?

The reason for using this particular illustration is that the benefits of advances in the medical sciences are so obviously ambiguous. Unfortunately, this has led to polarised responses, both of which tend to overlook the human needs of those involved — the infertile couples, any resulting children, and sometimes the donors of gametes or surrogates. My aim has been to demonstrate that the theological perspective I have sketched seems to place emphasis on a different aspect of the debate from the usual one (which in this example tends to focus either on human embryos or on infertile couples, to the exclusion of all the other participants).

Complexity of medical science

Medicine is no longer a simple area. Those in medicine cannot delude themselves that they are 'doing good', as though it were simply a matter of pressing a button marked 'good'. The complexities of ethical decision-making in medicine, as well as the complexities of the motives and goals of individuals within medicine, are basic to what modern medicine is all about. This has implications not only for ethical decision-making, but also for the Christian presence within medicine.

Christians, as those who have been redeemed and made new in Christ, are to represent him in all specialities within medicine, as well as in research areas in the basic medical sciences. Sometimes the more difficult the area, the more important that Christians be there. There are dangers, and the particularly dangerous areas are not for everyone. Moreover, whoever we are, we are never to go forward in our own strength. Yet if none of us is there, the reconciling and redeeming message of Christ will be neither heard nor lived out in crucial spheres within medicine.

An afterword

Everything I have said has been in general terms, and probably has been relatively non-controversial. My aim has been to show the relevance of theological principles for any Christian approach to medical and biomedical developments. However, as I ponder on the thinking and attitudes of many evangelical Christians to such developments, I am forced to conclude that some of these are far removed from the type of approach I have been advocating. The reason, I believe, is that we frequently seek simplistic and ideological solutions to the issues confronting us. It appears that we want answers that have immediacy and a compelling ring to them. Why do I say this, since it may be a harsh and very unfair conclusion to reach?

As I read books published by evangelical publishing houses, it is difficult to avoid the conclusion that evangelical Christianity in most of our countries is associated with well-defined stances. In the medical domain, these can be resolved into opposition to abortion, opposition to euthanasia, opposition to the use of human foetal tissue for therapeutic or experimental purposes and opposition to genetic engineering. Some go further and express their opposition to all forms of reproductive technology, perhaps even to any form of artificial contraception and in some specialties to medical technology itself. These are essentially negative stances, even though they may on occasion be phrased more positively than I have done. What is crucial, however, is that these stances (and others like them in non-medical areas) are all well defined, are rigidly circumscribed, and often allow no exceptions.

I wish to challenge these stances by suggesting that, at best, they have limited biblical warrant and at worst they fail to plumb the depths of an authentic Christian response. I admit this is a severe judgement and I do not have the time to work it out. What I do want to do, however, is to approach this matter from a different angle by asking whether, if we continue with these stances, we will be able to make any major contribution to the future direction of medicine. At present, we find ourselves at a crucial crossroads. We will become, or continue to be, a pietistic group with exemplary motives, high ethical standards, and concern for the spiritual welfare of individuals, but unable to influence medicine in a secular society. Alternatively, we are capable of becoming a group that will make a major contribution to framing the future directions of medical practice. The size of such a contribution, however, will depend on a number of factors and our response to these will be crucial. What are these factors?

Scrupulous honesty. We must determine to be scrupulously honest in our use of data, both biblical data and scientific data. I have considerable concern at this point. It is all too easy to use biblical data very selectively, utilising those data that support a position we hold on other grounds. Not one of us is immune from criticism at this point, when dealing with contentious medical issues. It is essential that we avoid giving the impression that the ethical position we adopt is, without further discussion, based solely on the Bible and is the only position any faithful biblical Christian can hold. This is very rarely, if ever, the case when confronted by the many specific ethical issues implicit within modern medicine. Almost without exception, honesty leads to differences of opinion within the body of Christ, as it does within medical circles. I would suggest that honesty is far more important (and also healthier) than conformity for its own sake.

Serious ethical analysis. It follows that we must be committed to serious ethical analysis. We may feel contented that we have expressed total opposition to euthanasia, or that we have advocated the saving of every individual human life regardless of the psychological and spiritual trauma involved, or of the financial costs. However well-meaning such positions may be, they almost invariably ignore detailed ethical analysis and hence are ill-equipped to deal with difficult cases. Serious ethical analysis should be viewed as an essential adjunct to biblical insights and to the leading of the Holy Spirit. They are two sides of the same coin, and our witness as Christians is diminished if either side is neglected or downgraded.

Consistency in ethical stance. We must be determined to be whole people in Christ, and this implies that our ethical stance is as consistent as possible across all areas of medicine and also of life in general. It is simply inadequate to respect human life in one area, but pay little attention to it in other areas. This is the way of one-issue pressure groups, but it should not be the way of those who have been redeemed in every aspect of their lives by Jesus Christ. I would argue that we have no option but to be holistic in our ethics as well as in our life-styles. However, once we accept this principle, it has dramatic repercussions for the way in which we approach ethical issues.

Diversity of responses. We must be willing to accept that there will be a diversity of responses within the body of Christ. There is no one 'correct' or 'orthodox' Christian response to most of the issues raised by the development of medical technology. I would expect agreement on broad principles by those within the body of Christ, but the specific outworking of many of these principles may, quite legitimately, vary. From this, I would suggest that we are to be known by our loyalty to Christ, rather than by some form of superficial conformity on selected ethical questions. That oneness in Christ should, in its turn, allow us to discuss productively those issues on which we disagree. In this way, we should build each other up as fellow Christians.

Vigorous interaction with others. We must be ready to interact vigorously, and even dangerously, with the thought-forms and attitudes of those within secular society. If Christianity is to influence secular society, it has to enter the debating chamber of biomedical ethics. It is not sufficient to be confrontational, always objecting to the directions society is taking. While there may be some place for this, it is more important that we act as salt and light to that society, seeking to influence its course by means of informed debate.

Those are my points. Inevitably, they have some important implications. The first is that we are to put aside all forms of 'easy answerism'. Under no circumstances are we to manipulate Scripture for our own ends, even if these ends are commendable ones. Neither are we to escape into some pietistic corner, from which we can hurl our darts at those around us. Integration into secular society, with the requisite separation from its ethos, is both difficult and dangerous. Yet this is precisely what Jesus Christ called us to. We are to be thoroughly immersed in the world as Christian doctors, dentists and research workers, and yet we are not to be enticed by its philosophies. However, if we are even to begin to do this, we have to cast aside the illusion that there are simple, cut and dried answers to all the ethical issues that confront us.

Finally, it follows from what I have said that we are under an obligation to work hard at knowing where we stand on medical ethical issues and why we stand where we do. It is exceedingly misleading to use labels that caricature our own position, as well as the positions of others. Labels such as pro-life, charismatic and creationist are generally interpreted in highly arbitrary ways, and even in sub-biblical ways. They serve to divide one Christian from another, rather than to unite the diversity of believers making up the body of Christ. All such labels should be anathema to us, since they tend to detract from the centrality of Christ. They may also be destructive when equated with that which is orthodox Christianity.

We are different in Christ. Our approaches to many medical dilemmas will vary, and yet the glory of what we are in Christ is that we recognise him as the focus of our faith, of our medical practice, of our professional lives and of every relationship we establish. It is from here that we should launch out to tackle all the dilemmas and possibilities that will inevitably confront us as medical technology continues to expand and diversify.

Christian ethics and Oriental culture. In order to meet the require-ments of life together, human beings must not only maintain their own individual life but also the lives of others. This requires that human beings share, care, and love each other according to the will of God. Christian ethics supports this meaning and tries to make it practical and active. It also requires a concern not simply for the prolongation of life but also for the meaning of life, in which life together, or collective life, is made possible.

YONG MAENG

ICMDA Seoul, Korea, 1990. **Yong G. Maeng.** *Dean, Presbyterian Theological Seminary, Seoul, Korea.*

THE CHANGED LIFE IN CHRIST

PABLO MARTINEZ

THE theme of the conference is foundation for change and we are experiencing all kinds of change. We start by considering 2 Corinthians 5:17. 'Therefore, if anyone is in Christ, he is a new creation; the old has gone, the new has come.' It is very important to notice that the verse starts with a condition, 'if'. There is a condition for change because change does not happen as a result of chance.

THE CONDITION FOR CHANGE: TO BE IN CHRIST

I remember a young woman who came to my office and told me, 'I want to go to the furthest point on the earth, where nobody knows me, where I can start again and afresh with new relationships.' She even said 'I wish I could have another name. I hate my name and I want to start again.'

Change is not a result of moving to another country or changing jobs or starting a new relationship or a new marriage or getting divorced or separated. If we really want a deep change the requirement is much deeper. This is the reason why Paul starts this paragraph with the word 'if'. There is a prerequisite for change, there is a condition. The condition clearly stated is, 'to be in Christ'.

Now what do we mean by this? What does it mean to be in Christ? Notice that the preposition is 'in', and this conveys the idea of location. The idea is that it is possible for the personal relationship between Christ and the believer to reach such a degree of complete intimacy, that Paul describes it as 'Christ dwelling in my heart through faith' (Eph. 3:17). This is a very important statement because it means that Christ in person, in some mystical sense that we cannot begin to understand, dwells within us. The British preacher Spurgeon said, 'It is a reciprocal indwelling'. The believer is in Christ and Christ is in the believer.

*ICMDA European Congress, Balatonoliga, Hungary, 1996. **Pablo Martinez.** Clinical psychiatrist, church elder, Barcelona. Chairman of UME Spain.*

Therefore we have to move from the objective reality that Christ is for us, which is truth, to the subjective reality that Christ is within us. We move from truth, Christ died for me, to experience, Christ is within me. This is a very important step. I come from a country that has been traditionally Christian, in this case Roman Catholic, for many centuries. Many people in Spain would call themselves Christians but perhaps we should add another word. They are 'cultural Christians'. They believe that they are Christians because they have some objective truth in their mind that makes their God to be an idea or an intellectual abstraction. This brings forth intellectual Christianity and cultural Christians who are against abortion, or euthanasia, etc, but this has nothing to do with the condition that Paul is mentioning here. To be in Christ means moving from the mere objective reality to the subjective experience.

Martyn Lloyd-Jones, the British preacher, in reference to this verse said: 'It is Christ dwelling within the believer, not as an influence, not as a memory, not merely through his teaching, not merely through the Holy Spirit; it is Christ himself dwelling within me in a mystical relationship.' The Lord Jesus Christ is in heaven but he is also in me. This is why in Galatians 2:20 Paul says '... I no longer live, but Christ lives in me.' So this is the prerequisite, the first condition, that we move from a cold objective reality of God as an idea to a deep subjective experience of Christ within us. We all need to become mystics in the right sense of the word. We should long for that kind of mysticism which means experiencing Christ as a reality in our hearts. This is the foundation for change. There is no real or lasting change, no profound change, apart from being 'in Christ'. So we must want to be Christians having Christ dwelling in our hearts.

THE RESULTS OF CHANGE

Being in Christ has three consequences that we can clearly deduce from the verse, 'If anyone is in Christ he is a new creation'. In more academic terms we would say this is the ontological result of the gospel. This is actually the deepest aspect of our transformation and the change that Christ works within. It starts with *being* a new being.

The new nature

This is indeed a change but so profound and so absolute that Jesus himself calls it to be born again or having to be re-created. How impressive it is to hear the testimony of people whose lives have been changed by the transforming power of Christ. The book *Born Again* by Chuck Colson, the former aide to President Nixon and one of the participants in the Watergate affair, is a most impressive account of how Christ can transform the being and the nature through re-creation. It is very important that we understand that change starts with being, not with the doing or even with the behaving, but with the being. If we start our Christian change just with doing we will either become legalists, which was very much criticised by Jesus, or we will become humanists, which is acting, doing or behaving for man's sake.

Christian life starts with a new character, but what do we mean by a new character? I am not thinking of this primarily in the psychological sense. The Holy Spirit does not change our temperament, nor the inborn features of our personality, nor our genetic code. We have to be very careful to understand this promise, 'If anyone is in Christ all things are made new', because understood wrongly it can be very misleading. The fact that the Holy Spirit gives us a new character does not mean that the introvert will become an extrovert. There are certain aspects in our personality, especially those connected with our temperament, that will not change. Christ and the Holy Spirit act in such ways that they mould and transform us but they do not change the basic patterns in our character.

Let us consider the apostle Peter, for example. Before Pentecost, Peter was a very choleric and quick-tempered person and cut off the ear of a soldier. Peter after Pentecost continued to have essentially the same temperament, an activist and always at the forefront, but as far as we know he didn't cut off any more ears! He behaved in a controlled manner and was moulded and disciplined in his temperamental features by the Holy Spirit. So there is some kind of change which is possible concerning our psychological make-up, even though we don't mean a new character primarily in the psychological sense.

What do we mean by changing character? Basically we mean a moral character. What is a moral character? A way of being like the character of Christ. It is exactly what Paul expresses in Galatians 5.

A moral character is someone whose attitudes, thoughts and reactions are permeated by love, joy, peace, patience and self control, etc. So this is the first result of Christ dwelling in our hearts, a new character that starts with the being and not with the doing.

Deliverance from the burden of the past

'The old things passed away'. In other words, God heals our past; old things are passed away. In this process of re-creation God firstly gives us a new character, but secondly he wants to stop all our waste of energy in complaining, struggling, remembering and crying about our past.

Many people live tortured lives, crippled by their past. They spend quite a lot of energy struggling against their past regrets, mistakes, decisions and steps. Because of my profession I see many patients coming from broken or abusing families. They often tell me, 'I wish I had another family', 'my father was an alcoholic', 'my parents were divorced', etc. Others have taken the wrong job or career, married the wrong person, or perhaps had some sinful experience with guilt attached, guilt related to the body being one of the areas where guilt is probably most intense. The new life in Christ unburdens all these problems because it gives us a new perspective. God restores our past in that he forgets our past. We as human beings cannot forget because we have a psychological feature called memory, but God forgets and if God forgets then this is therapeutic and healing.

Let's turn to Isaiah 43:18. These are God's words to the people of Israel so we have the right to apply them to ourselves. 'Forget the former things; do not dwell on the past. See, I am doing a new thing! Now it springs up; do you not perceive it?' God restores our past because he forgets it, and stimulates us to look forwards to the future and not backwards. In faith–life, the future is always the best. This is a concept that we find time and time again in both the Old and New Testaments. We as Christians are called to look not so much at our past but to the future which is always the best.

God's instruments of healing. In practical terms God has several tools or instruments to heal our past. Let's look at three of them.

Firstly, *forgiveness.* God forgives our past. This cleansing experience has a great therapeutic power both emotionally and spiritually. Feeling forgiven is one of the most refreshing experiences we can have as human beings. Secondly, God has to restore our past is *making sense of it*. God is provident. Do you know what this means? *Pro video* is Latin for seeing and watching from above. He gives meaning to our past, illustrated by the life of Joseph. Joseph had a very painful past life. He lost his mother at the age of seven, he was hated by his brothers, spoiled by his father's upbringing, exiled, tortured, spent thirteen years in prison and so on; what a miserable existence from a human viewpoint. Yet we find these words, 'Joseph said to them "Don't be afraid. Am I in the place of God? You intended to harm me, but God intended it for good ..." ' (Gen. 50:19–20). God intended Joseph's past for good, as he had a purpose to accomplish through it. There isn't a single event in our lives which escapes God's providence. I would like to say that God uses us, not so much in spite of our past but through our past.

The third tool that God uses to heal our past is that *he relieves pain*. He gives us rest. Therefore he gives us firstly forgiveness, secondly meaning and thirdly rest from the painful experiences. '... Come to me all you who are burdened and heavy laden and I will give you rest' (Mat. 11:28).

It is not so much that we will forget the painful past events because, as we have said, we have memory. If you want to completely forget then that is impossible. Wounds are transformed into scars, and there is a big difference between a wound and a scar. A wound is painful, can bleed and become infected whereas a scar is closed and if you touch it then it is not painful any more. God uses us through our past and also heals its wounds.

All things are made new

The new nature or being that we receive in the first place is like a window opening onto a landscape that is totally new for us. One window closes and a new one opens. All things are transformed and re-created and here we are experiencing the therapeutic power of the gospel, offering us new purposes and perspectives.

I am a psychiatrist and work in the area of mental health and I can assure you that the famous quotation by Jung, when he said, 'I have never seen any neurotic case that at the bottom line is not existential or religious', was totally right. Very, very often anxiety, depression, loneliness or guilt have an existential basis where the therapeutic power of the Gospel can be extremely healing and changing; Christ himself heals us.

How therefore can we view our relationship with Christ? There are two possibilities. You can be a cultural Christian and know all the truths about Christ objectively, or a healthy mystic (not all mystics were neurotic), Christ dwelling in you. If you really experience in Christ this reciprocal indwelling, then you will get a new moral character and your temperament will be moulded. You will find your past experiences relieved and given meaning, and you'll find a door to a new landscape in life and a new identity with new relationships.

❖

Failing to recognise a child's needs. Medical minds may revert to face-value judgement by assuming that whatever is there to do must be done. Even in the care of fragile, severely handicapped infants, the temptation is to subject the child to all possible medical and surgical advances even when this is not going to improve function and even though the process itself alienates the child from the family. Ideally, of course, we would like to restore every child to normal, but if in the attempt we are merely prolonging either misery or dying, we need to take stock and sometimes to change direction. Palliative care, in the context of family relationships, may take priority over the struggle to satisfy ourselves professionally. Palliative and terminal care may, even for babies, take place at home . . .

It could equally be someone's distorted view that such a child was 'not worth treating'. We must beware of inactivity as well as over-enthusiastic treatment, if by inactivity is meant total lack of care. There is never a time when there is nothing more to be done, but caring, understanding support and symptomatic relief all enhance the lives of the child and the family . . .

Amidst all our care for the physical and emotional needs of children, we can still fail to help their spiritual needs. . . . The only relationship which will last for ever is that with the Lord, their Saviour.

JANET GOODALL

ICMDA Cancun, Mexico, 1986. **Janet Goodall.** *Consultant paediatrician, Stoke-on-Trent, UK.*

❖

Section 4

Christian Practice

---------------------------------- ❋ ----------------------------------

Integrating Christian faith into
medical practice

THIRST FOR GOD

PABLO MARTINEZ

WE are going to read all of Psalm 63, which is a parallel passage to Psalm 42.

> 'O God, you are my God, earnestly I seek you; my soul thirsts for you, my body longs for you, in a dry and weary land where there is no water. I have seen you in the sanctuary and beheld your power and your glory. Because your love is better than life, my lips will glorify you. I will praise you as long as I live, and in your name I will lift up my hands. My soul will be satisfied as with the richest of foods; with singing lips my mouth will praise you. On my bed I remember you through the watches of the night. Because you are my help, I sing in the shadow of your wings. My soul clings to you; your right hand upholds me. They who seek my life will be destroyed, they will go down to the depths of the earth. They will be given over to the sword and become food for jackals. But the king will rejoice in God. All who swear by God's name will praise him, while the mouths of liars will be silenced.'

Introduction

Some words of introduction are needed before we expound the psalm in more detail. Before the Fall of humans, the relationship with God was perfect. God and man, man and God had a relationship of harmony, there was peace and balance. That is exactly the same kind of relationship we will have in Revelation 21 when we have a new heaven and new earth and God himself will be with us again in the full restoration of this relationship. In the meantime man is in conflict with God. Using the terminology of Psalm 42, our *thirst* for God has been distorted and repressed. I would like to summarise the main attitudes that man has towards God in three main areas.

Sometimes man hides from God. This attitude of hiding from God is seen as early as that amazing, deep and historical question,

ICMDA European Congress, Balatonoliga, Hungary, 1996. **Pablo Martinez.** *Clinical psychiatrist, church elder, Barcelona. Chairman of UME Spain.*

'Where are you?' (Gen. 3:9–10). This is a question that God still asks man. When Adam and Eve were asked where they were, they replied that they had to hide. They were hiding from God and escaping from faith. All the mechanisms that have to do with escapism, in very subtle ways, repress or distort our thirst for God.

Then, man does not want anything to do with God. We don't like God, we want to be free, let's not think of God, let's forget God who is a disturbance to our lives.

A third possible attitude, seen throughout history, is taming God. Making a god in our own image and according to our needs; in other words a self-made religion and a pocket God. Many people these days use pocket gods, a god that they have created. In this sense psychoanalysis was totally right in blaming people for inventing God instead of the other way round, God creating us. This is the attitude we find in Romans 1:21–23.

So many people today find themselves in one of these three attitudes. Yet when we are in Christ a great change happens in our relationship with God. Described in terms of thirst, when we are in Christ we have recovered our thirst for God.

I would like to consider three main points in this Psalm 42. Firstly, we find the thirst for God explained and described. Secondly, we find the thirst for God tested. Finally we will see the thirst for God recovered again.

The thirst for God explained

'As the deer pants for streams of water, so my soul pants for you, O God. My soul thirsts for God, for the living God.' There are three features in this description of our thirst for God according to the psalmist. Firstly, when we recover our new relationship with God *it is an intense relationship.* It is so intense that it is described as thirst. '... Earnestly I seek you; my soul thirsts for you, my body longs for you ...' (Ps. 63:1). Most of us here are medical doctors. Could you tell me one of the worst ways of dying? When you are really thirsty and are about to become completely dehydrated it is a very intense and painful experience.

The second feature concerning the thirst for God is that *it is very deep.* It comes out of the depth of our soul. In other words our desire for God is like that yearning that lovers feel for each other when they say 'I miss you'. There is a very interesting Spanish word (actually it is Catalan) *morena,* which is exactly the same word as homesickness and it means 'little death'. In other words you die a little when you are not with your lover. It comes from the depths of our souls and is deeply intimate. I was very surprised to hear the best expert in psychosis (delusions) in the whole country (he is not a Christian) say, 'It is interesting to realise that the subject that occurs time and time again in schizophrenic patients when they are suffering from delusions is God.' This is regardless of their previous religious faith and this happens to agnostics, atheists or Christians. Why is this so? Because God is very much in the depths of our soul and he comes out when we do not repress him.

The thirst for God is *intense, deep* and thirdly *unselfish.* Our thirst for God according to the psalmist should be centred on the lover, on God himself. Did you notice what the psalmist is searching after? It is not God's blessings, but God's presence, the very presence of the loved one, 'that I may dwell in the house of the Lord all the days of my life …' (Ps. 27:4). I want to contemplate him. The psalmist does not approach God in order to get things from him. This is selfish and natural religion. Many people approach God to get and get and get. The psalmist's thirst for God is motivated by love and therefore he wants God's presence, that is enough. He does not say that his soul thirsts for God's blessings and gifts. This is childish and immature religiosity. Our first concern is to seek after God's very presence.

How do people approach God today who are not Christians? A cultural Christian I know told me the following experience. 'I believed in God, in a God over there who is a creator, an all powerful God. But then my wife got leukaemia and I started praying that my wife could recover but she did not and she died. Therefore from that moment on I stopped believing in God.' I asked him why he stopped, and his sharp and quick reply was 'A God that does not give me what I want is useless; I don't want that God.'

There are three main idols in our society; the first is *individualism,* me first and then me and me still. Man has always been selfish but today we have a particularly individualistic society: 'If it's good for me it's good, if it's not good for me then it's bad'. This influences us and also our churches. How often do we approach God as in the beautiful hymn, 'O Lord, teach me thy way'? Here we find the essence and foundation of our relationship with God. Very often we approach God in the completely opposite way saying, 'Give me what I want'.

The thirst for God tested

Especially in verses 5–7 things apparently did not go very well for the psalmist. He had great faith, his thirst for God was all right, he was a mature Christian, he loved God earnestly and yet we find him in the midst of deep depression, turmoil and anxiety. Our thirst for God, even when it is mature and God-centred, does not exclude hard times, such as the valley of the shadow of death (Ps. 23:4). Sometimes it will bring forth struggle and tension, and, according to the teaching in the Bible, both things go together.

It is interesting to note that the word *faith* in Hebrew comes from a similar word which means tension. Faith always contains an element of tension, such as tension between our past state and our future state. We are not yet what we would like to be. Faith is a constant tension and in Christianity we cannot expect to feel better and better every day. Of course this does not exclude joy, because peace and joy are much more than feelings, but faith implies tension.

Again, another one of the great idols of our society is *hedonism.* What is the main purpose in life? To feel better and well! In fact, in some Christian circles it appears that the goal of Christianity is to feel good and be happy. If the purpose of Christianity was for us to feel good then is it not strange that straight after Jesus said, 'My peace I give unto you', he said, 'It is not like the world's peace. In the world you will have trials and tribulations' (John 14:27; 16:33).

Many people today want to experience hedonism not only in the sense of having pleasure (probably the most well known form) but also as the more subtle less known form, which is to avoid suffering at all costs. This attitude is a direct result of our hedonistic society. We are to enjoy everything that God gives us and not be bitter, gloomy Christians with long faces. Yet in another sense we have to struggle with the other aspect of hedonism which says that effort and suffering are stupid.

'Why are you downcast, O my soul? Why so disturbed within me …?' Faith is not a great vaccination that gives us permanent immunity to any emotional problem, tension or difficulty. I want to emphasise this because some Christians think that faith will give them an immunity to suffering, depression or anxiety in life. The psalmist experiences mature thirst for God and yet, together with this, has suffering. Freedom from difficult times will only happen when Revelation 21 is fulfilled.

The aim in Christian life is not to eliminate stress but to become more and more like Jesus; not to feel better every day but to be moulded into Christ's character every day. Remember that God uses us not so much in spite of our past but through it. We can also say that God uses us not so much in spite of our dark periods in life but through them.

The thirst for God recovered and stimulated again

First let us recall that God cannot just be someone outside cultural Christians but someone inside. We cannot tame God or have a pocket God, but there is a great third idol in our society, hyper-tolerance, *permissiveness*, mega-freedom. I would like to give a quote from Chesterton, the Christian thinker, in his book *George Bernard Shaw.* 'You may talk of God as a metaphor or a mystification. You may water him down with gallons of long words or boil him to the racks of metaphysics and nobody protests but as soon as you speak of God as a fact or a thing like a tiger, as a reason for changing your conduct or behaviour, then the modern world will stop you.' The attitude that I can do what I want is also influencing our churches very much. Why is it that we have such a crisis in ethics, for example in bioethics? I think the reason is that the idols of our society are influencing our churches very much.

Renewing thirst

We have three tools with which to stimulate the thirst for God. They are very simple. I have no modern recipes; my recipes are very, very old. The first tool is *to love and have real passion for God's commandments and God's Word.* 'How I love your Word, your commandments'; this sentence is repeated fifty-one times in the psalms.

I have a figure from a survey carried out in England in 1995. Of those who go to church regularly 43% never read the Bible. I am sorry to give a reference like this from a country I admire very much, but I am sure in Spain it would be much worse. This is something serious and for that reason the Bible Society in the UK is going to produce the Bible on tape, because at least if people don't read they can listen. The Bible is becoming boring and when the

Bible becomes boring to you or to a church then you have the embryo for stagnation and eventually the death of that church. The Word of God should be central. Where are we supposed to find the time to read the Bible? Recover the passion for the Word of God and read it with zeal.

The second secret for restoring a thirst for God is *prayer.* Speak directly with God. Bonner, one of the great Christians in Great Britain in the eighteenth century, said: 'By the grace of God and the power of the Holy Spirit I wish to establish the rule in my life of speaking to no man before I have spoken to God, of not reading any newspaper before I have been on my knees, of not doing anything with my hands before I have read some part of the Scriptures.' We need to recover this.

We indeed need to be stimulated by the Word of God, passion for prayer, but we must also *long to be with the people of God,* that is the church. We cannot pretend that we love Christ if we do not love the people of Christ. Again be careful with individualism. Let's enjoy that precious gift of Christian fellowship.

Christ changes our lives and the first thing he changes is our relationship with God. We are in the process of going back to Genesis 1 or forward to Revelation 21 with our thirst for God. In the meantime may God help us to be mature Christians and to use the tools he gives us — his Word, prayer and fellowship to restore our thirst for him.

FREEDOM PROMISED BUT DENIED

JOHN WHITE

DEFINING FREEDOM

FREEDOM is something which is easier to feel than to describe, but our feelings are not reliable guides as to whether we are free or not: they are not to be trusted. Sometimes when we feel free or think we are free we are deceiving ourselves; one example of this is the alcoholic. Scripture speaks of freedom by comparing it with slavery. For instance, in the Old Testament the contrast is made with the Israelites, 'You were slaves, you were in bondage in Egypt but now God has made you free', so they understood freedom by the contrast to the slavery which they had previously experienced.

In the New Testament sometimes Jesus, or sometimes Scripture, speaks of freedom in a paradox. We are told, for instance, that slavery to God is freedom. This would seem incomprehensible but as we submit our will to goodness and kindness we discover in fact that this slavery leads us to freedom. Jesus, addressing the Jews, expressed freedom in a riddle. 'If the Son shall make you free you will be free indeed' (John 8:36). Perhaps he was picking up the talk about political freedom, and often people think that when they are freed from the tyranny (military and political) of a power, then they will automatically be free. But Jesus spoke of freedom which was independent, which political oppression could not take away, and which political freedom could not give.

So what do we usually mean when we talk about freedom? We have many ways of expressing it. Let us take for instance intellectual freedom and its opposite intellectual suicide, or intellectual slavery or bondage. By intellectual slavery, I suppose we would mean that which prevents us from thinking freely, that which prevents us from exploring ideas with our minds, because suddenly we see stop-signs saying it is dangerous to think that. We may consider it dangerous because we are not used to such

ICCMS Oxford, UK, 1980. **John White**. *Associate professor of psychiatry, University of Manitoba, Canada.*

freedom or because people around us might suspect that we are thinking this way and come down on us.

Freedom as a feeling

Another expression from the past is 'free love'. People talked a great deal about it 60 years ago. By free love they meant neither something *free* nor something *loving*, but the freedom to lust after whomever one chose, whenever one chose, and in whatever form one chose. This was not only not love, it was not freedom because when we lust in this way, we slowly come into bondage as slaves to our own bodies and our own passions.

I find that when people talk about political freedom they not only define it differently (have different things in the back of their minds) but also have different ways to get at it. If I speak with the wealthy and powerful, either in the West or in the East — whether under capitalism or communism, it is all the same — the rich and powerful feel that freedom consists of keeping things exactly as they are because that is good for those who are wealthy and powerful and will ultimately prove to be good for everybody else. If I speak with the poor and the oppressed I find that they feel that freedom will consist of changing things because we are enslaved by our poverty, by our impotence, by our diseases, our hunger, by our lack of education. When they are thinking like that, neither the wealthy and the powerful nor the poor and the oppressed understand what freedom really is. Nevertheless, I believe that God listens to the cry of the poor much more than the specious musings of the rich and powerful.

When we were in school and now when we are studying, we experience some kind of freedom at the end of a year or a term because we no longer have to study. Suddenly we say we are free (we feel free) and then we may become bored. Freedom can be thought of in terms of experience and I would define it as, 'that experience of being able to do those things we most want to do and were not formerly free to do without becoming enslaved by them'.

Freedom in design and purpose

Freedom can be thought of as being free to do what we were designed or made to do. Fish, I suppose, by this definition, are most free when they are swimming in the ocean. We will not make them more free by taking them out of the ocean. Birds, similarly, are to be free when they are flying, when they are making nests, when they are migrating, when they are busy day and night, when they are dodging their enemies.

We might take the point of view that perhaps birds are not free at all. They are in bondage to instincts and to stimuli. They are forced to fly from north to south, or from south to north because of changing weather conditions, they have no freedom in the matter. They are driven to seek for food for their young, their lives are torn by ragged anxieties and fears. Perhaps it would be better to set them free from all this toil and fear and put them in a cage and give them a salary in bird-seed. But if we think in terms of design it would appear that birds were designed to fly, and to fly great distances, and to have little computer brains which can navigate by all sorts of forms of navigation, so, perhaps, there is something to be said for the idea that we are most free when we are doing with all our might what we are designed to do.

Normally we think of freedom in terms of the absolute removal of restraints, but of course this is in fact impossible. There are always restraints of some kind. Applying the idea that freedom may have something to do with design and purpose, it becomes helpful when we think of human beings designed to serve, glorify, to know, love and to enjoy God and to do all these things forever. That, as far as I can see from Scripture, means freedom and is the highest kind of freedom for a human being.

Let us turn again to sexual freedom and look at one or two passages of Scripture. In 1 Corinthians 6:9 Paul talks about forms of sexual gratification. He links them with swindling and stealing and being greedy and other things and, having discussed them, he says in verse 12, quoting the argument of somebody else, 'I am free to do anything, but not everything is for my good.' No doubt I am free to do anything in the sense that it is possible to do these things that he has been talking about, but I for one will not let anything make free with me. Instantly we see this idea that to be free to do one thing may be enslavement to do another and to put something else in control of me. 'Food is for the belly and the belly for the food', you say. True, and one day God will put an end to both so ultimate freedom is not to be found in gratification of our bodies. It is not true that the body is designed for lust, it is designed for the Lord, to know him, to serve him and to enjoy him forever.

Then again in verse 15: 'Do you not know that your bodies are limbs and organs of Christ? Shall I take from Christ his bodily parts and make them over to a harlot?' Again, the idea of purpose comes in here. We were designed to be part of the body of Christ and we function most freely when we are functioning as members of his body. We are doing something inconsistent with our design when we get involved with forms of sexual immorality. The argument that Paul is using against sexual immorality has to do with the nature of freedom. So often when people think they are being sexually free, they discover in the long run that they are facing not only sexual boredom but sexual slavery. So Paul says 'Shun fornication' in verse 18, by which he meant general sexual immorality. Every other sin that a man can commit is outside the body but the fornicator sins against his own body, meaning that he goes against that for which his or her body was designed. We were not designed to fornicate. This is emphasised in the last two verses of chapter 6, and again it is talking in terms of purpose: 'Do you not know that your body is a shrine of the indwelling Holy Spirit and the Spirit is God's gift to you? You do not belong to yourselves; you were bought with a price. Then honour God in your body.' We were designed to belong to, to honour, and to glorify God and we are freest when we are doing these things.

One other brief comment on sexual freedom and liberty comes in 1 Corinthians 7:35. Having discussed marriage and singleness Paul remarks, 'In saying this, I have no wish to keep you on a tight rein [that is, I am not trying to remove your freedom; he is very anxious to convince the Corinthians of this]. I am thinking simply of your own good, and of your own freedom to wait upon the Lord without distraction.'

Finally, he talks about Christian freedom and the well-being of others. Sometimes our freedom means somebody else's slavery. 'I am a free man and I own no master but I have made myself every man's servant to win over as many as possible to freedom' (1 Cor. 9:19). So, in making himself the slave of everybody, and in not using the freedom he has, we find if we read further that he has in fact made himself more free, and he has also introduced others to freedom.

THE NATURE OF PLEASURE
Let us now consider pleasure, which for many comes with drugs, sex, money and all these kinds of things. Some people get pleasure

from prestige, some from material wealth, some from power, others pursue sensual or intellectual pleasures. In my student days I was most helped by something that C.S. Lewis says in his book *The Screwtape Letters* (a series of letters allegedly written by a senior demon Screwtape to a junior demon Wormwood, instructing the junior demon in how to go about tempting a particular Christian). In the ninth letter to his nephew Wormwood, Screwtape says, 'Never forget that, when we are dealing with any pleasure in its healthy and normal and satisfying form, we are in a sense on the enemy's ground' (the "enemy" being God, of course). 'I know we have won many a soul through pleasure but all the same, it is His invention not ours. He made the pleasures. Our research so far has not enabled us to produce one. All we can do is to encourage the humans to take the pleasures which our enemy has produced at times, or in ways, or in degrees which He has forbidden. Hence we always try to work away from the natural condition of any pleasure' (notice this) *'to that which is least natural.* An ever increasing craving for an ever diminishing pleasure is the formula. To get a man's soul and give him nothing in return, that is what really gladdens our father's heart.'

There are — and Lewis is getting at this — two equal and opposite errors about pleasure. One is that pleasure is the supreme life and that the good in life consists of pleasure, and the other is that pleasure is essentially evil. Let's think for the moment about pleasure being the supreme good. In North America and Britain we see a magazine called *Playboy.* I comment on it not because of its pornographic nature — there are lots and lots of pornographic magazines in many languages — but because it has a superficial philosophy of eroticism. The philosophy is, pleasure is good so let's have as much of it as we can; if something is pleasant, let's have more. Pleasure is made for man and man for pleasure. But this is a self-defeating approach to pleasure and leads in fact to boredom.

People who think that they are chasing pleasure, sexual pleasure or any other kind of pleasure, often end up chasing not pleasure but things like novelty, and excitement and stimulation, which are not quite the same, though they may be associated with pleasure. There is psychological evidence for instance that if we pursue pleasure along the line of stimulation, we will need more and more stimulation to get the same amount of pleasure. This gets back to C.S. Lewis and Screwtape and the real enemy's aim being to give us less and less for more and more. If we think of pleasure as scratching an itch, the enemy wants us to do more and more scratching for less and less relief. If we are pursuing pleasure in this way, we find we want more and more novelty and, as Lewis said, we go from the normal to the bizarre. In sexual terms, we may be going from normal sexual relations within marriage to sexual relations before or outside marriage, or to bizarre forms of sexual behaviour — oro-genital, homosexual and the like.

This might lead us to suppose that pleasure is essentially evil but lest we fall into the opposite error, let us remind ourselves that the Lord God takes pleasure in his people. If God does that, then it must be good. The Lord finds delight in his people. He has no need of us, yet he finds delight in us. In Psalm 16:11, we read 'Thou wilt show me the path of life; in thy presence is fullness of joy, at thy right hand are pleasures for evermore.' It would seem, then, that not only is pleasure good but a lot of it is good.

MARRIAGE

Let me now take marriage to illustrate certain pleasure principles. What are the pleasures of marriage? Well, the pleasures of marriage have to do with mutual support and companionship and shared joys and shared secrets. There are sexual delights but they do not figure nearly so prominently as many today would make out. There are also the joys of children, of watching them grow, of enjoying them. But the pleasures of marriage are not the most important pleasures in life. If they were so, the supreme good in life would be to be married and the supreme tragedy in life would be to remain single and this is not true.

As we look at marriage, we discover that these pleasures are part of a greater whole. The whole includes responsibility, mutual faithfulness (sexual and in other ways) and mutual love. By love we are not now talking about romantic love but *'agape'* love (the love of the New Testament), where I consider the good of the other and serve the other and am patient and kind to the other person. The context of marriage also includes a lot of hard work. I have noticed that those couples, whether they are Christian or not, who seem to be rich in the pleasures of marriage exercise responsibility, mutual fidelity and love in this sense, and hard work.

EATING AND DRINKING

Similarly, in eating and drinking, both are necessary for our survival, but God has made pleasures of them. The pleasure is keenest when we are hungry, that is when we most need to eat, or thirsty, when we most need to drink. Cooking is an art which adds to the pleasure of eating and drinking. But the real danger comes when the pleasures of eating and drinking become ends in themselves and we live to eat rather than we eat to live. When eating and drinking become idols then we pursue the pleasure of them as ends in themselves.

So in this way pleasure is remarkably like freedom. It has some of those very same qualities — that when you pursue it you become enslaved to it and you do not find it.

Now let me throw in here a very good principle to guide you in your Christian life about pleasure. It is found in 1 Timothy 4:1 and is a sort of check on whether we have a right attitude to a given pleasure. 'The Spirit says expressly that in aftertimes some will desert from the faith and give their minds to subversive doctrines inspired by devils, through the specious falsehoods of men whose own conscience is branded with the devil's sign. They forbid marriage and inculcate abstinence of certain foods' (that is they deny pleasure) 'though God created them to be enjoyed with thanksgiving by believers who have inward knowledge of the truth. For everything that God created is good, and nothing is to be rejected' (and mark this) *'when it is taken with thanksgiving,* since it is hallowed by God's own word and by prayer.' In my personal Christian experience, giving thanks for something is a check on whether I am properly and legitimately enjoying it.

With regard to one's personal decision in relation to alcohol there are three factors to consider. First, is there any risk of my becoming enslaved to it? Secondly, what are the standards in my church and the group of Christians with whom I associate? The third factor is, 'What are the evils of alcohol in modern society?' Here we think about the yearly increase in alcohol consumption and in alcohol addiction throughout the West, and, as a consequence, the yearly increase in fatal road accidents, in divorces, murders and petty crimes.

Let us not become enslaved to our freedom.

THE CHRISTIAN PHYSICIAN AND CONTEMPORARY CRISES:

A keynote address

STANLEY BROWNE

WE come together from the ends of the earth, as Christian physicians, to deliberate upon some of the world's crises as they affect us and our patients and the community in which we serve, and we eagerly grasp the opportunity to discuss the relevance of a living Christian faith to the crises of today.

We cannot opt out of the world and its needs, to spend long hours in impractical contemplation, wistfully recalling the past or unrealistically pipe-dreaming the future. We are here to work and pray; to listen to others, and to God; we are here to submit ourselves to God our Maker, and then to apply ourselves to the contemporary crises that burden our society. If 'God has spoken', if he has broadcast any 'sure word' that is even now to be picked up, understood and acted upon, then it behoves us Christian physicians to tune in, to listen and to heed.

It is not presumptuousness or self-assertive arrogance that suggests that Christian physicians have something positive to assert. It is rather that, as ambassadors for Christ, we can humbly dare to claim that we actually represent, in this world of time and sense, the Creator God, that we have access to the divine oracles of his revealed will, and that we have a duty to bring the problems of our day to the touchstone of the spiritual, the eternal, the infinite. That is the starting-point, the datum line of our thinking and discussing. With humility, we look outside man and his environment — regarded by some as a closed and self-sufficient system; we see man and his needs in the context of an external moral standard; 'man does not live by bread alone'. We dare to assert that any attempt at solution of present-day problems that ignores God and the non-material component, is a partial solution that carries within itself the certainty of ultimate failure.

ICCP Toronto, Canada, 1972. **Stanley G. Browne.** *WHO adviser on leprosy. Director Leprosy Study Centre, London, UK. Past director Leprosy Research Unit, Uzuokoli, Nigeria. ICMDA Chairman 1972–75, President 1982–86.*

This congress, then, will provide opportunities for bringing the Christian mind, the scientifically trained and medically alert mind, to bear on the problems. Here in Toronto, as was so in Amsterdam, Oxford and Oslo, Christian physicians are meeting in an international atmosphere, and representing widely differing local and national backgrounds, yet all are in some way and to some degree facing the crises of modern man, crises of drugs and disease, of personal and professional ethical standards, of medical care in a society that is fast becoming depersonalised and computerised; of threatening divisions of race, ideology and material standards; of frustrations and fears unparalleled in the world's history. We sense the menace of global nuclear holocaust, and extinction — frightening prospects, science fiction becoming fact. We hear on all sides of poverty, population explosion, pollution, and we are confronted with crises of belief. What is man? Why are we here? Is there a beneficent — or malevolent — Being behind it all?

In the course of the next few days, we shall be studying selected areas of ethical confrontation and conflict, and I shall not now presume to prejudge the issues or anticipate the findings. I would here insist upon our duty as Christian physicians to think and act in our triple capacity:

- as scientifically trained professional practitioners of the healing arts who are personally and intimately concerned with the impact of the assumptions and mores of modern society on our medical work;
- as Christians who are part of a wider fellowship of faith that links religion with ethics and beliefs with morality;
- as citizens who have obligations to the society they serve and the larger community they influence.

These three overlapping and interacting functions generate their own inherent tensions for the individual physician, from the intensely personal physician–patient encounter, through his membership of team and guild, to his duty to the larger world. As members of a 'minority movement' — admittedly small, but by no means without significance — we recognise that our standards and our stand may sometimes provoke opposition and hostility; our fidelity to the Gospel may be misunderstood and misinterpreted; and our adhesion to certain codes of conduct may provoke charges of backward-looking obscurantism. It may well be that our intelligent and intelligible advocacy of the moral basis and context of our work as physicians may provide a much needed salutary and stable corrective to the loose talking and short-sighted action current in the profession today. If we have something important and relevant to communicate, then for God's sake — and I say it reverently — let us proclaim it with forthrightness and conviction. Far too often, the citadel of truth is captured while its guardians are fussily busy defending indefensible outposts long since abandoned.

Certain areas of acute crisis today force themselves on the attention of the Christian physician. These crises may seem at first sight to be of medical concern, but they have a considerable non-medical component — ethical, social, economic and political. They are symptomatic of the uncertainties and instabilities of a rootless society, and illustrate the plight of man without God, bewildered and groping after materialistic solutions to his essentially spiritual problems.

Medical ethics continues to be the occasion of discussion and debate. The Hippocratic oath is being examined and modernised in the light of the changing context of medical practice. This is all to the good.

Widespread concern is expressed at the possibilities opened up by the application in unethical ways of the newer knowledge, and the awful responsibility devolving upon the physician who is subject to pressures of many kinds. There are dangers of knowing what should not be known, and in discovering procedures that we are morally incapable of utilising aright.

Genetic engineering and manipulation and organ transplantation provide other areas of concern, in which research is opening up vistas of breathtaking potential for good and ill. In view of the probability that before long techniques will be available for programming cells with synthesised information, we should now be entering a caveat to the genetic tamperers who are, like us all, completely ignorant of the long-term consequences of such manipulation — physical, moral and ethical. This is not to put a damper on man's insatiable scientific curiosity, but rather to rein-troduce the apposite words of the sage of old: 'The fear of the Lord is the beginning of wisdom.'

A related area of concern — not yet a contemporary crisis, but likely to become one any day in many countries — is what is euphemistically and erroneously called *'euthanasia'*. All Christian physicians will utilise to the best of their ability drugs and other analgesic agents to relieve pain and distress, especially in terminal care. But, as currently understood, euthanasia includes some positive medical act that will tend to shorten life.

Further contemporary crises are concerned with the *control of conception* by drugs and devices. There are mounting pressures to persuade practising physicians to undertake *abortion* on purely social grounds.

Who would deny that *drugs and drug abuse* constitute a most important feature of the contemporary scene? Is it nothing to you, all ye comfortable Christian physicians? Have ye nothing to say and to do, in face of this traffic in death and degradation?

Has the Christian physician nothing to say to redress the investigational and ethical balance in all this, to insist on the moral utilisation of resources and skills, and to link life here with life hereafter?

We shall, I hope, eschew the temptation of thinking only within the framework of westernised society. In this shrinking world of international medicine and a shared faith in God through Christ, we must think globally and across denominational frontiers. We must grapple not only with the problems posed by the overfed and over-doctored and over-privileged communities, but also with the plight of those in the undernourished and under-doctored areas that make up two-thirds of our one world. They have their problems too — medical and spiritual, economic and moral. Their populations are increasing relatively faster than those of the Western world; their share of the world's medical services and facilities is actually diminishing; their problems of endemic disease and sheer human suffering — accentuated by war and political disturbance — are multiplying. And, while we give reluctant aid with one hand, on the other we entice and grab the medical graduates their countries need so desperately, and set them to work in our expensively equipped laboratories and clinics. Our selfish search for ever-rising standards of living for ourselves and our compatriots can only be pursued at the cost of economic pauperisation of others. Is this right?

The tremendous converging portents of population pressures, widespread pollution, the squandering of exhaustible fossil fuels and metals and water, the mounting economic and ideological tensions — all make for a sobering setting for our congress. You can't have medical ethics in a vacuum, or in the short-sighted materialism of the humanist. Nor can you have moral permissiveness and promiscuity without the risk of venereal disease and unwanted pregnancies and broken homes, and the rest. It is culpably naive, as well as grossly unscientific, to overlook the moral factor in our contemporary crises.

Our duty is clear; we have had diagnosticians aplenty, analysts and gloomy prognosticators without number. 'It is not knowledge that we chiefly need' — it is wisdom, 'all God's gifts to use aright'. Merely conferring together will make minimal impact on the contemporary crises we shall be considering. Mountains of reports, avalanches of resolutions and floods of high-sounding phrases will not put the world right. We must act!

Christian physicians do not presume that their faith excuses them from hard thinking and co-operative working. Nor does it supply them with sets of ready-made blueprints for righting the wrongs and redressing the ills of mankind. But it does provide the insights and the inspiration, the vision and the motivation, that are essential prerequisites to overcoming the contemporary crises. The larger dangers that now imperil the world and its inhabitants demand a religious solution, and not mere philosophical platitudes. No newfangled 'ecological morality' or refurbished humanism will suffice. We need renewal, not renovation.

This, then, is the challenge facing the Christian physician, confronted by the crises of personal faith, of slumping standards, of new knowledge: it must loom menacingly on his mental horizons as he looks out on a needy world. The challenge to put God back into his world, and to bring to the touchstone of the Christian faith the problems of our day, should constitute a rallying call to all of us here. It should bring us together, in unity and action, linking the individualistic with the more socially orientated, each learning from the other. It combines the God of the Old Testament — ethical, communal, national, cosmic — with the God of our Lord Jesus Christ — personal, compassionate, redeeming. It links a glowing personal faith to a community concern. It is worship and work, church and society, Bible based and community embracing. It looks up to God for forgiveness and strength; it looks out to men in service and help. Activated by a faith that has deep historical roots, and impelled by an acute awareness of today's predicament, the Christian physicians here will, I trust, in the next few days address themselves to the contemporary crises with conviction, courage and prayer. Who is sufficient for these things? Our deliberate and resounding answer must be, 'Our sufficiency is of God.'

May God be with us in all our deliberations.

❊

Euthanasia — a modern killing? A doctor has a dual responsibility, namely to preserve life and to relieve suffering. Medicine must always be practised with the recognition that ultimately all patients will die. Thus, to claim that a doctor must preserve life 'at all costs' is untenable. At the natural end of a person's life the overriding medical responsibility is to relieve suffering, not to prolong the patient's distress by 'meddlesome' interventions.

Euthanasia can be defined as a deliberate and specific death acceleration in a patient with an incurable progressive disease in order to relieve otherwise intractable suffering. This must be distinguished from 'letting nature take its course' in a patient whose life is naturally coming to an end, and the use of morphine and/or sedative drugs to relieve suffering in terminally ill patients, even though the use of such drugs may, as a secondary effect, shorten the length of survival.

The fundamental argument in favour of euthanasia is 'the patient's right to self-determination'. The fundamental argument against euthanasia is that patient autonomy does not extend to a right to physician-assisted suicide/euthanasia. These two viewpoints ('man as master' v 'man as steward') are not reconcilable.

This means that debate conducted at this level generally leads nowhere. In practice, it is necessary to argue mainly on pragmatic grounds. What makes a person request euthanasia? Can these factors be overcome? Much support for euthanasia stems from fear of an agonising death or a medically prolonged dying — often based on past family experience. Palliative/hospice care has clearly had a major impact in reducing the perceived need for euthanasia but cannot be regarded as a total answer to the 'self-determinist'. It is necessary, therefore, to accept that the argument will never be completely won either in the debating chamber or at the bedside. Pro-euthanasia voices will remain a feature of all secular societies.

ROBERT TWYCROSS

ICMDA Stavanger, Norway, 1994. **Robert Twycross.** *Consultant physician in terminal care, Sir Michael Sobell House, Oxford, UK.*

❊

PRIORITIES FOR CHRISTIAN PHYSICIANS

PAUL BRAND

Introduction

THE establishment of priorities, goals and objectives for a programme, for a mission, for an organisation, for an institution, for life, has become a very popular thing these days, and everybody's doing it. You have a little meeting, and you decide — 'Why do we exist, what are we here for, what are our objectives, what are our goals, how should we change, and how should we be able to accomplish that change?'

THE NUMBERS GAME

Everybody, no matter what they are doing or making, begins with quantifiable objectives. If they are making bicycles they would say that their objective for next year is to make 25% more bicycles, and we shall do that by making the tyres faster, or the wheels faster, or something of that sort. And the extraordinary thing is that when this 'management by objective' method is tried, it is successful. It may not have achieved absolutely the objectives, but always it is surprisingly effective in improving the thing which you are targeted at. If you really aim at a certain objective and put all your resources into accomplishing that thing, then it's much easier to do it.

But the most important things for us to achieve in our own lives are not easy to quantify, while others may be. If you're engaged in making shoes for the handicapped, it may be possible to say that 'I have an objective that this year we're going to make 12% more shoes than we made last year.' That's OK, so long as you don't drop the quality too at the same time. But it is harder to say that 'this coming year I will be 12% more sympathetic than I was last year, and that I will be 10% kinder to my daughter, and I will reduce by 15% the number of times that I am rude to the nurses!' The trouble is that these unquantifiable things, concerned with

ICCMS Bangalore, India, 1983. **Paul Brand.** *Chief of Public Health Services, Carville, USA. Past director Christian Medical College, Vellore and Karigiri leprosy centre, India. ICMDA President 1986–90, Vice-President 1982–86, 1990–94.*

character, with the spiritual qualities, mental qualities, the attitudes to our work and of our lives, not only are they not quantifiable, but they tend to get bypassed when people are setting goals and objectives. When you set quantifiable objectives and your attention gets turned on to them, these unquantifiable things are the first casualties along the way. This is very, very sad. As soon as you begin to say, in a hospital or in a medical practice, or in the work of a pastor, or anything else, as soon as you say 'I will accomplish more of certain specific things', then you find that because you only have a certain amount of time and energy, you find that in order to focus on the things which you can quantify, you begin to lose out on the things which you can't quantify.

Numbers don't always count

In the work of a Christian doctor, or anyone who is in Christian service, the very attempt to quantify, the very attempt to set numerical goals, is something which is fraught with hazards. For example, it's a very good thing to bring people to know the Lord Jesus Christ. And you may feel very happy that last year, as a result of your work, your witness, you know of perhaps two people who came to know the Lord Jesus Christ. So you say 'Good, next year I am going to increase that by 50%, I am going to win three.' Then you find that, in a very subtle way, as soon as you begin counting, as soon as you begin giving yourself a numerical objective, that number becomes unduly important. That number begins to assume the character of a command from God, as if it had some spiritual value.

Similarly, in medical practice you might think as a surgeon 'next year we're going to bring our mortality down from 2.5% to 1.5%.' That must be good — right? So you tell all your staff and all your nurses that next year we're going to do better, our objective will be to reduce the mortality even further on the surgical ward. I know instances where mortality has become the important thing, because the hospital was being judged on that account. So, in more than one instance the answer to this challenge has been to admit fewer and fewer serious cases. Somebody else is left to admit the desperately ill cases, and you'll take the early cases which haven't much wrong with them — and thus the mortality is easily brought down. Now, this obviously is not the right way to look at the thing.

THE HOLY SPIRIT GIVES PRIORITIES

What I'm saying is that it isn't good to set your priorities and your goals and your objectives on a numerical basis. I believe that, particularly for a Christian physician, or particularly for a person who is thinking about his life in relation to the guidance of God, it is very important that we should leave ourselves free to be guided by the Holy Spirit on a day-to-day basis.

Present yourself

I think perhaps one should say here that our priorities cannot be generalised, and even when they come to be specific we need to be very cautious in setting ourselves a goal, either in medicine or in religion, especially if there are numbers attached to it. Really our goal is best set for us in Romans 12:1: 'Present yourselves a living sacrifice, holy, acceptable unto God, which is your reasonable service. Be not conformed to this world, but be ye transformed by the renewing of your mind, that you may prove what is that good, acceptable, and perfect will of God.' I would add — prove 'today', prove 'now', for the acceptable and perfect will of God for you may be different tomorrow, and different again next week, but the first step in setting our priorities is to commit ourselves, now, today, as a living sacrifice to God. Make sure whose priorities we're talking about. Because without recognising it, sneaking up in our sub-conscious mind is going to come the priority of supporting the family, of making a name for ourselves, of riding high in the profession. And in our concern for the kingdom of God there is a danger in starting to think of getting numerical results that are visible — for these can redound to our credit, rather than neces-sarily to the credit of our Lord Jesus Christ. So present yourselves as a living sacrifice, make sure you are committed.

Be transformed

If you are committed, then the next step is to be transformed by the renewing of your mind, that you may prove what is that good and acceptable and perfect will of God for you, now. I could spend the whole of the rest of the time that I have with you telling you about my own witness, my history. I committed myself to the guidance of the Holy Spirit, and I believe that under the guidance of the Holy Spirit I learned the building trade. They offered me the chance to become a doctor but I said 'Oh no, I don't want to become a doctor'. And I believe that I was led to work in the building trade and learn carpentry and stone-masonry and brick laying and mechanical engineering, and then at the end of that period I was led into doing medicine. Then, at the end of that period I was led into coming out to Vellore, and then into leprosy work. When I came out to Vellore I had no idea that I'd be going to be treating leprosy. It wasn't until I'd got here and felt their hands and deformities and stood face to face with a man suffering with that condition, that God spoke to me, in that situation, and said 'Paul, this is why I brought you to India. This is your project.' If I'd prayed myself blue in the face, back in England, to get my priorities straight for the ten years ahead, leprosy would never have occurred to me. But, I had to be in the will of God. I had to be sensitive. And God spoke to me as the situation arose. So don't be worried that you can't see far ahead. The thing is that you've got to be committed, and you've got to be sensitive, to present your bodies, to prove God's will.

I'd love to spend some time on that word 'prove'. Prove God's will. You have a sense that you're in the will of God, and you start to do it, and in the doing of God's will it will be proved to you that that is his will. As Christ himself said: 'They that obey my word will know the doctrine' (John 7:17). It isn't that you know the doctrines first, then you obey. But you start obeying what you already know, and then more will be revealed to you. I think God wants to know whether he can trust us with his will, whether he can trust us with a certain job, and therefore he asks us to take the first step — which is usually the duty which lies immediately in front of you right now! Witnessing to the person who is your fellow medical student, to somebody in the ward, or to the patient that you're concerned with. Being faithful in some little thing. And as you do it, the Holy Spirit will bring some joy into your heart, and help you to realise that 'this is what I'm here for'. And as you do it, God will lead you on into the next step.

WE ARE PARTS OF ONE BODY

Continuing on in Romans 12, it says in verse 3 'I say to all of you, don't think of yourselves more highly than you ought to think.' Warning people that as soon as they begin to be blessed by God, as soon as they begin to prove the will of God, the first thing that's going to happen is that you'll think more of yourself than you should. You'll think that it's your strength, your eloquence, your skill, your dedication, that's doing all this work. And you thank God, you say to the Lord, 'Lord, I thank you that I'm not like other medical students are. I witness to my patients, I heal my patients, I work harder in the ward, I pray longer …' And before you know where you are you're a Pharisee! So, 'don't think of yourself more highly than you ought to think. For as there are many members in one body, and all members have not the same office, so we, being many, are one body in Christ.' Then you get the beautiful picture that some of us are a thumb, and some of us are an eye, and some of us are a liver, and some of us are a kidney. And we all have something to do, and we all are important. If someone got terribly excited and said 'the one thing is to be a hand!' — well, before you know where you are the body is going to die of kidney failure! Because there are no kidneys left to excrete all the toxins! Because we don't want to take the humble lowly part the whole body becomes sick and diseased and uraemic. So, let's remember that we are one body and that we are going to be taught how to fit into that body.

Knowing where we fit

When you are in the place where you fit, there will be a witness in your own heart from God, to say 'That's where you belong. That's where I want you. That's where you're fitted for.' Paul goes on, in 1 Corinthians 12:21–22, to talk about the gifts of the Spirit, and he says very specifically that 'the eye cannot say to the hand, I have no need of you, nor the hand to the feet, I have no need of you. Much more the members of the body which seem to be more feeble are necessary.' In other words, the most important members of the body of Christ are the feeble ones! 'And those members whom we think to be, humanly speaking, less honourable, upon those we should bestow the more abundant honour. And our unlovely parts should have more abundant beauty in our eyes. For our comely parts have no need. But God has tempered the body together, having given more abundant honour to the parts that lacked, that there should be no division in the body. Whether one member suffers, all the members suffer with it. And if one member be honoured, all will rejoice with it. Now you are the body of Christ, and members in particular' (1 Cor. 12:23–27). Then having said that all the members fit in together, and that the lowliest are the most important, and that we should honour the ones that seem to be feeblest, Paul finishes the chapter, v. 28 'And God set some in the church, first apostles, second prophets, third teachers, after that miracles, gifts of healing' (you notice, gifts of healing are fifth! If you want to know where you stand in the body of Christ, you're fifth!) . . . and then he goes on 'but covet earnestly the best gift' and he spends a whole chapter writing about love (1 Cor. 13).

The priority of love
I believe that in the medical profession this is something very, very significant for us. Because it's so easy to feel that the really significant gifts are given to the neuro-surgeons and the heart-surgeons and all the big noises that make all the headlines and do the spectacular things, while the person who goes out into the villages and helps illiterate village women to know how better to deliver babies, and helps to produce a clean water supply, and to do the simple things — we feel somehow that they are lower down. In the last verse of 1 Corinthians 12 Paul states: 'I show unto you a more excellent way.' Realise the real relationship between the members of the body of Christ, the relationship of inter-dependent love. So we could say, as a generalisation of the one overall priority, what Jesus said in Mark 12:30–31: 'Thou shalt love the Lord thy God with all thy heart and with all thy soul and with all thy mind and with all thy strength, and thy neighbour as thyself.'

THE PRIORITY OF DESIRABLE FRUIT
The other overall priority comes in the 15th chapter of John, where Jesus is talking about the vine, and here he gives as near as can be a kind of overall priority for our lives, whether we are physicians or surgeons or whoever we are. 'He that abideth in me, and I in him, the same bringeth forth much fruit, for without me you can do nothing. And this is my will for you, that you bring forth much fruit.' Jesus requires of all his disciples that they bear much fruit. Now, for some reason, in the evangelical Christian world, a person who 'bears fruit' is often spoken of as a person who has brought a lot of people to Christ. And if somebody has gone through the whole of their life and they can't point to anybody whom they have led to Jesus Christ, well then, too bad, they have no fruit! I think this is a wrong connotation.

Think where Jesus was when he spoke these words. Probably he was sitting beside a vineyard and said, 'Look, there's a vine. Now, I am the vine. You are the branches. And my will for you is that you bear much fruit.' Now, what does he mean? If you had been sitting beside a beautiful vine and had seen bunches of grapes hanging from the tendrils of the vine, what would be your immediate thought when you saw that parable in real life in front of you? If you saw those grapes, what would it mean to Christian converts? What do you see, what do you think, when you see a bunch of grapes? I say 'Boy, don't they just look delicious! I would like to eat them!' And I think that's what any ordinary, reasonable man or woman would think when they saw them. That's what the vine is all about.

There are so many different parts of a plant — the leaves are for respiration, the roots are for gathering the minerals and water from the soil, and the stem is for holding the branches, but all of this results in fruit. Fruit is the result of being alive. So I think that when Jesus was talking to his disciples beside the vineyard what he meant was 'I am the vine, you are the branches, and if you abide in me the result will be beautiful fruit.' Not only is the fruit the result of having a good root and a good branch, but it is the part of the vine which is appreciated by everyone. To me, the cluster of grapes is delicious. To me, it is nourishing. It quenches my thirst, it satisfies my hunger. I would go a long way to get a lovely fresh bunch of grapes. And that, I think, is what Jesus meant. I think he meant that, if we abide in him as the Vine, people will want to come to us, to partake of the result of the way we live. If you are a doctor in the service of Jesus Christ, if you are a physician abiding in Jesus Christ, people will want to come to you. Not just because you've got pills and injections and knives and things, but because you exemplify the love of Jesus Christ to them. The healing hand of Jesus Christ. And the whole quality of your life makes you attractive, and delicious. Do you know what I mean by 'delicious'? People want what you have. It's attractive. I believe that as Christians this should be a real priority of our lives. People will look at us, and say 'Lovely. Delicious. I want more of that.' And it speaks to them of the quality of the Vine.

The biology of Christ

But there is more to fruit than being good to eat. The grape is that part of the vine, and the only part of the vine, that contains the seed. And this is the biology of Jesus Christ. This is the biology of the Creator. The purpose of a vine, in one sense, is to propagate itself. To make new vines. To spread the seed. Now Jesus said to the disciples: 'Look at that vine! The fruit is delicious! And because it's delicious, people are going to pick it, and they're going to eat, and they're going to walk along the roadside eating grapes and spitting out the seeds to the left and to the right. And wherever they spit out the seeds, to the left and to the right, the purpose of the grape is being accomplished. Because grapes are delicious in order that they may be a vehicle of the seed.'

So therefore don't anybody dare say — 'Should I be a doctor primarily to treat patients or primarily to witness to Jesus Christ?' We are a total body of Jesus Christ, ministering in the love of God and in the power of God, in the power of his Spirit, to the people who are sick. And the total result of this, the total result of our abiding life in the Vine, is that people look at us and they love us, they feel the love of God and they want it. And so if they receive that love into their lives it serves as a means of propagating the kingdom of God, and so it contains the seed whether you're a preacher or not a preacher. Whether you're a preacher or not is not a fundamentally important thing, so long as you're abiding in the Vine.

Supporting others

May I remind you that, when you talk about the priorities of your life, it isn't just to decide whether you're to be a physician or a surgeon, because you are a person. You may be a doctor and an evangelist but you're also a husband, or a wife, or the father of a family, or the son of your father, or the daughter of your mother. You may feel that the priority of your life is to evangelise and to be a witness to Jesus Christ, and then your mother becomes ill and needs your help, and you have to leave your prime task, which pays your salary, to go and minister to your mother. If you are working according to 'management by objective' you might easily say, 'Well, this isn't my priority. My priority is to preach, or to do something else.' So you let your mother go, and your witness is ruined, because you have lacked that sensitivity, that under-standing of the body of Christ. You are a member of the commu-nity, you are a member of the church, and joined with all kinds of other things. The food you choose to eat, the quality of your lifestyle, all of these are witnesses of your total life. In this country of India more people are going to die from lack of proper gardening than they are from lack of proper medicine. And I believe that for a person to witness in the whole breadth of his life, care and concern for ecology, care and concern for the balance of food, and simplicity of lifestyle — all these are very important. We sometimes ask ourselves — quality versus quantity. Should I treat more patients more carefully, or less patients? God will lead us into these things. I believe that, providing we put our top priority first, which is to abide in him, he will teach us when to treat more patients, and when we should perhaps do more delegating.

Building others up

One of the great, priority tasks in the Christian church, particularly for people who hold responsibility, is to learn to delegate. Hand over your tasks to other people, build up people who feel they aren't worth very much, and demonstrate that they can do the things just as well as you, and then you can move on to something else. What others do because of you may be more significant than what you do yourself and gives a beautiful demonstration of being in the body of Christ.

The priority

God bless all of you, as you face all the difficult problems as to how to get the priorities of your life, but remember there is really only one priority — 'Abide in him', and then you will begin to bear fruit. Your fruit may not be in doing big operations, but will be more like the fruit of the Spirit in Galatians 5:22 — love, joy, peace, patience, gentleness, goodness, faith, meekness, and self-control. That is the fruit of the Spirit. And this is the will of God for your life. Amen.

FOR CHRIST'S SAKE IN STUDY AND PRACTICE

KURUVILLA VARKEY

Introduction

AFTER about eighteen years of work in the medical field, whenever I thought about a topic like this I thought of what I could *do.* Now the order is reversed for me. I take this time to share that because I think that there is something for you also in this. In other words what is primarily important for a Christian is your *being* and *not* your doing. I cannot emphasise this too strongly because I have learnt this rather late, but you are fortunate that you are able to learn this early and put the emphasis right: the *being* first, and an expression of the being will be the doing.

Being

What is the meaning of this *being?* What is your centre? What is the centre of your life? This first important point about your being is to have your centre right. In other words, when you look at your own heart and see your own innermost reality and find that it is in Christ, then I would say that you are Christ-centred. Let us at this moment briefly see if that is so in our lives. If that is not so there is no question of doing anything for him. We are unbalanced if everything we do is not centred in Christ.

The next important thing in Christian being is being with the Lord. This is well emphasised in the words, 'Abide in me', or stay with *him* … continuing with him. We read that Mary sat at the feet of Jesus. The Hindu Vedic word *'upanishad'* means to 'sit at the feet'. To sit at the feet does not merely imply to repose at the feet of someone. The same expression is also used of Paul who sat at the feet of Gamaliel. Sitting with the Lord is an inward activity. As medical students this must have a practical implication in our schedules with work and studies and examinations. But if when we go back to our regular work you are not willing to spend some

ICCMS Bangalore, India, 1983. **Kuruvilla Varkey.** *Medical superintendent and consultant physician, Christian Fellowship Hospital, Oddanchatram, India.*

time every day and sit quietly at the feet of Jesus, then this conference could go to waste. We must sit at his feet actively, learning from the Lord. It is very important to be with the Master. In practice, the morning is the best time for this meditation. It has been said that the battle for the morning meditation is won on the previous night. This is just a practical suggestion — that if we spend less time in the evening in talk and have an early night, then we will be able to wake up early for the morning meditation. Another practical suggestion is that once in a while we should get away from the activity and noise of the hospital or medical school, and go out somewhere alone and sit at the feet of the Lord. While I was working in the Laccadive Islands I found that I wanted to be at work all the time. Finally I discovered that I was empty inside. It was all doing, and no being. So it is very important that we have this time.

Another aspect of being is to be yourself. The first thing about being yourself is to be your true self, in the image of God as he created us. We become that only when we go to Christ. It is like the prodigal son whose false self was wandering around, but his true self was found in the Father. Secondly, being yourself should mean accepting yourself, being assured of God's acceptance of you. Sometimes we wish to be somebody else, especially in our spiritual lives. But what God wants is that you be yourself. You have a special role. Paul, writing to the Corinthians, said, 'By the grace of God I am what I am' (1 Cor. 15:10). He had made many mistakes, but he accepted himself, trusting in God's mercy in spite of his limitations.

The other thing about being is rest. We quote the familiar passage of Matthew 11:28–30: 'Come unto me all you that labour and I will give you rest.' We often quote it for non-Christians. But how much rest are you having? This was something very personal to me. I am referring to a time when I was able to look into my life, and to my surprise I found that there was no rest at all, there was all restlessness, there was all activity. And I will ask you this personal question: Have you experienced this inward rest in you today? Are you continuing in this restfulness? Psalm 131 tells us that this is the rest that the Lord is promising for you today and now while you are students and Christian workers and doctors.

The other thing in being is to be an integrated person. Being a unity, being integrated as a body, the body matters, not only the spirit. Thank God for a good physique. The Bible says that everyone nourishes and cherishes his body. Do we do that? When you go back and plan your time you must do that. That will bring glory to God.

Another thing about being is to be free. God has not given you the spirit of fear that you may come to his presence like slaves, but the spirit of freedom to come like sons and daughters. It was a great relief for me to hear this particular word. God is our Father. We as his children must be free to go to him. I think of my own young son coming home from school, his bag on his back and his school uniform dusty: he never knocks on the door, he just breezes in and enjoys his freedom.

Another thing about being is to be a transformed person, inwardly and constantly. Be a transformed non-conformist, not conforming to this world. I asked some of the Christian students who visited our hospital: 'What is the greatest temptation that you face in your campus?' They replied that it was the temptation to conform and compromise.

Doing

We have looked into the aspect of *being*. Now let us look briefly at the aspects of *doing*. God has shown me in a clear way that my doing is an expression of my being. What is inside me should come out. It must be spontaneous and natural. Medicine is a fascinating field, and I admit to being an ex-addict of medicine, because I was deeply fascinated by it. One difficulty in a profession like medicine is the 'helper–syndrome'. This is an occupational hazard for medical doctors. By occupation we tend to do more and more work because the demand is such. We go into what is called 'sterile medical activism'. If we stay on in the hospital, patients always come and we can be tied with work all the time. But in setting our priorities we must have time for the Lord and not for work all the time.

We must also try to distinguish between activity and activism. If you look at Martha you see an example of activism. That is a great danger. Activism is to start doing things when this is not indicated.

You can get very active and become symptomatically restless. You then begin to blame others like Martha did. Finally it leads to depression. Someone once asked Mother Teresa of Calcutta why it was that he never saw even one tired face in the whole of her institution. She said, 'The secret is that we have one hour of prayer individually and one hour of prayer collectively.' This is the best way not to get into activism, to spend time with God alone.

Let action come from being

If I were to analyse my old pattern of life, I would call it 'anxiously striving for results'. God has shown me the new pattern, 'restful through being'. This is the message that I wish to pass on to you. *For Christ's sake, in study and in practice, means being with him.* Out of that, as a natural outcome, will be your activity.

Here was the prayer of Dr Ida Scudder of Vellore: 'Father, whose life is within me, and whose love is ever about me, grant that thy light may be maintained in my life today and every day, that with gladness of heart, without haste, without confusion of thought, I may go about my daily task, conscious of the ability to meet every *rightful* demand, seeing the larger meaning of little things, finding beauty and love everywhere, and in the sense of thy presence may I walk through the hours, breathing the atmosphere of love rather than striving.'

This was a great personal message for me, not anxious striving but restful being. After several years of learning the lesson, if you were to ask me now the meaning of the words of the topic under discussion, 'For Christ's sake in study and practice', it would mean for Christ's sake being with him. And when you are really in him do not worry about what will happen. The doing will come — not the anxious striving but the wonderful natural fruit-bearing, restful fruit-bearing.

THE SPIRIT OF SERVICE

HANS GRUBER

IT is remarkable that in the German language the words 'to serve' and 'service', *Dienst*, have become unpopular. *Dienst* is being replaced by *Dienstleistung*. This word cannot be translated into English; it would just be 'service', but the second component *Leistung* means efficiency, accomplishment, attainment, achievement. The housemaid used to be 'serving-maid', but has been replaced by 'home-help'. There are few male servants any more in Germany and, if any name is used at all, the English 'butler' is now employed. The term 'Service–Organisation', *Dienstorganisation*, is being replaced by *Hilfsorganisation*, which simply means an organisation for giving help.

This trend has not developed just by chance. In today's world there is no longer any place for service, *Dienst*. 'Ministry' would really give a better idea of the German connotation, for we are not talking about service or gas stations, but about spiritual service — and minister means 'servant'. If we talk about a servant, we tend to think in terms of a hierarchy. However, today's society does not wish to have masters and servants. Man has rights and it is a duty of society to give him the demanded *Dienstleistung*, i.e. the required 'service–efficiency'.

The new ideological framework

Current trends call for the integration of physicians into some of these ideological patterns of modern society. We doctors are asked to free ourselves from the idea of finding fulfilment in our profession but to find it instead by 'participation in the process of society'.

Recently our sixteen-year-old daughter brought home an instructional pamphlet from school written by a pastor. This is what it said:

> 'We do not understand work as a blessing; it is unfortunately a necessity. The ethics of labour consist in doing your bare duty. The

ICCP Davos, Switzerland, 1978. **Hans L. E. Gruber.** *Medical director Deutsche Mission Gemeinschaft, West Germany. Past professor of pharmacology, Christian Medical College, Ludhiana, India.*

work should not be contrary to our liking, we expect to get as much money as we can for as little labour as possible. This is the way of thinking today. My work is only a job, which I do without personal involvement. If I have a better offer, I can forego it at any time.

I can hear the protest of the older generation. "This is incredible." But I do not think it is. It is simply a promising process of getting rid of old myths about work. I will not be tempted any more to make my work my god, regardless of whether I am a mason, a turner or a pastor! The new type of man will not "give himself" any more for his work or whatever similar phrases he may know! He has to earn money, therefore he works. That is all!

If there are really still some young people who enter the world of labour with innocent faith, it is only an indication that their parents have educated them in an old-fashioned, outdated manner.'

In contrast to encouraging a sense of individual responsibility, an artificial sympathy for those who have taken criminal actions is being irresponsibly promoted. Laziness and absenteeism are now euphemistically called 'rejecting pressure of achievement' and 'working to rule', so making the idea of service a farce. Physicians who still give real service to their patients (and perhaps just for that reason earn well) are objects of jealousy, and jealousy sometimes suggests political motives. They are, in consequence, being attacked as 'greedy egotists', 'rapacious money grabbers', or 'demigods in white'.

We have to note in this context that a practical spirit of service hinders the development of ideological ideas of equality and the process of levelling. Within the high walls of social security (as for instance in England and Germany) it is, unfortunately, far more convenient to work within a 40-hour week than to show readiness for service, sacrifice and risk.

Ethical standards of service are basically Christian, but they are getting shaky even amongst doctors. The breakdown is part of a process within society as a whole, and is being furthered by massive external legislative intervention. Every loss of professional ethical standards, however, will also promote disintegration of the general ethical order of society. It would not be wise to regard this as a specifically German or European problem. We are dealing with a topic of particular importance for individual Christians and it is also a key subject for our social order at large.

The meaning of service

Originally, God took man into his service. Adam had not been put into a self-service restaurant. He did not spend his days in doing sweet nothing. 'The Lord God placed the man in the Garden of Eden as its gardener, to tend and care for it' (Gen. 2:15). Man had to work physically and to use his brains, for one of his first tasks was to give names to the entire contents of the garden! The original biblical vision of service included some characteristics which are still valid today.

The mandate comes from God. God appoints man into his service, therefore the activities of man are not related to himself but to God.

There is a responsibility to God. He is the one who distributes the tasks of service but who also asks questions; 'Where are you? … Who told you that you are naked? … How could you do such a thing?' The motive for responsible action is primarily not getting gain out of service, but voluntary subordination.

Man's goal was to keep the property of God, to tend and to care for it. Here is an important point for us physicians. Everything was related to God.

The resources for service are given by God. The Creator gives not only the mandate but also the productivity. (This already disproves the allegation that the ruthless global exploitation of resources stems from Christian philosophy!) The riches of the Garden of Eden were created by God and put at the disposal of man, expressly for tending and caring.

There is 'freedom' but within limitations. ('You may eat except from the tree of conscience.') The limitation simply gives the enabling freedom necessary for truly serving God. Autonomous, disobedient man can only perform a parody of service, which is tedious labour. He loses immediate communication with God.

Since that time godless humanity has been desperately trying to find an image of a new man. The present and the future are not likely to stimulate our hopes either. Yes, we have everything wonderfully at our command. We hardly know anymore where the borderline is between life and death; we can save a few hundred people by organ transplantation, whilst tens of thousands die unnecessarily. Is this latter unavoidable?

Even if we have electrochemical and genetic manipulation of man as our vision for the future, the question still stands: 'What is our goal when we thus manipulate?' 'What use is an evolutionary humanism (according to Julian Huxley) if we have no image of what is human? Fallen man has found the technical means, but he has not found the model of a new man. Science, by restless labour, tries to widen the horizons which God has set.

The example of Christ

Into this situation Christ, God incarnate, enters; not only as a model, a demonstration, or an example, but also as an inspiration in the true sense of the word. He is the 'Spirit of service'. He re-establishes the original relationship of service between man and God. For this reason he makes it plain that service is the essence of the incarnation! 'He made himself nothing, assuming the nature of a slave' (Phil. 2:7 *The New English Bible*). 'The Son of Man did not come to be served, but to serve, and to give up his life as a ransom for many' (Mat. 20:28).

The person who has received new birth by the Spirit will invariably be put into service: 'If any man serves me, he must follow me; where I am, my servant will be' (John 12:26). 'Among you, whoever wants to be great must be your servant and whoever wants to be first must be the willing slave of all, like the Son of Man' (Mat. 20:26).

We all know these words well, but what do they mean to us in day-to-day life? I asked Dr K.N. Nambudripad, now director of Christian Medical College, Ludhiana, India: 'What significant changes happened in your life when you were converted from Brahminism and became a Christian?' His reply was: 'Previously the patient was for me an object of prestige, or of research, or one from whom I could get gain. Since my conversion the patient is a *person* to be served and to be loved, a Christ-given task.'

The character of a servant

It is not always easy (Mat. 25:14–30). Let us recall the parable of the master who put his capital in the hands of his servants. Two of them think and act as true stewards of their master. One does not truly serve, he functions only as a safe, a locker, a depository for his master's capital, and apart from that he cares about nothing except his own business. The foolish virgins, too, do not think ahead. They have all the trappings, but they do not have the right attitude. It may be good to spend just a few seconds in self-reflection. Are we identifying ourselves with God's mandate for service? Are we investors of the capital which God has entrusted to us or are we unprofitable to him?

Surrender of independence

'Equality with God' was a legitimate position for Jesus Christ, but he yielded up this right and took the form of a servant. It makes all the difference in my life whether I am a *helper* or a *servant*. As a voluntary helper I may come and go as I like and do what I think is best. A servant has to surrender his independence to his master. A surgeon's assistant, for example, may be involved in some very important and perfectly legitimate research. But if he is needed to assist his 'chief' in the operating theatre and decides to leave at a crucial point of the operation in order to attend his research work, it may amount to an act of disloyalty and could have serious consequences. Important as his research may be, he does not do just what he likes and certainly not at a time of his choosing. His first task is to be an assistant to his 'chief'. How does this kind of service work out for me in my office or in my laboratory or out-patient department? What does it mean when planning my time or my holiday? What does it mean in my choice of professional career or in my attitude toward my family?

We need humility if we are to let go our independence. The Greek New Testament word for service is not *leitourgeo*, which means 'honorary service for the community', 'service for the government', or 'service in prominent positions for the public'. No. It is significant that 'to serve' is *diakoneo*, from which we get our word deacon or deaconess. For the Greek this signified the lowest order of society, one who was willing to fetch and carry.

What man considers to be foolish, yes, even disreputable or suspicious, *that* has been revalued by God. In Christ, God has demonstrated that not only does service take precedence over mastery, but that we can be true masters only as we become servants.

THE CHRISTIAN IN SURGICAL PRACTICE

EVAN THOMSON

No distinction between secular and sacred

WHEN I was a medical student and a very young Christian I worked during vacations for a businessman who introduced me to the idea from which our thinking must necessarily commence. He felt that the life of a Christian businessman should be divided into two compartments, his religion and his business, and that he should not let his Christianity intrude too much into his business life. A similar attitude has been adopted by others better informed and more famous. Pasteur declared that when he entered his laboratory he left his religion outside (quoted by Schlemmer, 1957). Should we maintain, too, that when the Christian surgeon enters his wards, his operating theatre, his lecture room or his laboratory he should do the same?

Now this distinction between secular and sacred has been a common one down the centuries. Commencing in pagan philosophy and developing in the Gnostic and other systems it stems from the false assumption that the spiritual is good, the material evil. For the Christian there must be no dichotomy, for Christianity, although much more, is a way of life. Christ is Lord of life and Lord of all and cannot be excluded from any department of the Christian's life, any 'secular' activity. Despite Pasteur, the Christian must contend that personality cannot be divided into compartments — citizen, scientist, surgeon, Christian. He must also remember that secularism in its many modern forms — naturalism, humanism, humanitarianism and so forth — leads to belief in mere materialism and in the self sufficiency and self redeemability of man, and God is ignored. Moreover, the Christian must teach, and illustrate by his life that, of all the great religions, none is more concerned with material things and human welfare than Christianity. How this can be done in medicine is part of the story of history.

The Christian surgeon must synthesise his Christianity and science in the practice of scientific therapeutics. Though

*ICCP Oxford, UK, 1966. **Evan Thomson**. Consultant surgeon, Brisbane, Australia.*

Christianity will not figure in a textbook of scientific therapeutics, the Christian must bring his Christianity into this sphere to the extent of making scientific therapeutics a Christian vocation. Christianity, then, has a place in scientific therapeutics and, indeed, it must pervade the whole of a Christian surgeon's practice. Philosophy and science may meet best in medicine and I believe the Christian doctor has more to offer than anyone else towards a true philosophy of medicine.

The Christian surgeon has a potential impact on the practice of scientific therapeutics. He, more than anyone else, should practise medicine from the right motive, the constraint of the love of Christ. He, more than anyone else, should be able to bring 'the feeling heart' which, as Lister said, 'is the first requisite of a surgeon'. He, more than anyone else, can follow Lister's 'one rule of practice' — 'to put yourself in the patient's place'. Sir Herbert Seddon has written that, 'It is difficult to be a good medical scientist and at the same time a completely human person'. That this is true we can all confirm from experience.

It is platitudinous to say that the Christian surgeon must have the highest standards of ethical, academic and scientific practice. But beyond this he must maintain, and illustrate in practice, that therapeutics introduces factors that are not 'scientific', where by scientific we mean based on the exact sciences, developed by scientific method or amenable to measurement. So much involved in the practice of therapeutics is not measurable. Patience to listen, to explain and explain again, understanding, sympathy, kindness and that form of treatment described as 'tender loving care', are not measurable. But aesthetic and religious experiences are as real and fundamental as measurable scientific ones.

Real treatment involves the interaction of personalities — the 'I–Thou' relationship of the theologians — and commences the moment patient and doctor meet. Real clinical surgery cannot be practised from the foot of the bed through the mediation of a colleague. This is why thoughts of computerised medicine give us the horrors. If, then, by scientific therapeutics we mean treatment based on the exact sciences and developed by the application of scientific method we fall far short of real patient management. The Christian surgeon must not be a mere purveyor of such therapeutics. He must not be a mere surgical scientist and technician.

Even the simplest operation must not be to him just a mechanical business akin to the artisan's craft. His therapy ought to exemplify all those immeasurables that constitute good total patient care.

Lip service is given to the treatment of 'the whole man', to the treatment of people rather than of diseases, but the principle is rarely well practised. Our training is largely responsible, stressing as it does the physical and 'scientific'. Who better than the Christian surgeon is fitted to guide and implement the treatment of the whole man? Haemorrhage from oesophageal varices, for example, is amenable to surgical treatment, 'scientific' if you will. The hepatic cirrhosis is 'treatable', if less successfully. But for the basic personality problem, addiction to alcohol, more is required than scientific therapeutics, although the psychiatrist may contribute his aid. I dare to suggest that only Christianity has the real therapeutic answer. The course of treatment can be prescribed but is, unfortunately, much less willingly followed.

The Christian must be in the vanguard of those whose practice is guided by the principle that the fascinating problems of disease and its treatment must not take precedence over the true interests of the individual patient. The real value of each individual, so basic in the Christian message, must be paramount.

'To cure sometimes, to relieve often, to comfort always'. The busy surgeon, and the busy Christian surgeon too, finds it difficult to be as effective as he might be in the real management of those whom his skill in therapeutics cannot cure. The incurable and the dying have many false comforters. To the Christian surgeon Christ is the only answer in this situation and his faith must affect his practice. But the practical problems are great and demand a policy of the greatest circumspection. Time is required and in busy practice time is at a premium but, despite this, he must himself provide, or secure through others more able, the help the patient needs.

We commonly have under our care patients, often young, who have been kept alive, sometimes decerebrate, after major head injury. Where should our endeavours cease for such tragedies and how long in these and other similar conditions should we keep patients 'alive', if that is the correct term? This is not the place for answering the question, but it has to be asked.

The Christian surgeon must play an active role in the development of scientific therapeutics. He must make his influence felt in many of the problems in this field, the problems of clinical research. This is equally a Christian vocation and a call to which some Christians must respond. In this sphere the Christian attitude to the significance of the individual must be constantly maintained. The Christian research worker must never allow the moral problems of clinical research and controlled clinical trials to be shelved. A clouded vision is so easily acquired in this context. But if the one rule of practice is to put yourself in the patient's place, this applies equally well to investigation and research as to treatment.

The Christian surgeon should play an active role in the teaching of scientific therapeutics. By precept, and particularly by example, he can influence developing minds. He should regard his teaching as a Christian vocation and remember that the Christian position can be illustrated and others influenced by the practical Christian vocation — both the practice of and the teaching of true scientific therapeutics.

The Christian doctor brings Christian ideas and values to medicine. He brings the potential for a Christian medical philosophy. The Christian surgeon has a potential for impact in many fields including his therapeutic art — its development, its practice, its ethics and where conventional treatment is found wanting. His prayer should be for wisdom, rightly and adequately to use this potential.

THE CHRISTIAN HOSPITAL CONSULTANT

PAUL BREMER

Some questions and answers

SOME of the various demands and pressures in the life of a hospital consultant:

Pressure of work; night work.

Teaching and examinations.

Keeping up academically.

Administration and committee work.

Frustration, particularly with authorities who have no insight into the necessities required to run a department.

Financial considerations.

The place of the spiritual approach to the consultant's problems

Is the Christian in any way different from the non-Christian consultant?

He should definitely be different although there are many non-Christian men and women whose lives are particularly exemplary. The Christian should have an answer to problems where the non-Christian in certain cases has no answer.

How should the committed Christian consultant react when problems arise?

His daily life should be lived in such a way that he is *strengthened from within* (Rom. 12:1–2) and enabled to react to problems in a Christian way and not in a frustrated, irritated way.

This implies a *personal daily devotion* to the Lord Jesus Christ, his Saviour, by reading of his word, meditation and prayer.

The application. *His work should be well done.* The patient is of the greatest importance and should enjoy primary consideration, not the income or convenience of the consultant. He should be willing to go the second mile, and must maintain the highest ethical standards.

ICCP Singapore 1975. **Paul Bremer.** *Consultant and senior lecturer in obstetrics and gynaecology, University of Pretoria, RSA. ICMDA President 1990–98, Vice-President 1982–90, Chairman 1975–80.*

When the opportunity arises, he must be *ready to witness* to the patient (and student) regarding his personal faith.

The failings and temptations a consultant faces

To seek success for its own sake
When Jesus refers to laying up treasures on earth, it does not only mean money or possessions, but also success, position, power, etc. — anything which is more precious to us than Christ himself (Mat. 6:19).

The desire for riches
Motives must be very carefully watched when you reach the position of launching out as a consultant, especially with the possibility of having a very remunerative practice. The desire for riches has overcome more than one Christian and spoilt his witness and testimony, because he has sought first not the Kingdom of God, but riches for their own sake.

A lowering of ethical standards
Perhaps the biggest temptation is not to commit the most glaring transgression in the ethical field but to operate, or make certain investigations, when they are not strictly necessary but mainly in the interest of the doctor and possibly less so in the interest of the patient. Unnecessary operations are unfortunately a very frequent example of this temptation and failing.

To neglect your responsibilities at home
Care should be taken not to forget this. Especially when success comes your way and you are earning a good living, you may become very self-sufficient. Without even recognising it as a temptation, you can begin to rely on yourself and not on God (Deut. 8:17–18).

ETHICS IN DENTAL PRACTICE

FRED BERGAMO

I HAVE been asked to address you on the subject of ethics. I am not a professional ethicist, but simply a practising dentist. Because of that distinction my remarks will be rather practical, reflecting the opinions and experiences of those in the reality of daily practice, in contact with the tensions of the marketplace, working through the moral dilemmas that confront people of conscience daily.

Public reluctance to discuss ethics

Ethics has to do with morals, and is *concerned with the goodness and badness of human action and character.* Though we may enjoy debating ethical issues, we can be assured that there will be disagreement over what is right, and what is wrong; what is evil and what is good. In a pluralistic society, and even within the framework of this congress where people of diverse tradition and culture are gathered, the consensus might be to agree to disagree, and go our separate ways, doing our own thing. That attitude is not at all uncommon in the local church where, in matters of social behavior, some might consider it safer to keep quiet, rather than risk confrontation.

Peters and Waterman, in their best-selling book *In search of excellence* observe that most businessmen are loath to write about, talk about, or ever take seriously value systems. To the extent that they do consider them at all, they are regarded as vague abstractions.

Should silence or evasion be the normative response when matters of ethical behavior are broached? Lewis Bird has noted that: 'to do ethics, to reason about decisions that have the potential to do good or harm, introduces a burden to the mind that can overwhelm the best of souls.' That may be true, but can we allow ourselves to be detoured around ethical problems because of either intellectual uncertainty or emotional overload?

We must also acknowledge that the mood of uneasiness that

ICMDA Cancun, Mexico, 1986. **Fred Bergamo.** *General dental practitioner, USA. Activist in Medical Group MIssions.*

often prevails in discussions of ethics can be symptomatic of man's need to *stand in the shadows where his deeds are not clearly visible.* Jesus said that 'men loved the darkness rather than the light, for their deeds were evil' (John 3:19). As redeemed men and women, we should have no affection for the darkness Jesus speaks of. We are obliged to walk in the light, to fulfill, by the power of the indwelling Holy Spirit, God's standards for holy living. Jesus declared: 'He who practises the truth comes to the light that his deeds may be manifested as having been wrought in God' (John 3:21).

Some ethical challenges in practice

It has been my goal throughout twenty years of dental practice to deliver a high level of dental care to my patients, and I have been confident of my ability to do so. However, I am not absolutely certain that my personal and professional ethics are always beyond reproach. The maturing process that one works through in twenty years of professional practice inevitably contains many humbling experiences. Therefore I, too, at times am *reluctant to go public with my opinions on ethical issues.* In the reality of daily practice, those principles, values, and standards that form the foundation of my ethics are often severely tested, not only by patients and staff members, but also by that small corner of my nature that wants to compromise and cut corners, usually to my own advantage.

Recently a patient came to my office from a practice for which I am the covering dentist. The patient was upset that a fixed prosthetic restoration that the dentist had inserted last year had fallen out. The patient requested that I re-cement it. I examined the abutment teeth and determined that, because of recurrent caries, the abutments would not be able to support the bridge again. As I listened to further details from the patient my mind began to race, attempting to formulate an explanation for the patient. *Should I try to cover for the other dentist?* Should I attempt to re-cement the bridge and say nothing about the caries? What do I owe to the patient? What do I owe to my dental colleague? What do I owe to myself?

The American Dental Association Principles of Ethics and Code of Professional Conduct advises against making disparaging statements against another dentist but, in applying that principle, am I not in conflict with the very basic ethical principle that preserves *the patient's right to the truth?* How can I reconcile these apparently opposing principles?

In another situation a patient offered to pay cash in return for a discount on the fee, and then suggested, with a wink, that I pocket the cash. 'Everybody else does it, Doc,' he remarked. My receptionist observed the dilemma and awaited my response. Do I humor the patient and accept the cash, allowing him to think that I will pocket the money, even if I don't? What sort of precedent do I set in his mind if I accept his terms? If I accept his terms, is it only to avoid creating an embarrassing situation for him?

There are two issues here:
- Rendering unto Caesar that which is rightfully Caesar's (Mat. 22:21);
- Avoiding the appearance of evil.

The issue of one's financial fidelity and political responsibility, though relevant here, is not the primary one. However, to allow a patient and perhaps even a staff member to suspect complicity in some questionable activity is to ignore Paul's advice: '... to hold fast to that which is good, abstain from every form of evil' (1 Thes. 5:21–22). If one is tolerant of the appearance of evil in this situation, what guarantee does the patient have that a similar compromise, unbeknown to him, will not be made in the course of his dental or medical care?

Similar experiences have forced me to take a hard look at my *personal value system.* Do I subscribe to the morality of the herd, the 'everybody else does it' ethic? Can I, as a Christian, live comfortably according to the uncertainty of man's sliding scale? Or have I adopted a lifestyle, a value system that is responsive to the discipline of God's order, as revealed in Holy Scripture? The latter is not always a comfortable lifestyle. Paul, writing to Timothy, suggests that to follow after righteousness, godliness, faith, love, patience and meekness involves a fight, 'the good fight of faith' (1 Tim. 6:11–12). Unless I am willing to be that man or woman, ready to stand for God's highest standard, I, as a Christian, am shortchanging the world.

Gordon McDonald makes this interesting comment in his book *Ordering your private world:*

> 'Driven people tend to have a limited regard for integrity. They can become so preoccupied with success and achievement that they have little time to stop and ask if their inner person is keeping pace with the outer process. Usually it is not, and there is an

increasing gap, a breakdown in integrity. People like this often become progressively deceitful; and they not only deceive others, they deceive themselves. In the attempt to push ahead relentlessly, they lie to themselves about motives; values and morals are compromised. Shortcuts to success become a way of life. Because the goal is so important, they drift into ethical shabbiness.'

For those in training

Though we may recognize this stage as a particular period in life, the responsible person is never out of training. All of us should be challenged to rigorously maintain our spiritual, physical, and professional fitness. I would like, however, to address some thoughts directly to students. The rest of you are invited to listen in!

First of all, I would like to remind you of the Socratic charge: *'To know thyself.'* Have you identified the value system by which you live? That's critical. Too many young people are without a moral rudder, sailing along with the tide. As you proceed through dental and medical school, give more than just a passing thought to the ethical dilemmas you encounter. When you are in practice, they will be yours exclusively to deal with. Become the responsible man or woman that Bonhoeffer refers to when he states: 'It is he himself, the responsible man who must observe, judge, weigh up, decide and act.' That's ethical responsibility.

As Christians we are obliged also to *know what we believe:* '. . . to always be ready to make a defense to everyone who asks you to give an account for the hope that is in you' (1 Pet. 3:15). The ethics of the New Testament rest upon dedicating one's whole life to God daily. Have you done that? Unless you are committed to knowing God personally, daily, you will never consistently practise the great Christian virtues that are the fruit of God's presence in one's life, '. . . love, joy, peace, patience, kindness, goodness, faithfulness, gentleness, self control' (Gal. 5:22–23).

The Christian must also be careful that his *personal and professional ethics complement each other.* In other words, practise what you preach! Establish for yourself high professional standards. It is so easy to drift into mediocrity. Strive for technical excellence. That commitment will pay dividends in ways you never dreamed of. If your patients respect your professional skills, they are more likely to respect your Christian witness and you will find it much easier to take a stand for what you are convinced is right.

Be gracious, benevolent, truthful, competent, and conscientious. *Be careful how you treat those who work for you.* Even if your values are not the model they have chosen for themselves, they judge you by yours, not by their own. You may have formulated an air-tight position on abortion, or some other popular bioethical issue, but if your attitude toward subordinates and associates is condescending, they won't respect you or your opinions. It is the ordinary issues that become the measure of our ethical standards.

Recently I received a letter from a dentist who was a dental resident at the hospital where I work. He writes:

> 'I've just finished reading your editorial on ethics and I must say thank you. After finishing my residency, I began working in private practices and I, too, found my ethical standards challenged too often.
>
> The pressure to produce almost always led to the testing of my ideals and values, yet I resisted as much as I could, and have felt better for it. In these times of trial I draw upon my religion and the morality fostered in my home. I am no angel by any means, but I aspire to be as ethical and fair as I can be.'

Such a letter is both encouraging and discouraging. Discouraging in that it reveals the awful dilemma many young graduates face. Usually in debt, with insufficient funds to set up their own practices and survive, they are at the mercy of the case-load of clinic operations where they are pressed to produce, often at the expense of quality and commitment to excellence. Yet such a letter is also encouraging in that it confirms the existence of those who are still ready to maintain their moral and ethical standards in difficult times.

Jesus has directed us — Christian doctors, nurses, paramedics, homemakers, mothers and fathers — to be witnesses where we are; to be salt and light; to be the mentors the world so badly needs. We cannot be that in our own strength. To the Philippians Paul wrote: 'My God shall supply all your needs according to his riches in Christ Jesus' (Phil. 4:19). He does this, even supplying the desire and ability to live and practise ethically. In the modern world, a morally sensitive practice has become a way by which we can gain the right to be heard about the faith that guides our lives.

PHYSICAL HEALTH RELATED TO SPIRITUAL HEALTH

RAMON DE LA TORRES

Introduction

'GREAT crowds came to him, bringing the lame, the blind, the crippled, the mute and many others, and laid them at his feet; and he healed them' (Mat. 15:30). This verse cites one of the examples in Matthew where Jesus heals a multitude of individuals gathered at one location. Once, when meditating on this passage, I realised that there were some considerations here which apply to people such as ourselves who are in a ministry and yet can be spiritually sick. This passage points out those who came with the crowd to Jesus, among whom were the lame, the deaf and the blind. Rather than the English version which uses 'crippled', the Spanish version mentions specifically those who have trouble with their arms. It says that these people were placed at the feet of Jesus and he healed them. The physical limitations that we read of here speak to me of at least four spiritual conditions.

The pathology

First of all, Jesus healed *the blind.* In the midst of all of our Christian activity and hard work, we can lose our eyesight. Jesus dealt with those who thought that they were rich and comfortable. He said that you don't realise what situation you are really in. You have become spiritually blind. Now it's really tough to be physically blind, but you will at least know it. What is worse is to be spiritually blind and not know it.

Now my Bible tells me that a bitter spirit and a critical attitude towards my Christian brethren are strong evidences of spiritual blindness. When I think of examples of bitterness between Christian workers within hospitals or churches, I realise how prevalent spiritual blindness really is. If you remember, John in his letter wrote that, 'He who hates his brother is in darkness and he

*ICMDA Cancun, Mexico, 1986. **Ramon de la Torres.** Pastor, Baptist Church, Pueblo, Mexico.*

does not know where he is going because this darkness has blinded his eyes' (1 Jn. 2:11). Part of the problem is that we have forgotten that we were purified and so we are blind because this kind of blindness affects both the mind and the spiritual heart of man. One of the handicaps that it brings is that when such an individual reads God's Word, he gets nothing out of it because God's Word must be perceived by spiritual insight.

The second group that I would like to look at are *the lame.* Eric Liddell, who was immortalised in the film *Chariots of Fire,* said something profound when he stated, 'God made me fast.' Even Eric Liddell could not win a race if he had a broken foot or if he had had a withered leg. Not only are we to win the race that is set before us, but we are to walk the walk with Christ. Many Christians are so lame they cannot walk this walk. They cannot walk with Christ, their Lord.

In Paul's letter to the Ephesians, he mentions that God has given us great gifts and has prepared us that we might walk with him (Eph. 2:4–10). So not only if the Christian is blind can he not walk, but stumbles; but also if he is lame he cannot walk with his Lord. Paul follows this up by saying that 'I pray that you will be worthy to walk in this way that you have been called' (Eph. 4:1). In verse 17 of the same chapter, Paul points out that the Christian is not to walk as the other Gentiles do. Next he admonishes them that Christians are to walk in love (Eph. 5:2). The Christian is also to look with diligence at how he walks, not as a fool does (Eph. 5:15).

A few years ago, while preaching in Tunisia, I was in an automobile with a young Arab man of about 21 years old who could not speak any Spanish or English. Through an interpreter I sought to discover how he had come to know Christ as his Lord. When I asked him how he had become a Christian, he told me that for a year and a half he had watched the life of an older lady missionary who all her life had never married, but had the single purpose of sharing God through her missionary work. He said that it was in those 18 months of close observation of everything that she seemed to say and do that he decided that Christianity was really true. I wonder how many months of watching our lives it would take somebody to become convinced that Jesus Christ is real, is the truth. Now I ask you, are we lame or do we have a walk that makes the non-Christian ask us what it is that makes our life so different?

There were some among those who were brought to Christ who

were *unable to express themselves* — they were called dumb. The question now for us is this: Do we suffer from being unable to confess Jesus Christ, to own him publicly? A long time ago I told God I never wanted to be a pastor in the United States. Eventually he called me and told me that I was to go there and for four years I did pastor a church in the United States. I find it interesting how often God makes us do our 'nevers'! After I had been there about two weeks, two of the founding members of that congregation, a husband and wife, came to me and said, 'Pastor, it is important that you know that we cannot participate in any of the visiting on behalf of this church because we are so timid we cannot publicly say anything about our salvation.' My own belief is that this is a form of a spiritual disease. To this day I really believe that one of the evidences of spiritual health is the ability to talk in your own or other languages to anyone about Jesus Christ.

Now one of the reasons that I mentioned the Spanish Bible and the value of my bilingual concern is that I want not to just speak of lameness with reference to crippled legs and feet, but I want to refer to *limited hands.* I want to parallel the state of those who had limited ability with their arms and hands to the actions of Christians. The actions that Christians perform result from the special gifts that God has given us each one. I believe that God has made these gifts to be our hands.

I presume that one of the gifts that God has given to many in this audience is the gift of surgical technical skill with the hands. That truly is a God-given gift, brought to perfection by careful practice. The things that God mentioned as gifts many of you have in abundance — the ability to give, the ability to preach, to counsel, to comfort. These are gifts of God and yet how many of us have allowed these hands to wither and dry up simply because we have not practised. We have not used the gifts that God has so generously given us. Some of you also have a gift that I admire so tremendously, and that is a cross-cultural gift, the ability to move from one culture to another and to behave gently and responsively and sensitively. What a magnificent gift that is.

The cure
We've said enough now about the pathology. It's time to talk about the cure. It's right here in the fifteenth chapter of Matthew.

First we must come to the feet of Jesus. Unfortunately for many this is a very humble location. It's a position of great humility but it is an essential first step. The cure does not proceed without first coming to the feet of Jesus. The source of this power is even more humiliating because you must come to the feet of Jesus when he is on the cross, even if somebody has to carry you. Some of you have been carried by prayer to this location of healing. Some of you have been carried by the good wise counsel of those who love you, others by strong advice and scolding. Some come on their own when they recognise where the cure is.

Secondly, the disease must be recognised. In other words, the diagnosis has to be stated. The realisation has to be made openly to ourselves and to the Lord. Sometimes it's not so easy to admit the diagnosis. Just because one is on his way to preach Christ to 3,000 people does not mean that he cannot speak to somebody at the gas station where he stops. Just because you have the skill to go on caravan missions and apply hands of great healing to the needy around the world does not take away the necessity of speaking to your neighbour of your Saviour, Jesus Christ. How often am I reminded in Scripture how God resists the proud and gives grace and kindness to the humble.

The third fact is that we must realise that we are not capable of healing ourselves. We do not already possess the cure; rather we must believe that God holds the cure for our lameness, for our inability to see, for our limited actions. We must recognise, we must admit to ourselves, that God holds these gifts. It is he who gives these through grace.

Next, God says, we have to do something. If you remember, when they brought the paralysed man to him, even though the officials were all concerned when he said, 'Your sins are forgiven you', Jesus said something else very important to the man. That was, 'Take up your bed and walk.' When the man with the withered arm came to Jesus, he said, 'Stretch forth that arm.' Remember when God asked Naaman through his prophet to wash seven times in that filthy Jordan River? Do you want the cure if God tells you that what you have to do is go and talk to that spiritual brother that you have offended? What if God asks you to speak to that concerned individual in your church to whom you've been so insensitive?

Those of us who are in the medical and nursing professions have seen such terrible physical limitations and diseases that we must recognise each day the importance of seeking the physical cure that is available. May we each one also be willing to meet at the feet of Jesus for the sake of spiritual health, spiritual wholeness, for being the complete individual God wants us to be — healthy and walking with him, using the gifts that he has given us that others may know of his love and grace.

The ministry of the physician. Christian physicians are ministers of Jesus Christ like any other Christian laymen. Physicians sometimes fail to realize that they are lay ministers because as members of a profession they look on *other* people as laymen. We have all confused vocation and occupation. As Christian physicians we are called to serve the living and true God, our vocation. The way we fulfill that calling depends upon our occupation. The physician's first obligation is to minister to the physical needs of his patients, but he has a spiritual obligation as well. The latter he tends to keep separate from his professional life because of a tendency we all have to compartmentalize our lives. These compartments of our lives tend to compete with each other for time and priority, and a sense of balance is essential. The physician probably has the most advantageous occupation for a combination of physical and spiritual ministries, but accordingly the temptations to failure are also great.

EVERETT KOOP

ICCP Amsterdam, Netherlands, 1963. ***C. Everett Koop.*** *Professor of pediatric surgery, University of Pennsylvania and surgeon in chief to the Children's Hospital of Philadelphia.*

THE CHRISTIAN CONTRIBUTION TO THE DRUG PROBLEM

DUNCAN VERE

Introduction

WHY should Christians become involved with problems of drug misuse? There are three primary reasons: *Love,* or care for others; the doctrine of *Christ's Kingdom,* which opposes any other influence threatening to divert from God's control (Mat. 12:25–28); and the doctrine of *redemption,* denied when a damaged body prevents its proper use by God's Spirit (1 Cor. 6:12–20).

Having agreed that Christians should become involved with these problems, what can we contribute to lessen them? The answers lie in understanding and action.

Christian understanding

Refining analysis and identification of drug problems makes a distinctive Christian contribution to understanding. Repeatedly, studies attempting to identify the antecedent psychopathological factors in drug abuse have failed. Adverse family backgrounds or personality disorders are common amongst both drug dependent and non drug-dependent persons. Many drug takers are deeply wounded by experiences early in life, whilst others lack these features. When no cause can be seen, there is still one cause which cannot be detected because it is characterised only by the absence of what might have been there. This is an empty heart. At root a spiritual problem, this is not susceptible to normal psychological investigation.

As studies of the drug problem unfold, it becomes increasingly clear that for most drug dependent people, theirs is not really a *drug* problem at all! The real problem is a personality which wants surrogate satisfactions. Most ordinary people, even if they can easily obtain diamorphine, never consider taking it for other than therapeutic reasons. Yet the drug dependent person, if he cannot obtain

ICCP Toronto, Canada, 1972. **Duncan W. Vere.** *Consultant physician, head of the department of pharmacology and therapeutics, the London Hospital Medical College, UK.*

his drug, will get any other he can. His problem is really *dependence*, not the drug on which he depends. It is absurd to argue that if the drug were not available he would not be a dependent person. He would — on alcohol, or on other persons, or even on food.

The problem of distorted dependence has been clearly discussed by many experts, one of whom (Sharpley) described the 'strange, sterile energy' of the drug dependent person.

Now, here is a splendid secular insight. What is its Christian complement? Surely, it can only be this: Scripture teaches us that the strong man is not the one who is independent, but instead is the one who depends by faith upon God.

To present relevant spiritual facts is the next distinctively Christian contribution. The results of conventional programmes for the relief of drug dependence are poor in terms of numbers. Experts often admit that only a tremendous emotional impact can replace the power of drug dependence over a person, yet they seem reluctant to agree that a religious conversion can achieve this. Though I know of the histories of many drug dependent people, I have only known half a dozen who have found lasting relief. In one it was marriage and a new baby that proved to be the stronger force. In the others it was a new religious faith.

Informed critique of partial views about social problems is another potentially Christian contribution. By social convention, much of the Western world mistrusts cannabis but accepts alcohol and tobacco. This is not the place to plead the cause of one more than another, but since they are likely to be about equally damaging there is no rational basis for prejudice. It is all too easy for Christians to accept faulty ideas rather than to criticise them. Thus we can become conformed to this world.

There is now massive evidence in Britain that the medical profession is the guilty party in conditioning people to accept drugs as the primary solution to all their problems. This begins in small ways, but the prescribing figures are enormous and there is reliable evidence that dependence is thereby induced.

It is known that drug dependence is more frequent when society is changing and value systems come under attack, or when recreational and cultural facilities, or family stability, are denied young people, or cease when they leave home. Yet social structures in capitalist societies continually force up the price of land and property, making it harder to provide parks, sports areas, church buildings and houses for younger people. If there are social factors which tend to enslave people in dependence, they must be identified and criticised in the name of Christ until our cities are planned for people's enjoyment rather than for individual wealth.

Emotional deprivation and drug dependence can emerge from both religious and wealthy homes. One may provide the harsh pursuit of an unattainable ideal and the other be lavish with material gifts. Yet both can be lacking in the warm, personal relationships which would do so much to fill a gradually emptying heart.

Christian action

Actions complement understanding. A proper Christian understanding would be to give compassionate aid to all who suffer and this includes drug dependent people. All realise that the important phase in therapy is not drug withdrawal but aftercare. This needs immense patience, love and sacrifice and is therefore a very Christian work. Numerous Christian institutions exist, but they often find it difficult to gain a place in a neighbourhood or in the established medical organisation, even when seeking help from fellow Christians.

Proper Christian action should also involve the dissemination of accurate information about drugs to young people and their parents. Such information should understand, explain and 'God-centre' the problems of dependence.

Young casualties are met by society with a stereotyped set of reactions — denial of the problem, blame of minority groups, fear for the good name of family or society and belief that the epidemic will be self-limiting. Treatment is neglected because of a partly justifiable pessimism. It needs a constant effort to see drug dependents as they actually are. Whatever their past and present background, they are above all needy people for whom Christ died.

It is easy to assume that because they reject and attack our social order this in itself proves that that order is right. This is not so. Neither capitalism nor socialism nor the status quo are enjoined by God, but equity and love are required of us. Whatever suppresses these is opposed to God. The most effective therapy we can offer is the love of God, to restrain, constrain and then to fill the empty life.

DRUG ABUSE IN HONG KONG –
A SPIRITUAL PROBLEM

LIK-KIU DING

AT the root of the problem of drugs lies a spiritual one. In Hong Kong today the drug problem is spreading, particularly amongst young people, many of whom come from families with status and education. We have so emphasised material achievements that we have lost spiritual resources.

Whilst all might agree that this is a spiritual problem and that it must be dealt with on a spiritual basis, the question is, how do we do it? How can we recover spiritual life? How can we recover spiritual depth in our daily lives?

First, we must see clearly that many of our traditional ways have failed. In the past, emphasis on the spiritual life has ended up in separating an individual from the world in which he lived. It has frequently given a rather rigid ideological view and made spiritual growth an end in itself. This approach has been self-defeating. In many instances, our church worship has become institutionalised or superficial.

Recovery of spiritual depth involves grasping a new image of the church — not as an organisation going out to get people to join and support it financially, but rather as a group of people who are giving their lives on behalf of the whole world. It must communicate loving concern and service for all men everywhere, providing adequate structures for this to happen.

Young people can and must be challenged to see their own lives in terms of this responsibility towards the whole world. Yet challenge without commitment will be ineffective. Recovery of spiritual depth will come only as they 'give themselves first to the Lord' (2 Cor. 8:5), so finding a relationship with him through his Spirit. Head-knowledge is replaced by heart-allegiance and a joy to be shared in worship and witness.

*ICCP Toronto, Canada, 1972. **Lik-Kiu Ding**. Medical consultant and narcotic researcher to the Chinese University Social Research Centre, Hong Kong. Past physician Christ Hospital, Kapit, Borneo.*

Recovery of spiritual depth depends in large measure upon the recovery of our sense of responsibility towards God for the whole world. That is what I mean by mission — the church carrying out its responsibility to the world. Within this context, the church will be enabled to deal with drug abuse, which represents an escape from this responsibility, from relationships with others and from oneself.

To face the drug problem seriously is to face the problem of what it means to be a Christian community in our modern society. It also means facing deeper questions to do with one's own personal commitment, in faith and in life, within that Christian community.

✳

Working prayer. An early instance of the value of overt support for local authority was quite unpremeditated. Years ago, when a team from our hospital was running evangelistic camps in a forest tribal area, we had stopped outside the village to be visited as we awaited the settling of buffaloes and the completion of other household evening chores, and so were praying. Some men entering the village stopped by and overheard. It transpired later that they had heard us ask God to give wisdom and help to the village headman and all others responsible in the area. They realised from the first that we and our God were out to help and not to threaten, a factor which laid the foundation early on for mutual confidence and communal activity.

KEITH SANDERS

ICCP Bangalore, India, 1982. **R. Keith M. Sanders.** *General Secretary ICCP and CMF, UK. Past medical superintendent Duncan Hospital, Raxaul and regional superintendent, Emmanuel Hospital Association, India.*

✳

GOALS FOR CHRISTIANS IN MEDICAL EDUCATION

SAM FEHRSEN

Introduction

A GOAL is a vision or dream we strain forward to as we try to make it a reality. It also means we have not arrived! Today we as Christians stand very much within Western medicine and perhaps take too many things for granted. We should spend more time reflecting about where we are and where we are going in medicine so that we can make up our minds whether this is compatible with our first allegiance. How many of our goals are determined by our faith and Christian world-view and how much by the trends in our profession and in the world of education? Paul (Rom. 12:2) warns us not to let the world squeeze us into its mould, but that we should rather let God remould our minds from within.

Nobody can look back over the last two centuries and not be impressed by the phenomenal results of scientific methods. Many Christians have been in the forefront of these developments. But alas, we are today not only reaping the benefits, but also the toxic effects of these developments. We have allowed the scientific method too much authority over areas of life and death where it has no place. It has moved from being an instrument that we use to advance knowledge and technology, to become a religion for many, even those who claim allegiance to Christ.

PROBLEMS WITH SCIENTIFIC ADVANCE

Let us look at some of the problems that have arisen along with an almost unbridled advance of the sciences.

Mechanisation

When the stethoscope arrived, there were those who bemoaned the fact that it would cause a separation between the physician and

ICMDA Cancun, Mexico, 1986. **Sam Fehrsen.** *Professor of family medicine, MEDUNSA, RSA.*

his patient. James McKenzie was also to demonstrate how doctors committed people to a life of invalidism and misery with this instrument when they were perfectly healthy. Many a child with an innocent heart murmur was denied a normal life due to the use of the stethoscope. In spite of this 'misuse' of the instrument, the advantages of its use far outweighed its harm and it has continued in use up to this day.

It has been followed by an avalanche of instruments and machines that have all done some good and some bad. Today we even find doctors of one machine. From the time of the simplest to the most complex instruments and machines the fascination and wonder of doctors have been pulled away from the person they were dealing with to the machine and its results. Thus the chief toxic effect of mechanisation resulting from the advances in the wake of the scientific method is *dehumanisation*. Mechanisation has some brothers and sisters.

Bureaucratisation
Bureaucratisation has grown during this same period. Medicine has grown from a cottage industry into large organisations, often operating on a national scale either via the stock exchange or parliament. This third party intervention between the doctor and the patient brings both good and bad. The net effect is that it reduces access to and joy in using the system. And we are in the business of being accessible to people!

Industrialisation
Industrialisation or the industrial process has been introduced into medicine. All of us have probably seen highly efficient clinics organised for single conditions without considering other aspects of the patients' needs. Henry Ford discovered that this system works just fine for manufacturing cars in a short time. Not long afterwards, we discovered that we could do the same (for example for ante-natal care) and go home earlier and less tired than before! On the other hand, what is also disturbing is that there is a possibility that the patient has not had the feeling that she has seen anybody in particular or that anyone has accepted responsibility for her. The information she has gained was from the pamphlet she was given and the lecture to the uninformed crowd in the waiting area.

Medicalisation

In the words of Ivan Illich we are medicalising even the smallest problems. We are thereby infantilising people and making society more and more dependent on ourselves. This means that as doctors are overproduced in many countries today, they can still to a large extent continue to make a comfortable living.

Implications for learning and teaching

The impressive advances in science have brought with them increasing specialisation and fragmentation in the teaching and practising of medicine.

Subspecialists often become so isolated that they would, for instance, never dream of attending a faculty board meeting or they avoid teaching undergraduate students at all costs as these are bothersome things that will delay the advance of science, technology and careers. The net result is that very few people look at 'wholes' today. Students feel that there are voids in their knowledge and experience of patients; that they are visiting organ and body mechanics rather than doctors of people. Accompanying this is the *information explosion* that we as teachers and students need to cope with. I advise students who are struggling through this overload of information and cannot see the wood for the trees, to put aside their textbooks for a while and work with a synopsis, until they have a feeling for the whole before learning any more detail.

GOALS IN LEARNING AND TEACHING

I prefer to think in terms of learning, as teaching often has little relation to what is learned. Three curricula may be described: the explicit one, the implicit or hidden curriculum and the one not being addressed at all, the null curriculum. This last is communicated through role models who ignore and often belittle such aspects of personality as honesty, empathy and joy; hence students learn that it must be totally irrelevant and unimportant. The implicit curriculum becomes deeply ingrained in their attitudes and ethical behaviour especially, and they memorise the explicit curriculum with great efficiency for the hurdle of examinations and thereafter function to a large extent with only the 'rules' of practice and frames of reference that they have picked up from the implicit curriculum.

Students to become learners

The first main goal will, therefore, be to enable students to become *learners.* They should be able to bring all three curricula as much as possible to the level of consciousness, reflect on them, and learn to decide if what they see in their mind's eye is compatible with their life of faith. In this way we will hopefully move away from over-stimulation by sensation and passive imagination and masses of information, towards a more active imagination and reflection. We need to stop living at the top of our heads and out of touch with our feelings, and learn to integrate that which we learn and prac-tise into our life of faith. How do we set about learning to think and reflect in a world of technology, where a lot of thought and reason-ing is replaced by remembering to do the right battery of tests and get the solution from a list of options on the computer? The first thing is to shift from learning only information to also learn the management of information, as this is irrevocably with us. We will never be able to master all there is to know at one time, neither will we be able to keep up with future developments. There is too much to learn and the half life of 'facts' is just too short. No longer can we specialise to be able to know and control the whole subject.

Another trend in medical education is *to get students to parade their knowledge and strengths* before colleagues and teachers on ward rounds and in group discussions. This may be good for things that have to be memorised, but it does not help people to grow. It produces an atmosphere in which the student is continually being put down and discouraged if he does not know something. We need to create a 'safe space' where students and teachers can both feel free to bring their ignorance and weak-nesses, so that they can learn and build, instead of devouring one another.

A greater emphasis on what kind of doctors we should be will help to reduce the harmful effects of just concentrating on knowing and doing. Research seems to indicate that the being aspects are largely related to the role modelling influence of teachers rather than the overt curriculum. Because of this, my hunch is that teachers should spend far more time on developing as persons themselves and evaluating their own attitudes and values than those of their students. Again, students should learn how they can grow and develop as people, rather than going through a prescriptive programme about attitudes and values.

Specialisation and fragmentation

The second goal in education for me will be to learn to deal with the problems accompanying specialisation and fragmentation. It has become abundantly clear that we need specialists and generalists, though many only give lip service to the idea. To quote Nouwen, we need to move from hostility to hospitality and get real teamwork within the profession. Patients need the generalist to serve an integrating function, helping them to interpret the physical, psycho-social and spiritual aspects of their illness, if medicine is to be rehumanised. Having faced their feelings about the practicalities of, and perhaps also the meanings of their illness for themselves and their families, a visit to the medicine of high technology becomes an experience within a whole and not a fragmenting episode. If we do not teach the next generation of doctors and other health professions to live together and co-operate, the way they relate to one another will be decided upon by those who make laws and regulate society. Not only does fragmentation dehumanise, it also costs more. Our students must know how to become specialists or generalists, whichever direction they choose, and also learn how to relate to one another.

For generalists especially, there is a lot of hard work ahead, to understand what holism is. Holism for many is just a trash can into which all kinds of hocus-pocus therapies and philosophies are thrown, to be produced on demand. We need to work at understanding the relationship between psychological, spiritual and physical well-being. How does hatred and an unforgiving spirit affect cancer and acute and chronic disease, for instance? We must develop the tools to study and communicate these issues with our colleagues in a way that allows validation. These tools will probably not be the empirical methods used almost exclusively in traditional scientific analysis.

Synchronism

The third goal to aim for is mainly for us generalists in primary care/family practice. To some extent it also applies to specialists. We must learn to work simultaneously with the patient's agenda as well as our own.

It is the concentration on the doctor's agenda to the exclusion of the patient's that has allowed medicine to go so far down the road towards alienating people. The books on clinical method used by our generation of students actually used vocabulary such as, 'systematic interrogation', 'the patient admits and denies' and so forth. Not only does this sound like a charge office, but it leads to guilt. A patient recently said to me, 'They asked me so many questions that I felt guilty for being ill.'

Conclusions

I think we as doctors should have an agenda that has more breadth than that which most medical schools presently teach. We should give attention to health and not exclusively to disease. We should think in terms not only of the patient before us, but also of the population we are responsible for. Even so we must learn to curb our own agenda till we are more sure of what the patient's agenda is. For this we need new skills. We also need to learn to negotiate with our patients and communities what the problem really is before we move on to a mutually acceptable management. This will require the kind of love Paul Tournier describes. 'Really to love is to listen, to love is to give one's time, to love is to try to speak in his language, to love always means going to others.' When we do this and restore the patients' agendas into our clinical method, truly giving attention to their expectations, feelings and thoughts, the processes of dehumanisation and medicalisation will be reversed.

I have been trying to give you my responses to medicine past, present and future, speaking as someone who reads the Scriptures and tries to integrate my 'medical life' with my 'life in the Spirit'. I hope you will, with me, continue to look at what medicine is doing to us, whether we are teachers or students (and we are usually both), and to weigh what we see. Oppose the negative and strain forward to those things that foster service, caring, neighbourliness, respect, the release of captives, those things that heal wounds, build community; but above all bring hope, love and worship of God, our creator and healer. I end with Paul the apostle as translated by Phillips (1 Cor. 8:1–3):

> 'While knowledge may make a man look big, it is only love that can make him grow to his full stature. For whatever a man may know he still has a lot to learn, but if he loves God, he is opening his whole life to the Spirit of God.'

CHRISTIAN MEDICAL STUDENTS IN A CHANGING WORLD

EWE KONG SNG

THERE is an old Chinese proverb which says: 'The same man never steps into the same river twice.' What it means is that life, like a river, is moving all the time. No two days are exactly quite the same. We live in a constantly changing world. New discoveries and innovations are being introduced all the time. It has been estimated that each year over sixty million pages of scientific and technical publications are produced. This is a remarkable amount of knowledge to be churned out. Sooner or later, our lifestyles and habits are bound to be affected by them.

In medicine, the sweeping changes are no less apparent. The remarkable advances at both the research and clinical levels in recent years are well known to all of us. So fast is the pace of development that in some disciplines new textbook editions on the subjects have to be produced every two years — much to the consternation of students and teachers. There is no doubt that the advances will continue. New and exciting possibilities will continue to be opened for mankind. But with every advance there also come along fresh challenges and responsibilities for the medical practitioner. If he has new tools to wage war against human suffering and disease, new insight into disease patterns and their aetiologies, then he also has new roles that he must play. He can no longer confine himself to the mere prescription of pills and mixtures. A new world of possibilities is being opened up and the practitioner must be prepared to accept the new responsibilities. We want to examine some of these possibilities and to see their implications for us as Christian medical practitioners. We also want to ask how as medical students we can prepare ourselves today for the world of tomorrow. For the purpose of our discussion, I want to borrow an expression used by that great reformer John Calvin in his description of Christ's ministry: 'The physician today must play the roles of prophet, priest and king!'

ICCP Singapore, 1975. **Ewe Kong Sng.** *General Secretary, Graduate Christian Fellowship, Bible expositor, Singapore.*

The physician as prophet

Some years back, in Minamata, a small Japanese town, an estimated 300 people were killed and almost 1,000 others were crippled by poisonous mercury waste which had been systematically discharged into the local harbour. Fish which had fed on the waste were in turn consumed by the local population, resulting in the tragedy. This incident highlighted once again the intimate interlocking of the health of a community and its environment. Man is both a product and a prisoner of his environment. When his environment is poisoned, man suffers. There are today some two million known chemical compounds. Every year about 25,000 new ones are developed. Of these about 10,000 will ultimately have commercial uses. Although most of these are 'harmless', their long-term effects are uncertain. Man is therefore constantly exposing himself to new sources of possible poisoning, some of them chemicals that did not exist a century, a decade or even a year or two ago. Environmental disease is becoming the disease of the century.

Probably even more fundamental to the problem of pollution as a contributive factor to ill-health is the kind of society we live in and the kinds of values we subscribe to. For after all, man ultimately determines the kind of environment with which he wants to surround himself. Think, for instance, where the pollutants would be if a society really determined not to transform itself into a free-for-all consumer society. Where would the problem of massive malnutrition and hunger be if a nation were willing to tackle seriously its social impediments of corruption and greed, and to rechannel its resources from armaments to food production? In Asia today, we still have societies that venerate all forms of life. To what extent would the problem of hunger be met if some of these sacred cows could be used for food? To what extent is the preservation of disease-carrying insects and rodents a contributive factor to a people's ill-health?

The links between a people's health and all these factors cannot be ignored by the physician. Diseases and human suffering have to be fought not only at the personal level but also at the social level. We must not only be concerned with our patients' micro-environment but with their macro-environment as well. We must be prepared to make prophetic judgements on society. Its deleterious cultural values, myths and taboos, food habits, its quest for the mirage of a 'better' life, its insensitivity to the aged, poor and handicapped because of their poor economic returns, its short-sighted social goals, etc., are as much our concern as the immediate management of our patients. In short, the practice of good medicine cannot be divorced from a genuine desire to reshape society and to redirect its values. The physician today has a prophetic ministry.

The physician as priest

Recently I spoke to a group of patients addicted to heroin. There were about forty of them, many still in their early twenties. After the meeting, we had an informal discussion. What struck me was that many of them realised their error and expressed their desire not to go back to the drug after their treatment. But again and again they asked: 'How can I be sure that I won't go back to heroin?' It is clear that, in this instance, the mere prescription of pills, fresh air and sunlight are not going to be sufficient. The crucial question is: To what kind of life are we restoring them? If these patients are to be helped at all, then their needs must be met at the deeper level of their existence. After all, it was largely the lack of spiritual ballast and undergirding that had led many of these patients to turn to drugs in the first place.

With the kind of society we are moving into, this need for spiritual undergirding will become increasingly important. Modern man is haunted by a sickness of the soul. His very technological advances have undermined his sense of self-worth and the significance of his own existence. It was Sigmund Freud who once said that there have been three great revolutions in man's history — the Copernican, the Darwinian and the Freudian (of course!) revolutions. Note how each of these have in turn undermined man's self-estimate. The Copernican revolution exploded the myth that the earth was the centre of the universe. Man's planet home is just one of the countless billions of stars and planets that fill our universe. Mother earth, and man's ego, could not have been more humbled. The Darwinian revolution suggested that man emerged from the animal kingdom. Any idea that man is unique and the result of special creation is dismissed. Freud's own revolutionary teachings suggested that man is but a prisoner of his subconscious. He is not autonomous and his religious ideas and behaviour are nothing more than the by-products of his upbringing.

With each of these discoveries man takes a step nearer to committing existential suicide. He loses meaning of himself and any hope of discovering his own uniqueness is mercilessly crushed. Added to this are the tremendous psychosocial pressures of modern urban life: its competitiveness, its overcrowding, its many anxieties and uncertainties about the future, its many rapid changes allowing no time for adjustments, etc. Is it any wonder therefore that so many find themselves confused? Is it any wonder that so many have decided to opt out of life by turning to drugs and aberrant behaviour? Without any firm bearing in life, they are like ships cast adrift amidst a turbulent sea.

In his book *Future Shock,* Alvin Toffler, having examined some of the common areas of tension in modern life, suggests: 'To help tide millions of people over the difficult transitions they are likely to face, we shall be forced to "deputize" large numbers of non-professional people in the community — businessmen, students, teachers, workers and others — to serve as "crisis counsellors".' The physician is precisely in a unique position to serve as a crisis counsellor. He is often called at those times when help of this kind is most needed, e.g. an attempted suicide, a patient with an incurable condition, a mother with a deformed child, a business failure, etc. What these people need is more than just tranquillisers and sedatives. They need a soul therapist — someone who can minister strength and courage to their souls to enable them to cope with life again. I believe this priestly function of the physician will become increasingly important in the days ahead.

The physician as king

In the time-honoured Hippocratic Oath, one of the statements declares: 'I will abstain from whatever is deleterious and mischievous. I will give no deadly medicine to anyone if asked, nor suggest any such counsel.' That the physician has within his means tremendous power over the lives of men has been recognised from early times. His understanding of bodily functions and his knowledge of the potency of various drugs give him the responsibility of seeing that this power is never abused. It must at all times be exercised for the good of his patients.

Today, as a result of the various medical advances, the physician's power over the bodies and lives of men has reached frightening proportion. For instance, understanding physiological processes has enabled patients to be resuscitated who have actually died. The doctor can now prolong indefinitely the patient's metabolic functions long after his brain has ceased to 'live'. He can replace malfunctioning organs and change a patient's sex. The scientists' unlocking of the genetic code will soon enable the physician to tamper with life's fundamental building blocks. He will be able to treat genetically-linked diseases in the prenatal stage. What is alarming is when geneticists begin to speculate on the possibility of breeding new species of human beings. Highly gifted individuals could be multiplied through cloning. Again, the physician's knowledge of the various centres in the brain will soon enable better control over a patient's behaviour. This may be done either through specially designed electrical stimulators appropriately implanted in the brain and remotely controlled, or through the use of psychopharmaceutical compounds.

All these God-like powers have imparted to the physician unparalleled opportunities for good or for evil. Also, he has taken upon himself responsibilities which transcend the previous duty of simply prescribing pills. He has, for instance, to decide which patient should receive the kidney transplant and which other patient be allowed to die. He has to decide whether to terminate an unborn life with a proven genetically-linked disease, whether to switch off the resuscitative machine which is sustaining a vegetative patient, whether to alter the genetic code of the unborn, to change the sex of his patient or to alter the behaviour of the mentally maladjusted. These are not decisions that are easy to make, for they affect the very life of his patient, or at least the quality of that life. However much he may dislike his new God-like role, the physician cannot turn the clock back. Man's aspiration to be like God (Gen. 3:5) has never been closer to fulfilment than today.

The religious dimension

The physician's prophetic role today calls him to join in the task of reshaping society and to make judgements upon our cultural and social lifestyles. His priestly role calls him to act as a soul therapist and to minister to the deeper and more existential needs of his patients. His God-like role has invested him with power to tamper with the very fundamentals of life and to create exciting possibilities for the human race.

With these new responsibilities, a number of crucial questions begin to emerge. For instance, what is life and non-life? Upon what ethical criteria does the physician decide who to save and who not to save? What are the limits of experimentation on the human embryo? What makes man man? What kind of counsel can the physician give that will meet the deeper needs of his patients? What has he to say to the dying? These questions are not only disturbingly fundamental, but some of them are also engaging the minds of the laymen.

The pivotal question which all of us must ask ourselves is: Can we adequately fulfil our new roles in medicine and do justice to our patients if we do not have a religious outlook on life? I believe the answer is in the negative. The ultimate questions about man and his existence are religious in nature. If man is to retain his significance and medicine to retain its human dimension, then as practitioners we cannot afford not to cultivate a religious perspective to life.

The Christian physician

The Christian physician is in a unique position to provide that religious perspective in medicine. His understanding of man and his existence enables him to make valuable contributions to the fulfilment of these new roles.

Firstly, his recognition of the distortions of evil means that, *in his prophetic role, he cannot ignore the real forces he has to contend with.* He realises that the deeper problems of human greed, selfishness and corruption have as much to contribute to the problems of environmental and social ills as have the lack of proper legislations and their enforcement. The Old Testament prophets of course had always recognised this. They repeatedly traced the roots of their social problems to the hidden recesses of the human heart rather than to external structures and influences. This does not mean that as Christian physicians we are going to overcome the problems of malnutrition and environmental pollution through the preaching of the Gospel alone. These will have to be dealt with through social means and legislation. But it does imply that there can be no lasting transformation of society if our effort is not also directed at the deeper level of man's moral and spiritual life. Man's biggest problem is not his environment but himself.

Secondly, the Christian physician's recognition of the uniqueness of man means that *in his priestly role he will not fail to ignore that deeper homesickness of the soul.* St Augustine has well expressed man's soul sickness in this way: 'Thou hast made us for thyself, and our hearts are restless until they rest in thee.' If that is so, then it means that we must be willing to struggle with our patients' fears, doubts and anxieties and to help them to see beyond themselves. Man may be a creature of Today, but he has Forever engraved in him. When our patients begin to realise this, the dying will find hope, the defeated will find strength, the bereaved will find comfort and the anxious will find peace.

Thirdly, the Christian physician's recognition of a more final reality means that *in his God-like role he will never make himself the final point of reference.* His new-found power may be awesome, but it is never absolute. What knowledge and skills he has have been entrusted to him by God. To God he remains accountable as to how he uses them. This means that there is a certain frame of reference within which he exercises this power. When there is the temptation to transgress beyond this frame, then he must have the courage to say 'No'. He may have God-like power, but he is not God.

The Christian medical student

In the light of the above, what implications are there for us who are still students? How can we prepare ourselves for the tasks that are before us? I want to make three suggestions.

Firstly, we need to be *aware of the trends in today's world.* Let us learn to identify the various psychosocial and technological forces that go to shape our society. Let us learn to understand the impact of these on man and his existence. This means that we need to read widely. Our medical textbooks are often most wanting on those points we have just been discussing.

Secondly, we need to *define our own Biblical worldviews.* Let us not be content with having just a religion of the 'hereafter'; we need a religion of the 'here-and-now'. What has the Bible to say about man's existential impasse, his ethical dilemma, his ideological tensions and so on? Often, there are no neat and ready answers to these questions. There is therefore all the more urgency for us to have a comprehensive Bible study scheme so that we can look at these problems theologically.

Thirdly, we need to *recover our sense of Christian vocation.* There is probably no other need more important in our time than this. Unfortunately, the word 'vocation' has lost much of its original force. Today it is taken to mean either a person's occupation or the so-called 'full-time' Christian ministry. Of course it is nothing like that. Our Christian vocation is nothing less than our calling as the people of God (Eph. 4:1). Why are we Christians? Why are we here? What is God's mission for his people? These are questions that are crucial to our understanding of our vocation. To recover our vocation, therefore, is to discover our true selves. Only then can we adequately fulfil those roles that God has called us to.

In a world that is confused and sick, my prayer is that a generation of Christian physicians will emerge who will take their Christian vocation seriously, for it is only in so doing that we can point our patients to the Lord Jesus Christ who alone is the true prophet, priest and king.

Jog your mind too. The priorities committees, the postgraduate educational bureaucracy and the audit committee do not have the appeal of the operating theatre, the rural dispensary or the cancer research laboratory, but do not despise them; God has his jobs for Christians here, too.

The *New England Journal of Medicine* advertises itself with a picture of two muscular physicians jogging round the block and the caption 'Jog your mind too'. If God has blessed you with a mind that enjoys being jogged he may present you with an unglamorous but necessary intellectual challenge.

DAVID KERR

*ICCMS Oxford, UK, 1980. **David Kerr.** Professor of medicine, University of Newcastle, UK.*

A SERVICE OF COMPASSION AND STEADFASTNESS

HEINZ GOTTSCHALL

Introduction

WITHIN the word compassion lies not only the idea of shared suffering but the suggestion, too, of endurance, tolerance and patience. All are needed when meeting those who are clearly sick in body, or who have less obvious primary or secondary disturbance of their minds.

Steadfastness is the ability to persevere in a certain conviction, commission or challenge. This type of steadfastness is an important part of medical care and personifies the love of Jesus Christ in a way which should be the main concern of the Christian doctor.

Where does the physician find the ability to do the so-called best for each patient? There are three points to consider:

- Intelligence and skill are individual talents, given to us by our Creator.
- The way in which these talents develop in us depends both on our political, social, cultural and educational conditions and on our mental and spiritual upbringing and development.
- The so-called best for our patients must be in accordance with their personal background.

As Christian physicians, we also have a responsibility to practise and preach to individual patients the love of God, as shown in Jesus Christ.

The Christian doctor's professional education, linked with the conscious responsibility for acquiring medical know-how and practical skills along with the ability to evaluate a patient's social, religious and mental background, all call for deep spiritual maturity. It is also helpful to evaluate the moral status of patients, their own views about illness, life and death and, if also Christian, their degree of spiritual maturity. In this way, the illness may be

ICCP Bangalore, India, 1982. **Heinz Gottschall**. *Internist, Winterthur. President AGEAS, Switzerland. ICMDA Chairman 1986–94.*

viewed biblically, with a spiritually aware physician who seeks to understand the patient's socio-cultural background.

The spiritual maturation of the Christian physician

It is nothing but the grace of God, as we understand it in Jesus Christ, to be born into a family or to have those around us who show us the love of Christ by word and deed. Every human being has the God-given ability to be religious, but it needs to be cultivated. Natural religiosity, though, is not the same as Christ's appealing to me personally, or at all comparable to the gift which enables me, by grace, to subject my will to the will of God. To understand and then experience God's grace and to be at peace with him through the atoning, all-forgiving sacrifice of Christ Jesus — that is the highest expression of God's love to men. For God is not just lovely: he *is* love. He is not just a nice father.

The natural man is void and empty without an opening *for* and an outlook *to* God. This emptiness is the opposite of the fullness promised by God to those who believe. Neither talents nor knowledge, neither noble efforts nor privileges, enable us to live a life of fullness and purpose as God meant it to be. It is purity of heart that gives clarity of vision.

In today's world, with its frightening total relativity, stands the firm claim of God to be the highest authority. Only the person who realises deep in his heart who God really is, in the light and clarity of his son Jesus Christ, only that person will find purpose for life and peace with God. Becoming personally transparent *before* God and *for* God brings the necessary purity of heart. This purity is not according to established human morality, this being more intellectual and social, but is essentially that of the Ten Commandments and the Sermon on the Mount. So, I repeat! It is purity of heart that gives clarity of vision.

To what extent a Christian doctor is devoted to his patients and fellows is, after all, determined by the extent to which he is true, compassionate, loving and helpful — that is, in compassion and steadfastness. In shared suffering and persevering service to the sick as much as to every other creature, you will experience God and the power and working of the Holy Spirit in your fellows and even in yourself.

Modern man is no longer persuaded to believe in God by mere logic; he asks for a living experience. Only in such measure as we let Christ break through into our lives are we able to escape from our self-centredness, our wrong ambitions and our preconceptions. In the legendary arrogance of scientists, we can too easily forget that we are God's children and so lose our original trust and confidence in the divine and wise decrees of our Creator God.

Illness seen from secular and Christian viewpoints

People begin to evaluate the nature of illness and health — or in common parlance of fortune and misfortune — according to their own standards. It is only by faith, by experiencing reconciliation with God through the death of Jesus Christ on the cross, that a breakthrough to a genuine Christian existence can happen. Being a Christian is not just being born again; it also entails growth. It is only as God's Holy Spirit is expressed in our daily work that our original trust in God can grow. Our fear (expressing as it does our separation from God) can then be conquered.

The secular view

The World Health Organisation defines health as a state of physical, emotional, social and spiritual wellbeing. Illness therefore includes very different aspects of existential insecurity, both for the natural man and also for the spiritually inactive, traditional Christian.

According to a widespread Western misunderstanding, sickness is often spoken of as an act of God, in punishment for sin. The biblical message is quite different. Think only of Job, or the man born blind who was healed by Jesus, both of whom were cleared of blame for their illnesses. Even psychosomatic medicine has problems in avoiding the error of interpreting emotionally induced illness as punishment. Thus, infective colitis is considered an 'honourable' illness, whereas to have an irritable colon suggests sin affecting the patient's emotional reserves of strength and is regrettably labelled as psychosomatic.

Just as widespread is the view that illness stems from failure of someone's physical or mental machinery. It therefore endangers one's career and has to be concealed. Society today demands that everyone functions and operates perfectly. This high expectation leads to the successful manager or super-athlete becoming the ideal and every form of training for physical fitness, be it purposeful or absurd, is also idolised. Sickness and healing in the Bible have never been an end in themselves: Paul even says, 'For me to live is Christ *and to die is gain'* (Phil. 1:21).

The Christian view

If our understanding of the purpose of life is godly, then, viewed from the divine perspective, childhood, middle age or death are not mere phases offering differing qualities of life, but parts of one and the same course. With this attitude, all kinds of Christian experience, whether of different age-groups or even in different states of health, offer the possibility of development in a way that will please both God and ourselves.

Sickness with its resulting sorrow is thus a form of living in a world cut off from God's fullness. It poses the problem of how to cope with the inner and outer conflicts which arise. Especially in our Western world, physical illness may be the expression of a psychic injury, an attempt to repair an inner loss or to resolve an unconscious conflict. Very often, then, physical illness is an attempt by the self to heal the psyche.

Have we understood and learnt to interpret illness as the language of the entire organism? What is the message of a particular illness to the afflicted individual and what is the message to me through his or her perspective of being weighed down by it? We have to hear and understand these silent questions to be able to find the proper moment to speak first to God about the patient, rather than to the patient first about God.

We also have to consider the possibility that the illness may well be an attempt by the patient to repair damaged relationships. Think, for example, of an exhausted housewife, spouse and mother, who has to be hospitalised. Suddenly, her husband and children develop strengths never known before, which enable each of them to become more independent and to take more responsibility. Out of this mutual assistance grows a new solidarity, good for all of them, including the mother.

It is in such situations that we, as Christian doctors, must have an open ear and be more sensitive to what is going on at the emotional level. In any case, our medical help is only *one* side of the necessary support. Silent intercession and an open testimony to our Lord Jesus Christ will also help and, as illustrated, can open the way for the inner healing of the whole family.

Health is not the same as perfection, neither in a spiritual nor a secular sense. The fictional image of a physically and intellectually perfect human being arose out of the 19th century confidence in science. Today it is just as common. It matches well with the self-righteous arrogance of good works and self-sufficiency.

Summary

Christ leaves us in this world and puts others at our side, Christian and non-Christian alike. In every situation, we must allow Christ to equip us, through his Holy Spirit, with the necessary wisdom, spiritual insight and vision, as well as with much courage and patient endurance.

This is the service of compassion and steadfastness, for the life of the physician and patient alike is not static. Times of rest are followed by times of change; security and safety can suddenly become conflict and crisis; phases of health can alternate with phases of sickness. It is into this field of tension that our Creator God has put us and only by abiding in Christ shall we find the necessary balance. Through such a dynamic process, we are enabled to hand over to God in prayer our compassion and fellow suffering as we also offer time, as well as physical and emotional support, to individual patients.

We can only get the balance right by surveying all the medical resources available to us with reverent humility before God, then restricting ourselves to offering that which will serve to restore the patient to wholeness. Curable and incurable people equally need our help, because help should always be for the whole person. There is no such thing as a worthless life, even when it comes to death. Let us bear up all our patients with prayerful hearts, then the appropriate distribution of time, effort and professional activity will fall into place. Professionally speaking we work *with* our patients *before* God; spiritually speaking we testify *to* our patients of our relationship *with* God.

Compassion on its own can blind us, but linked to a Spirit-given steadfastness we shall become perceptive and understanding tools in the Master's hand. Let us pray daily for such wisdom and understanding.

Section 5

Responsibilities

---✱---

Facing facts and meeting needs
at home and abroad

❖

AN ICMDA CONGRESS

Objectives of ICMDA world and regional congresses expressed through the Introduction to the 5th ICCP, Singapore 1975.

OON TECK KHOO

Mr President, your excellencies, distinguished guests and friends. This is an opportune time to consider co-operation between medical practitioners and health extension workers, medical missions and national health service, the clergy and the doctor, the lay and the profes-sional, in achieving maximal health care and promoting a comprehensive health care delivery to the community. The great importance of health care centres in rural areas where 80% of the population live in developing countries is increasingly realised by governments and funding agencies. Therefore the concept of primary health care and the critical role of the health extension worker will be discussed in some depth. More important still, the emphasis will be on a Christian partnership with all its many implications of mutual giving and sharing, as in a marriage. There will be a need, for example, to consider situations where one partner is more prominent.

This is a gathering of Christian physicians, and time will be laid aside each morning to consider the relevance of God's word in the Bible to the practice of medicine. We recognise that there is a spiritual dimension in the nature of man and that Scripture speaks of God's concern for the wholeness of the individual. In other words, man's body, mind and spirit are indivisible and to be truly healthy, every part of man's nature must be given care and attention.

*ICCP Singapore, 1975. **Oon Teck Khoo**. Professor of medicine, Academy of Medicine, Singapore. ICMDA President 1975–82, Vice-President 1986–94.*

❖

OUR VOCATIONAL SERVICE

JOHN STOTT

WHAT I propose to do this morning is to take three words, all of which are in fairly common use among us and all of which have to some degree been misunderstood, and together we are going to seek a biblical understanding of these words. The first word is 'vocation', the second is the word 'service', or 'ministry', which are synonyms, and the third is the word 'work'.

Vocation is of course a word of Latin origin and its Anglo-Saxon equivalent is calling. Our calling. Now in the New Testament the Greek verb *kaleo*, meaning to call, is used of God at least 150 times. Of course, sometimes the word is used in a secular context and it means to invite, such as to a wedding or a feast. It is also used to summon somebody, as when King Herod summoned the wise men. Now when God calls us, his calling includes both these ideas. It is on the one hand a gracious invitation to a banquet and on the other it is an authoritative summons.

The point I want to make from Scripture about our calling or our vocation is that when God calls us he is not calling us primarily to *do* something but to *be* something. In other words our calling, according to Scripture, concerns much more our character and what kind of a person we are than simply what our job is. It is interesting that there are non-Christian people who are saying this very thing today and sometimes they seem to have a better biblical understanding than some of us Christians.

Let us look into the New Testament and find out when this word calling is used and what it is to which God invites us, to which he summons us, to which he calls us; in other words what is our vocation as Christians? Let me summarise it for you in seven short sections.

Our Christian vocation
He calls us to Jesus Christ (1 Cor. 1:9). 'God is faithful, through whom you have been called into the fellowship of his Son Jesus

ICCMS Oxford, UK, 1980. **John Stott.** *Rector Emeritus, All Souls Church, London, UK.*

Christ.' What a marvellous verse that is. We could spend all morning meditating on it as it speaks of the faithfulness of God and the fellowship of Christ. God's calling is that we should come to know Jesus Christ and have fellowship with him. Similarly Romans 1:6 says, 'You have been called to belong to Jesus Christ.' Now it is quite clear in the gospels, that when Jesus called people, he said, 'Come unto me, follow me.' It was a call to know him, a call to be with him, a call to have fellowship with him, a call to belong to him. That is what it means fundamentally to be a Christian. To be a Christian in its very essence is to know Christ and to belong to Christ, so that he is our Saviour, our Friend and our Lord.

He calls us to freedom. It is essential to take this next because when we talk about being called to belong to Christ, it means called to be his slave and his servant. We then have to define what this slavery is. We have to say that according to the New Testament it is authentic freedom. Galatians 5:1 says, 'Stand firm in freedom with which Christ has set you free', and verse 13 of the same chapter, 'You were called to freedom', that is, freedom from guilt and freedom from self-centredness — what Malcolm Muggeridge calls the 'dark little dungeon of my own ego'. We are made free from fear, free ultimately from death, and free to live in love for God and man. This is our call to freedom.

He calls us to fellowship, not only now with his Son Jesus Christ but with one another. Colossians 3:15 says, 'Let the peace of Christ rule in your hearts to which you have been called in one body.' What is this peace to which we are called in fellowship with others? Paul goes on to define it. Peace — the famous Hebrew word *shalom* — is a social concept in the Bible. It doesn't just mean inner tranquillity, which I enjoy by myself in sweet solitude. Peace is reconciliation with one another as well as with God and the context in Colossians 3, within which verse 15 comes, makes it plain that this is the peace to which he is referring. The same is taught in Ephesians, the parallel letter, which is all about God's new community into which we have been called. So I hope nobody is attempting to live in isolation. The New Testament knows nothing of that grotesque anomaly, an unchurched Christian. God calls us to belong to Christ and to the new community of Christ. It is inconceivable that we should belong to Christ without belonging to one another. We are called to Christ, called to freedom, called to fellowship.

He calls us to holiness. We are 'called to be saints' (Rom. 1:7), or, as in 1 Corinthians 1:2, called to belong to the holy people of God — people set apart to belong. We are set apart from the standards and values of the world in order to develop new standards and a new value system, given to us by God. We are called to be saints. The Christian calling is 'a holy calling' (2 Tim. 1:9). 'As he who called you is holy, so you must be holy in all your conduct' (1 Pet. 1:15). 'God has not called you for uncleanness but for holiness' (1 Thes. 4:7). So you see, it is repeated many times in the New Testament that we are called to be holy. If you don't like the word holiness try Christlikeness as a substitute. We are called to be like Christ in character and conduct.

He calls us to witness. Part of our Christian vocation as the people of God is to spread abroad his wonderful deeds throughout the world. 'You are God's people that you should declare the wonderful deeds of him who has called you out of darkness into his marvellous light. For once you were no people, now you are God's people, once you would not receive mercy, now you have received mercy' (1 Pet. 2:9–10). This is a striking contrast between what we were and what we are. We were in darkness, now we are in his marvellous light. We were no people, alienated, now we are his people, reconciled. Once we were under his wrath, now we are under his mercy. We cannot keep these truths to ourselves. He has called us into his marvellous light in order that the light may shine and that we may spread abroad his excellences throughout the world.

He calls us to suffering. 'What credit is it' (and Peter is writing as the stormclouds of persecution gathered on the horizon and Nero was known to be hostile to the Christian church) 'if when you do wrong you are punished for it and you take it patiently' — there is no particular credit then; you have deserved your punishment and you get it, 'But if when you do well and suffer for it and take it patiently, this is pleasing to God' (1 Pet. 2:20–21). Why? Because you have been called to this. And why have you been called to this? Because Christ suffered for us that we should follow in his footsteps. We are called to suffering and called to bear suffering patiently. It comes as a surprise, even as a shock, to many Christians that suffering should be part of our vocation, but it is. It is part of the Christian calling to suffer. It has always been so. Jesus warned us of it. The apostles warned us of it and it is still so today.

He calls us to glory. 'After you have suffered a while, God who has called you to his eternal glory in Christ Jesus will strengthen, stablish and settle you' (1 Pet. 5:10).

I don't know what your reaction is to our Christian calling. It is probably not new to you; you may well have studied it already in the New Testament. But it seems to me to be a beautifully balanced picture of the Christian vocation, the Christian life.

Our Christian service

Now I come on to my second word which is the word service or ministry. They are interchangeable terms. They describe a Christian life-style in which we live not for ourselves but for Christ and seek to be the servants of others for his sake. I have three things to say about the word service or ministry.

Every Christian without exception is called to service. No, I did not say that every Christian was called to *the* ministry (I will comment on that in a moment), but I said every Christian is called to ministry; *diakonia* is the Greek word for it. It is very misleading to use the definite article and talk about *the* ministry when we mean the pastorate, because, whenever we do that, we are giving the impression that there is only one form of ministry and 'the ministry' is the title. But that isn't true, it isn't biblical and, because it is misleading, I hope we will give it up. Whenever anybody now says to me, 'I'm hoping to go into the ministry', I say immediately, 'Really, which one?' because there are many different kinds of ministry. If we mean the pastorate, then let us say the pastorate or the pastoral ministry. There are many ministries, many Christian ministries, many full-time Christian ministries. In other words, there are many different ways of giving our lives in the service of God and man.

How can I be so dogmatic in saying that every Christian is called to the ministry? How can I be sure about that? Well, the answer is because of the Lord Jesus, who is our model. 'He took on him the form of a servant' (Phil. 2:7). He fulfilled the prophecy in the latter part of the book of Isaiah about the servant of the Lord. He gave himself without reserve in service, preaching, healing, feeding the hungry, comforting the sad, forgiving the sinful. He never thought about himself, he gave his life in service. He was the servant par excellence. He said once, 'The Son of Man didn't come to be served but to serve and to give his life', and in particular for him, 'to give his life as a ransom for many' (Mat. 20:28). In the upper room, you remember, when the disciples were quarrelling with one another as to which of them would be the greatest, Jesus said, 'I am among you as a serving man' (Luke 22:27). He exhibited this in action. He put on an apron (a symbol of servitude), he got on his hands and knees and he washed the apostles' feet, and then he said, 'If I, your Lord and Master, have washed your feet, you ought also to wash one another's feet, I have given you an example that you should do as I have done' (John 13:14–15). So if Jesus was the servant, took the form of a servant and gave himself in service, then of course every Christian is called to the same thing.

We are not called primarily to greatness, we are called to service. Indeed, greatness is measured in the kingdom of God according to service. I hope all of us are well aware of this, that the concept of greatness or leadership is radically different in the kingdom of God from the concept of greatness and leadership in the secular world. The world measures greatness by success or power but Jesus measures greatness by service.

What is your ambition? I hope it isn't to be great in the secular sense of that word, to hit the headlines, to become a famous physician or surgeon or even missionary. I hope it isn't to get rich: there can be great wealth in medicine. I hope it isn't to live comfortably. I hope your ambition is greatness in the kingdom of God, which is service. As one writer has put it, service is not a stepping stone to nobility, it is nobility and the only nobility that is recognised in the kingdom of God. Give your life in service — every Christian is called to serve.

Our Christian service includes our life work. In other words we must see our life-work as a vital part of our Christian ministry or service. Indeed, the one thing that is certain about our career, if we are Christians, is that we shall give our life in service. Since we are followers of Jesus this point is non-negotiable. I say this because there are too many Christians, even too many doctors, who see their job as an unfortunate, an unavoidable necessity, or even a downright nuisance. They have taken to themselves a wife, or a husband, and have got children. They have got to earn their living, they have got to support them and the job is the means to that end.

Others see their job in terms of personal ambition. They want wealth or status or power or security, and I say again, it is unthinkable that a Christian will decide his life-work by such criteria. Other Christians, even doctors I am afraid, see their job primarily as a useful sphere of evangelism, a way of reaching people that you could not otherwise reach for Christ, but that is a totally inadequate reason for becoming a doctor. We must not see our job simply as a sphere of evangelism. It is maybe a sphere of evangelism but this is not the reason we go in for it. We must never see our job as a means to some other end. Whether that end is money, status, power or evangelistic opportunities, we must see it as being in itself the Christian ministry or service to which God has called us.

There is a wide diversity of ministries. The fifth chapter of the book of Acts is very important from this point of view. The Greek-speaking Christians complained against the Aramaic-speaking Christians. The apostles did a very wise thing. They called a church meeting and they said it isn't right that we apostles should give up the Word of God in order to serve tables, so choose seven men filled with the Spirit and set them over the job.

Now this was a very wise sharing of ministries. The apostles were called to the ministry of the Word. The seven were called to the ministry of tables but both were ministries. In Greek the ministry of the Word is *diakonia,* to serve tables is *diakonein;* it's the same word used in both instances. Both were Christian ministries. Both required Spirit-filled Christians to do them. It wasn't that one was ministry and the other was not, or that one was secular ministry and the other was spiritual. No, one was the ministry of the Word that we call pastoral ministry, the other was the ministry of tables that we call social service; both were Christian ministries. Both could have been full-time Christian ministries.

There are a wide variety of ministries. God calls different people to different ministries, largely according to their natural and spiritual gifts, so that they fit into a particular niche for which God has fitted them and to which he has called them. Now don't misunderstand me, some of you are medical missionaries and I want to be the first to say that to be a missionary is a wonderful form of Christian ministry, an immense privilege, and a great responsibility if God has called you to it. Worldwide evangelisation is a permanent responsibility, indeed priority, in the Christian church. It is also a privilege to be a pastor, or a doctor, or a teacher, but Christians are also needed as politicians and industrialists and in the media. There is a wide variety of Christian ministries and we mustn't despise any.

The question is, 'What is God calling me to do and how does he mean me to serve him?' There is many a girl who, like the men, is going into a professional ministry. Nevertheless, there may be others who are called to give their lives full time to marriage and homemaking and motherhood. To build a Christian home and raise a Christian family is a Christian ministry as much as any other, and it can be full time. Only eternity will reveal how much society owes to Christian wives and Christian mothers.

Our Christian work

So far we have talked about vocation, and we have talked about diakonia, service, and now we come thirdly to the biblical doctrine of work. We know that the Fall has turned work into drudgery in some cases, particularly for agricultural workers. The ground has been cursed, thorns and thistles grow in it and cultivation is by toil and the sweat of the brow. But we need to realise that work is not a consequence of the Fall, it is a consequence of creation. 'God said let us make man in our image after our likeness and let them have dominion over the fish, birds, cattle and over all the earth and every reptile. So God created man in his own image, male and female created he them, he blessed them, he said be fruitful, multiply, fill the earth and subdue it' (Gen. 1:26–27). Verse 31, 'God saw everything that he had made. Behold, it was very good', is a marvellous example of divine job satisfaction. Chapter 2 verse 2, 'God blessed the seventh day and hallowed it because he rested from all his work' (his work which he had done in creation).

So in the very first chapter of the Bible, God reveals himself as a worker. Day by day, stage by stage, his creative plan unfolded. Then when he created human beings in his own image, he made them workers too. He gave them some of his own dominion and he told them to subdue the earth that he had made, which means to harness its resources and develop it for the benefit of mankind. From the beginning, human beings were given the privilege of being God's representatives, God's stewards, to take care of the environment and to develop it on his behalf.

In the light of these revealed truths about God and man — God the worker and man the worker; man created in the image of God with whom God shared his dominion — how can we develop a biblical doctrine of work? I have three things to say.

Work is intended for the fulfilment of the worker. We are to find employment and fulfilment in creativity which our work brings to us. It is very important to put together the two affirmations that God made man in his own image and he gave man dominion. The dominion that man has is due to the divine likeness that has been stamped upon him. Our dominion over nature is because we share God's image and his dominion; our potentiality for creative work is an essential part of our God-likeness. Work, therefore, is an indispensable part of our humanness. This is the reason why unemployment is so extremely serious in Christian eyes. We must remember, however, that work and employment are not identical. There are many people unemployed who are still workers. Wives, for instance, don't ask to be given wages for their homemaking but they can scarcely be considered unemployed. They are workers and there are many other voluntary workers in the community. Nevertheless, unemployment is very serious because it does deny many people their God-given calling to be workers. Even dull jobs can afford some measure of satisfaction to the worker who does them in the right spirit and from the right perspective.

Work is intended for the benefit of the community. Adam cultivated the garden, not just for his own fulfilment but to feed and clothe his own family. Throughout the Bible productivity for the benefit of the community is clearly taught. God gave Israel a land flowing with milk and honey. Why did he give Israel this fertile land? He commanded that the poor, the orphans and the widow, and the alien and all residents in the land should enjoy the fruits of it. It was for the benefit of the community. In the New Testament, for example, the thief is told to stop stealing and to start working.

Why is he to work? In order that he may give to those who need. He is to become a benefactor. His work is to be productive in order that he may serve the community. So the Bible sees work as a community project undertaken by the community for the community. Work is service for others and that is not difficult for doctors to see.

Work is intended for the glory of God. We need to understand that in creation God deliberately humbled himself in order to require the co-operation of man; he didn't create an earth that would become productive on its own. He gave dominion over the earth to mankind, who were to subdue and cultivate it. God deliberately depended on human beings for their co-operation. He did not plant a garden that would flourish on its own; having planted a garden, he appointed a gardener.

You know the story of the rather pious pastor who was being shown round a beautiful garden in the height of summer. The gardener was taking him along the herbaceous border and there was a profusion of magnificent colour. The pastor, as pastors are wont to do, waxed pious, and said, 'How wonderful is God the Creator.' The gardener replied, 'You should have seen this 'ere garden when God 'ad it to hisself'. When God had the garden to himself, it was in chaos, it needed the gardener to cultivate it. God has deliberately humbled himself in order to require human co-operation.

We emphasise the necessity of the divine co-operation, but we can put it the other way round. It is no good God giving the increase, if we don't do the planting and the watering, and it is no good the divine hand blessing the earth unless we plough the fields and scatter the good seed on the earth. We depend on God but he depends on us. Luther put it beautifully in his down-to-earth way, 'God even milks the cow through you.' There is plenty of milk in cows, but they are no help to us unless there is somebody to milk them.

The same truth applies to the doctor. You know the famous words written on one of the walls of the École de Médecine, in Paris, 'I dressed the wound, God healed it', but you could put it the other way round — God did the healing but I dressed the wound. It was necessary for me to dress the wound and I was co-operating with God in doing it. So God is the creator but man is the cultivator and each requires the other. Creation and cultivation, nature and culture, raw materials and craftsmanship belong together and each requires the other.

Now this concept of divine human collaboration applies to all honourable work. God has so ordered life on this planet as to need our co-operation. In living life to its fullness we don't only depend on God, we also depend on one another. Life would not be nearly as rich if it wasn't for the contributions of our fellow men and women. So you see, whatever our job, if I were talking to people in industry, business, teaching, law, whatever it was, this principle is true. It should be very easy for you to see it.

Let me just give you an example. I like the story of a man who was walking down a country lane one day. He passed a stone-quarry in which he heard a lot of noise, so he turned aside into it to watch the men working. He was interested to see how hard they were working so he talked to several of them. He went up to one of them and said, 'What are you doing?' and the man answered, rather irritably, 'Can't you see what I am doing? Use your eyes; I am hewing stone.' So he went up to the next man and said, 'What are you doing?' 'What am I doing?' he replied, 'I am earning £150 a week.' 'What are you doing?' he said to the third man. The third man put down his pick and stood up to his full height and stuck his chest out and said, 'If you want to know what I am doing, I am building a cathedral.' Now here are different attitudes to work. Some people can't see beyond the work they are doing, others can't see beyond the salary they are earning, but we need to see the ultimate to which our work is leading. In this case it was a cathedral, in ours it is the fulfilment of God's purpose for mankind. In your case, it is health and the fighting of disease for which we have divine warrant in the ministry of Jesus, who was indignant in the face of disease and death, and compassionate towards their victims.

So, what is work? Let me give you a definition of work as God intended it to be. 'Work is the expenditure of energy, whether manual or mental or both, in service to others, which brings fulfilment to the worker, benefit to the community and glory to God.' May God enable us to work like that.

CHRISTIAN INFLUENCE IN MEDICINE WORLDWIDE

STANLEY BROWNE

Introduction

THE title calls for several detailed surveys embracing history, research, ethics and the whole of medical practice. It presupposes more knowledge and competence than any individual can hope to possess or acquire. I can only do my best within the limitations imposed by my limited resources and experience. Any discussion is incomplete without a brief reference to certain basic facts.

Our pre-Christian heritage

This consists mainly of the principles of hygiene, food handling and sexual morality enjoined in the Mosaic code drawn up, as it was, for a nomadic pastoral people in the process of becoming a settled agricultural community in Palestine. While many of the regulations and taboos may be difficult to understand and doubtfully applicable to twentieth-century society, the insistence on personal and communal cleanliness, the importance of a regular rest-day, and the recognition of Jehovah as the source of well-being and righteousness and the one to whom all are accountable — these truths are of universal and timeless validity. Of less authenticity are the derivations of the association of ritual uncleanness with specific diseases, and the whole corpus of Talmudic comment.

Our Lord's attitude to disease and death

To him, disease was not necessarily a sign of divine displeasure or punishment, though it might be. It was abnormal, an intrusion, a foreign element. It was an inescapable part of life. The radical element of our Lord's attitude to the sick individual was that he mattered to God, and should matter to himself, his family, to society

ICCMS Oxford, UK, 1980. **Stanley G. Browne.** *WHO adviser on leprosy. Director Leprosy Study Centre, London, UK. President Baptist Union, GB. Past director Leprosy Research Unit, Uzuokoli, Nigeria. ICMDA Chairman 1972–75, President 1982–86.*

and to the religious establishment. He was not to be neglected, or despised, or ostracised. The 12, and then the 70, were sent out on their medical missionary itinerations with specific instructions to heal, to cleanse and to exorcise as well as to preach.

The early and medieval church

The caring component of the apostolic church, with its emphasis on compassion for the poor and the underprivileged, was in the medieval church overlaid by a curious ambivalence: the Christian conscience showed itself in commendable care for the sick, and an unprofitable blind-alley series of activities in witch-hunting and exorcism; an orgy of footwashing of 'Christ's poor' (the leprous), and a wholesale condemnation of the especially sinful who had thus incurred God's wrath. The Church had to await the birth of scientific medicine — notwithstanding its conception in an environment of non-Christian materialism — before it could offer real medical help to the 'heathen' and the poor whose cause it was increasingly espousing.

The Christian doctor and society

This brief and superficial historical survey could end with a listing of Christian doctors and their contributions to medicine world-wide in research, in medical education and in introducing scientific medicine.

Rather than enumerate these people and their contributions, I submit that it will be an exercise of greater relevance and profit to stand back and deduce certain principles that have actuated Christian doctors worldwide in exercising a Christian influence yesterday and today, so challenging the rising generation unashamedly to apply their faith in an honest and convincing way to the problems of tomorrow.

BIBLICAL PRINCIPLES

God calls individuals to faith in Christ and service to their fellows in his name

These individuals are first and foremost Christian; those whom we are thinking about happen to be doctors — they might have been bricklayers or plumbers, farmers or preachers. They arrive at personal faith in the risen Christ by a diversity of routes, and a variety of agonising conflicts; but they enter with fellow-believers by the same Arminian portal, 'Whosoever will may come', with its Calvinistic counter-claim emblazoned with equal clarity: 'I have chosen you, and ordained you.' God calls them all to dedication and to service, taking and transforming and enlarging the gifts of character, knowledge and skill placed unreservedly on the altar. It is Christian men and women practising medicine, and not an insubstantial and non-existent entity called 'Christian medicine', attracting those who happen to be Christians, who constitute the whole thrust of Christian influence in medicine worldwide.

Thus, the Christian doctor (and the Christian student) will face the same limitations and the same opportunities as his non-Christian counterpart — in innate intellectual ability, in gifts and insights, in diagnostic acumen and surgical skill. But he has the inestimable and incalculable advantage of seeing needy men and women in the light of God's concern for his suffering creatures, and in the additional context of the spiritual dimension. In this sense, he is — or should be — a better doctor. It is Christian character that counts, always. He should necessarily be more caring, which means more thorough, in every aspect of his work — in study and in research, in medical contact with patients and colleagues, in sympathy and compassion. He always goes the second mile, curing sometimes, relieving always. His personal and professional integrity is beyond suspicion, despite the dangers of subtle pressures and erosions.

Concern for the sick, suffering and deprived

The worldwide influence of these men of God who happened to be doctors has been predominantly exemplified in their concern for the sick or suffering or deprived individual. Historically, of course, this was a revolutionary attitude; the sick person was no longer (as in Hebrew thought) a sinner above all others, called upon to suffer as a just recompense for his misdeeds, nor worthy of neglect or revulsion (as in Greek philosophy) because he failed to attain the physical ideal in form and fitness. He is a person, made in the image of God, a fellow-man with whom we could and should identify, a fellow-citizen, with inalienable rights to care and shelter. In the world of today, this compassionate concern should show itself in every part of our practice as Christian doctors — in lifestyle and consumption, in conscientious utilisation of medical resources, in genuine sharing of the best we have (be it the Gospel, medical education, food or technology) with our less privileged brothers and sisters for whom Christ died. Thus it is his motivation, his God-honouring and patient-benefiting concern, that determines the Christian doctor's choice of priorities and use of resources for the greatest good of the greatest number.

The biblical view of sickness and suffering

A third great principle actuating the Christian doctor is the biblical view of sickness and suffering that he willingly embraces. This is God's world — the world, the wonderfully complex and intricate world, of genes and DNA, of micro-organisms and immunological defence mechanisms, of limited ecological resources and burgeoning populations, of sin and sickness. Before the bewildering and numbing immensity of the problems confronting us today, we have the reiterated scriptural assurances that God rules, that he is righteous, and that he will have the last word. Meanwhile, the Christian doctor exemplifies and advocates the unchangeable and impregnable moral and ethical bases for right conduct and right relations. He is not hesitant or reticent in his advocacy of the highest principles in patient care and consideration, nor in his condemnation of the indulgences that inevitably favour sickness — the promiscuity that means venereal disease, blocked Fallopian tubes, abortions and broken homes; the indulgence in tobacco and alcohol that may produce carcinoma of the lung and cirrhosis of the liver and a whole array of social ills; the overeating that often paves the way to obesity, diabetes and hypercholesterolaemia and their consequences; the selfishness and greed and anxiety that are frequently the prelude to coronary disease and cerebro-vascular accidents.

Basing their practice of the healing art on the high biblical concepts of a holy God and accountable creatures, Christian doctors exert an influence on medicine worldwide out of proportion to their actual numbers, for the ethic of medicine is still based on the essentially Christian attitude enshrined in the Golden Rule. Hence the crying need today for doctors to stand out against the increasing depersonalisation of medicine and the unfeeling anonymity of computerised mass treatment. They stand up for the inarticulate majority who suffer in silence, who starve and die. In lands where Western medicine has been introduced, theirs should be the brave voices calling for the observance of high standards of doctor-patient relations, of honest diagnosis and honest treatment, of compassionate care of rich and poor indiscriminately and of both the influential and the mass of ordinary folk. They stand courageously for the sanctity of human life, and oppose all that threatens this truth.

This Christian influence is also seen in the varied pioneering response to human need in many spheres. The sight of deformities occurring in neglected leprosy may drive a Paul Brand into applying his knowledge of reconstructive surgery to the succour of leprosy's victims, just as it impelled me into abandoning surgery and advocating measures for preventing leprosy's ravages.

The whole new realm of preventive medicine owes much to Christian doctors who see their efforts, at home and abroad, as a necessary modern corollary of the Master's injunction to heal and to relieve; preventing the disabilities of neglected pathology — making the road to Jericho safe for travellers. Public health enactments, health education, the provision of adequate food and pure water, family limitation — all are part and parcel of the newer positive attitudes to health. By extension, the Christian influence reaches out to the compassionate caring of the deprived and the handicapped, children and their mothers, the victims of disaster, of flood and famine, earthquake and volcanic eruption. The Christian doctor is there, where the action is, where the need is, treading in the footsteps of his Master and showing forth his love and concern, and inspiring others so to do.

Patient-orientated research

Christian influence worldwide has shown itself time and again in patient-orientated research. Sensing the real needs of sick individuals and communities has been the concern of alert Christian doctors in many lands, and today these doctors are called to play a specifically Christian role in recalling a noble profession to its basic obligations to minister to the sick person in his sick environment. The availability of new techniques and sophisticated (and ever more expensive) technologies is no impelling imperative for their use; we cannot afford to do every-where — or anywhere — what we could do; nor should we necessarily do it. Good medicine may mean doing first-class work in second-rate surroundings with third-rate equipment, as many a missionary doctor would testify. And good research should bring us back to the best in patient care, serving the whole man and the whole of man with compassion (a much overworked and debased term today) in the spirit of the Lord Christ. The Christian research worker sees and seizes the opportunities to investigate reverently what God the Creator is waiting to reveal. In Kepler's fine phrase, popularised in English by Lord Kelvin, he can 'think God's thoughts after him', avoiding the sensational and meretricious in seeking God's glory. Research into the conscientious reappraisal of the use of resources of finance, technology, medication and skills, will provide a continuing challenge to the Christian doctors of the future.

Who is sufficient for these things? we might well ask. 'Our sufficiency is of God' comes back the challenging reply. The God who has called us in Christ to follow him, and to minister to his sick and suffering creatures, is the Creator as well as the Saviour. The one who impresses the scientific mind with his infinite knowledge and wisdom, is the one who reveals himself in the Jesus who went about doing good and healing all manner of sickness and all manner of disease among the people, and it is he who calls upon us to follow in his steps.

THE HEALING MINISTRY IN THE MISSION
OF THE CHURCH

ERLING KAYSER

IT is a basic belief of mine that medical missions should not merely be the response to the need we see, able to be withdrawn if the needs were met by others, but the spontaneous, integral and vital ministry of the church, the overflow of compassion and love. This means that we should not withdraw, but on the contrary go on, undertake new ventures and look forward to a new and rich era in medical missions. It has to be admitted, however, that some people, even medical missionaries, do not agree.

This is an important matter which has to be considered in depth and a theology of the healing ministry is developing. Jesus says: 'You know that in the world, rulers lord it over their subjects, and their great men make them feel the weight of authority, but it shall not be so with you. Among you, whoever wants to be great must be your servant, and whoever would be the first must be the willing slave of all — like the Son of Man; he did not come to be served, but to serve, and to surrender his life as a ransom for many' (Mat. 20:25–28).

Jesus was incarnate in the world and he is living in his church today. The church is the continuing incarnation. As there was a healing ministry of Jesus, so there is and always must be a legitimate healing ministry of the church. Therefore the theme for a conference on medical mission in Tübingen two years ago was, 'The healing ministry in the mission of the church'. In the findings the following basic points were made: 'There are insights concerning the nature of health which are received only within the context of the Christian faith. The church cannot surrender its responsibility in the field of healing to other agencies.' And further, 'Health in the Christian context, is a continuous and victorious encounter with the powers that deny the existence and goodness of God. The church's ministry of healing is thus an integral part of its witness to the Gospel.'

ICCP Oxford, UK, 1966. **Erling Kayser.** *General medical practitioner, Hordaland, Norway.*

The consequence of this is that the healing ministry of the church primarily belongs to the congregation. As it was said in Tübingen, 'If healing is understood as above, it will be clear that the entire congregation has a part to play in it.' 'One of the most urgent needs of today is that Christian congregations, in collaboration with Christian medical workers, should again recognise and exercise the healing ministry which belongs properly to them.'

The history of medical missions

Let us now look very briefly at the historic development of medical missions. In the early church the service was primarily inside the congregations, the deacons serving the apostles and the ministers of the word. About AD 300 the church began to build institutions, which in the Middle Ages were run by the various monastic orders; these were usually cloistered and isolated from the congregations, so that the healing ministry was not an integral part of the whole congregational life.

As a result of the Reformation, a new sense of responsibility for the healing ministry, the service of the sick, the handicapped and the aged swept through the congregations but as time went on the service was again institutionalised.

We have seen the same trend in medical missions during the last 150 years. At first medical missions were an integral part of the whole missionary enterprise, but since 1900 there has been a trend towards medical missions as a separate enterprise in their own right. This development was good and necessary because hospitals and other institutions were built, in which outstanding work was done. But institutions have walls, often thick walls, so that the healing ministry became less and less an integral part of the congregational life. The young congregations and the young churches had big buildings which they saw from the outside only. In these the sick were greatly helped, but it was difficult for the congregations and the individual Christians to canalise their compassion, their *agape* or their therapeutic function through these institutions.

I feel, then, that medical missions are working too much in isolation. The German expression 'Arztliche Mission' (*Arzt* = doctor) spotlights this overemphasis on physicians and hospitals. The new approach in medical missions should also aim to establish means of channelling the therapeutic function and healing ministry of the congregation.

Modern problems and medical missionary work

When touring the mission fields today one is over and over again met by three big problems. The first has already been mentioned, namely the *isolation* of the institutions. The second is the ever *increasing cost* of running the big hospitals, leprosaria and other institutions. The third is the problem of better *co-operation* with governments.

As to the first point I should like to quote again from the findings of the Tübingen conference. 'The time is long overdue for the complete integration of the hospital and clinic into the life and witness of the church.' This means: 'that the congregation must recognise itself as the healing community which knows the hospital to be an essential channel of its witness to the world. The doctor, the nurse and other hospital personnel are only a specialised section of a team composed of the people of God performing its healing ministry in each local situation. Where there appears to be no evidence that this integration of a healing function is going to be understood, the continuance of the institution must be seriously questioned.'

Here two serious questions arise. The first is whether to *close a hospital* if it is not a living witness of the congregation, not working adequately as a teaching body, or not meeting a special need in the area. There are such hospitals on mission fields today, and the possibility of closing some of them has been seriously considered.

The second question to consider is if it is desirable to *turn hospitals over to the government.* Usually economic pressures force this consideration and these economic problems may be very great indeed, if only because health work must be of a high standard. This is, however, something never to be undertaken lightly. It is an entirely different matter if the government demands to take over; it is also another matter if the church or mission has the opportunity to run a government hospital. This should be done as far as we can afford it.

Future trends

As for future strategy, I would like again to stress the legitimate therapeutic function of the congregation. The principles must be to promote the role of the congregation in the healing ministry. This will then bring knowledge and inspiration into the congregations. They will form the nucleus of the new medical missions. The key figures will no longer be the doctors, but the nurses and social workers working in health centres, in rural areas and in the inner city. These small groups can be an integral part of the life of the village in rural areas, and of street life in the towns. They will live more in contact with people and congregations and can be the nerve centre of a richer health work in the congregations. At the same time they can do excellent prophylactic as well as curative medicine treating minor ailments, tuberculosis, leprosy, etc, in addition to caring for the sick and old people at home.

I should like to quote the Tübingen findings again. 'Other forms of service through which the church should continue to express its healing ministry lie in the fields of leprosy, tuberculosis, care of the chronically ill and aged, rehabilitation, psychiatry and maternal and child health. There still exist many areas of pioneering service in rural health, as well as inner city clinics, which for more adequate therapy should be linked to a central hospital. This need not necessarily be church-related. It is especially in these areas that the congregation can assist in domiciliary care and in health education through practice and precept.'

It is necessary to make one last point about the future strategy of medical missions, namely the *necessity of joint planning and the use of resources.* The Tübingen findings declare: 'The Consultation believes that churches in all parts of the world, at the local, regional and national levels, must increasingly join together in survey, study and planning for the most efficient and effective means of carrying out the healing ministry. In all localities and regions such joint planning will make more effective each individual church's medical ministry. Beyond this, in some places it may be desirable not only to plan together, but to conduct additional united medical programmes.'

Travelling in developing countries makes one aware of the enormous need on every hand. We must answer this call. But it is still more important to accept God's calling to be filled with his Holy Spirit and be outlets for God's compassion and love.

ALLOCATION OF HEALTH CARE RESOURCES

GUNNAR HOLMGREN

The national picture

WHENEVER resources in a community are scarce it seems that the only way to maximise their use is by involving the local communities in decision-making about priorities in health care, on the basis of accurate health information. It would seem that any centralised health care system will always favour the urban, the better-off, those with political clout, and curative rather than preventive measures.

One of the most exciting decentralisations of a national health system is taking place at present in Zambia. This is occurring against a backdrop of a country in a severe economic crisis. It has the highest debt-burden per inhabitant of any country in Africa. Its main industry, copper mining, is running at a loss. Agriculture, which is the main hope for the future, has had the worst year on record with most of the commercial farmers now technically bankrupt. Inflation is running at an annual rate of around 120% and interest rates at commercial banks are running at 134% for 28-day loans. The structural adjustment programme has widened the gap between rich and poor, and now 70% of the rural community are said to be below the poverty line.

And yet despite this gloomy picture Zambia has successfully launched one of the best prepared and most soundly constructed health reform programmes in the developing world.

The main pillars of the reform

- *Massive decentralisation:* giving nearly all decision-making about district health programmes to the newly formed and trained district teams;
- giving them the means to *construct a sound district health plan,* with advice and training in the process from an enthusiastic reform-facilitation team;

ICMDA Stavanger, Norway, 1994. **Gunnar Holmgren.** *Physician, International Child Health Unit, University of Uppsala, Sweden. Past director of mission hospital in Zambia.*

- *planning a realistic budget* to carry this plan out;
- having the *freedom and funds to implement their own district plan;*
- thorough *training in book-keeping* to control the flow of funds;
- a good central audit team which, helped by provincial staff, is able to carry out an *annual audit of performance and finances.*

After only nine months, the positive health impact of the reform is already being seen. The enthusiasm generated by seeing the health plan as being their own possession is creating a completely new morale in the work force.

An example of this is seen in a central hospital, Kitwe Central Hospital. By giving the Hospital Board the freedom to decide their own agenda and their own priorities and by having an enthusiastic medical superintendent who has inspired his staff to see the hospital as their own, the place has been transformed into a 'pearl' by Zambian standards. It now has a high work morale and good reception of patients on arrival, very clean wards and neat surroundings and markedly improved drug supply. This has not needed a massive injection of funds but has been done on a relatively modest budget.

The district picture

My own experience over a period of 16 years was trying to allocate resources and make ends meet at a mission hospital functioning as a district hospital in rural Zambia; this was prior to the national reform process.

This was a 130-bedded rural district hospital with an average 100% bed-occupancy. We had around 60,000 out-patient visits and 5,500 in-patient admissions a year. We carried out around 125 major and 450 minor operations annually and had over 800 deliveries a year.

We had at most 20,000 visits a year to our mobile MCH clinics, linking up seven stationary rural health centres run by medical assistants and 23 village clinics run by community health workers. For most of the 16 years I worked there I was the only doctor but during the last two years there were two. We had on average 10 registered nurses and 15 enrolled nurses. We had to depend on a whole range of measures to match income and expenditure.

Income

1. The Zambian Ministry of Health gave a fairly generous *grant-in-aid* to the missions for their medical work and paid the salaries of over half our workers. This constituted 40% of our total income and was considerably more than in many other African countries. However this *grant-in-aid* was still only around 6% of the national health budget for undertaking 38% of the total health care in the country! Salary support from Sweden amounted to 20% of our running costs.

2. Our hospital was able to obtain funds from a *major donor* for three capital projects, which included building a farm training centre where families would be brought in for training in better farming methods. This centre was also the training unit for community health workers in our Primary Health Care programme. Health and agriculture linked up naturally.

At times we were able to finance external purchases of drugs, equipment and even vehicles for the hospital by channelling project funds for other necessities via external suppliers and then paying the project its local construction costs from the hospital accounts. This is an excellent way of maximising the benefit of external funding of projects and is often termed 'project funding'. It has the risk that when the project is over, a vacuum appears that can be difficult to fill.

3. The mission farm, as a *production unit*, became a major source of funding for our running costs. Over a number of years it was contributing around 15% of our total income. However even this has its dangers and can become a millstone around the necks of institutions.

4. In the last two years of my stay in Zambia *patient fees* were introduced; previously they were not allowed. In most mission hospitals these fees will gradually become the major source of cost recovery and only a very limited number of the poorest can have their fees waived if the books are to balance. Such decisions are best handled by local staff.

5. Many mission hospitals have side-wards for *private patients*, who pay a fee that helps to subsidise the rest of their work. However this can also be a trap should more and more time and space be given to private patients from the middle and upper classes in order to strengthen the economy, whilst the poor, for whom the hospital was originally built, become marginalised.

Expenditure

1. *Food* is provided for in-patients in Zambia and was a significant cost (around 25%). If a production unit can be a source of food as well as funding it serves a double purpose. Local farmers must not lose out in this process. Our experience was that local farmers could produce vegetables at half the price of our mission farm and so it made sense to phase out our vegetable section.

2. *Drugs* are the biggest expenditure after food and staff wages (i.e. around 10% in our hospital but likely to be higher in most units). Here new flexible thinking will be necessary. Cheaper alternatives to standard treatments in industrialised countries are absolutely essential, especially those to be used in common and in chronic diseases (e.g. hypertension). Even more important is the continuing training of staff to see the benefits of cost-effective prescribing, reduction of over-prescribing and remembering that *most diseases will get better even without any treatment* except for a sympathetic ear and a good explanation. Local safe remedies, which the patient can arrange himself for all minor ailments, are to be encouraged.

Alternative cheaper suppliers may need to be found overseas if the country's own medical stores' prices are too high. Donations of drugs can be a major benefit, but these must be thoroughly sorted before despatch by those knowing local needs so that valuable money is not wasted on transporting, clearing, and distributing useless and out-of-date drugs.

3. *Staff wages* accounted for 56% of total costs. In Zambia the staff wages for most of the hospital staff are already fixed but for some of the newer untrained staff we had some flexibility.

We were able to have many workers with multiple functions, e.g. the driver working in the mobile clinic for the outreach services had full employment during the day whilst on the visits, weighing children, doing clerking, and even taking part in health education. This is not only good for the economy but also very stimulating for job satisfaction.

4. It was always easier to find funds for capital expenditure rather than for running costs. Aspects of major *running costs that could be reduced by investing in suitable capital projects* were therefore a high priority. An example was the high cost of running a diesel engine for generating electricity. A water turbine was built on a nearby stream and within two years it had paid for itself.

5. A central office for controlling costs *reduces the risk of corruption, theft, and carelessness* in the use of resources. In Kenya it has been found that, generally, married women bookkeepers, treasurers, store attendants and pharmacy assistants are more dependable than men! The biblical principle is still valid in all countries: 'The love of money is the root of all evil' and money matters must be handled with great circumspection.

Two central precautions are important:

- *Personal money and public money must never be kept together;*
- *Responsibility for public money must be shared.* Every transaction should be written down and cross-checked by a second person. *Open accounting* where any staff may inspect the books, dispels rumours and leads to good relationships amongst all the staff.

Conclusion

I want to end with a quotation from John Stott about Christian responsibility in sharing: 'The present situation of North–South inequality ("a gap so wide that at the extremes people seem to live in different worlds") is not God's fault (for he has provided resources in earth and sea), nor is it the fault of the poor (since they were mostly born into it, though some government leaders are to blame for corruption and incompetence), nor is it necessarily our fault (although our colonial forefathers may have had a share in creating it). We become personally culpable only if we acquiesce in its continuance. In Jesus' story of the rich man and Lazarus there is no hint that the rich man was responsible for the poor man's plight. Dives went to hell not because he had exploited Lazarus, but because of his scandalous indifference and apathy.'

WHAT MAKES A HEALTHY FAMILY
AND SOCIETY?

HIROMI KAWAHARA

Introduction

BEING Eastern orientated may not be an exact description of the lifestyle of many who currently live in Asia. In a sense, it may equally be true of some of the philosophies found in Pacific and African tribes as well as among North and South American Indians. To be Eastern orientated may indicate the influence of non-Christian religions and philosophies such as Buddhism, Taoism, Confucianism and forms of nature worship. In contrast, those of Western orientation may have been influenced by a Judeo-Christian or Islamic perspective, or the much older Greek philosophical tradition.

Historical and philosophical characteristics of the Eastern orientated

Philosophically, to be Eastern orientated may mean being in harmony with nature, reflected in very old Chinese paintings which portray natural scenery towering over man. This kind of thinking emphasizes the primacy of nature, with man constituting an integral, if not negligible, part of life on earth. In Western orientation, whether in the pre-Christian, Medieval or Renaissance periods, man is put at the center, with emphasis on drawings and sculpture adorned by human figures, or gods and goddesses in the likeness of humans. In Christian art, even God is drawn to look like a human being.

Ancient Japanese people were very Eastern orientated. For example, when making his acceptance speech, a Japanese Nobel Prize winner for literature named Yasunari Kawabata cited a poem of Dogen, a 12th century Zen priest: 'Spring cherry, Summer a little cuckoo, Autumn moon and Winter snow. Beautiful are four seasons in Japan.' Kawabata was trying to express that the

ICMDA Seoul, Korea, 1990. **Hiromi Kawahara.** *Director, Asian Health Institute Foundation, Tokyo, Japan.*

Japanese tradition is one of living in harmony with nature. There is also a 13th century Noh song which contains a verse saying that human life is just like a bubble floating on a stream. It appears, stays for a while, then disappears and returns to water. The writer wanted to emphasize that people may appear and disappear but still exist eternally in the great life of the universe. This is entirely different from the Western idea of nature as a gift from God, the creator. In Hindu tradition, the great stream of life is 'Karma', or fate, which no one can resist.

Especially as demonstrated by traditional Chinese medicine, the Eastern way of thinking led to a different attitude towards health and disease. No actual intervention or experimentation was practised on the human body or its functions. Instead, health and disease were regarded as an interaction of opposites, *yin* (negative) and *yan* (positive). Disease may arise from an imbalance between the two which must be corrected for renewed health. This philosophy of health, which combines elements of nature (such as metal, wood, water, fire and earth) to explain human physiology and pathology still baffles us today, although practitioners of this ancient traditional medicine come to similar diagnostic conclusions as doctors in the West.

The contemporary situation

Does the Eastern orientated way of thinking prevail in the East today? Except for some residual influence, as in areas where such thinking ensures the individual's subservience to group activities, it has largely been supplanted. Selfish forms of individualism and the search for quick material gain, regardless of consequences to the environment, mean that the social, human costs of rapid economic growth have been high.

Paradoxes of urban and rural Asia

In most parts of Asia, there is a race by governments and corporations to achieve rapid industrialization. Combined with agrarian reform, this has proved beneficial to Asian countries like Japan, mainland China, Taiwan and the Koreas, but has often been pursued at the expense of human and environmental health. Japan, an economic superpower, is notorious for mercury poisoning (Minamata disease). Farmers in rural areas have been ruthlessly evicted from their farmlands to make way for airports and other so-called developmental projects. Today, Japan (together with the comfortable nations of the First World) is guilty of continuing to plunder the Third World's natural and human resources, for example in Asia, Africa and the Latin Americas. Here, for decades, past and present authoritarian régimes have provided cheap raw materials and cheap labor in exchange for economic and political support.

On the other hand, most of the peoples of Asia are rural, landless people. There is a widening gap between rural and urban areas and the creation of urban slums as these neglected people flock to the cities in search of jobs. Land reform remains a challenge if the poverty of millions of rural Asians is to be ameliorated.

Family life and mental health

The rapid growth of materialism is affecting and distorting the quality and purpose of many lives. It is still true that the Eastern orientated have relatively strong family ties. Throughout Asia, 80% of people depend on agriculture, in which close co-operation between family members is essential for survival. Even in Japan, the most industrialized country in Asia, the number of three-generation extended families is almost three times as great as that in countries of the West, though these Japanese family ties are gradually being eroded. Because Japanese working fathers are usually out of the house until late at night, children cannot eat with both parents except at weekends. (In any case, though, it has been traditional for the mother to serve the father separately before eating her own meal with the children.)

The stresses of industrial societies are taking their toll on mental health. Irritability, insomnia, nervousness and mental disorders, chronic alcoholism, drug abuse, suicide and crimes of various kinds are all products of this stress-filled society. As an example, when economic growth brings material prosperity the consumption of alcohol goes up. According to Japanese statistics, 90% of male adults and 45% of female adults drink alcohol, two million of them being thought to be alcohol dependent.

Medical problems

Strict production schedules exert pressure on personal and family life and create stress-related problems, such as cardiovascular disease, made worse by alcohol. In the rush to fulfill work quotas and targets, people neglect periodic and regular rest as well as relaxation with family and friends. They become too much orientated to hospital-type cures and forget that a holistic approach to health is preventive, so is ultimately the best medicine.

Other medical problems arise from contact with chemicals which, in modern technological society, are to be found in the food we eat, the clothes we wear, the air we breathe and the water we drink. The very chemicals which so revolutionized some aspects of life can also pose hazards to life itself. This is especially so in the industrialized and newly industrializing countries.

As we go to the countryside, where most Asians live, medical problems take on a different character. Most of them are connected with material poverty, aggravated by lack of education and lack of access to health care, which is so much easier to reach in populated centers. The majority of Asians die of diseases which could be prevented by proper food and sanitation. Because Asian delivery systems for health care are mainly hospital based with cure as the goal, the rural poor either find such care to be financially (or physically) inaccessible, or they end up sick again because the social causes of malnutrition have not been properly addressed.

As medical professionals, should we be getting involved with the ills of society and of the environment? Why not strictly confine ourselves to physical disorders? In fact, our biggest challenge is to take a traditional Eastern orientated (holistic) attitude to health, whilst using Western methods, to combat the enormous problems which face us, not only in Asia and the East.

The Christian health challenge in Asia and the Third World

Action towards community-based health
In dealing with medical problems, we need to be concerned not only with their direct medical causes but also with their social and environmental background. In attempting to deal with these causes we will need to work with all kinds of people besides health professionals. In the end, this may be more cost-effective than any further emphasis on cost-intensive and technology-dependent medicine. Yet this approach should not be made an excuse for neglecting scientific investigation and diagnosis, the legacy of

Western orientation. In short, we have to combine the orientations of East and West, both the holistic and the reductionist approaches, if we are better to understand and deal with the problems of ill-health, especially in Asia and the Third World.

The challenge for Christian health professionals in Asia and much of the Third World is to encourage the people in the rural and urban poor communities to form their own organizations. These can provide basic health care, education and livelihood projects which could supplement the family income and improve nutrition. These community-based organizations should also eventually confront the root causes of their ill-health, such as land tenure, caste systems and exploitation by governments, corporations or other sections of society. In many parts of rural Asia, we do now find such community-based programs and organizations, many of which are non-governmental.

In 1978, these developments were further stimulated by the World Health Organization's Alma Ata Declaration, calling for 'Health for all by the year 2000'. To achieve this object, it was stressed that the people should be involved in taking a holistic approach to their own health problems. In addition, all effective means of health care, both modern and traditional, were to be put at the health worker's disposal. Based on these principles, the Asian Health Institute was formed to help local self-reliant efforts in Asia, through primary health care training programs. The Institute's principle of 'sharing for self-help' did not arise from any feeling of superiority towards the least of our Asian brethren, but because the least of our brethren represents the Lord Jesus Christ himself (Mat. 25:40). Yet it would seem that providing health for all by the year 2000 is still a remote goal.

Working with people of various countries, religious and cultural backgrounds

As problems have become global, approaches to solve them would now need international, inter-denominational and inter-cultural co-operation. The First World has to be more sensitive to the needs of the Third World. These, the most impoverished countries, have been the victims of previous colonial plunder as well as the currently unequal patterns of trade with the First World. Despite this being largely composed of Christian nations, especially those of Europe and America, their political and economic practices toward the Third World have not been exactly exemplary. With this largely Christian background it is to be hoped that the First World will exert more effort, in genuine acts of repentance, to assist the victims of its former colonialization. The Third World (a mixture of Christian, Hindu, Muslim, Buddhist and Socialist nations) needs help to stand on its own two feet. Japan, though not a Christian nation, also has a responsibility to transform its purely trade-based relationships with the Third World into a genuine partnership between peoples, aiming for self-reliance, genuine democracy and social justice.

As Christians in the healing ministry, we can play a significant part in bringing together people of the First and Third Worlds. With health as an entry point, we can make the people of the First World recognize their overindulgence and overconsumption of the world's resources whilst people in the Third World wallow in poverty. Health, or the lack of it, in the Third World (or even in the First World itself, amongst the homeless, the unemployed, victims of drug abuse, AIDS and so on) can provoke Christians in the healing ministry to examine themselves. Amongst the sufferers we can find the Lord Jesus Christ himself, teaching us to show compassion and justice toward the least of our brothers and sisters.

Except for countries like the Philippines, Christians in most Asian countries form a small minority. In Japan, they form only 1% of a population which is mainly Buddhist. So it is very important for Christians to live as witnesses to the Lord, as the salt of the earth (Mat. 5:13).

Since Christians are in the minority, they should respect and seek to understand those of other faiths. Yet they themselves will clearly stand out as they work toward true justice and peace. In thought and action, they will be following the Lord's pattern of self-sacrificial service. As the apostle Paul found, becoming a servant of all is the very way to see others won over to our Lord Jesus Christ (1 Cor. 9:19).

CHRISTIAN WITNESS IN MEDICAL PRACTICE

Hospital Administration

J.E. SIREGAR

Our commission

CHRIST'S command to his disciples 'to go to the whole world and preach the gospel to all mankind', as is written in the Gospel of Mark 16:15, is very clear in its brevity, and therefore there is no reason for it to be misunderstood or misinterpreted. The first disciples and the first congregations in their humility and weakness have done this with great enthusiasm and spirit, thereby ignoring death and persecution.

As a simple layman it is not my intention to dig into the theological background of different churches. In my position as an ordinary hospital administrator I will only try to define how to fulfil the command of the highest commander of us all, Jesus Christ. This command is given to all who call themselves Christians, disciples of Christ, without exception and without reservation and has still its full power and meaning even at the present time. Every Christian has to follow this command in full obedience and surrender, whatever function or position he may have in daily and social life. He cannot hide himself behind special or exceptional conditions, but in all these he has to communicate directly with the highest commander, the living Christ, a privilege we have received from him since we accept him as our Saviour, who has liberated us from slavery of sins and customs and the law.

It is only in this act of obedience that we appear before our Lord when we have to apply his commandment in the very real situation and opportunity he has given to us. Our preparedness to fulfil his commandment must be without doubt or reservation. Regrettably, it is not often well understood by the church, including the official leaders. Instead of encouraging someone who is obedient to the Lord's commandment, Christians are more inclined to criticise him as somebody who is not obedient to the church and its regulations.

ICCP Singapore, 1975. **J. E. Siregar.** *Director Immanuel Hospital, Bandung, Indonesia.*

Our Immanuel Hospital in Bandung is no more than an ex-mission hospital inherited by the local church 25 years ago. The mission board has withdrawn gradually from this hospital. There is only one mission doctor and one mission physiotherapist left, and although the mission board is still willing to support in incidental needs, the whole policy is in the hands of the local church and Christians. When questioned, the simple local Christians and in particular the Christian workers in the hospital only see the hospital as a means to proclaim the gospel to their fellow men in the old 'traditional and pietistic' way. If theologians come with new theologies about the changing situation and condition, concluding that we have to change our way of service and witness so that the high commandment will fade away, our people simply will not accept it. Proclaiming the gospel in the traditional and 'pietistic' style is still a living challenge in the hearts of the Christians 'in the street'. And I believe that we are wrong when we try to suppress this spirit. On the contrary we have to encourage and to support them therein as obedient followers of Christ.

Fulfilling Christ's commands as hospital workers

A hospital is usually seen as a place where sick people come for medical treatment. Both patients and doctor are already very happy when the patient can be restored to his previous physical condition. Later on, when the WHO came with its formulation that, 'Health is a state of complete physical, mental and social well-being, and not only the absence of disease or infirmity', more attention was paid to the non-physical aspect of sickness and health, including the psychological, spiritual and sociological sides. Although the common doctor–clinician cannot fulfil this comprehensive task alone, awareness about the non-physical side of sickness is of the greatest importance in attracting the attention of other hospital workers, e.g. hospital chaplains, social workers, public health workers etc, so that a well co-ordinated and concentrated effort can be made for the total well-being of the patient.

This new concept about health has given rise to the development of community medicine also, which urges the hospital to step down from her ivory tower into the community. It opens the insight that individual health is only part of the community health.

This concept brings the doctor and the hospital much more

intensely face to face with the problems of life — its purpose and sense — than all other professions on the technical field.

Seeking for the sense and purpose of life, we only have to listen to what the Creator has decreed for his creature. Jesus Christ, the Logos, has formulated in Matthew 4:19: 'Come with me and I will teach you to catch men.' And after having trained his disciples for three years, he sent them away by saying: 'Go then, to all peoples everywhere and make them my disciples, baptise them in the name of the Father and the Son, and of the Holy Spirit, and teach them to obey every thing I have commanded you' (Mat. 28:19–20).

As to my humble opinion, the sense and purpose of life is to be found between these two poles: following Christ as a professional man and going to all peoples everywhere as a professional man. Therefore, it is most decisive for a man, including the sick, whether he is a follower of Christ or not. Calling a (sick) man to be a follower of Christ in this sense must not be seen as interference, but as an act of love to our neighbour to guide him into the true purpose of life. This is particularly important for those patients who no longer have hope of being cured and for those in the terminal stage of their sickness.

Preaching the gospel to sick people is often said to be unlawful, because it is thought to be abusing the patient's weakness to Christianise him. Or, proclaiming the gospel to sick people will only disturb the healing process, so it is thought not to be fair to Christianise people under such circumstances.

But, bringing the gospel to our fellow men in the words of the Master in Mark 16:16, 'Whoever believes and is baptised will be saved; whoever does not believe will be condemned', is only an act of love. It is an expression of our concern for our fellow men, including patients in the hospital. How will other people, including patients, know that, 'God loved the world so much that he gave his only Son, so that everyone who believes in him may not die but have eternal life' (John 3:16), if this truth is not told to them by other people? Experiencing God's loving care during one's sickness will only bring healing more speedily and totally, something even many secular doctors have come to realise. Is it not an expression of love and concern for our fellow men, also those who are sick, when we tell them this good news and not remain silent?

Training for sharing the gospel

Our care for the sick, however expert and good, will not be complete if we refrain from telling the patient about the true and only salvation.

Seen from this background, we have made it our aim to make every Christian hospital-worker an obedient disciple of Christ, ready to fulfil his commandment. They must be given training for this, something they never had before, and by doing this we train our people in their Christian calling and ethics at the same time. They must at least be conscious of the importance of sharing their joyfulness in Christ with the patient.

We have estimated that our hospital in Bandung, with its 352 beds, is visited by more than 500,000 people per year, patients and relatives included. This provides a real opportunity to do community medicine, to introduce the gospel and to make people followers of Christ. Here is a great mass of people at hand, which we may not reach even if we go out into the villages.

For this purpose we are scattering daily Bible readings and devotions into the different divisions of the hospital, under the responsibility of the head of the division. Bible reading and morning devotions must be seen in the real context of the daily job in each division, not only in the medical department, but in administration, laundry, kitchen, workshop, etc. The head of the division is responsible for this kind of job also and has the task of interpreting God's word within the daily problems. Once a week they get training from our hospital chaplain. Besides these activities, we also organise Bible study and prayer groups, weekend retreats for the whole personnel, including doctors.

Preaching the gospel does not mean using long words and great learning, with skilful words of human wisdom (1 Cor. 2:1), but bringing the living Christ to everybody, with the convincing proof of the power of God's Spirit. With the power of the Holy Spirit, the most humble and simple hospital workers can touch even the most influential and wise patient.

As for our non-Christian personnel, who make up about 35% of the whole, they automatically take part in the morning devotions, because these form an integral part of the job. On acceptance they have to promise that they will follow all the regulations and policy of the hospital.

A broadcasting system provided in the wards and waiting

rooms not only brings the gospel, but also informs and educates about problems of health and health care, prevention, family planning, i.e. things related to community medicine.

Results

One may wonder: What is the result of all these activities? It is not up to us to make an evaluation. With some new converts every year, we feel that these activities have undoubtedly their broader impact on the spirit of the whole community, a kind of spirit we would not have experienced if we just functioned on a secular base.

Our aim is to make Immanuel a hospital in which even the simplest people in the city can feel themselves at home and where they can find healing and security in an atmosphere of loving care, thereby showing the way to Jesus Christ as the true and only life and salvation.

We are not pretending that we've already come to this point, nor that our fellowship is perfect in its witness and service. We believe that the total impact of Immanuel Hospital as a Christian community of loving concerned service is much greater than the individual efforts of its staff members. It is this feeling of being within a true community which is first noticed and commented upon by the patients and visitors and it is within this atmosphere that the individual witness of staff members can then be made, both in quiet words to patients and relatives as the opportunity is given and in their attitude to their daily duties in their own departments. We only enjoy ourselves in the belief that our Lord pleases to make use of us in our imperfection. Any one of us can come and tell our Master in deep humility: 'This is our response to your commandment. Tell us how to work according to thy will.'

It may be that the Master will speak to us through your criticisms and advice also. We are listening.

MORALS AND COMMUNITY MEDICINE

SHUN-ICHI YAMAMOTO

Introduction

IN modern times, the progress of biomedical science and technology has necessitated a review of the ethics set out by Hippocrates. Recent developments in community medicine also demand modification of traditional medical ethics. Whilst considering a Christian view of ethical issues, problems arising in community medicine will be compared with those being faced in clinical medicine.

Individualistic versus community medicine

Ethics is in principle an individualistic duty. It holds in the one-to-one relationship, as when a patient consults a doctor in the clinical situation. In contrast, in community medicine, the complexities of the structure involve a 'mass to mass' relationship, formed between the providers of health care (doctors, nurses, social workers and other paramedicals) and its recipients (a given community of basically healthy people).

As there are many members of a community and their value systems are also manifold, leakage of health information by health professionals can cause grave consequences within that community. As confidentiality is more easily broken when community, rather than personal, health is involved, providers of health care need to be particularly careful when sharing information with a multiplicity of recipients who may have conflicting interests. However, maintaining confidentiality is not quite so simple in modern community life. For example, health checks are made on the employees in Japanese enterprises in order to prevent occupational illnesses and industrial accidents. Although the primary purpose of such exercises is to protect the health and safety of the workers in accordance with the Labour Law, the data obtained has a double edge. Whilst it enables the workforce to

ICMDA Seoul, Korea, 1990. **Shun-ichi Yamamoto.** *Professor, St Luke's College of Nursing, Tokyo, Japan. ICMDA Vice-President 1986–94.*

keep healthy, any information shared with their employers could violate the workers' privacy, particularly when physical or mental defects have been exposed as a result of the examination.

Even if the health data relating to members of a community were fed back exclusively to that population, confidentiality could be broken should the information have some negative significance (as when a shop has to be closed for selling contaminated food). In general, the infringement of human rights is more serious when health information leaks out locally rather than in remote, unfamiliar areas.

This demands the highest degree of care from health care providers. However, it should also be understood that excessive caution in releasing information can act against the original intention, demoralise the participants and so incur other types of difficulty.

Qualitative versus quantitative ethics
Essentially, the element of ethics in an ordinary clinical situation is qualitative. The choice lies between two alternative courses of action, with no possible compromise between them. In contrast, the substance of ethical issues in community medicine is how to allocate inadequate resources between a multitude of health problems. Possibilities are infinite, but health professionals have to establish an order of priority in the midst of the competing value systems existing within a community. It is like being asked to solve a complicated equation in higher mathematics.

By having to consider the cost-effectiveness of any and every decision, community health professionals make a substantially quantitative approach. In this sense they are like administrators, reponsible for serving the health needs of the people in their jurisdiction to the best of their ability, yet with only a limited budget. Both parties are likely to feel guilty as they cannot afford a full health service for those who need it. Quantitative ethics will always leave health professionals dissatisfied, yet with a raised level of consciousness for these particular ethical issues.

Deontological versus utilitarian ethics
When a lawyer asked Jesus, 'Who is my neighbour?', he told him the famous parable of a good Samaritan (Luke 10:25–37). As every one of us knows, a man was on his way from Jerusalem down to

Jericho when he fell in with robbers, who stripped him, beat him and went off, leaving him half dead. It so happened that a priest and a Levite came to the place, one after the other, but when they saw him went by on the other side. It is supposed that both priest and Levite were hurrying back to Jerusalem for some urgent task, such as preaching in the synagogue. Unexpectedly, each was confronted with a difficult problem, whether to stop to care for the wounded man or not. Without hesitation they went past him on the other side of the road to serve all the people who were waiting for them. From an ethical viewpoint, neither of them was acting immorally. Each chose to act by the utilitarian ethic, esteeming the good of the many to outweigh the needs of the individual.

After them, a Samaritan came on the scene. When he saw the wounded man he was filled with pity. He went up and bandaged his wounds, bathing them with oil and wine. Then he lifted him onto his own beast, brought him to an inn and looked after him there. Next day he produced two silver pieces and gave them to the innkeeper saying, 'Look after him and if you spend any more, I will repay you on my way back.'

The good Samaritan took his stand on deontological ethics, or the ethics of duty, in which motivation is of prime importance. When he saw the man half dead, he stopped to care for him as he should have done. The Lord Jesus praised what he had done and said, 'Go and do what the Samaritan did.'

As Christians, we always try to follow the example of the good Samaritan. However, it should be noted that deontological ethics are not necessarily Christian in themselves. The 18th century author of a book on Bushido, the Japanese way of chivalry, praised the tradition of *harakiri* (self-disembowelment) as the supreme deontological virtue. The same author warned his readers not to ponder the utility of harakiri before executing it, else no one would dare to obey the rule and kill himself. This shows how deontological and utilitarian ethics can be incompatible with each other.

Generally speaking, ethical decisions in clinical medicine tend to be regarded as deontological and those of community medicine utilitarian. In the latter case, lofty motivation is like a painted cake which cannot be eaten, or a political party with a beautiful slogan but poor executive ability. Yet the value of utilitarianism can only be assessed by looking at the successful consequences of community health planning.

Deontology points out duties common to us all, but utilitarianism has to include more complicated value systems when trying to determine the probable usefulness or otherwise of a decision. Community health professionals should therefore pay attention to such complexity of interests within a community, seeking to make impartial decisions on health problems which affect both community development and personal relationships within that community.

Christian versus Confucian ethics

In Asian countries, Christian doctors of Chinese culture are subject to close scrutiny by patients, curious as to how their Christian ethics will differ from traditional Confucian ethics. In the Confucian sense, medicine is the art of practising the highest virtue in his teaching, namely benevolence. Physicians are therefore expected to be ethical.

Whilst Jesus taught us to treat others as we would like them to treat us (Luke 6:31), Confucius taught us not to treat others as we would not like them to treat us (Analects of Confucius). Superficially both statements are similar in content, but they are opposite in expression, one being positive and the other negative. However, there is an essential difference between the two.

Eight out of the Ten Commandments are expressed negatively, as prohibitions. Yet to keep a prohibition needs self-restraint. Jesus expanded to the full the commandment, 'Thou shalt not commit adultery', when he said, 'If a man looks on a woman with a lustful eye, he has already committed adultery with her in his heart' (Mat. 5:27–28). It should be noticed that the teachings of our Lord were generally positive and so were even more demanding than the Old Testament prohibitions. As he said, 'Do not suppose that I have come to abolish the Law and the prophets; I did not come to abolish but to complete' (Mat. 5:17). The prohibition, 'Do not hate others', allows us either to love them or to be indifferent to them. It is relatively easy to observe. In contrast, the positive command, 'Love others', means that one should love even his enemies and pray for his persecutors (Mat. 5:44). This is harder to achieve.

The apostle John said in his first letter, 'It is by this that we know what love is: that Christ laid down his life for us. And we in our turn are bound to lay down our lives for our brothers' (1 Jn. 3:16). This is the true meaning of the positive command to love. Thus, we can see how Confucian benevolence is self-limiting and Christian love is boundless.

Conclusions

Recently, community medicine has had to face problems which have arisen from a utilitarian approach. As people are living longer, the cost of health care has become a heavy burden to the public. The budget has been cut, particularly endangering the health of the elderly. At the other end of life, controversial genetic screening is being applied to prevent the birth of handicapped babies. Unbalanced utilitarianism inevitably leads to such dehumanising concepts.

Christian ethics in community care should seek to combine the best of both deontology and utilitarianism. Projects should be motivated by the love of the good Samaritan and fulfilment found in healing individuals, as our Lord showed in his time. If this seems impossible we must pray to God, for Jesus said, 'With men this is impossible, but with God all things are possible' (Mat. 19:26).

Missionaries have always been pioneers. Medical practitioners have gone to the farthest parts of the world because they have been called by God to do his work there. Often they have felt cut off from the 'ivory tower' in which research is conducted in the large centres. By numerous examples it has been shown that 'front line' observations on diseases, and where and how often they occur, contributed greatly to the clarification of the causes. Even the absence of certain diseases among the more primitive cultures can help us suspect the reasons why they are common in the so-called 'developed countries'.

DENIS BURKITT

ICCP Toronto, Canada, 1972. **Denis P. Burkitt.** *Member of the external scientific staff of the Medical Research Council, London, UK. Past surgeon, Kampala, Uganda. Described 'Burkitt's tumour'. Fellow of the Royal Society. ICMDA Vice-President 1978–93.*

MEDICAL EXCELLENCE IN POVERTY

JOHNSON LULUA

The situation

UGANDA is a small country in the heart of Africa with an area of 236,000 square kilometres, 85% of which is useful agriculturally. A good rainfall of between 75 and 125 cm per annum adds to the rich tropical fertility of the soil.

With a population of about 14 million people, of whom about 90% live in rural areas, about 50% are below the age of fifteen. Such distribution has its far-reaching effects in the provision of health services, let alone effects in other social services. Education and its once well established structure has over the last 16 years disintegrated following the despotism of Idi Amin. With a very low female literacy, the care and health of a family and children in particular becomes staggering.

The services were well integrated from the smaller units in villages and towns to the larger regionally placed hospitals. There was good staffing at all levels so that referrals and follow-up care was well placed. The nearest health unit would be about 10–15 km from the village dweller.

But with the changes over the past sixteen years, many professionals have fled the country, the economy has become fluid, and breach of professional ethics is a more normal practice than otherwise, so now Uganda is counted among the 'least developed countries' of the world. Facilities, equipment and personnel in the health services have so disintegrated that only one referral hospital enjoys any reputation in the country. Communication and transportation is so degraded that travel to better equipped health centres becomes a never realised alternative for patients.

With about 80% of services being curative and over 95% of the medical training being so oriented, very little impact is exerted on the real problem of the 90% rural dwellers in such a degraded and yet underdeveloped structure. No wonder the doctors, nurses and other paramedical workers seek jobs outside Uganda for these

*ICMDA Cancun, Mexico, 1986. **Johnson Lulua.** Physician and surgeon, Kuluva Hospital, Uganda.*

reasons. Every year, of the 100 doctors qualifying, about 30–40 leave the country and another 30–40 remain self-employed in the five or so larger towns.

With all this today, it is estimated that the church-related health units, both Catholic and Protestant, provide up to 50–55% of the total beds in the country. The basic reasons are apparent:

- most of the senior staff in these church-related units are expatriates or missionaries;
- the supplies and equipment available to them are donations, with good continuity;
- the staff have a commitment to serve despite the circumstances.

Practical aspects

My practical experience is drawn from a typical church-related rural hospital in Uganda. Kuluva Hospital is located in the north-west of Uganda and was founded by two missionary doctor brothers in the early 1940s. Only a 75-bed hospital, we accommodate up to 120 patients. Over the years it has served a growing population of about 150,000 and more people come from nearby Zaire and Sudan. The steadiness, perseverance and Christian love that Kuluva staff have maintained has created a reputation, besides the specialist services in ophthalmology and leprosy which continue to attract many over the years.

We have developed a general curative and community-based health programme. Most of our time is spent in dealing with mainly preventable disease problems. However, with the nearest referral hospital 500 km south of Kuluva, we have developed broad-based experience in clinical management. We face a wide variety of infections and infestations with widespread anaemia and dehydration, including 5,000 or more cases of malaria and of respiratory tract infections per year. Four or five obstructed labours a week result in many major repairs. Surgery is available for all emergencies and other procedures done as time permits, with a total of some 1,000 operations a year, 350–400 being major. Our lighting is chiefly of the sun with generated electricity for two hours each evening. (Our battle with insects does not appear to affect wound sepsis!)

Treatment is basic, dependent largely on history and clinical judgement. The doctor must necessarily be able to do simple bacteriological tests for meningitis, tuberculosis, etc, as well as be the consultant for obstetrics, surgery, medicine, ophthalmology, paediatrics, orthopedics and relieve intra-cranial pressure with burr holes! There is no blood bank so blood is taken from relatives as required. Water supply is irregular; sometimes in the dry season water has to be hauled from a deep well. Most of the staff are locally trained. Usually one trained nurse has the care of the 120 patients. Much of the time only one of the four doctors is available and the other two or three are taken up with leprosy, ophthalmology and community based health centres which cover about 20 villages.

Conclusion

I am sure as I conclude, the question that remains in your mind is, what is excellence here? In a suffering, poor, sick and neglected population, I believe that excellence does not depend on material sufficiency or high technology. The fight is for survival and that God-centred commitment to service and perseverance amidst difficulties of different degrees. The love of God must be channelled through man as the main factor, counteracting the triad known in most developing countries today — namely, disease, poverty and ignorance. Kuluva, like many such hospitals in the country, is a necessary component of the health network in a structure where the government's free health service is coming to a halt.

I subscribe firmly to the Christian medical worker's seeking God for clear guidance about priorities for medical service in his own locality. Nearly 90% of our training, even in such poor set-ups, assumes high-tech status, aware that only 20 miles away all these gadgets are unknown. Christians ought to read between the lines, helped by the Spirit. Only those things that will be appropriate and available to us can be used. With five years in such situations, I can say that only the man that lives in a locality knows best what other facilities are appropriate.

The hospital's solid circle of dedicated, hardworking, Christian staff have been conscious of their role in the service and extension of God's kingdom within our clear limitations. They have included the doctors and nurses, showing Christian love directly by joining in prayer with despairing patients and relatives and indirectly by giving themselves tirelessly to work. In all respects this is not only appropriate to us, but to all Christian health workers.

We have also recognised the role of honest and Christian stewardship as an integral part of the level of excellence. Equipment-wise, the trust and confidence God has continued to invest in us by opening the hearts of friends and Christian organisations to give towards the work, according to their means, has added much. The understanding and will of the relatives have added to the care of patients. Due to limitations, we do not provide food to patients, and so relatives bring foodstuffs from home to cook and share with patients. In other ways this could be seen as good therapeutic management of a family, though not without problems.

In such a set-up, which may be similar for over 2 billion of the people of our world, medical excellence in poverty consists of being available, being committed to persevere, cultivating all appropriate possibilities of facility and mind, and to be loving. In this way we all exist, the rich and poor, the educated and uneducated. We are counted with them as human beings and therefore share the same rights spelled out by no one less than the Creator of all, on whom we constantly depend and in whose practice we are as stewards to his glory.

MEDICAL EXCELLENCE IN AFFLUENCE

INGE SCHARRER

IN German medicine, affluence becomes apparent above all in the classic social security system which is admired all over the world and which has three different branches within the social network: health insurance, accident insurance and disability insurance. However, we have reached the limits of growth. In the year 2000, medicine will be dominant as an economic factor as well as a psychological factor (health passes for the greatest good) and a political factor. Excellence will become apparent in the relationship between doctor and patient. This partnership between doctor and patient will be one of the most vital tasks of the world of tomorrow. We are confronted with an important transition from a curative, malady-related technique of therapy to preventive and health promoting therapeutics. Today, many doctors believe that their main task is not so much repairing organ defects as attending their patients, above all the chronically ill. In many areas this recent patient oriented medicine is concerned with the quality of the patient's life. Thus, future medicine aims more at resocialisation of the whole person than at rehabilitation of organ system functions.

How can a Christian doctor stand as the patient's partner, or as a researcher and a teacher, amid those medical changes?

Like Denis Burkitt, I would like to answer this question according to my personal spiritual belief:

> 'I have frequently stated in public that if I were to be asked what I considered the most important lesson that I learned during my medical student days, the reply would not be in the realm of medicine or surgery. It would be the appreciation of the importance of starting the day with a deliberately planned time of Bible reading and prayer, studying the chart and attempting to pay attention to the compass needle of the Holy Spirit's promptings.'

ICMDA Cancun, Mexico, 1986. **Inge Scharrer.** *Clinical professor of internal medicine, Frankfurt University Hospital, West Germany.*

The following verse from Matthew 6:33 does apply to the Christian doctor: 'Seek ye first the kingdom of God and all these things will be added unto you [and all the fearful questions will be answered].' On the 'chart' of the New Testament, the compass shows us two important parables: in Luke 18:23–25, the parable of the rich ruler; and in Luke 12:16–21, the parable of the rich farmer.

In the parable of the rich ruler, the rich man is very appropriately characterised as being upset. The parable teaches us that he especially has one great and basic shortcoming and Jesus says, 'You still lack one thing.' The rich ruler who has treasure on earth lacks treasure in heaven. 'He is a prisoner of his great possessions', defines Karl Barth. His possessions possess him, and money reigns over him. Jesus offers him, 'Sell everything you have, become rich now and in eternity.' Jesus is aware of the great difficulties caused by affluence, and he says to his disciples, 'How difficult it is for those who have great possessions to enter the kingdom of God. A camel could squeeze through the eye of a needle more easily than a rich man could get in the kingdom of God' (Mat. 19:24). Jesus is asking us, 'Are you willing to be freed from the sin of worldly love?'

Jesus confronts us with this question, 'What and whom do you love?' He does not say, 'My own should no longer have families; they should not be interested in science or professions.' He is only concerned about what has the *first* place in our hearts — what our hearts are most attached to.

Characteristics of Christian excellence amidst affluence

We cannot serve God and money — or God and medicine! Our life-style, our *biggest* house and car, how we deal with the surplus income, reveals an attribute of Christian excellence amidst affluence. Our compass, the Holy Spirit, leads us by the chart of the New Testament to another parable, the parable of the rich farmer in Luke 12. It is the story of a man who today would be considered as being very successful. And yet, Jesus called this rich man a fool. Jesus, the simple and poor man from Galilee, dared to call this man a fool — despite his affluence, good reputation and great economic power. Jesus did not call him a fool because of his affluence. Jesus never fought affluence. He just condemned its misuse. Like every other power, money can serve good and bad purposes. It can give rise to blessing and cursing. There is nothing wicked about affluence and nothing virtuous about poverty. The rich man was a fool, for he did not understand the sense and purpose of his life. He was a fool because he did not understand how much he was dependent on others. His monologue consists of about sixty words, ten of which are the words 'I' and 'my'. So often had he said 'I' and 'my' that he was no longer able to say 'us' and 'our'. He had become a wild individualist. Jesus called the rich man a fool because he would not understand his dependence on God. He attached imperishable importance to transitory things, and made trivialities his main occupation. When the rich man had stored his treasures, when he had made great profits from his possessions, when his palace was the talk of the town, he became acquainted with the master of man, which is death.

The Holy Spirit, compass of the New Testament, shows us that the rich ruler went off very sadly, and that the rich farmer was dissatisfied and restless. Both were dependent on money and therefore never did learn to share, distribute, feed the poor, clothe the naked, heal the sick or live as a brother among brothers. Their affluence gave them no peace, no satisfaction, no genuine joy and no happiness.

Christian excellence amidst affluence means taking into account the spiritual need of people (patients and colleagues). The fear and love of God is one essential component which is so often excluded in the problems and diseases of our patients. This exclusion is very often the root of drug, sex and alcohol abuse.

We believe that God has created men and women in his own image and that rebellion against him is the root cause of suffering and death. As Christians we realise very quickly how many of the problems we see in surgery, in general practice, or in people's homes have their roots in disordered family relationships. We are confronted with the misery of extramarital affairs, separation and divorce, and are asked to 'get rid' of unwanted pregnancies.

As compassionate and sympathetic listeners, we can offer encouragement and support for people to face up to the reality of their situations and their responsibility for their own health, to work and fulfil themselves as human beings according to God's plan. 'Our bodies are the temples of God's Holy Spirit' (1 Cor. 3:16). We doctors must be prepared to emphasise and demonstrate that health depends far more on the way we live than it does on the provision of adequate therapy.

Christian excellence amidst affluence stands for health education (in the sense of prevention). Primary prevention sees to the maintenance and protection of health and leads to a healthy way of life. Secondary prevention takes measures which serve to remove certain risk factors which are supposed to evoke diseases, such as obesity and the abuse of nicotine. Tertiary prevention is directed towards the recognition of already existing diseases. Christian excellence amidst affluence stands for: helping people to become independent of medical aid and expense so that they can look after themselves and not be brought back for frequent appointments, in which they may become addicted to the doctor besides wasting a lot of money.

Christian excellence amidst affluence is characterised by true and merciful communication based on the New Testament. Our compass leads us to the words: 'Let your speech always be gracious, seasoned with salt' (Col. 4:6) — not seasoned with honey, but seasoned with the salt of honesty. Communication in close interpersonal relationships with patients, with colleagues, with other members of the health team or with administrators becomes more and more important. Here, Christian excellence amidst affluence stands for taking the risk of going along the right road which appears narrow and difficult. In every situation we have to find out what the Lord wants us to do (Eph. 5:17) and wants us to say. What are his goals and the aims in our professional life, or do we want to rule?

Christian excellence amidst affluence stands for caring and working in those fields of medicine where there is the greatest need. The inner cities and some industrial areas are not popular, but are in great need of real care. Similarly, community medicine, geriatrics and terminal care for dying people are not regarded as professionally interesting, but the need is great.

Difficulties amidst affluence

Christian excellence amidst affluence is much more difficult than Christian excellence amidst poverty. Amidst poverty we learn to do the most important, only the relevant, and help people as inexpensively as possible. In the Third World it is obvious that one of the most important aspects of medicine is to educate people on how to prevent illness and promote health through hygiene, food, inoculations, etc. Prevention and treatment must go together. Amidst poverty, we do the most important as inexpensively as possible — amidst affluence, we do all possible diagnostic and therapeutic interventions, expensive or inexpensive. But we must ask ourselves: Are these measures always so necessary? Can they be paid for? Do they correspond with our categorical imperatives — as much as necessary and as little as possible?

Professional life and Christian excellence amidst affluence is more difficult because, among often unlimited possibilities, we must choose what is for the patient's real benefit and therewith for our benefit as well. Decisions made now determine our destination later, and the failures and disappointments that can follow the freedom to make selfish choices are emphasised in Ps. 106:15: 'He gave them their desire, but sent leanness into their souls.'

The subject 'Christian excellence amidst affluence' asks every physician in his special field as general practitioner, as clinician, as scientist or teacher, if he wants to take the role of the rich man or of Lazarus in the well-known story of Luke 16:19–31. This subject asks us if we want to be the rich poor man like Lazarus or the poor rich man, successful, admired and popular. This poor, rich man had travelled and missed his destination. All he could do was to warn his friends, hopefully to persuade them to alter their priorities and values and to make sure that the road they were travelling on led to the destination they desired.

The following questions remain to be answered
- Does my work make sense?
- Are the principles of my work compatible with the rules of the New Testament?
- Am I prepared as a Christian to swim against the tide and thus face disadvantages?

Christian excellence amidst affluence — this subject is a personal challenge for me, being a Christian doctor, teacher and researcher, especially since it tests in a very hard way the genuineness of my Christian faith. When speaking of Christian excellence amidst poverty, the need is evident and the work is urgent. This work is physically difficult and often marked by failures. In this area, too, Christians must struggle and hold out. However, Christian excellence amidst affluence is personally most challenging in view of the vast array of seducing temptations, all accepted by mankind as 'good'. Affluence is a challenge for a doctor who is competent in working as a researcher, teacher or practitioner and who is at the same time a persevering and unshakeable Christian — firmly attached to the New Testament and daily led by prayer and the Holy Spirit, and living from the love and forgiveness of Jesus Christ.

✳

Excellence in practice amidst poverty is to be available and willing to meet the need even with limited conventional means and to constantly depend on God in whose practice we are as stewards to his glory.

We understand God as being one, yet we also recognise the concept of the Trinity. We generally understand man to have three aspects: body, soul and spirit. Another threesome. I believe that this model of three in one is relevant to medical care, particularly in poverty situations to cure, to promote health and to console.

Although we all recognise the need for these three aspects I find that I tend to focus upon the curative and preventive aspects of health care. When both we and our patients see the efficacy of modern treatment (and preventive programs such as measles vaccination) in poverty situations, we find we are often 'pushed' into these aspects of health care to the neglect of consolation and relief.

I, for example, learn from Aboriginal people who have an understanding and a commitment to the consoling, caring and loving aspects of health care, that I can only hope to have. I thank God for what I have learned from them.

If we are to be interested in all three aspects, it will require a working together for health, a partnership with our patients, their family, nursing staff, health workers, as well as teachers, community poor, the educated and uneducated. We are counted with them as human beings and therefore, share the same rights spelled out by no one less than the Creator of all.

TREVOR CUTTER

*ICMDA Cancun, Mexico, 1986. **Trevor Cutter.** Physician with the Aboriginal people, Australia.*

✳

A CHRISTIAN PHYSICIAN'S RESPONSIBILITY TO HIS COUNTRY

A Latin American Viewpoint

ARTURO CABEZAS

Healing involves more than the body

THE principal duty of the Christian physician is to have a healing ministry to each of his patients. Of course, the healing of a person involves more than merely taking care of his immediate physical problems. Often, a man's emotional, economic, and spiritual problems are so intertwined with his physical condition that it is impossible to deal with one kind of problem without touching the others also. Almost always too, the healing of a personality depends to some extent on the healing of an environment, and although the home and church environments are of utmost importance, the general conditions prevalent in a geographical region have a great impact on each individual. In the long run then, a Christian physician's responsibility to his patient leads him to a special responsibility for his country.

If I had listened carefully to all the prophets, I should have learned this lesson sooner, but I find that, in reviewing my own practice in Costa Rica, these truths were not always so obvious to me as they are now. My personal philosophy concerning the responsibility of a doctor to his country has gone through a considerable process of evolution, forced upon me by a consideration of the social conditions present in Latin America.

Let me give a simple illustration of the kind of change to which I refer. When I first began practising medicine in Costa Rica, I considered my duty to a child with amoebic dysentery to be the treatment of his disease. Soon, I came to realise the futility of sending the child back to drink water from the same polluted stream that had caused his disease. This led me to see the necessity to teach basic health concepts myself when possible and, more

ICCP Toronto, Canada, 1972. **Arturo Cabezas.** *Medical director of Clinica Biblica and of Goodwill Caravan Program, Costa Rica.*

importantly, to help sponsor government and church programmes of health education. It is only in the last few years that I have come to see that the final solution to this problem is not just teaching the parents of the child to boil the water. Until the government assumes the responsibility of supplying pure drinking water to each citizen, the problem of amoebic dysentery will not be solved.

Eventually, then, I came to feel that my responsibility as a Christian involved me in helping those forces which are pushing for programmes to help marginal groups who are usually without power to help themselves. In other words, it led me to political awareness. I will admit that I was helped to this understanding largely by listening to Christian university and seminary students who are also facing the problem of the need for social change.

The situation we face

Latin America is the fastest growing region of the world at the moment. Accompanying problems to this population explosion have been the great internal migrations of rural dwellers to the great urban centres, usually the capital city of the country, in search of work. As a result, nearly half of the population of Uruguay lives in Montevideo, a third of Argentinians live in Buenos Aires, and fifty per cent of Costa Ricans live in San José and its surrounding communities.

The great tragedy of this internal migration is the formation of the so-called belts of misery that are growing up on the outskirts of these cities. They consist of pitifully inadequate shacks, usually without water or sanitation, where the unemployed, or newly arrived country people, live while trying to come to terms with city life, for which they are unprepared. The national economy does not increase at a fast enough rate to furnish jobs for most of these people.

Most often it is the wives and daughters of these families who eventually find jobs as maids for the well-to-do. A good many of the girls who cannot find work drift into prostitution, where they discover they can make a better than average living, and with their reputations permanently lost they generally are doomed to continue with this ancient trade until their looks deteriorate. In most cases the girl prostitute is working to feed her brothers and sisters. Caught in the trap of misery and unhappiness, many of the men turn to cheap bootleg whiskey as an escape, starting a dreadful cycle that increases the problems of the families. Recently, the director of our psychiatric hospital said that he felt the most serious social problem of the country was the large number of children who are growing up with emotional problems as a result of the insecurity caused by living with alcoholic parents. Latin America is fighting a double battle against hunger and ignorance.

Projects for health and education

Faced with this series of conditions I have mentioned, I had to decide as a Christian doctor just where my responsibility to my country lay. In the last few years I have channelled most of my efforts to help towards the activities of a group called 'Goodwill Caravans'. In 1960 the Evangelical Alliance of Costa Rica formed a committee to promote rural work to help in the zones which are not adequately serviced by the government. I was a member of that committee. We began by studying the social problems that I have outlined for you and making a list of resources that could possibly be tapped.

From the beginning we decided that the work should be a volunteer programme, that it should be inter-denominational, and that it should minister to the whole man. We decided that we would coordinate our programme as far as possible with the government, so as not to appear as competitors and not to waste our energies by duplicating existing services. We decided to go to those areas where a local Protestant church would sponsor our programme, but would minister equally to people of all religions and races. We would not only aim at helping to solve immediate problems but, through a programme of education, show people how to solve some of their own problems. Whenever possible we would try to secure the help of local teachers and municipal authorities.

We began to organise teams to go into the rural areas for a week under the supervision of leaders from our central office. Our medical team usually consists of a doctor, a dentist, and one or two nurses. In addition to seeing those of the community who are ill, we have vaccination campaigns, instruction in health and nutrition, and have organised a carefully directed programme of family planning. The most common health problems discovered on the caravans are parasites, anaemia, intestinal infections, respiratory infections, malnutrition, fungi and other skin diseases.

The agricultural technicians, who form an important part of the team, treat sick animals and carry on a vaccination programme for cattle and poultry. They teach modern practical techniques of agriculture, distribute seeds and small grafted fruit trees, and organise poultry and rabbit growing projects to supplement the protein-weak diet.

A number of people, especially university students and seminary students, have learned the Alfalit method of adult literacy, which is a Spanish version of the Laubach system. The persons trained in this method of Alfalit go with the caravan to teach adults to read — a process that can sometimes be accomplished in five days because of the fact that Spanish is a completely phonetic language. Taking into account the large number of people who can just barely read, our programme concentrates on making functional readers of all learners and attempts to supply simple reading material graded for new readers, to gradually improve their level of reading. For this we use the series of books which Alfalit has developed to teach basic subjects such as mathematics, Spanish grammar and science. The literacy team also tries to make contact with the local school teachers in order to teach them the method so that they can follow through after we leave.

In the evenings we have audio-visual programmes with lectures and movies on health or farming. This programme is made possible through a portable generator, for most of the towns to which we go do not have electricity. It makes something of a sensation for the country people to have this service offered in the isolated areas.

The final movie is usually a religious one and is generally followed by a brief evangelistic message. With the illustrated lessons given to children in the afternoons while the doctors are seeing patients, this forms the evangelistic basis of our programme. Of course, the team looks for opportunities to witness in its contact with people and there is always a chaplain available to talk with anyone who shows interest. We do not think of our ministry as bait to catch souls, but rather as an opportunity to show Christian love. Caravans have resulted in many conversions and, in some instances, the founding of new churches. We could not fulfil our goal of ministering to the whole man without this religious emphasis, because healing of an ultimate kind is always related to our salvation through Christ.

The programme of Goodwill Caravans has been made possible

because of the professionals who volunteer their help, many of whom are not from an evangelical background. We gratefully accept the help of those Catholic and Jewish doctors who are in sympathy with our programme. Then we receive medicines through Medical Assistance Programs, the Board of Missions of the Methodist Church, our own Bible Hospital, and the Ministry of Public Health. This past year the government granted Goodwill Caravans permission to import medicines and medical equipment without paying duty, the first time such a right has been granted to a Protestant group in our country.

Although we have been encouraged by the great improvement in health evident in an area revisited by our caravans, we have, from the beginning, been disturbed by the 'hit-and-run' nature of our programme. As a result we are experimenting with two new schemes in addition to the caravans.

One is the establishment of a small dispensary or rural health centre in an isolated country town staffed by two nurses who rotate between the clinic and the caravans. Because this clinic has a permanent outreach in the community and surrounding territory, and provides long-term results, we would like to establish others in the future.

The other project is an educational project in one of the worst city slums. Volunteer workers from the churches gather groups of women to teach them to read, to sew, and to cook. The response to this new service has been very encouraging also.

Conflicts of interest

I face a number of conflicts in my own thinking as far as my responsibility as a Christian in the remaining years of my service is concerned. The rural areas of the country are generally neglected because doctors and nurses do not want to go there to live, and often whole sections of the population are left out of government health programmes completely.

As the medical director of a small Protestant hospital under independent management, I have been forced to consider whether members of our staff should quit practising private medicine and join in with the government programme or whether there is still a need for the kind of individualised attention we try to give both to private patients and in the outpatient clinic. As of now, we have decided to enlarge our hospital and better it. We feel that we can treat the whole person better under the circumstances that we now have, unencumbered by any government regulations. So, while I politically endorse the increasing government responsibility for medical coverage of its citizens, I still feel led to work in a private hospital and with the church-related caravans programme.

One last conflict shared by many of you is of finding a balance of responsibility between the demands of church and medicine. Because of the shortage of professional people in the evangelical churches, a doctor in Latin America always finds himself in demand for church positions, lectures, and community projects where the church is represented. Often one feels a deep conflict between accepting these offices and just dedicating oneself to being the best doctor possible. Some kind of balance must be found.

Conclusion

I should like to say that no discussion of responsibility should end without a mention of the personal joy that goes hand in hand with an attempt to live up to those responsibilities. Although I often feel overwhelmed by the challenge of the enormous opportunities I see, I would not change places with anyone in the world. Surely there is no greater joy for a doctor, than to feel that one is in the place God has chosen at an hour when one is needed.

CO-OPERATION RELATING TO GOVERNMENTS, COMMUNITIES AND MISSIONS

KEITH SANDERS

Introduction

IN discussing the place of co-operation under the Congress theme of 'Christian challenges to present day concepts of health care', with specific reference to governments, communities and missions, I would first like to briefly state what I think we in health care should be aiming for through co-operation, then to describe some present-day examples of co-operation by answering the questions: How do we co-operate? What are the stumbling blocks to co-operation? Does co-operation work? Finally, I think it will be worth while saying a little about maintaining Christian identity, a point which worries many when called to co-operate.

The basis of co-operation

The grace of co-operation is one of the most valuable gifts given by God as method or tool for his people to fulfil his purposes in the world. Co-operation includes two principles of the Almighty's creational policy which we need constantly to bear in mind.

God works through multiple agencies to fulfil a single objective. There are innumerable examples of this principle. The life of any individual is dependent on a complicated mutually sustaining complex of ecological and social systems. In literal truth, no man liveth unto himself! Take the food we eat. There is no such thing as a multi-purpose food; what we eat for a necessary diet is a wide variety of specific entities. It is essential, too, that each item in a balanced diet maintains its specific uniqueness — a bean is only worth having if it is a real bean. Similarly, as is emphasised so often in Scripture, our bodies are a superb complex of innumerable specific components working together to allow the whole to function as a single unit.

ICCP Bangalore, India, 1982. **R. Keith M. Sanders.** *General Secretary ICCP and CMF, UK. Past medical superintendent Duncan Hospital, Raxaul and regional superintendent, Emmanuel Hospital Association, India.*

From these examples I would emphasise two points: firstly, that we are obviously designed to be co-operative beings; secondly (and we will come back to this again later), to co-operate effectively we must be good at what we are called upon to contribute. As we have said, beans are of value only if they are good beans, and a hand can best serve the body by being a good hand.

God works through civil authorities (as well as individuals) to fulfil his purposes. The Old Testament is full of instances demonstrating how God used kings and authorities as the means of blessing or punishment. Pharaoh was his instrument, Cyrus his servant, and David his appointed. The New Testament no less emphasises the necessity to respect, to co-operate with, and to pray for civil authorities. If God works through civil authorities, why shouldn't we?

The health care objective

A concise definition of what all of us should be aiming for in health care was given in the formative policy statements of the Emmanuel Hospital Association twelve or more years ago, and I would recommend it to you. It is to establish *ongoing, indigenous, self-propagating, comprehensive community health.* Many of you will recognise this as a parallel to Latourette's definition of the mission of the church, which is to 'establish ongoing, self-propagating, indigenous Christian communities'.

The objectives for health care and the mission of the church are inevitably similar. Both are concerned with the whole man, body, mind, spirit, in his relationship to God, to society and to himself. This is not the place to elucidate the implications of our health care objective. I would, however, make two comments in passing for your further consideration. First, even as the beginning of wisdom is the fear of God, even so the fear of God is the basis of health. Secondly, we are out for *comprehensive* health care, that is, curative, preventive, educational, hospital based or itinerate, and it is high time we gave up arguing which is more important.

In achieving our objective of establishing ongoing, indigenous, self-propagating, comprehensive community health care I would emphasise just three relevant axioms to which we must adhere if we are to succeed. They are obvious, but so often they can be forgotten or not applied.

Health care involves many disciplines. Doctors may not like to recognise it, but they are dependent on a host of other services in order to function effectively. Comprehensive health care is far too complex a service for any one discipline to dominate; it is too big even for the medical profession.

Health is for all. This means that all should have the knowledge of how to keep healthy. So often doctors appear to resent the prospect of everyone knowing the basic rules for health. Are they afraid of losing their status or running out of work? How foolish: You might as well think of ministers of the Gospel making themselves redundant by effectively teaching all how to relate healthily to God.

The work we do should continue after we are gone. To establish a service which ceases when we depart is to fail. Our Lord Jesus on several occasions defines the glory of God in terms of the fruitfulness of the disciples. In other words, it is not so much what God himself can do which he counts as glory, but rather what we do because of him. Thus, surely, real success for us is not what we have done but what others do because of us.

With these guidelines in mind we will now turn to the practical implications of co-operation in relation to governments, communities and missions.

How do we co-operate?

In relation to governments

(a) Aim to do what governments want done. For example, some of us have been fighting a heresy which has been propagated over the past twenty years or more, the belief that India is closed to missionaries. This is not true. India is only closed to those who want to do their own thing. We all heard at the inauguration of this congress the open invitation given by the honourable Minister of Health. He promised a welcome and support to any from overseas who would care for the indigent, for leprosy sufferers, and for the rural poor. India is not the only country which restricts the entry of foreigners to those committed to doing what fits in with national policies.

(b) With relatively limited financial and educational resources, governments must control overall policy. The Christian who is really out to serve will co-operate to make national resources go as far as possible. Fifteen years ago the then Minister of Health for India presented a paper to the Prime Minister showing how missions made one rupee go as far as seven rupees in the hands of state agencies, and thus recommended a greater allocation of central and state funds to the voluntary sector.

(c) Go where governments can't fill needs from local resources. This is something which Christian doctors in the West especially need to consider seriously. Even the best national health services leave gaps which only voluntary agencies can fill. Often, from the medical point of view, they are 'uninteresting' gaps, but that is not how our Lord views the needs in health care.

(d) Most governments are prepared to learn from those who succeed in fulfilling their objectives. The Christian, if he is good at doing a relevant service, will find his example welcome. There are many examples approved by governments, such as the Christian Medical College of Ludhiana and the United Mission to Nepal.

In relation to community and local authority

(a) Avoid repetition and duplication. Find out what is already being done and what is needed and where. This enquiry should include all aspects of health care and educational and preventive medicine, as well as curative and specialised services.

(b) Make yourself accessible in terms of centres of population and easy communication. The Christian has come to serve as a light for all to see, and not to be hidden in some irrelevant corner. It is a tragedy when, as still occurs, excellent curative centres are built without the site having been selected by the relevant authorities, but instead are located principally at the convenience of the funding agencies.

(c) Understand local life-styles and indigenous facilities and adapt to them. Western standards of architecture, equipment or administration are by no means the criteria of excellence for all peoples and places.

In relation to Christian missions and other agencies

(If you think co-operation with governments and local authorities poses difficulties — they are nothing to what can be encountered with some Christian missionary agencies!)

(a) Recognise how wide a field is covered by comprehensive

health care, and that no one agency can do everything. Even the national health services of so-called developed countries leave big gaps which have to be filled by voluntary agencies.

(b) Decide what is the most relevant contribution you can make and do that well.

(c) Don't compete with other agencies nor duplicate unnecessarily. Instead, aim to complement.

(d) Remember that our objective is an ongoing self-propagating service, so help other agencies to achieve their particular aims to the benefit of the community. To withhold any co-operation which might be given is to assist failure. Remember, the characteristic of the Christian is *'agape'* love, to give oneself to others, and Scripture makes it quite clear that when we withhold such love we kill.

Stumbling blocks to co-operation

There are at least four stumbling blocks to co-operation, one or all of which seem to be constantly present to defy the Almighty's creative policy of co-operation.

Pride is first. The professional pride of the individual physician who wants to be king, or the pride of the medical profession which is convinced that it holds the ultimate keys to all aspects of health care. Institutional pride is a fault of mission and government. In India over 20% of all hospital beds are provided by Christian missions as voluntary hospitals, and some 70% of trained nurses come from less than 3% of the total population, the Christian community. Yet, should you ask a State Health Minister (as I have done) why the voluntary hospitals are not publicly listed among the health units serving the State, you will be told that it is not politically expedient to do so. Again, the insistence by all too many Christians on maintaining their own independence can easily be a cover for religious bigotry — 'this is what God has given us to do, and we are not going to be contaminated by anyone else's help'.

Second is selfishness. 'I must do my own thing', 'I'm a surgeon/community health expert, etc and I must do just this'. Such attitudes lead to selfishness, not only in unwillingness to cover the work of colleagues, but also in sharing equitably the resources of staff and finance needed for other aspects of the comprehensive service. Institutions and missions can be guilty also of refraining from co-operation because they wish to keep all the credits to themselves.

Third is ambition. 'I want to be the best, to excel'. Centres of excellence are fine if they are relevant, but irrelevant excellence is idolatry. Putting it another way, professional excellence which develops out of phase with other necessary aspects of ongoing comprehensive health care becomes a neoplasm, a debilitating tumour in the overall service.

Fourthly, but not necessarily the least effective stumbling block to co-operation, *is fear.*

- Fear of losing one's theological or mission identity. (Some Roman Catholics are as fearful as some Protestants of co-operative ventures in health care.)
- Fear of losing one's professional identity. 'I won't be a proper doctor/surgeon' or 'It will no longer be a proper hospital'. But what are we here for? To fulfil our own concepts of medicine, or to contribute to a relevant service? Are we called to serve medicine, or to serve people?

Basically, the stumbling blocks to co-operation lie in the hearts of health care professions which are not prepared to recognise that they are only one part of the overall service. Doctors are notoriously guilty of this. Ask yourself this question: 'If you as a doctor were able to choose which part of the "health care body" you would wish to be, would you choose to be the face or the liver? Which most closely resembles your concepts of the contribution doctors make to the health of all?' We can't be everything.

Does co-operation work?

In answering this question I shall keep myself to personal experience. Even then the examples to be mentioned must be limited.

The United Mission to Nepal (UMN) is an outstanding example of where Christian dedication and integrity, in fulfilling agreements made with government, have played a vital part in achieving great benefits to the people of that country, and much honour to our Lord. From the first the UMN has offered services in the name and spirit of Jesus Christ, and has been careful to observe the restrictions imposed by the authorities on proselytisation by UMN workers. Today the UMN is trusted and respected by government, while the Church in Nepal is growing as fast as anywhere in Asia.

Bihar, the Cinderella, the most backward State in India, has given birth to a number of remarkable phenomena including Nalanda (the source of science and philosophy before the time of Christ), the goddess Sita's incarnation, the Buddha's enlightenment and Mahatma Gandhi's 'non violence' movement. Less than twenty years ago was born another inspiration, the Bihar Voluntary Health Association, the first of India's State voluntary health associations, which together now form the Voluntary Health Association of India (VHAI). With the encouragements of the Christian Medical Commission, many countries now have this most valuable instrument for wide-ranging consultation and co-operation between many voluntary health care agencies and governments. In Bihar we established a system whereby each member unit was prepared to provide immediately, on telegraphic request, a known facility of drugs, food, personnel, or a vehicle. In this way we were able to establish emergency relief teams for flood disasters etc. within 24 hours — often two days or more before even the Indian Red Cross could arrive. During the Bangladesh refugee crisis the Bihar VHA maintained a relay of personnel for months. None of us could have provided any of these vital services on our own, but together we did, and also won the support of authorities. The VHAI in turn has won the confidence of State and Central Ministries. The current health care proposals for the next Five Year Plan of India are in no little measure the results of VHAI and government consultations.

Another miracle brought about by co-operation is the Emmanuel Hospital Association, the Indian registered charitable society which maintains some 18-20 hospitals in North and Central India. The EHA was formed by the bringing together of a number of Christian mission hospitals whose parent bodies could no longer run them. The result is a viable ongoing Indian medical missionary society through which national and overseas churches and missions can fulfil our Lord's great commission. None of the hospitals in the EHA could stand on its own, but together they serve most effectively the needs of many millions of the rural communities.

Maintaining identity

Lastly, I want to touch on the subject of maintaining identity, which is such a stumbling block to many, with the hope that unwarranted fears and assumptions may be dispelled.

Remember that our objective is to establish ongoing, indigenous, self-propagating, comprehensive community health. We have seen how this can only be achieved by the integration of many agencies, as no one can do everything. Recall again the analogy of a balanced diet, which is dependent on each item being true to itself — beans are no good unless they are good beans. Similarly a hand best serves the body by being a good hand.

Hence in co-operation, instead of fearing to lose your identity, aim to be yourself. Be yourself in terms of theology or profession, as a voluntary agent or as government. In doing so, recognise your particular gifts or characteristics. If they are of God they can be used to build up the whole; so contribute those very things which make you what you are. Each of us is necessary for the other, and we best help each other by contributing what we really are. Co-operation does not mean everyone trying to become like everyone else. This can only lead to unwarranted duplication, competition and the lowest-common-denominator type of socialism.

Co-operation does mean, however, the contribution of our strength to help others achieve what they can't do on their own, even as we accept assistance from others. These gifts which we contribute are spiritual as well as material. Governments welcome the specific Christ-like commitment of Christians, and missions need the support of legislation in many aspects of health care. Involvement in service with other agencies need not in any way compromise one's Christian standing. How you express yourself may be modified, but this does not alter what you stand for. The witness of the UMN is such an example. Similarly, the church in East Germany maintains a very positive Christian witness through work which is welcomed by Communist government despite the often severe restrictions imposed by the same authority. The only loss of identity that we have to fear is that of being known as a Christian. The world calls for more people to be more Christian, and to show this by the way they love others. To love as Christ did is to put yourself out for others, and to do so you can't help but co-operate.

Finally a few aphorisms or mottoes! We are in a land of helpful sayings, we see them written on station platforms and taxis. May I suggest, as a way of summarising what we have been talking about, that we write the following on our hearts and minds:

- Aim to help others to do their jobs better.
- To heal is to enable people to live without dependence on a doctor.
- Boast not of what you have done, but rejoice in what others have done because of you.

THE SICKNESS OF MAN

THE SOLUTION

MARTYN LLOYD-JONES

WE have seen that the sickness of man is that he is under the wrath of God, as the result of his rebellion against God, and his transgression of God's holy law. All of men's troubles both individually and collectively arise out of that condition. There is no peace, in any sense, saith my God, to the wicked. There is the diagnosis and, we make bold to assert, the only diagnosis. Now we move on to consider the treatment, and here again I start with the assertion that there is only one treatment.

Man's opposition to the diagnosis

I'd like to put this to you in the form of an exposition of a statement in the Scripture. The apostles Peter and John had been arrested, not only because of their preaching, but because they had healed a man who had been born lame, a man for whom the medicine of those days could do nothing. They had healed this man by a word. Peter had said to him: 'Silver and gold have I none, but such as I have give I unto you. In the name of Jesus Christ of Nazareth, rise up and walk' (Acts 3:6). So this man, forty years of age, who had never walked in his life, sprang to his feet and in a few minutes could be seen walking and leaping and praising God. The result of this was that the Jewish authorities met together to decide what they could do to put an end to this kind of teaching and activity. So Peter and John had to appear before this great council and were examined and cross-examined as to what they were doing. Peter gives his answer; he makes it quite clear that there was nothing inherently miraculous in him or in his colleague John. He said: 'If this day we be examined of the good deed done to the impotent man, by what means he is made whole; be it known unto you all and to the people of Israel that in the name of Jesus Christ of Nazareth, whom ye crucified, whom God raised from the dead,

*ICCP Oxford, UK, 1966. **Martyn Lloyd-Jones**. Minister, Westminster Chapel; past chief clinical assistant to Lord Horder, King's physician, London, UK.*

even by him doth this man stand here before you whole.' Then he makes this statement, and this is the basis of my remarks: 'This is the stone which was set at naught of you builders, which is become the head of the corner. Neither is there salvation in any other; for there is none other name under heaven given among men, whereby we must be saved' (Acts 4:10–12).

The picture here is the attempt of mankind to build a civilisation; civilisation, mankind and the good of mankind are all represented as a kind of building. The idea is exactly the same, so we might very well translate it like this: this is the remedy that has been dismissed, set at naught by you physicians which, nevertheless, is that which has been successful. I want to consider therefore the claim of the Bible that this, and this alone, is the treatment for the sickness of men by contrasting it with what the 'builders', or physicians, of today and over the centuries, have been proffering and suggesting.

Man's self-confidence

Here inevitably is our starting-point. We look at the state of the world and we see that it is in grievous trouble. This is not through lack of treatment; indeed, mankind has never been quite so busy in attempting to cure its disease than in this present century. When Peter says: 'This is the stone which is set at naught of *you builders*', he is describing those who claim that they will deal with the situation. He refers to their confidence — their pride of intellect, their pride of understanding, their pride in human reason. The world rejects Christ's Spirit for this same reason, as it rejected him when he was here on earth; and that is because of its confidence in self.

Now, this has been true, of course, right through the long story of the human race. It was the original sin. The devil tempted man along that line, 'Hath God said that you are not to understand certain things? Don't listen to him. You are capable of it. You can be as gods yourselves.' That has continued to be the attitude of mankind ever since.

The consequence of man's self-confidence

What has all this knowledge and understanding and reason and confidence really led to? What has it achieved? The builders reject God, they reject his Christ, because they are confident that they can build a civilisation. They can build a durable society, they are confident that they can solve the problems of mankind. Yet what have the builders done? Where is the building? What success has followed their confident claims and prognostications? There are physicians that were assuring us that everything was to be put right. Has it?

The builders have said that sin and evil and pride were merely the result of *ignorance,* and that the moment people were educated they would live good and decent and responsible lives. It was believed that education was going to solve the problem. The other thing, of course, was *poverty.* Crime, we were told, is almost entirely due to poverty. But now we are also being told that crime is due to *affluence.* The people are committing crimes because they've got too much money, and don't know how to spend it! All this is a part, you see, of the great claim that has been made; they had confidence in these things. The builders have claimed that they can deal with the situation. What have they done? Where is the building? What achievements have they made?

Now, I think it is time that we became realistic and faced this great question. We are facing a most grievous situation at the present time. Now, this isn't new, of course. It's happened many times before. Civilisations arise; they are confident, they think that they can put everything right; they flourish for a while, then they decline. I think we are witnessing something of that at the present time.

Man's need of reconciliation with God

Why have the builders thus proved false in all their prophecies and prognostications? The real answer is their complete failure to realise that men's ultimate need is to be reconciled to God. That's the diagnosis we arrived at and the failed attempts of the builders support our diagnosis. They have tried everything. Everything has failed. When will they come back to the fact that this is men's fundamental need, to be reconciled to God? Or let me put it in another way, it is their failure to recognise the Lord Jesus Christ.

Now, this is something that is emphasised in the New Testament. The apostle Paul brings this charge against the builders, and the rulers, and the great people of his own day and generation. Referring to our Lord, he says: 'whom none of the princes of this world knew', 'for had they known him they would not have crucified the Lord of glory'. Here are men who claimed to be experts, they are builders, they can recognise (they say) the very thing that is needed — but when the very thing appears, they dismiss it. They said, 'Who is this fellow? Away with him, crucify him.' They rejected him, they failed to recognise him when he appeared amongst them.

Now, in contradistinction to all that, our position as Christians is to assert that there is only one cure for this sickness of men, there is only one treatment that we need consider. We assert that this is God's own way of salvation —and this is the very essence of the Christian message — that man has failed to deal with his own case, but that God has done something about it. 'God was in Christ, reconciling the world unto himself.' God was in Christ, it's God's way. Also, 'God so loved the world, that he gave his only begotten Son, that whosoever believeth in him should not perish but have everlasting life' (John 3:16). This is the tragedy of the world, that men find in it terrible sickness, grief, pain, sorrow and suffering, yet are in their pride rejecting the certain cure, the only cure, because it is God's cure.

Christian responsibility

Our business as Christian physicians and as those who will increasingly have to do a kind of pastoral work, owing to the state of the world at the present time — it is our business, not merely to make statements to people, but to explain and substantiate them. As Christian physicians, we must not be content with a mere 'Come to Jesus' evangelism. The name of Jesus is used, at times, almost as some kind of incantation, or some form of psychological treatment. That is not the biblical message. We must be clear as to the content of this, and we must be able to explain it and expound it to people.

I'm pleading that we give ourselves to a study of this so that we can present it in a biblical manner and in its own biblical setting. This is God's way, and it is something that God himself planned before the very foundation of the world. God's way of salvation is not an afterthought. It is something that God planned before he even created the world at all. As the apostle Paul says: 'We speak the wisdom of God in a mystery, even the hidden wisdom which God ordained before the world unto our glory' (Col. 1:26–27). This is to me one of the most thrilling things about being a Christian, that we are looking into and are believers in this great and glorious plan thought out by the everlasting God himself, even before the foundation of the world. This plan comes to fulfilment in the person known as Jesus of Nazareth.

Now God planned this even before the foundation of the world, and in the Old Testament you have God's repeated promises with respect to this. You first find the gospel in Genesis 3:15 where the promise is given that the seed of the woman shall bruise the serpent's head and the promise goes on right through the Old Testament. God promises that he is going to send someone into the chaos that man has made of life and of the world who will be capable of delivering — a Messiah, a Deliverer, a Saviour!

The basis of Christian certainty

All comes to a focus in the birth of the babe in Bethlehem. And here, according to the claim made by the apostle Peter, is the Saviour. This is the stone which was set at naught of you builders, which is become the headstone of the corner, and it is on this one alone your building can be erected. Notice he says, 'Neither is there salvation in *any* other, for there is none other name under heaven given amongst men, whereby we must be saved.'

Let me just underline what this means: Jesus of Nazareth, the Lord Jesus Christ, is *the* Saviour. What does that mean? Well, it means this. That it is what he has *done* that delivers us and cures us. He doesn't merely teach us how to save ourselves. Neither has he come merely to give us an example. There are many people who think that the word 'Saviour' means that he is just an example. You look at his life, you see how he lived in the same world as ourselves, and you try to imitate him and as you do so you'll be saving yourselves. Now that is, actually, the very antithesis of the Christian message. The message is that he is the Saviour. As Peter talked about the healing of the impotent man, his point was, 'John and I haven't done this. It is his name, through faith in his name [referring to this Jesus], which hath given this man this perfect soundness in the presence of you all.' As the living Christ had enabled that man to rise and walk so he, by his action and power, saves, heals and cures mankind from this terrible illness and sickness.

Now this is a most important point. We are not saved by trying to live his teaching. We are not saved by trying to imitate and emulate his example. We are saved by something that he himself has done on our behalf once and for ever. He is the Saviour — he has said this himself. He said: 'The Son of Man is come to seek *and* to save that which was lost' (Luke 19:10). He said again: 'The Son of Man is not come to be ministered unto, but to minister, and to give his life a ransom for many' (Mark 10:45). It is what he *does* that saves us. He doesn't merely instruct us how to save ourselves or how to help ourselves. This is absolutely crucial and essential to this message, but how misunderstood today! The apostle goes on to say that not only is he the Saviour, but uses an exclusive term: he is the *only* Saviour.

The Christian Gospel is unique

A gospel which is not exclusive and not intolerant is not New Testament Gospel. We must be exclusive and intolerant. 'For there is *none other name* under heaven among men whereby we must be saved.' There is no second name, there is no other name at all. This is the one and only name. In saying this the apostle is only repeating what he'd heard his Lord and Master say so frequently. We are considering One who could stand up and say 'I am the light of the world: he that followeth me shall not walk in darkness, but shall have the light of life' (John 8:12). He says: 'I am the way', and he means the only way, 'the truth, and the life: no man cometh unto the Father, but by me' (John 14:6).

I say, therefore, and we must continue to assert this: we mustn't put him into the same category as anybody else. I'm tired of reading of men who say, 'Ah, yes, these are the men who have helped mankind, Moses, Isaiah, Jeremiah, John the Baptist, Jesus, Paul, Plato, Socrates, Aristotle', and they may add even some of the moderns too. Now that is a complete denial of this entire message. There never has been, there never will be, neither is there any other. There is none another name under heaven given amongst men whereby we must be saved. I am going to put that still more exclusively and, if you like, improvidently. He needs no help, he needs no assistance, he needs no supplement. This one and only Saviour has done everything himself; he doesn't need the help even of his own mother. Mary is not a co-redemptress. When it has all been done, there is no need of co-operation, no need of supplement, no need of help. We don't need the saints to pray for us; we don't need priests to do anything on our behalf. Here is one who's done everything. He was able to say: 'It is finished', and it was finished.

Neither is there salvation in any other. For there is none other name under heaven given amongst men whereby we *must* be saved. Today there is nothing more appalling nor ultimately destructive of the Christian faith than the increasing tendency at the present time to a kind of false universalism of religions. This is a denial of the Gospel.

Why is he the only Saviour?
Why must we ask this? Why this plea of exclusiveness and this kind of intolerance? Why must we say that he is the only Saviour? People will ask us this question: are you not just being arrogant? Are you not just claiming for yourselves some superiority and dismissing everything else? Have we a right to do this? I say we must do it and here are some of the reasons why we must do so.

The first answer then is that *the very nature and character of God* makes this statement quite inevitable. Of all the fallacies that are current today there is none that is commoner and none so fatal as the fools' views with respect to God, that the deliverance of men, the cure of this sickness of men, is something comparatively easy, and especially for God. God, we are told, is love. Because God is love, there is no problem. Surely there is no difficulty about forgiveness; we forgive our children, we forgive other people. If I come to God and say, 'I'm sorry', God says, 'All right, don't worry, everything's all right.' That's the common notion. But you know if that were true, most of the New Testament would never have had to be written. According to the New Testament, this problem of the sickness of mankind presented a problem even to the mind of the eternal God. The deliverance, the salvation of man, is the most difficult thing that God has ever done, infinitely more difficult than creation. We are told about creation, that all God had to do in connection with the creation was to say 'Let there be light', and there was light — a word is enough. But God cannot deal with the sickness of men by a mere word. If he could have, he would have. But it's quite clear from the whole of the biblical teaching that he couldn't do this. Why not? Well, because of the character of God. God, we are told, is not only love, but God is righteous, and God is holy, and God is just. Habbakuk says, 'Thou art of such pure countenance, that thou canst not look upon sin.' We can't conceive of God and that is the essence of our trouble; we think we can, and we make gods after our own image. God was pleased to give us a revelation concerning himself when he gave the Ten Commandments through his servant Moses and there he gives this revelation of his own holiness. It's often summarised like this: Be ye holy, for I am holy, saith the Lord.

He is just and he is righteous and he is holy. God can't pretend that he hasn't seen sin. Sin must be punished, so the problem is: how can God ever forgive anybody at all? That's the problem; that's the problem in the heart and the mind of the Eternal. As Paul puts it in Romans 3:26: How can God at one and the same time remain just and be the justifier of him that believeth in Jesus. How can God remain eternally just and yet forgive anybody? That's the problem. And it is, I say, the profoundest, the greatest problem that the universe has ever known, the greatest problem for God himself. The nature of God makes it an insoluble problem from the human aspect.

Then think of the *condition of man.* Man's first problem is that he is guilty. Our trouble is not that we are sick, we are guilty. The first thing we have to realise is our status, our standing before God — and we are guilty. The whole world lieth guilty before God, for we have broken his laws. You may say, 'Oh, I don't believe that', but ignorance is no plea. The fact of your ignorance of the law won't save you in the law court, still less before God. We've got it in a written form. We are all guilty, before God. Not only that, we are fallen, our natures are polluted, we are all twisted and perverted. We are under the power of sin and of Satan, and we are completely helpless. And there, facing us at the end, is death. It's the last enemy, and there we all are moving steadily in that direction.

Very well, what is man's need? Well, *man's need is to be delivered.* Man doesn't merely need help. He doesn't merely need instruction. He doesn't merely need a fillip to his good intentions. He needs this deliverance that he is incapable of within himself. What does he need? Well, let me put it in a different way. He needs to be able to speak to God, but he can't find him.

How can man find God?

Paul puts the question and the question is still there, and your modern philosophers are no nearer. But that's not the greatest problem; there is something infinitely more impossible to us. Even if I could find him, how could I stand before him? As Job exclaimed: 'Oh, that there were somebody who could come between us, who could take hold of me with one hand and take hold of him with the other, and bring us together. Oh, that there were someone who could represent me' (Job 9:33). Here's the problem; the moment we get some dim little realisation of the nature and the being of God, we see how vile, how unworthy we are, how inadequate, all our ideas become nothing.

I need a new nature. Here is the problem, you see, of the treatment of this disease. The moment we realise that this is the problem, you see how utterly hopeless are the remedies of all the other physicians, how futile are all the efforts of the builders, in all their pride and self-confidence, to build this building of salvation. So we come to the inevitable conclusion.

There is only One who can do this and One alone; 'Nothing in my hands I bring, simply to thy cross I cling; Not the labours of my hands, can fulfil thy law's demands. Could my zeal no respite know, could my tears for ever flow, all for sin could not atone; thou must save and thou alone.' I can't do it, no man can do it for me. That is why all the world's greatest men have no right to use the word 'Saviour' with respect to themselves, as some of them in their folly have done from time to time. No man can save me. Why? Because he can't save himself. He can't deal with his own problems. And yet if we are to be saved, we must be saved by a man. Why? Well, because we are men, we are human beings, and here is the problem. Man alone is not enough, and yet the saviour must be a man. And you see there is only one solution to the problem: Jesus of Nazareth. He is truly man, but he is not only man. He is the Son of God.

Here is the message. This is why he is unique. This is why we mustn't put him into the list and category with these great men of the world. They were men, nothing but men, they were all sinners, they were all failures. Here is one who is God and Man. Here is our message, which sounds so ridiculous: God and Man. The divine Man with two natures in one person. He is truly man, so he can represent man, but he is more than man, so he can save man.

The first problem is the *problem of our pardon*. Let there be no mistake about that. We don't need just to be made better in this respect or in that respect. The problem of mankind ultimately is not just that of not committing this sin or that, or not suffering from this disease or that. One great problem, I repeat, confronting us all is the problem of our guilt, of standing before God, and facing the demands of his holy and eternal law. We need to be *pardoned.* How can we do this? How can a man's pardon be obtained? There's only one answer. God's law *must* be honoured; it is the law of God, and the law *must* be honoured. It must be kept, and this is God's way of delivering us and of healing us. He sent his only Son into the world — Jesus of Nazareth, Son of God. Here he is — he is entirely without sin, and he lived his life in this world; was tempted in all points like as we are and yet he never sinned. He had lived a perfect life. God's law had been honoured in its entirety.

Well, that's the first step. But it's not enough. *What about my past sins?* What about my guilt? He is able to deal with this also. Even before he did that, he met our great adversary, the devil, Satan, in single mortal combat, and he defeated him and routed him utterly and absolutely. We need someone who can enable us to do that. He's done it, and then he comes with this great question of the guilt and punishment of our sins. I say, with reverence, God must punish sin. If God doesn't remain just and righteous and punish sin, he is no longer God; he is like one of us. But God *must* punish sin, and there is only one way whereby you and I can, therefore, be forgiven and delivered. It is the way of God's own devising. He sends his only Son into the world.

When God sends him to the cross on Calvary's hill, what's happening there? Is that the action of men only? Is this the death of a pacifist? Is this just the death of another Socrates, a man ahead of his time, whom his contemporaries don't understand? A thousand times No. He is sent deliberately by his Father. He has his agony in the garden and he sweats drops of blood. He says to his Father, 'Father, if it be possible let this cup pass me by'. What is this? Is this the human Jesus shrinking from the fear of death? Of course it isn't. The martyrs have never shrunk from death. They knew where they were going, and he'd be less than his own followers if it was a mere natural human shrinking from the fear of death. No, no, he knows what's involved in the cross and what's going to happen. What is it? Well, it's this. What is happening on the cross is that God is there, laying on him the iniquity of us all. Or as Peter puts it, 'Who his own self bore our sins in his own body on the tree, that we, being dead to sin, should live unto righteousness: by whose stripes ye were healed' (1 Pet. 2:24) God hath laid on him the iniquity of us all. He has been smitten, stricken, for us.

What is happening is this. God is punishing sin as a just and righteous and a holy God. He *is* punishing it in the person of his only son. Your sins, my sins; my guilt, your guilt, borne by him. Dealt with by him, so Paul can say triumphantly in Romans 3:25 and 26, 'Whom God hath set forth as a propitiation through faith in his blood, for the covering of the sins that are past'. Why? In this way — that God might be just and, at the same time, the justifier of him that believeth in Jesus. 'Behold the Lamb of God! The Lamb of God that taketh away the sin of the world' (John 1:29). That's what's happening, he has borne the punishment. It means his death, for the wages of sin is death, and he dies.

They take down his body and they put it in a grave. Is that the end? No, no, because he is not only perfect man, he is God. It was impossible that he should be holden of death. He bursts asunder the bands of death. He rises triumphant o'er the grave, the resurrection morn arrives. Literally, physically, in the body, he comes out of the grave and manifests himself to chosen representatives. He *has* overcome the *last* enemy. So that we are able to say 'O death, where is thy sting?' 'O grave, where is thy victory?' The sting of death is sin, and the strength of sin is the law. But thanks be unto God who giveth us the victory through our Lord Jesus Christ' (1 Cor. 15:55–57). And he has not only conquered death and the grave, he has opened the way unto heaven.

The treatment of man's sickness

From there, to all believing in him he gives this new nature. He makes new men of us. This is a gospel of a new life, a new birth, not a mere improvement. You must be born again, he says, you must be born of the water and of the Spirit. 'If any man be in Christ,' says Paul, 'he is a new creature, a new creation.' Not merely a better man, he's a new man, entirely new. 'All things are passed away, behold, all things are become new.'

In this and with the power of the Spirit that he puts within us, we are made strong to fight the battle against the world and the flesh, and the devil. Again, in the ringing words of Paul, 'Sin shall not have dominion over you, for you are not under law but under grace' (Rom. 6:14), re-echoing the very words of the Lord himself: 'If the Son shall set you free, you shall be free indeed' (John 8:36). This is the position into which he puts us. He has dealt with our every need. At any time we can turn to him and say: 'I need thee every hour, stay thou nearby, temptations lose their power when thou art nigh.' That's what's happened. Neither is there salvation in any other.

Is there any other? Where is it? Where is he? You builders, if there are any present, what have you to say? What have you to offer? There is nothing. The story of civilisation proves that you are complete failures. Here is the only Saviour. He *is* the Saviour, and a Christian is one who knows something of the power of this salvation in his own personal life. We say with Paul: 'The spirit of life in Christ Jesus hath made me free from the law of sin and death' (Rom. 8:2).

Here is our message for this unhappy, defeated generation to which we belong. Christian physicians, you are living epistles declaring this, 'known and read of all men', or as Paul puts it to the Philippians, 'you are to be blameless and harmless, the sons of God without rebuke, in the midst of' — listen — 'in the midst of a crooked and perverse generation' (Phil. 2:15). And that is this generation, crooked, twisted, perverse. We are living amongst it and we are to be as lights in the heavens, holding forth this Word of Life. We are to tell men and women about this only salvation, provided for us by the only Saviour, the Son of God. This is our message, that when man has completely failed God himself has intervened and put into practice the plan that he had worked out before the very foundation of the world itself. We are living in thrilling times. The world is getting darker and darker. Oh that our light were getting brighter and brighter. We are to be like stars in the heavens on a dark night, showing that there is a light in the darkness and that there is a way whereby man can be delivered individually, and more than individually, by the action taken so long ago and now mediated to us by the Holy Spirit, by the Son of God. Neither is there salvation in any other, for there is none other name under heaven given amongst men whereby we must be saved.

I wonder whether we have all recognised this. I wonder whether we will bow the knee to him. I wonder whether we will acknowledge our failure, our utter impotence. I wonder whether we will cast ourselves in our helplessness upon him. 'Nothing in my hands I bring, simply to thy cross I cling; naked come to thee for dress; helpless, look to thee for grace. Foul, I to the fountain fly; wash me, Saviour, or I die.' Having said that to him, that is all we need to do. If we have never done it, may God give us grace to do it, quietly, and experience repentance toward God, and faith toward the Lord Jesus Christ.

SUBJECT INDEX

Article or page reference to most but not all main subjects

AUTHORS

OTHER ICMDA PUBLICATIONS

GOD AND THE HANDICAPPED CHILD
Selected papers presented to the joint conference of ICCP/Innere Mission of the Lutheran Church of East Germany, Dresden 1981.

THE DOCTOR'S LIFE SUPPORT
Maintaining Christian vitality.
Readings with short commentary for each day of the year.
Revised edition 1994.

AMAZING
The first quarter century of the International Christian Medical and Dental Association.
1990.

PROCEEDINGS of all World Congresses

Obtainable from the Secretariat
82-88 Hills Rd, Cambridge CB2 1LQ, UK.

NOTES

NOTES

NOTES